A PLUME BOOK

THE BASEBALL ECONOMIST

J. C. BRADBURY is an associate professor of economics at Kennesaw State. His research has been featured in the *New York Times* and the *Los Angeles Times*. His op-ed pieces have appeared in the *Wall Street Journal*, and he writes about baseball, economics, and the Atlanta Braves on his blog at www.Sabernomics.com.

Professor Bradbury coined the term *Sabernomics* to describe his way of combining the tools of modern economics with the statistical revolution in baseball made famous by Bill James and his sabermetrics (derived from the acronym SABR, which stands for the Society for American Baseball Research). J. C. Bradbury lives in Marietta, Georgia.

The Baseball
ECONOMIST
The Real Game Exposed

J. C. Bradbury

A PLUME BOOK

PLUME
Published by the Penguin Group
Penguin Group (USA) Inc., 375 Hudson Street, New York, New York 10014, U.S.A. • Penguin
Group (Canada), 90 Eglinton Avenue East, Suite 700, Toronto, Ontario, Canada M4P 2Y3 (a
division of Pearson Penguin Canada Inc.) • Penguin Books Ltd., 80 Strand, London WC2R
0RL, England • Penguin Ireland, 25 St. Stephen's Green, Dublin 2, Ireland (a division of
Penguin Books Ltd.) • Penguin Group (Australia), 250 Camberwell Road, Camberwell,
Victoria 3124, Australia (a division of Pearson Australia Group Pty. Ltd.) • Penguin Books
India Pvt. Ltd., 11 Community Centre, Panchsheel Park, New Delhi – 110 017, India •
Penguin Group (NZ), 67 Apollo Drive, Rosedale, North Shore 0632, New Zealand (a division
of Pearson New Zealand Ltd.) • Penguin Books (South Africa) (Pty.) Ltd., 24 Sturdee
Avenue, Rosebank, Johannesburg 2196, South Africa

Penguin Books Ltd., Registered Offices: 80 Strand, London WC2R 0RL, England

Published by Plume, a member of Penguin Group (USA) Inc. Previously published in a
Dutton edition.

First Plume Printing, March 2008

10 9 8 7 6 5 4 3 2 1

 REGISTERED TRADEMARK—MARCA REGISTRADA

The Library of Congress has catalogued the Dutton edition as follows:

Bradbury, J. C. (John Charles), 1973–
    The baseball economist: the real game exposed / J. C. Bradbury.
      p. cm.
    Includes bibliographical references and index.
    ISBN 978-0-525-94993-0 (hc.)
    ISBN 978-0-452-28902-4 (pbk.)
      1. Baseball—Economic aspects—United States.   I. Title.
    GV880.B73 2007
    796.357'640973—dc22   2006027888

Printed in the United States of America
Set in New Baskerville
Original hardcover design by Kate Nichols

To my father,

the man who taught me how to throw and hit.

Contents

Preface

Economics is the study of mankind in the ordinary business of life.

—ALFRED MARSHALL, *Principles of Economics*

ECONOMICS has a nickname: the dismal science. To say the least, this gives the wrong impression. It earned this moniker not for its supposedly dull subject matter, but from the ideological bent of one of its founders. In the nineteenth century, infamously racist social critic and historian Thomas Carlyle came up with the nickname in a dismissive retort to the brave classical economist John Stuart Mill, who had openly argued that slavery was wrong. I'm happy to say, the dismal science nickname turns out to be a badge of honor.[1]

A popular misconception is that economics is just about money, which does make it sound dismal. But economists study behavior in all aspects of our lives. Nowadays, anywhere human beings make choices, economists will be watching. Whether it's deciding what to buy at the grocery store, whom to vote for in the voting both, how fast to drive a car, or whether or not a pitcher decides to plunk a batter, economists have something to say.

A couple of decades after Carlyle's dismal jab, Alfred Marshall, one of the fathers of modern neoclassical economics, described his discipline as "the working of common sense aided by appliances of organized analysis and general reasoning, which facilitate the task of collecting, arranging, and drawing inference from particular facts." I like his emphasis on common sense and a general approach. His most famous student, John Maynard Keynes, echoed these sentiments, stating, "[Economics] is a method rather than a doctrine, an apparatus of the mind, a technique of thinking which helps its possessor to draw correct conclusions."

It is a method, not a doctrine. Most recently, Steven Levitt, an award-winning economist at the University of Chicago, has gained notoriety for daringly applying the economic method to matters as diverse as cheating in sumo wrestling and racial discrimination on television game shows. He and his coauthor, Stephen Dubner, wrote in *Freakonomics*, "Since the science of economics is primarily a set of tools, as opposed to a subject matter, then no subject, however off-beat, need be beyond its reach." Baseball isn't exactly offbeat, but it is my favorite place to apply economic method.

In the economic way of thinking, the first rule in analyzing human behavior is that *all choices have trade-offs.* Baseball players have choices to make in their job just as most non–baseball players do in their workplace or around the home. Attempting to steal second base is a choice that involves sacrificing a safe position at first in order to move into scoring position. With this choice, the runner risks making an out; conversely, choosing to stay at first has the cost of not advancing to a better scoring opportunity. No matter what he does, the player must decide to sacrifice either his safe position on first or the better scoring opportunities of second base. There is no way to make a costless choice. There are many other aspects of the game to which economic thinking about trade-offs applies. Should a manager play a left-hander or right-hander at catcher? Should owners want Major League Baseball to act like a monopolist or a competitive firm? Should a player use steroids to enhance his performance or not? These are just a few of the choices that require trade-offs that people in the baseball world must make.

The second rule in understanding human behavior is that *people respond to incentives.* Human beings are predictable creatures that tend to engage in activities with high rewards and low punishments. Raising and lowering rewards and punishments predictably affects the choices people make. This is a very simple and powerful assumption. Baseball is a game full of well-defined benefits and costs, which makes it a fantastic laboratory for economists. It is easy to predict what a player will do once we understand the relevant incentives. Why do pitchers hit more batters in the American League than in the National League? How does arguing with the umpire affect the way he governs the game on the field? Do pitchers treat batters differently according to the ability of the on-deck hitter? The economist's job is to predict behavior based on the expected punishments and rewards.

Economists also love disentangling data, and baseball has plenty of data to play with. As evolutionary biologist and baseball enthusiast Stephen Jay Gould wrote, "If philately attracts perforation counters, and Sumo wrestling favors the weighty, then baseball is the great magnet for statistical mavens and trivia hounds."[2] We can theorize all we want about what we think *ought* to be going on in the game, but we really want to know what *is* going on. The answers are in the numerical records of the game, but it's hard to extract information about individual contributions in a team game. How responsible is the pitcher for preventing runs? What is the best statistic for measuring offense? What is the effect of city size on winning? To decipher the numerical records, we need tools that can condense huge tables of numbers into more comprehensible measurements. Economists call the combination of economic intuition with statistical methods *econometrics*. They use it to test the validity of their economic theories. Without these tools, patterns in the sea of individual observations are often unrecognizable or misleading. I'll be using these methods to answer the questions I raised above. The answers are often counter to ingrained beliefs about the game.

I'm not the first person to look at baseball more or less in this way. Bill James, who not coincidentally was an economics major as an undergraduate, is the Johnny Appleseed of analytical baseball research. Many years ago James became annoyed that the established conventional wisdom of baseball was not entirely right and that few baseball insiders seemed to care. He wanted objective answers. What is the best statistic for measuring a player's ability to create runs? How many more runs is a single worth than a walk? Is a strikeout worse than any other kind of out? Very few other people seemed to be trying to find out, so he decided to do it himself, publishing his findings in the annual *Baseball Abstracts*, along with several other books, over the years. James was not the first person to dabble in this, but he was the most vocal and popular member of this community, not to mention a very gifted writer. A certain segment of the population ate it up. *Sabermetrics* is the name that James gave to his pursuit, in honor of the acronym of the Society for American Baseball Research (SABR).

James defined sabermetrics as "the search for objective knowledge about baseball." Though sabermetricians often use mathematical and statistical tools, it is the methodological approach that differentiates sabermetrics from the traditional approach to understanding baseball. Erroneously, sabermetrics has been labeled the application of statistics or computers to baseball. Statistics and computers are common tools of the sabermetrician, but these tools are utterly useless without critical thinking. However, sabermetrics does not quite describe my approach.

I apply a wide range of economic principles to baseball, so I think of what I do as *sabernomics*. Sabermetrics involves analytical and statistical methods, but the analysis is often narrow and is not based on economic assumptions about human behavior. For example, sabermetricians have studied whether or not the on-deck batter can protect a star slugger. I'm interested in this, but I'm also concerned about how the man on deck might influence the opposing pitcher, and how this effect applies to all hitters in the lineup. Baseball and economics are to sabernomics what peanut butter and chocolate are to a Reese's Peanut Butter Cup. While both subjects can stand alone, they are quite good consumed together. I hope to demonstrate that economics has a lot to say about not just baseball, but all human behavior. Yes, economists do talk about boring, even dismal, subjects such as cash flows, deficits, inflation, and taxes; but, it's the economic way of thinking that inspired me, and most of my colleagues, to follow economics as a vocation.

Broadly, we start with economic decisions on the field, then progress to off-the-field choices. The issues are interrelated, and therefore to build a successful baseball team, a general manager, or fantasy baseball player, must understand both. By the way, I expect the dominant team for years to come will not be the mega-market New York Yankees, but the smaller-market Florida Marlins. The reasons will become clear in the later sections of the book.

One of the more complicated tools that I use, *multiple regression analysis*, merits an appendix in which its genius is explained. In short, multiple regression analysis isolates the individual impacts of many factors on a single event. It can quantify the impacts of latitude, altitude, and proximity to water on the snowfall in towns in the United States. While all of these factors are important, multiple regression analysis can give each factor a specific value, taking into account the potential influence of all of the factors, based on the historical record. In understanding individual contributions in team sports, this analytical tool is invaluable. Also included is an appendix listing all major-league players by team, along with a calculation of each player's dollar value to his team. Turns out, some players have negative values, and they too are listed.

Writing on my blog, *Sabernomics*, led me to this book. Many of the ideas in the chapters that follow were debated by readers of my site. I thank them for tempering my thoughts. What started out as a few questions about puzzles in baseball has turned into an obsession. As most economists find out, working with a universal theory of human action often leads to close examination of previously unexamined corners of our daily lives. I've been hooked by sabernomics. Baseball is a fantastic game, full of unsolved puzzles, and I find myself thinking of little else on many days. I hope you'll find the discussion as consuming as I have.

Part One

ON THE FIELD

1

Accidents Happen . . . but More So in the American League

Are you seriously going to throw at somebody when you're facing Randy Johnson?

—CURT SCHILLING[3]

ONE WARM SATURDAY AFTERNOON in New York City, Roger Clemens hit Mike Piazza in the head during an interleague matchup between the crosstown rivals Mets and Yankees. The Mets felt that the fastball that gave their star slugger a concussion was intentional, and wanted payback. But the game was played (on July 8, 2000) at Yankee Stadium, an American League ballpark, where a designated hitter (DH) bats for the pitcher. Clemens was safe, but the Mets would not forget. Nearly two years later, on June 15, 2002, Clemens came back to New York to pitch at Shea Stadium where the game was played by National League rules—no DH. Like a child pulling a snowball from the freezer in the middle of summer, Piazza crouched behind the plate and called the pitch. The pitcher, Shawn Estes—who wasn't even on the Mets when the first incident occurred— reared back and aimed some payback right at Clemens's backside . . . and just missed.

There is no concept more sacred to economists than the *law of demand.* Though the study of economics began without it, its discovery yielded a vital tool for social scientists studying human behavior. The law of demand states that there is an inverse relationship between the price of a product and the amount of a product consumed. If the price of a product goes up, expect the consumption of the product to fall. If the price falls, expect the consumption to go up. It sounds pretty simple, right? Maybe that's why Alfred Marshall believed economics to be nothing more than the organized analysis of common sense.

Economists have traditionally illustrated the law of demand in a retail context. Shelf prices in stores move up and down, and customers adjust their purchases of goods based on the price. It's a useful way to learn the concept, but the law of demand has much broader application. Prices aren't only paid in dollars; a price can be just something a person gives up in order to get something else—an "opportunity cost," as economists refer to it.

On the baseball field, managers and players are constantly making decisions based on the "prices" of their actions even though there is no money involved. For example, the price to the manager of pinch-hitting for his ace starter is to lose his skills in preventing runs for the rest of the game; because, once a player leaves the game, he cannot return. When a starting pitcher takes his turn at bat in the early innings, and his arm is still fresh, the manager loses a lot by replacing him with a superior hitter. But in the eighth inning, when the pitcher might be running out of gas, forgoing his services for the rest of the game is cheaper than it was earlier in the game. According to the law of demand, we expect managers to pinch-hit for their pitchers later in the game (when the price is low) more often than early in the game (when the price is high). Again, this just seems like common sense, because that is exactly what we do observe.

To examine players' behavior where large differences in prices suggest obvious choices is a bit boring. What is interesting is that the law of demand is a powerful force that influences seemingly trivial areas of human behavior. We often view a pitch that hits a batter as an inadvertent event: a hiccup in a pitcher's performance. However, hitting a batter has a price to the pitcher and his team. So even though it might not seem to make a difference to who wins the game, as the price changes for hitting batters, we should expect pitchers to change the frequency with which they plunk opposing hitters. It just so happens that the adoption of the designated hitter rule in the American League had an interesting effect on hit batsmen. It lowered the price of hitting batters, which yields an obvious prediction from the law of demand. The designated hitter rule demonstrates how sensitive humans can be to even the tiniest of price changes.

The Price of Hitting Batters

In 2004, when Major League Baseball adopted the policy of assigning home-field advantage in the World Series to the league winning the All-Star Game, FOX television advertised the game with a montage of clips of hit batters while the voice-over boomed, "This time, it counts!" It's funny that a major network sought to promote a baseball game using an event that happens barely more than once per hundred times that a batter steps to the plate. And when a batter gets hit, it normally results in about as much excitement as a base-on-balls, with the hitter trotting down to first base.

The bloodlust provoked by a pitcher hitting a batter can be quite exciting. Of course, batters don't like being hit by a ninety-mile-an-hour hardball. Most batters don't think the free trip to first base is sufficient compensation for the inflicted damage. And even if it's something the pitcher didn't mean to do, the victimized batter surely doesn't appreciate the pitcher's lack of care and doesn't know for sure that the blow wasn't intentional. Sometimes the batter will stare or yell, or maybe even charge the mound to brawl, which gets fans to their feet, makes for good television, and sells advertising. Turning a game children play into a blood sport, played by men of honor who don't shy from taking the law into their own hands, boosts ratings.

However, even when a batter feels he's been wronged by a pitcher, he rarely responds with immediate violence. The punishment for fighting is quite severe, with most participants receiving multi-game suspensions, fines, and not to mention a few extra bruises. Instead, teams are said to employ Hammurabi's code of retributive justice. Hammurabi ruled Babylon nearly four thousand years ago and became famous for his laws, some of the first ever written, which pronounced punishments equivalent to the damage the crime caused. Plunking pitchers are sometimes reminded of the discomfort of being plunked when they take their turn in the batting order. It's this punishment according to an unwritten "eye for an eye" code that is thought to deter pitchers from being careless.

If plunking pitchers are criminals negligently inflicting harm on fellow players, a useful framework for analyzing the phenomenon is an economic model of crime. After all, negligence is a legal term that describes the failure of a party to take proper care in protecting other people or property. Developed by Nobel Prize–winning economist Gary Becker in the 1960s, the economic approach to crime begins with treating criminals as rational human actors who base their choices regarding illegal activity on the potential benefits and costs. Simply stated, the greater the expected benefits—based on the likelihood of success and the size of reward—and the lower expected costs— determined by the probability of getting caught and the severity of the punishment—the more likely it is for a criminal to commit a crime.

Becker's model is a fascinating application of the law of demand. The higher the price of committing a crime, the fewer people we expect to see engaging in criminal activity. The price may be due to a new law or a private response of potential victims. For example, to reduce auto theft the government could increase the length of prison sentences for stealing cars, or car owners could purchase alarm systems. Both of these activities raise the cost of committing a crime, and correspondingly ought to lower the "consumption," that is, auto theft.

The written official rules of baseball dictate that the price for hitting a batter is that the plunked hitter goes to first base. Given this punishment, pitchers will hit batters at a rate commensurate with costs of putting men on base. Though pitchers don't want to hit batters, the optimal number of batters hit isn't zero. Why not? Because, avoiding hitting batters at all costs can have some pretty disastrous consequences. To ensure that the ball doesn't hit a batter, the pitcher will have to throw softer and err on the side of leaving the ball over the plate, which results in the increased likelihood of the batter depositing the ball in the outfield bleachers. Therefore, the pitcher must make a trade-off between batter safety and pitching success.

When a batting team feels the opposing pitcher is neglecting batter safety too much, one response is to raise the price. It's impossible for a team to rewrite the rule book, awarding the batter two bases instead of one or sentencing the pitcher to forty lashes. Instead, according to the unwritten retributive justice code of baseball, the team will plunk the offending pitcher when the time is right—an eye for an eye. How is punishing a person for a past indiscretion supposed to stop him from misbehaving in the first place? Certainly, he can't go back in time and undo his misdeed, but he, along with any other pitcher who takes the mound against that team, expects this justice will be served. By establishing a reputation for punishing plunking pitchers, the retaliating team will credibly raise the price to future offenders in order to deter them from negligent pitching.

From the pitching team's perspective, hitting a batter on the opposing team is a pretty poor deal. Giving the other team a man on base isn't the best way to prevent runs. That's why most hit batsmen are legitimately accidental. But losing a player to injury from being hit by a pitch is also costly to a team, possibly more costly than the benefits of the compensation of a free base. This is why teams often feel retaliation is not only justified, but necessary to protect the interests of the team. The Mets didn't mind putting Roger Clemens on first if it sent a message to opposing pitchers that the Mets would be exacting revenge against those who plunked their star slugger.

How effective is this long-standing unwritten code if hitting batters is largely unintentional? While it's clear that rarely does a pitcher intentionally hit a batter, not all accidents in life are random, and therefore they don't render a guilty party faultless. For example, the motorist who drives sixty miles per hour through a dense fog is much more likely to crash than the motorist who slows down. While neither driver intentionally wants to crash, the slower driver is being more careful in trying to avoid a collision. Certainly, the fast driver bears more culpability for his actions than the slow driver. A pitcher who isn't being as careful as he should has to know he will be punished, and with this in mind, he might take a little more care in keeping his inside pitches away from the batter. As Cy Young Award–winning pitcher Randy Johnson describes it, when a pitcher doesn't have to bat, "you may have a tendency to throw inside a little bit more knowing when that ninth hole comes up, you won't be hitting."[4]

A Price Change

If the threat of retaliation really does raise the price of hitting batters, then this yields a prediction that we can easily test. In the American League, where a designated hitter bats in place of the pitcher and the pitcher faces no threat, pitchers ought to hit batters at a higher rate than in the National League. The lower the price for hitting a batter, the greater number of batters a pitcher will hit. Veteran NL manager Dusty Baker states the theory more bluntly: "You can be bold in [the American] League and get away with [hitting batters]. It's different in our league where you have to hit."[5]

The test of any theory is how well it conforms to the real world. The American League adopted the DH rule in 1973; therefore, if the law-of-demand explanation is correct, then hit batter rates should rise in the American League relative to the National League after 1972. The National League acts as a control group, because it lacks the rule the American League added.

Figure 1 shows the hit batters rates in both leagues from 1921 to 2005. This picture shows a startling, if not surprising, change. From 1921—the start of the modern baseball era of the home run and the end of the spitball—until 1972, the rate at which batters were hit in both leagues moved together from year to year, but no league had a consistently higher rate than the other. Following the introduction of the DH, the hit batter rate in the American League was higher than in the National League for the next twenty-one years. From 1973 to 2005, on average, the hit batter rate in the American League was 15 percent

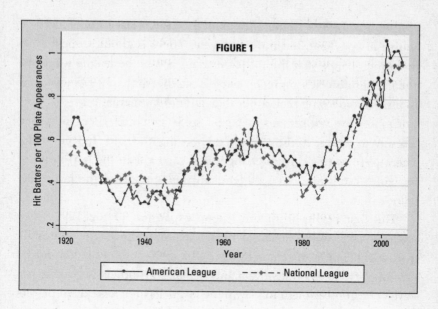

higher than in the National League. This is pretty strong evidence that pitchers are responding to the price difference in hit batters in accordance with the law of demand.

However, this picture is a little more complicated than it appears. There are several excellent objections to be made to the argument that the difference in hit batter rates in the leagues is the product of a law-of-demand response by pitchers.

Retribution in the 1990s

The most obvious strike against the law-of-demand explanation is that in the 1990s, the interleague difference in hit batters shrinks. In 1994, the National League hit batter rate rose above the American League rate for the first time in twenty-one years. And for the next few seasons that followed, the rates were much closer than in the past, with the National League rate exceeding the American League rate three more times over the next decade. Is it possible that the twenty-one-year run of American League dominance in hit batters was just a run of luck? Of course it's possible, but not very likely. There is about a one-in-one-thousand chance that the hit batter rates across the league would be equal; therefore it's more probable that the shift in 1973 was a response to something real rather than a random fluctuation.

Do we have any reasons to expect the league differences in hit batter rates to change in the 1990s in the way that they did? In fact, we do. There were two significant changes that can explain the narrowing of hit batter rates; one of which lends further support to the law of demand.

The first results from the league expansion in the 1990s—two teams in 1993 and two teams in 1998. Expanding the league dilutes the quality of talent in the game by letting in, at the minimum, a hundred new players (four twenty-five-man rosters) who otherwise would not have been good enough to play in the league. These less skilled players included pitchers who were more likely to accidentally hit batters, and batters who were less able to get out of the way of inside pitches. This expansion was heavily concentrated in the National League, with the addition of the Rockies and Marlins in 1993 and the Diamondbacks in 1998. The Devil Rays joined the American League in 1998, with the Brewers switching from the American to the National League. In the first year of expansion (1993) the leagues' difference in hit batsmen fell to 10 percent, while it had been nearly 20 percent over the previous twenty years.

However, the concentration of lower-quality talent in the National League has more to do with the way new talent was allocated than with the league the new teams joined. The rules for the expansion draft of the 1993 teams, from which the new teams stocked their rosters, favored the selection of talent from National League teams: American League teams were allowed to protect more of the talent on their rosters than National League teams. Some support for this explanation is that three of the four years in which the National League rate exceeded the American League rate occurred during the first five years of expansion. In the second round of expansion, neither league had an advantage in protecting its rosters in the expansion draft, and only once since that time did the National League rate exceed the American League rate.

The second explanation has to do with a rule change that directly affected the price of hitting batters. In 1994, major-league baseball adopted the "double-warning" rule for hitting batters, in hopes of halting plunking wars between teams. The double-warning rule requires the umpire to warn both teams if, in the umpire's view, a pitcher throws at an opposing player intentionally. Once the umpire issues the warning, a future hit batter by either team results in the immediate expulsion of the offending pitcher and his manager, along with monetary fines and suspensions. While the intention behind the double-warning rule is good, it has the unfortunate side effect of reducing the retaliatory threat that kept pitchers in check in the first place. Unintended consequences of good intentions are a popular theme among economists, and this is a perfect example. The double-warning rule raises the price of retaliating against offending pitchers, and it is very likely that the high price of hitting batters in the National League deters pitchers from hitting batters. But with the rule change, pitchers in the National League now know that retaliation for plunking has become more expensive, and in accordance with the law of demand, teams ought to consume less retaliation. The code of *lex talionis* (law of retaliation) loses its teeth.

As a result, the double-warning rule actually gives protection to National League pitchers, because the opposing team would likely have to forfeit its own pitcher and manager if it chooses to retaliate. Retaliation now carries a pretty steep price, so it is no surprise that the National League hit batter rate has ticked a bit closer to the American League rate in recent years. The relative price of hitting batters decreased in the National League with the lower threat of retaliation, and therefore National League pitchers began to behave more like their brethren in the American League. It's interesting to note that something similar occurred in Japanese professional baseball. The Nippon Professional Baseball League, which also has the DH in its

Pacific League, experienced a similar convergence of hit batsmen—following several years of a higher hit batsmen rate in the DH league—after the implementation of new disciplinary measures for hit batters.[6] But wait, maybe the change in price of retribution is not the whole answer. . . .

Ceteris Paribus,
Another Aspect of Demand

The law of demand makes perfect sense intuitively, but it can be confusing to identify in practice. The definition above is a little misleading. When we predict an inverse relationship between price and quantity we assume that nothing else about the product in question has changed. The Latin phrase *ceteris paribus* is attached to the definition—if not explicitly, it is always implied. The Latin translates as "all else being equal." When looking at the difference in hit batters between leagues, even beyond the fact that pitchers don't bat, all things are not equal.

The introduction of a designated hitter into American League line-ups changes the pitcher's costs and benefits in different ways. Perhaps most importantly the pitcher has to face another good batter—the DH—in the lineup, instead of the weak-hitting pitcher. Typically, pitchers are very poor hitters, as even most pitchers considered to be good hitters barely bat over .200. Due to his poor hitting, the pitcher at the plate represents an easy out for the pitcher on the mound. The last thing a pitcher on the mound wants to do is allow the batting pitcher, who will produce a near-certain out, to reach base. It is possible that pitchers feel that requiring them to bat has almost no effect on their decision to hit batters. The fact that putting the opposing team's worst hitter on base is a bad strategy may cause the pitcher to assume that no team would attempt retaliation. If true, the price-change explanation cannot be correct. And we must remember that all the evidence regarding plunking as an effective retributive threat is anecdotal folklore, which is not the most rigorous evidence.[7] Therefore, the increase in the quantity of hit batsmen in the American League following the introduction of the DH may not be a response to a change in the price, but rather a change in the benefit to hitting batters. This highlights an important distinction between the economic phrases *change in demand* and *change in quantity demanded.*

A change in quantity demanded describes a *behavioral response to a price change,* in accordance with the law of demand. For example, as the price goes up for a product, we can expect humans to consume less of the quantity of that product. Nothing about any particular person's preference for a product has changed, only the price. Pitchers in the National League face a higher price for hitting batters than pitchers in the American League. But a change in demand refers to a change in someone's willingness to consume a product *at the same price.* Something else about the consumer's preference for the product has changed, which caused a change in consumption. Overall, pitchers are less willing to hit batters in the National League because there is always at least one very bad hitter in the lineup to whom they do not want to give a free pass to first base, which is not the case when the DH bats in place of the pitcher.

This adds up to an interleague difference in the willingness to hit batters that violates the "all else being equal" assumption that accompanies the law of demand. Rather than a price difference causing the quantity of hit batters demanded to differ, maybe a different degree of preference for hitting batters explains the greater number of hit batsmen in the American League. Note that pitchers in both leagues are still beholden to the law of demand. There is an inverse relationship between the price and quantity of hit batters for pitchers in both leagues; however, at the same price pitchers in the leagues have different preferences for the amount of batters they are willing to hit.

The difference in the demand schedules is produced by having the good-hitting designated hitter in the batting lineup in the American League. Even without a price change, we have a competing hypothesis that explains the hit batter differential without employing the law of demand.

A Solution

Just because we have two competing theories to predict the same phenomenon does not mean we have to throw up our hands in the air and guess which one is right. There is no need to let the confusion of a complex world get in the way of an economic analysis. Many statistical tools exist that allow us to isolate individual impacts among many overlapping relationships in the world. The problem with using some of the most basic tools to evaluate the hypotheses is that they don't give us the power to distinguish between them. A particular problem in this case is the rarity with which hit batters occur. Even in an era where hit batters are at an all-time high, a hit batter occurs in about only 1 percent of all plate appearances. This means the totals can be heavily influenced by a few instances where hit batter totals are high or low based on game situations that induce pitchers to be extra careful or not so careful.

An altercation between the Houston Astros and Chicago Cubs in August 2004 reveals the importance of the conflicting strategic incentives within the game in regard to the decision to plunk a batter.

After giving up a home run to the previous batter, Roy Oswalt of the Astros plunked Michael Barrett of the Cubs in the back. Barrett took exception and walked toward the mound before order was restored. The umpire ejected Oswalt from the game, so retaliation wasn't an option for the Cubs. But Barrett sent a message to Oswalt through the media: "I thought he was better than that. We're going to see him again." Five days later when the teams met again, the situation was tense, not just because of the animosity between Oswalt and Barrett, but because both teams were neck and neck in vying for a wild-card playoff berth. When Oswalt stepped to the plate in the second inning, he and Barrett argued, but Oswalt was not hit. The Astros led 4–2, and it was much too early for the Cubs to give the opposition a free runner, especially in such an important game. However, when Oswalt stepped to the plate in the sixth, the state of the game had changed quite a bit. With the Astros now leading 8–4, Cubs reliever Kent Mercker hit Oswalt in the thigh on his first pitch.[8]

All of the activity in this game was in response to a perceived intentional plunking the week before. When the lead was two runs, a relatively close game, the Cubs decided it was too costly to punish Oswalt; however, when the Astros extended their lead later in the game, the Cubs retaliated. The cost of putting Oswalt on base—Oswalt had a career .194 on-base percentage—was much lower at this point in the game since there was a high probability that the Cubs would lose the game.

The problem of controlling for all of the factors that might influence hit batters is what my friend, Doug Drinen, and I set out to solve. Doug is a math professor and a former colleague of mine at the University of the South. In addition to being an excellent mathematician and critical thinker, Doug is a former All-Conference college pitcher who brought a few personal insights to the issue. Doug and I decided we would have to use play-by-play and game-by-game data to control for the incentives faced by pitchers in any given situation. What is the importance of the configuration of runners on base? What is the score of the game? How good is the hitter? Is the pitcher coming to bat in the next inning? These are just a few of the things we looked at to determine the factors that impacted the likelihood that a batter would be hit. Once we "controlled for," or held equal, all of these factors, we could then estimate how much influence the law of demand had over the frequency with which pitchers hit batters. Any difference in hit batters between leagues that persisted after we excluded the other competing possibilities would lend support to the law-of-demand explanation. If the difference disappeared because it was, in fact, the product of something that we could not see on the surface, then this would cast doubt on the law of demand explanation.

With play-by-play data we were able to look at eight seasons' worth of data (two four-season samples—1969 and 1972–1974, and 1989–1992) to estimate the determinants of hit batters.[9]

Here are some interesting things we found.

- Pitchers were more likely to hit good batters. Also, pitchers were much less likely to be hit themselves than other players.

This is consistent with the change-in-demand theory that pitchers are more willing to risk hitting good batters than bad batters.

- Good pitchers were less likely to hit batters than bad pitchers. This suggests that pitchers with good control are less likely to hit batters accidentally compared to those with poor control.
- Teams who were losing were more likely to plunk the other team. And the larger the run deficit, the greater the likelihood that the pitcher would hit a batter. As the chance of winning a game falls, the price of plunking, in terms of contributing to the loss, also falls.
- Pitchers who hit batters in the previous inning are more likely to be hit than those who did not hit batters. This provides evidence of retaliation against offending pitchers.

Most importantly, we found that after controlling for these many factors—especially the quality of the batter, which should capture the unequal factor that generates the change-in-demand theory—having a DH increased the likelihood of a batter being hit by 11–17 percent. Even after we accounted for the fact that pitchers were much less likely to be hit than other batters, the existence of the designated hitter is associated with a greater incidence of hit batsmen. Therefore, it is very likely that the law-of-demand hypothesis is a partial reason for the difference in hit batter rates across the leagues, explaining between 60 and 80 percent of the league differences over these two data samples.

Unfortunately, at the time of our initial study, play-by-play data for games after the 1992 season were not freely available to the public. This would be a good sample of data to examine because the nature of the hit batter difference changed quite dramatically in the 1990s. Luckily, game-by-game data does exist from 1973 to 2003, the entire DH era. Although we could not control for play-specific factors influencing hit batters in this sample, we could look at the game-specific factors, such as score and the average offensive and defensive abilities in scoring and preventing runs.

The beginning of interleague play in 1997 provided a unique opportunity to see how the use of the DH by National League teams, and lack of it by American League teams, affected the hit batter rates. Because of the DH rule difference, Major League Baseball adopted the policy of having a DH based on the league rule of the home team. This allowed us to determine whether or not the identified impact of the DH on hit batters in our play-by-play study was due to a price response or if it was just a difference in the American League style of baseball that we had yet to identify.

The results from the game data were consistent with the play-by-play data. Having a designated hitter was associated with about an 8 percent higher rate of hit batters than without. And interestingly, when we looked at interleague games we found that the DH was associated with an 11 percent increase in the incidence of hit batters. This is strong support for the law-of-demand hypothesis. In regards to hitting batters, National League teams acted more like American League teams with the DH and American League teams behaved more like National League teams when they lacked the DH. We also found that for each batter the batting team plunked when pitching, the incidence of hit batters by the pitching team increased by 10–15 percent. This provides further evidence that teams do retaliate for pitchers hitting batters.

Incentives Everywhere

Economist Steven Landsburg wrote, "Most of economics can be summarized in four words: 'People respond to incentives.' The rest is commentary."[10] Indeed, this chapter provides a clear example of how even small changes in incentives in a trivial sporting contest can affect human behavior. Pitchers respond to the price of hit batters in a predictable manner. When the "price" of hitting batters changes, pitchers change their actions accordingly.

Pitchers respond to other incentives, as well. If the batter isn't much good, why risk hitting him with a harder-to-control pitch? Pitchers are more likely to hit good batters, who are more likely to punish pitchers for leaving balls out over the plate. Additionally, they are less likely to hit pitchers on the opposing team, who represent an extremely poor class of hitter. In these ways we begin to build the best intuition about how a pitcher or any player in any position will behave.

The law of demand, which is deemed a "law" because its powers of foresight are so great, is something we should never ignore when analyzing human actions in baseball or anywhere else.

2

The Legendary Power of the On-Deck Hitter

*Nomar Garciaparra has something fundamental in common with
the security guard at the ATM, the rent-a-cap patrolling the mall
and the bouncer at the dance club. He was hired to provide
protection. Pitch around Jeff Kent? Answer to Garciaparra.*

—STEVE HENSON[11]

A S MATT MORRIS toed the rubber during the first inning of
the 2004 World Series for the St. Louis Cardinals, his focus
should have been on the batter, Manny Ramirez. But how could
it be? He'd just given up a double to Johnny Damon and hit Orlando
Cabrera with a pitch—two runners on base. There were no outs and he
was now facing a man who'd swatted forty-three home runs that season,
more than any other player in the American League. As if the pressure
weren't enough, he couldn't ignore the sight of David "Big Papi"
Ortiz—who'd hit forty-one home runs—standing in the on-deck circle.
Should he put some more gas on the fastball or go with something off-
speed? He had to do something, because it wasn't going to get any easier. While he certainly wished the situation were better, he must have
been thankful that at least there wasn't anybody on third. . . .

Baseball fans like statistics in part because the team game can be quantified into many mini-contests between individuals. Batting statistics
especially seem to reflect individual achievements that don't rely on
teammates helping one another out, which is different from individual
performance in other team sports. A basketball player might score a lot
of points, but maybe it's because other good players on his team freed

up the defense. Or in football, a receiver might have a lot of receiving yards, but is it because of his speed and catching ability or the result of an excellent quarterback? In these sports it's hard to evaluate players independently of other players.

In baseball, a hitter steps up to the plate to face a team of nine men all alone. The outcome of this event is surely the triumph or failure of the individual who stands against his rivals. And the statistics he puts up over a given time frame, whether it is a season or a career, indicate a certain level of individual skill demonstrated over that span. There-fore, baseball fans feel a degree of comfort in evaluating batters using well-worn statistics such as batting average or slugging percentage or on-base percentage. However, there does seem to be one exception to this view. In fact, it's a widely held belief that a man who isn't even par-ticipating in the game at a given moment can influence a batter's suc-cess. Many people believe that the hitting prowess of the on-deck hitter—the batter who follows the current batter—influences the per-formance of the batter. How could that possibly be?

It's the pitcher's job, while facing a series of hitters, to minimize the runs produced by the opposing team. One way to do this, which we looked at in the last chapter, is to avoid giving good batters pitches right over the center of the plate, because they are easier to hit. On a team with very few good players, a pitcher may decide to "pitch around" a dangerous hitter—even putting him on base by walking him—in order to pitch to a less threatening on-deck hitter. The logic behind this move is that this limits the runs scored by the opponent by limiting the opportunities for good batters to produce runs through hitting the ball. Pitching around a good batter is something that gets more costly for a pitcher to do the better the on-deck batter is. Putting one runner on base so that he can throw to another good batter is something a pitcher tries to avoid. Therefore, it is often assumed that hitters can "protect" one another in the lineup. A hitter who is good enough to help the preceding batter get better pitches to hit is said to offer *protection*.

The concept of protection is so commonly thrown around between baseball commentators that it's come to be accepted as fact. I often hear comments like "The Giants need to acquire a slugger to protect Bonds, or opposing teams are just going to pitch around him," or "His numbers may look impressive, but that's mostly a product of having a slugger hitting behind him in the batting order." The impact of one person's actions spilling over onto others is a phenomenon well known to economists. A discipline that assumes individuals always act according to their own self-interests ought to be concerned when the behavior of one individual has consequences for other individuals. Economists refer to any action that imposes costs or benefits on other parties as an *externality*.

The externality is simply the amount of the cost or benefit that spills over onto a third party. Externalities can be both positive or negative. Actions that have good consequences for third parties generate a positive externality, and those that have bad consequences produce negative externalities. It's not a hard concept to understand, because we experience externalities in everyday life. When someone cuts you off in traffic, that's a negative externality. Your next-door neighbor who keeps a well-manicured lawn generates a positive externality.

Whenever externalities are present, they generate problems for society. Negative externalities are overproduced, because individuals who engage in behavior that causes a negative spillover don't always take into account the negative consequences of their action. For example, a woman who lights a cigarette in an elevator has the pleasure of the nicotine rush, but often doesn't appreciate the irritation to the lungs of her fellow passengers. Positive externalities are underproduced. A man who paints his house will reap monetary benefits when he sells it, but he probably won't factor in the benefit that his neighbors' houses will sell for more because of the pleasant view he creates. Rather than paint it every year, he might do so every five years.

Sure, most individuals do care about other people, but it would be a stretch to say individuals care as much about others as they do about themselves. After all, the Golden Rule doesn't say "love your neighbor as you love your neighbor." And even if you did care about others as much as you did yourself, you would lack the information to know how your decisions impact others . . . that is, unless you can read minds.

The problem with externalities is that people make decisions that they would otherwise not make if they reaped the rewards or bore the costs of those decisions in accordance with their impact on other people. For example, let's say we have an elevator with eleven passengers, one of whom wants to smoke a cigarette. If ten passengers in the elevator value having their lungs clear of smoke for the ride at ten cents a piece, and the smoker would prefer to be a dollar richer than enjoy the cigarette on her ride, the world would be a better place if this transaction took place. The smoker gets a dollar and the passengers get clean air, and all parties are happier than they would have been had the trade not occurred. In a situation like this, a transaction doesn't often take place, simply because the cost of organizing the transaction is too high. So the smoker will end up smoking and the passengers will bear the cost of her decision to do so. Therefore, we often adopt rules (like prohibiting smoking on elevators) to mirror the likely outcome if such a market did exist.

The house-painting positive externality is a little more interesting. Externalities in real estate transactions can have huge financial and quality-of-life rewards. Everyone likes a good neighbor, and we would all like to live in neighborhoods where people keep up the appearance of their property. Unfortunately, few people are willing to undertake projects because they benefit neighbors. A popular solution to this problem is the use of restrictive covenants in real estate developments, which require owners to adhere to certain appearance standards to guarantee positive spillovers to neighbors. While you might think that buying a piece of property with a catch is not as desirable as buying one without—most certainly you would prefer not to be burdened by rules—these covenants are popular because they ensure that all of the owners in the area do the things necessary to keep neighboring property values high.

But now back to baseball. The hitting externality in baseball doesn't have the negative consequence of influencing market transactions. It's just a spillover, and this spillover is interesting for a different reason. Quantifying the impact would be of great help to general managers, agents, and arbitrators in evaluating talent. Managers might learn how to better arrange their batting orders for the best run production. If player hitting abilities do influence one another, then we ought to learn how to evaluate the influence of talent properly.

Measuring the On-Deck Influence

In order to properly estimate any potential externality in hitting, we need to hypothesize about the possible external effects we are looking for. The traditional model of protection states that a good on-deck hitter prevents a pitcher from pitching around a good batter. This means that the batter is more likely to see good pitches to hit, which will result in more frequent and powerful hits. It should also lower the likelihood that he walks. For simplicity, we'll assume that the improved hitting is more valuable to the hitting team that the forgone walks. Conversely, a poor on-deck hitter means a good hitter will see fewer pitches in the strike zone, which limits his ability to hit. He may walk more, but his hitting production will suffer. In economic terms, a good on-deck hitter generates a positive externality, while a poor on-deck hitter generates a negative externality.

However, there is another possible spillover that we need to consider. It's also possible that good on-deck batters have a negative impact on the batters who hit in front of them. A good on-deck hitter becomes even more dangerous if the hitter in front of him reaches base; that is the reason we expect pitchers not to walk protected batters. However, it's also reasonable to assume that the pitcher will put forth more effort against protected batters with the pitches he throws in the strike zone. The traditional hypothesis of protection discussed by baseball fans assumes that pitchers can only vary their pitches by throwing in the zone or out of the zone, which is not really the case.

Pitching a baseball game is like running a marathon. Going full speed all of the time is not the way to succeed. If a pitcher throws as hard as he can on every pitch, he's going to wear out quickly. This is why most pitchers vary their pitch speeds throughout the game. The difference in effort from batter to batter may be small, due to the quality of all major-league hitters, but pitchers do pitch slower to some batters and faster to others. Veteran manager Tony La Russa explains it this way:

> If you have a veteran pitcher who may know what he's doing out there, he may throw 140 pitches—but of the 140, he's only max-ing out on 40. The other 100, he's taking a little off, putting a little on. But when the slop is flying, he'll reach back and make his best pitch.[12]

This impacts the hitting externality in an interesting way. While having a good on-deck batter may help the current hitter see more pitches in the strike zone, the pitches he does see may be tougher to hit than if he had a stiff hitting behind him. When there's more to lose from letting up, that's when we expect a pitcher to reach back for more. In the language of La Russa, a better on-deck batter creates more "slop." And more slop for a hitter ought to make it more difficult for him to hit the ball.

If pitchers do vary their effort according to the game situation—and we have good reason to think that they do—then we need to modify the traditional protection argument. The externality of a good on-deck hitter may not be positive, but negative. If the good on-deck hitter causes the pitcher to ratchet up his effort, the batter might actually have a tougher time hitting. Having a poor on-deck hitter may cause the pitcher to be less fearful of the hitter reaching base, and therefore save his effort for a more crucial situation. In this case, a poor on-deck hitter would provide a positive externality. I can easily see a pitcher letting up on an eight-hole batter in the NL, because there is a weak-hitting pitcher on deck. The pitcher may say, "If I don't get this guy, I'll just get the pitcher."

A Scientific Test

While, theoretically, it's easy to see why the traditional view of protection might be wrong, we don't know this. This is a problem that we can examine, but it requires some advanced statistical techniques. My math professor colleague, Doug Drinen, and I pondered the existence of hitting externalities over several lunches and decided the subject warranted further investigation. So we designed a test that would measure hitting externalities if they existed.

Using individual plate appearances of batters, we were able to observe how the hitting prowess of the on-deck hitter affected the hitting outcome. We had to be especially careful because there are many other factors that could impact the hitting of a batter. Therefore, we used a multiple regression technique to "hold constant" these other factors. As long as we could include in the model other factors that might influence the hit probability of the batter, we could isolate the impact of the on-deck hitter on the outcome. These were the outside factors we controlled for:

- The hitting ability of the current hitter and pitcher—measured by OPS and OPS allowed for that season (See Appendix B for definition of OPS)
- The handedness of the pitcher and hitter, to control for the "platoon advantage," which is that opposite-handed batters and pitchers increase offense
- The situation of the game (the number of outs, the base runner configuration, the inning of the plate appearance, and the score of the game)
- The park in which the game was played (parks substantially affect run production)

For data from 1984 to 1992, we measured the influence of on-deck-hitter quality (measured by OPS) on the likelihood that a batter would walk, get a hit, get an extra-base hit, or hit a home run. Doug and I were a bit shocked by what we found. Though the conventional baseball wisdom—a better on-deck hitter does protect a batter from being walked—is partially correct, the hitter also lowers his ability to hit for average and power. Therefore, a good hitter imposes a negative externality and a bad hitter imposes a positive externality on the batter who

Table 1: The Percentage Impact of a 100-point Difference of the On-Deck Batter's OPS on a Hitter's Batting Outcome

Outcome	Percent Change in Likelihood
Walks	−2.61 percent
Hits Safely	−1.09 percent
Hits an Extra-Base Hit	−3.70 percent
Hits a Home Run	−2.99 percent

precedes him in the batting order. This is completely counter to the conventional baseball wisdom.

However, there is one crucial caveat. Though we found the impact to be real—it's more than a product of random chance—the size of the effect is tiny. So tiny, in fact, that it's best to say that on-deck hitters have virtually no effect on the performance of a batter. It takes a very large difference in the ability of an on-deck hitter to have a tiny impact on the outcome for the batter at the plate. Table 1 shows the magnitude of the impact of the ability of the on-deck hitter on the current batter. A one-hundred-point increase in the OPS of the on-deck batter lowers the probability that the current batter will walk by 2.6 percent, get a hit by 1 percent, get an extra-base hit by 3.7 percent, and hit a home run by 3 percent.[13] Even with this rather large difference in on-deck hitter ability, the impact is very small.

Although protection is a regular topic of concern in the banter of sports commentators, it turns out that it's not something to worry about at all. Protection is a myth. While pitchers do seem to fear walking batters when there is a good hitter on deck, the benefits of seeing more pitches in the strike zone are offset by greater pitcher effort. Sports announcers have more important things to worry about than protection.

3

The Extinct Left-Handed Catcher

left-hand • **ed** ($l_e$ft′h$_a$n′d$_i$d), *adj.*
4. Of doubtful sincerity; dubious: *left-handed flattery;*
a left-handed compliment.

—THE AMERICAN HERITAGE DICTIONARY
OF THE ENGLISH LANGUAGE, FOURTH EDITION

CATCHERS TYPICALLY have two qualities: good arms and bad legs. Adam LaRoche ought to be a perfect fit. As the son of former big-league pitcher Dave LaRoche, he has a cannon for an arm. Many teams wanted to draft him as a pitcher, but he wanted to hit. And no one would describe him as speedy. He broke into the majors with the Atlanta Braves in 2004 and has shown the potential with the bat to be a good-hitting catcher. Instead, he toils at first base—a position typically manned by hitters much better than Adam—which makes him seem very ordinary. Why? Because Adam is a victim of discrimination: he's left-handed, and left-handers don't play catcher in baseball.

Benny Distefano is a player whom you might know only as the answer to the trivia question: "Who was the last left-hander to play catcher in the major leagues?" In 1989 Distefano played three games at catcher for the Pittsburgh Pirates, becoming only the fourth southpaw to step behind the plate since the AL and NL merged. The fact that the catcher is a right-handed position has always puzzled me. There seems to be very little gained from excluding one class of players from a sport that generally favors left-handedness. But, as an economist, I'm a big believer in persistence signaling the superiority of a practice. As Nobel Prize–winning economist George Stigler wrote:

> Mistakes are indeed made by the best of men and the best of nations, but after a century are we not entitled to question whether these "mistakes" produce only unintended results? Alternatively stated, a theory that says that a large set of persistent policies are mistaken is profoundly anti-intellectual unless it is joined with a theory of mistakes. It is the most vacuous of "explanatory" principles to dismiss inexplicable phenomena as mistakes—everything under the sun, or above the sun, can be disposed of with this label, without yielding an atom of understanding.[14]

In answering this puzzle, it's clear that I should heed Stigler's advice. The strict use of right-handers at catcher is not the result of some whim or official policy of Major League Baseball. It's a practice that has existed for nearly a hundred years. There has been too much time and too much incentive for teams to discontinue an inferior practice for this to be some sort of historical accident in the guise of traditional wisdom. In this chapter, I reveal what is desirable about limiting catching duties to right-handers, which causes this practice to persist.

The Role of Handedness in Baseball

The handedness of a baseball player matters on the field, and we tend to think it matters most in the matchups between pitchers and hitters. Typically, batters perform better against pitchers of the opposite hand, which is known as the "platoon advantage"—because two opposite-handed players on the same team sometimes take turns at a position based on the handedness of the pitcher. The handedness of players would probably be of very little interest in baseball if left- and right-handedness were equally distributed among the general population. Because humans tend to be right-hand dominant (87–90 percent of the population), this creates unique advantages and disadvantages in baseball. A left-handed hitter who is of equal hitting ability as a right-handed player is a more valuable offensive weapon than a righty because a left-handed hitter will have more opposite-hand at-bats than a right-hander, and will therefore produce more offense than a righty of equal hitting skill.

Conversely, the advantage for pitchers would *seem* to be the exact opposite. Right-handed pitchers will face more same-handed at-bats than lefties, thereby reducing offense of the opposing team. However, because lefty batters and switch-hitters populate lineups at a rate greater than in the general population, left-handed pitchers are actually quite valuable commodities. Left-handed hitting is something that right-handed fielders can learn to do, while handedness in throwing is an inborn trait. In 2004, 14 percent of position players threw with their left hand, which is not much higher than the incidence of left-handedness in the general population. However, out of this same group of players, 45 percent had the ability to hit left-handed—29 percent were pure left-handed hitters, and 16 percent were switch-hitters. The platoon advantage has created a strategic use of left-handed pitchers in order to limit the effectiveness of left-handed batters. Many teams carry a "LOOGY," which stands for Lefty–One–Out–GuY, on their rosters to use as a relief specialist against left-handed batters. In 2004, left-handers pitched to 27 percent of all batters faced. Due to their rarity in the general population, being left-handed in baseball, both as a hitter and as a pitcher, is generally considered to be a desirable trait.[15]

Handedness also plays an important role in fielding. The rules of the game dictate that players run the base path in a counterclockwise direction, which results in a high frequency of plays at first base. Due to the angle and distance at which the non–first basemen infielders must throw the ball to first base, right-handed infielders have an advantage in getting the ball to first. Therefore, the positions of second base, third base, and shortstop are almost exclusively manned by right-handers. As evidence, since the birth of the American League in 1901, a left-hander has played second base 86 times, third base 55 times, and

Table 2: Left-Handed Catchers Since 1902

Player	Year	Team	Games
Benny Distefano	1989	Pittsburgh Pirates	3
Mike Squires	1980	Chicago White Sox	2
Chris Short	1961	Philadelphia Phillies	1
Dale Long	1958	Chicago Cubs	2
Homer Hillebrand	1905	Pittsburgh Pirates	3
Jiggs Donohue	1902	St. Louis Browns	23
Joe Wall	1902	Brooklyn Superbas	5
Jiggs Donohue	1901	Milwaukee Brewers	19
Joe Wall	1901	New York Giants	2
Fred Tenney	1901	Boston Beaneaters	2
Jiggs Donohue	1901	Pittsburgh Pirates	1

shortstop 8 times.[16] Handedness poses no such advantage/disadvantage in the outfield or first base, and players of either hand play these positions.

But now we reach the curiosity of the catcher. The catcher doesn't face the same problem with fielding the ball that the other infielders do. In fact, a catcher who is left-handed will have an easier time making a throw to first base on a bunt than a right-hander. Yet left-handers have not played catcher with any more frequency than the other infield positions. Table 2 lists every player and the number of games he's played at catcher by team and season since 1901. Jiggs Donohue is the only player who has logged any significant time at catcher, playing in two-thirds of the sixty-three total games in which a left-hander has played catcher. Since 1905 only four left-handed players have played catcher.

Poor Excuses for Right-Handed Catcher Bias

I listen closely when I hear commentators discuss their explanations for the lack of left-handed catchers. Here are some that I find unconvincing.

• A quickly thrown baseball will fade in the direction of the catcher's throwing arm. For a right-hander the ball will tail toward a runner stealing a base, and for the lefty it will tail away.
• The "framing" of pitches—so that the umpire is more likely to call borderline pitches strikes—is harder for lefties.
• The limited availability of left-handed catcher's mitts prevents left-handed players from learning the position as they grow up.

The first two explanations involve skills that are too minor to explain the complete exclusion of lefty catchers. All baseball players can throw hard and straight without much fading. Framing pitches is more about acting than the positioning of the catcher and offers no obvious advantage to catchers of either handedness. The last explanation doesn't fit with what we know about players learning new skills at the major-league level. Many players learn new positions and skills that they never played or used before. If a lefty could play catcher, the fielding instructors would be able to teach him how to do it.

The answer most commonly given, and the one I've found most convincing, is that left-handed catchers have a harder time throwing out runners at third base on steal attempts. The way the catcher positions himself to receive the pitch creates a difficult throwing angle for left-handers. A lefty must pivot and possibly throw behind a right-handed batter. This is similar to the difficulty that a left-handed shortstop faces when throwing to first. It's possible that the difficulty in throwing to third base allows runners at second a greater opportunity to reach third on a steal. Problems solved, right? I'm not so sure.

Is this really that much of a problem? Right-handed catchers don't seem to have too much of a problem firing pickoff throws to first base (the equivalent of left-handed catchers throwing to third base). Just ask Manny Ramirez, whom right-handed catcher Javy Lopez picked off first base at a crucial time during the 1995 World Series. To examine the potential advantage that right-handers have at preventing opposing runners from producing runs by stealing third, we need to know how valuable it is to keep runners on second base from getting to third base.

What Is Third Base Worth?

We can gauge the value of third base by quantifying the change in the runs a team is expected to score in a given base/out situation. The farther a runner is around the bases, the more likely it is that a runner will score. Additionally, each subsequent out in the inning lowers the number of runs we expect a team to score in an inning, because each out limits the opportunities for a team to knock in runners on base.

Thankfully, the tools we need to measure the trade-off are available and were first presented by George Lindsey in 1963. At the time, Lindsey was an Operations Research Scholar for the Canadian Department of Defence, who had an interest in baseball. With the help of his father, Lindsey tracked the individual plays of baseball games to gather the frequency of different events in baseball.[17] There are eight possible runner configurations (empty, first only, first and second, etc.), three out situations (zero, one, or two), for a total of twenty-four possible states in an inning. From his data, Lindsey calculated the frequency of and the expected runs to be scored from every base/out situation. Lindsey's chart is a helpful tool, because baseball games produce a multitude of outcomes from the same initial starting state. The chart is simply a compilation of the average of all of the run outcomes at the end of the inning in which the state occurred. For example, with a runner on first with no outs, the expected number of runs to be scored from this situ-

Table 2: Expected Runs per Inning Based on Outs and Runner Configuration

Runners	Outs		
	0	1	2
Empty	0.461	0.243	0.102
1st	0.813	0.498	0.219
2nd	1.194	0.671	0.297
3rd	1.390	0.980	0.355
1st and 2nd	1.471	0.939	0.403
1st and 3rd	1.940	1.115	0.532
2nd and 3rd	1.960	1.560	0.687
Loaded	2.220	1.642	0.823

Table 3: Frequency of Events per Inning

	Outs		
Runners	0	1	2
Empty	24.3%	17.3%	13.7%
1st	6.4%	7.6%	7.8%
2nd	*1.1%*	*2.4%*	*2.9%*
3rd	0.2%	0.7%	1.2%
1st and 2nd	*1.4%*	*2.6%*	*3.3%*
1st and 3rd	0.4%	1.1%	1.6%
2nd and 3rd	0.3%	0.7%	0.8%
Loaded	0.3%	0.8%	1.0%

ation is .813; however, a runner on second with one out can be expected to produce .671 runs in that inning (that's right, *on average*—not in all instances—sacrificing an out for a base in this situation *lowers* the expected number of runs scored in the inning).

We also need to know how frequently runners are in a position to steal third base. Even if keeping a runner off third base is valuable, opportunities to steal the base happen infrequently. A player can steal third only when there is a runner on second with third base open. By adding up all of the event frequencies for a runner on second and runners on first and second, italicized in Table 3, stealing third is an option only 13.7 percent of the time.

What we need to do with the information in these tables is to estimate the change in expected run-scoring from stealing third, which catchers try to prevent. A successful steal of third changes the game situation in three ways:

- Going from a runner on second to a runner on third
- Going from runners on first and second to runners on second and third
- Going from runners on first and second to runners on first and third

Since the change in the third state is rare—almost always the runner on first goes to second when the runner on second goes to third—let's exclude it from the analysis. Table 4 shows the change in expected

Table 4: Expected Runs Gained from Stealing Third

	State	State Run Expectancy		Raw Gain	Weighted Gain
Base/Out State	Frequency	Initial	Safe	Stealing Third	Stealing Third
2nd, 0 out	1.1%	1.194	1.39	0.196	0.002
2nd, 1 out	2.4%	0.671	0.98	0.309	0.007
2nd, 2 out	2.9%	0.297	0.355	0.058	0.002
1st and 2nd, 0 out	1.4%	1.471	1.96	0.489	0.007
1st and 2nd, 1 out	2.6%	0.939	1.56	0.621	0.016
1st and 2nd, 2 out	3.3%	0.403	0.687	0.284	0.009
		Total Change in		Per Inning	0.044
		Run Expectancy		Per 9 Innings	0.393

runs per inning from changes in the base/out situation for all out con-figurations, weighted for the frequency with which they occur. We can use this table to compare the expected runs gained by stealing third to the expected runs from staying on second. The final columns of the table show the expected raw gain in runs from stealing third and the gain weighted for the frequency of times the initial state occurs in a game. The bottom right corner of the table sums the runs gained on a per inning and per game basis. The numbers tell us how much stealing third is worth if a runner on second successfully steals third every time the opportunity arises. The result: on average, stealing third nets the team about 0.4 runs per game, which conversely means keeping a run-ner from stealing third base lowers the opposing team's expected runs by that same amount. The difference is not huge, but it's large enough to be relevant—about sixty-four runs a year. If you are having trouble thinking of this number as small or large, you can view it as we view a pitcher's ERA difference of 0.4 earned runs per game. As a manager, would you have preference between pitchers with 3.01 and 3.41 ERAs? I would.

However, this difference is actually very small, probably too small to be the only explanation for the bias against left-handed catchers. Four-tenths of a run is the amount of runs a team gains if it *successfully* steals third base *every time* a runner reaches second base with third base open. Teams don't steal third base every time the opportunity exists. Failing to steal third is costly because the team gives up a runner on second and an out, which are both valuable inputs to run production. An extra out means fewer opportunities to push runners across the plate, and the forgone runner removes a player that was previously in "scoring position." That is why steals of third base are rare.[18]

So the gains from keeping runners on second from stealing third are small, and this is where the advantage of the right-handed catcher is supposed to be. Even if we made the extreme assumption that runners successfully stole third every time they got the opportunity against lefty catchers, and righties always put them out, it would net the opposing team only 0.4 runs per game. Since we expect teams to steal less than this, the expected gains are less.[19]

However, why don't teams put lefties behind the plate if the benefits from excluding them are so small? As George Stigler warned, simply claiming managers have just been making a mistake for so long isn't the best path to understanding. So let's dig a little deeper. While the benefits of using right-handed catchers are small, maybe the costs will yield some answers. What is the cost of excluding left-handers from catching?

The Cost of Southpaw Bias

A large benefit of playing a left-hander in the field is gaining his left-handed bat in the batting order—nearly all left-handed throwers possess the valuable trait of batting left-handed. Lefties can play four positions in the field: all of the outfield positions and first base. All of these positions, except for center field, are considered to be easier to play than the infield positions reserved for right-handers. This gives a team three positions to stash even a defensively poor left-hander in the NL, with the DH as a fourth option in the AL. Unless a manager has an overabundance of left-handers on his team, it's very unlikely that he will need the catcher's spot to get a left-handed bat in the lineup, especially considering the fact that many right-handed fielders possess the ability to bat left-handed. For all non-catching fielding positions played from 1998 to 2004, left-handed throwers have manned those seven positions 24 percent of the time. This means that it's the average base-ball manager's job to find a place for about two players (24 percent times 7 equals approximately 1.7 positions) to play among the seven positions in the field. Even after allotting three of those positions to right-handers only, the manager still has four slots to play lefties in the field without having to squeeze one into the catcher position.

An outfielder has to be able to run and a catcher must have a good throwing arm, while first base requires the least amount of fielding ability on the diamond. The only real reason a manager would be tempted to put a lefty behind the plate is if he had a not-so-agile lefty with an excellent throwing arm and first base reserved for another player. This is a situation that very few teams face. There may be situa-tions in the career of a left-handed player that would make his playing catcher a worthwhile move for the team to do at the moment. For ex-ample, a team has an up-and-coming lefty with a good bat, but he can't run well enough to play outfield and is blocked by an injury-prone All-Star at first base. If he's got a gun for an arm, you might consider put-ting him behind the plate just to get his bat in the lineup. However, the investment in training a lefty to catch probably isn't worth the effort. Catcher is not an easy position to play, and it takes a toll on the bodies of the men who play the position. Why train a left-hander to catch when the odds are that he won't have the role for long? The long-run returns to the player's effort would be higher in working on other ar-eas of his game, and the team would rather have its catching instruc-tors working with long-run catching prospects. It's just cheaper for the team to trade the player to a team without a logjam of players at first base, the traditional home for not-so-agile lefties.

The Simple Answer

We could conclude that the main reason that there are no left-handed catchers is that there simply isn't a need to use that position to get a left-hander playing time. Even though the advantage of being right-handed at catcher may only be slight, there seems to be no real cost to keeping left-handers out of the role. Using only right-handed catchers is like locking your car door in a small town with no crime. The chances that someone will break into your car are tiny, but the cost of protecting yourself against the small likelihood of the negative consequences is so low (pressing the lock button) that it's still worth locking the door. Similarly, in those rare instances where the advantage of having a right-handed catcher is the difference between winning and losing a game—runner on second base in the ninth inning of a one-run ball game—you'll be glad you have one.

Even if we grant that there is an advantage in keeping opposing runners off third base for right-handed catchers, the advantage is very small. It's small enough that a left-hander with an excellent arm could overcome it. But herein lies a second issue, which adds one more reason why lefties don't catch. In Bill James's opinion,

> The biggest reason there are no left-handed catchers is natural selection. Catchers need good throwing arms. If you have a kid on your baseball team who is left-handed and has a strong arm, what are you going to do with him?[20]

The opportunity cost of using a lefty who's good enough to catch behind the plate is using him as a pitcher. If you have a left-hander with an excellent arm in a world where left-handed pitching is in short supply, you're probably going to want him to throw to a catcher rather than become one.

4

Lobbying for Balls and Strikes

*[The Braves] beat the umpires down. It's really bull and beneath
the class of the organization. It's a joke.... There's no doubt in
my mind. Maybe that's their strategy. It's not to be admired. It's
not to be copied.*

—TONY LA RUSSA[21]

WAS STANDING in the first base coach's box on the local Little League field, when the ball zoomed down the line. I turned to watch the ball as it passed me, and I saw it land on the chalk and roll into foul territory. Without looking back, I waved my arm and hollered to my player, "It's fair, go for more!" As the runner coasted into third, I saw the home plate umpire waving his arms and yelling in my direction with anger, "That was a FOUL ball!" Without even thinking I responded, "What are you talking about? It hit the line!" The crowd snickered, because they knew I was right. I'd had the best view of the play in the whole park. The umpire covered his icy glare with his mask, while still staring in my direction. "FOUL BALL!" I was punching myself on the insides, thinking, "Why did I do that?" My team didn't get a close call for a week.

It's quite common to hear people rant against the evils of profits. When a business sells a product that generates more revenue than it cost to produce, this seems unfair. But economists are normally quick to defend profits. Profits are something that entrepreneurs chase, and in doing so they yield new products and ideas that benefit society. However, one form of profit seeking that economists will not defend is *rent seeking.*

Rent seeking is one of those economics terms that can be misleading. It's not about landlords searching for tenants. Rent seeking occurs when parties try to capture profits by transferring wealth from one party to another. It is most often studied in the field of public economics, a field where economists analyze government decision making. Governments of all types—although some are more susceptible than others—possess the power to grant special privileges to . . . well, whomever they can get away with granting these privileges to. Dictators may grant privileges to almost anyone, but in representative democracies politicians tend to give special favors to those who support their re-election campaigns. And what type of favors do politicians grant? Some privileges help promote the interests of the lobbying company, such as subsidies for a product, favoritism in winning government contracts, or loopholes in regulations. Some favors indirectly help lobbying interests by harming competitors by taxing competing products, adopting strict regulatory standards, or outright banning of substitute products.

A common example of rent seeking is protectionist trade barriers. American car manufacturers really wish Japanese car companies didn't sell their wares in the United States. In the late 1970s, several Japanese automakers began to offer cars to American consumers at prices lower than what was available from U.S. dealers. One way to prevent this competition from "destroying" profits was to keep Japanese imports out of U.S. markets by lobbying the U.S. government to place quotas and taxes on foreign automobile imports. With less foreign competition, American consumers would have to pay higher prices for U.S. automobiles, leading to greater profits for U.S. companies. Of course, an alternate path would be to reform U.S. car production to become more competitive with Japanese imports. It turns out that a little of both happened.

On its face, rent seeking seems like pretty nasty business, and something that almost no one likes. Self-consumed politicians responding to the whims of greedy businessmen in search of easy profits? It is not the way we like to see decisions made in government. However, the search for profits through lobbying as opposed to generating superior products through innovation is not always undesirable to economists. What's wrong with rent seeking is not the transfer of wealth from one party to another. Transferring wealth from American drivers to American car sellers doesn't make American society any poorer. Drivers may be a little poorer, but this is offset by the extra wealth of stockholders in U.S. automobile firms. I think this kind of transfer is morally repugnant; however, it's not because society was made poorer. Dollars were just shuffled around.

Rent seeking *is* very bad for society; it just turns out that the transfer of wealth isn't the problem. The problem is that the effort that went into transferring the wealth is effort that could have been devoted to something productive. Think of what it takes to get majorities in two houses of Congress and the President to agree to a law that grants favors to a particular group. The President seems easy; one person is all you have to convince, right? Moving to the Senate, you'd have to get 51 senators on your side. And the House has 435 members, so you'd need 218 representatives. How are you going to convince 270 people to support legislation that benefits a group of already rich people who just want some help earning more money? It's going to take more than a few postcards expressing support for the law.

Politicians are well aware that helping one group necessarily hurts another group. Potential losers from favors given to one group may be pushing just as hard to prevent the legislation from being put into place. In addition, elected representatives must serve the needs of their constituents or fail to be reelected to office, and some political favors may require a politician to vote against constituent interests. Thus, convincing politicians to dole out favors is not a simple task. Interest groups spend large amounts of money hiring lobbyists, lawyers, and experts to make their case. Rent seeking requires putting on a happy face for the public. Companies advertise on television to sway politicians' constituents that these special programs are a good idea.

All of these expenses are the costs of rent seeking. The expenditures on lobbyists and advertising could have gone into R&D to develop new and superior products that could be sold at lower prices, which is the goal of profit seeking. The difference between rent seeking and profit seeking is easiest explained through the metaphor of a pie. Rent seeking is the attempt to get more pie by taking pieces from others. With profit seeking, individuals seek to generate profits by innovating to create new low-cost production techniques. These individuals get more pie by making more pie. The effort that goes into arguing over who gets the slices could be spent on enlarging the pie for everyone, which is why economists consider rent seeking to be social waste.

The social loss of rent seeking was the discovery of Professor Gordon Tullock, whose lectures I was privileged to attend as a student. In his seminal article on the subject, Professor Tullock made the case that not only is rent seeking social loss, but that the amount of resources individuals will devote toward rent seeking will be equal to the amount of the profits to be gained from "winning" the special interest legislation. If I were to offer an auction on a $100 bill on eBay, how much do you think it would sell for? $100. We expect rational human beings to exploit profit opportunities until they are gone. A bid of $75 would most certainly be matched by other bidders. The ability of governments to grant special privileges creates the incentive for rent seeking, which is why public economists spend large amounts of time trying to design and advocate for political rules and institutions to discourage rent seeking.

The end game of a rent-seeking contest is a sad outcome. Because, in the end, winning the contest puts you right back where you started. If you pay $100 to get $100, you're not gaining anything. So this begs the question: why does anyone participate in a rent-seeking contest to begin with? Well, the problem is that if there are profits to be gained, someone is going to go after them. Not going after them can be deadly to your livelihood. If you make a product, and your competitors see your inaction, they will lobby to put you out of commission. You can't just not play the game. If you are in business, the game is being played.

And as long as the rules allow it, rent-seeking players will engage in this behavior. Again, the ending is not a happy one.

But what does this have to do with baseball? Certainly, we see owners, players, and agents in front of Congress on a frequent basis on issues ranging from steroids, to labor disputes, to franchise relocation. This is certainly posturing that may affect some rent seeking for privileges by the many parties with a stake in the business of baseball. But that's all just politics. I want to look at a particular brand of rent seeking that is quite unique to the game of baseball and is so much a part of the game that it's hard to imagine the game without it.

Managerial Rent Seeking

Baseball managers have many jobs: keeping players happy, setting the batting order, picking the right players, etc. We generally think of managers handling the strategic choices of the team that lead it to win or lose the game. However, one very important aspect that a manager rarely gets any credit or blame for is lobbying umpires to ensure that his team is getting calls to go his way. Old men kicking dirt, spitting, and base-throwing tantrums all seem like a sideshow. But this is much more. It's all done in an attempt to influence how umpires enforce the rules of the game in a way that benefits the manager's team. This is rent seeking, plain and simple.

While certainly any manager will tell you that the goal is make sure the umpire "gets the call right," not to seek special treatment, the game of baseball requires umpires to pick winners and losers on many close plays. Anyone who watches a lot of baseball will admit that though umpires make incorrect calls from time to time, the vast majority are correct. Obvious mistakes are rare, and normally understandable given the speed of the game. It is during the moment just before the umpire makes his public judgment—safe or out, ball or strike—that the manager wants him to think, "I don't want to hear an earful from that guy." And if a manager can make an umpire feel insecure enough, maybe he'll be more deferential to that team on future close calls. Tony La Russa, who has managed the White Sox, A's, and Cardinals, sums it up nicely:

> When you go against somebody who is complaining all the time, you worry about how it affects the umpires. . . . When I was a young manager, Earl Weaver at Baltimore played it that way. They challenged every strike. If your wife is getting on you every minute, you get fed up. Pretty soon, you may tune her out and do whatever it takes to get through it.[22]

Every call an umpire makes has a zero-sum outcome. That is, one team's gain equals the other team's loss. A called strike helps the pitching team at the expense of the batting team. A manager understands that gaining an advantage on close calls is not just something he wants, but also that any advantage the opposing manager gains is something he wants to prevent. This sets up a rent-seeking contest within the game. Every manager tries to make his influence felt just to keep the other manager from gaining the upper hand. One manager yells, "Hey, Ump, that ball was high!" The other manager, if he thinks the comment has been influential, responds a few pitches later, "The strike zone goes all the way to the letters. A high strike is still a strike!" Most of this banter stays on this level, to where it's not always obvious that this game is being played from the shadows of the dugouts and behind the mask of the umpire.

Sometimes the lobbying spills out onto the field, where the exchanges become heated and the antics begin. If the manager goes "too far," he'll get tossed, and return to the clubhouse and run his team just as effectively through a relay to the dugout. Why does a manager allow himself to be tossed? There's no bigger insult than to say to the umpire, "You blew it," in front of the thousands in the stands and the millions watching highlights. The manager may be wrong in a particular instance, and he may even know it, but he's sent a message to the umpire: "If you cross me, I'll make life difficult for you." There are superiors to answer to, umpire review hearings, maybe even questions from the media. It's all a pain that the umpire would prefer to avoid if possible. And to make matters worse, the umpire has to keep both sides happy.

Let's think about the end result of this little game by comparing two worlds: one where managers can argue and one where they cannot. For both worlds we'll assume that we have a home plate umpire who is an impartial judge of balls and strikes. He's going to call it the way he sees it. He may make mistakes, but they will be random and will even out over time. In the world without manager arguing, there will be mistakes but no bias in the calls of the umpire.

In the world with arguing, we'll assume that each comment by a manager makes the umpire slightly more inclined to choose in favor of the complaining manager. "The squeaky wheel gets the grease," as they say. Managers know that complaining about anything but borderline calls will only make the umpire mad and hurt his case. Therefore, each manager has the incentive to complain whenever the call is close but goes against him. And once the first complaint starts, the other manager knows he must respond or risk losing future calls. Each counter-complaint reverses any developed bias back toward unbiased calls. So what happens at the end of the day? There is no bias in the calls of the umpire, just as in the first world, but there is also a lot of complaining. This effort that goes into complaining is rent-seeking loss.

The costs of riding the umpire include: noticing the opportunity for a double-switch, identifying a minor defensive adjustment, stealing signs, or talking up a player who's in a funk. These certainly seem minor, and may be minor, but often these are the kinds of sensitivities we hear about when players talk about great managers.

The fans pay a price too. MLB is constantly trying to speed up what many perceive to be a slow game. Those instances where umpires must engage in banter with managers and players add up. I'd guess that lobbying takes up between five to ten minutes of every baseball game. That's time that could have spent working, playing with a daughter, going fishing, or getting to bed just a little bit earlier. The loss may be small, but when you consider that there is nothing to be gained from all of this arguing, it doesn't seem like we'd be losing much but the spectacle of manager tantrums.

Which Managers
Are We Talking About?

Still, lobbying umpires is a skill that some managers possess or lack. After hearing Tony La Russa complain about Bobby Cox's on-field banter
during a Cardinals-Braves series in May 2005, I set out to try and identify how much influence particular managers have over umpires during the course of a game. It is hard to find. The parties involved could
not be expected to give up much information. Managers and umpires
tend to exaggerate their ability or inability to influence calls. A manager who says he doesn't influence calls could lose his job, as could an
umpire who admits to being influenced by managers. No one has an
incentive to be honest, but economists don't give up when witnesses
get hostile. To gauge manager influence, all we need is a situation
where we can view calls where influence isn't likely. Luckily, an experimental automated pitch tracking system, known as Questec, used in
ten ballparks, creates the conditions for a natural experiment.

The Questec system uses computerized imaging technology to map
balls and strikes during a game. While Questec requires a human oper-
ator to set the top and bottom of the strike zone for every player (so
must the umpire), the system maps each pitch location and identifies
each as a ball or strike, based on whether or not a pitch passed through
an objective strike zone. These calls have no impact on the game; in
fact, the balls and strikes are not "called" by the computer until after
the game is over. Umpires still call the official balls and strikes; however, unlike in non-Questec parks, there is a historic trail to which the
umpire's record can be compared by league officials. Any pressure an
umpire feels to bias close calls in one direction or another will be a
matter of public record within MLB. And umpires know that there are
plenty of umpires waiting in line to take their jobs if they should be
deemed anything but impartial judges of the rules of the game.

While there may be some influence on balls and strikes in Questec
parks, it is reasonable to assume that it will be less pronounced. So we
can compare the balls and strikes—as measured by the strikeout-to-walk

Table 5: MLB Ballparks with Questec in 2002–2003

American League	National League
Anaheim	Arizona
Boston	Houston
Cleveland	Milwaukee
New York	New York
Oakland	
Tampa Bay	

ratio—in games managed inside and outside Questec parks over a two-year span. We use the strikeout-to-walk ratio because a pitcher that is getting more beneficial calls is going to be able to strike out more batters and walk fewer batters. While not all of the pitcher's strikeouts will be the result of called strikes without a swing, batters will be more likely to strike out and less likely to walk if they have to defend a bigger strike zone.

To begin, I looked at the strikeout-to-walk ratio on the pitching side of the baseball. That is, how did the ratio of strikeouts-to-walks change for a manager when his team pitched inside and outside of Questec parks? To avoid the influence of the home crowd of the manager, I only looked at a manager's away games. The ballparks in which Questec is used are listed in Table 5.

One problem with looking at the raw difference between how pitchers perform inside and outside of Questec parks is that there may be other influences that are to blame for any difference. Therefore, I used multiple regression analysis to isolate the effect of individual managers on the strikeout-to-walk ratio in Questec parks. Multiple regression allows me to control for outside influences on the strikeout-to-walk ratio other than the managers and Questec. Some other potential impacts on the strikeout-to-walk ratio are the quality of the pitchers on the manager's team, the quality of the batters on the opposing team, subtle differences in the park (e.g., the hitting background, altitude, etc.), and the use of the designated hitter. Therefore, I included the following "control variables" in the multiple regressions to account for these potential influences:

- The average strikeout-to-walk ratio of the pitchers on the manager's team on the road in that year
- The average strikeout-to-walk ratio that year of the batters on the opposing team at home in the park in which the game was played
- The league of the home team

I also included variables that indicated who the manager was and when Questec was in use. This information allowed me to see how each manager's impact on the strikeout-to-walk ratio changed when his team played in a Questec park. Table 6 lists the impact of each manager in Questec parks on his pitchers' strikeout-to-walk ratio. The greater the negative number, the greater the manager's decline in the ratio (meaning fewer strikeouts and/or fewer walks) in Questec parks, which indicates that this manager's pitcher performed better outside Questec parks. It is outside these parks that managers will have influence on balls and strikes.

Most managers experience no statistical difference between Questec and non-Questec parks (rounded to three decimal places). Only two managers have a statistically significant impact on the strikeout-to-walk ratio, which means we can say with a high degree of confidence that these impacts are very unlikely to occur via random chance. And right at the top of the list is Tony La Russa (who managed the St. Louis Cardinals during this time frame), whose quote about Bobby Cox (of the Atlanta Braves) working the umpires started this chapter. It turns out that maybe Cox should have been the one doing the complaining.

La Russa's ability to sway umpires is not surprising considering that he is a lawyer, the most popular pedigree for professional lobbyists. I wouldn't be surprised if La Russa is quite adept at manipulating umpires on the field and off through MLB's umpire evaluation system. Certainly Tony La Russa has no moral high ground to accuse any other manager for influencing the game through umpires, since in Questec parks his pitchers' strikeout-to-walk ratio falls by nearly one. And if Bobby Cox is low-class for his manipulation of umpires, La Russa must be the scum of the universe.

Table 6: Manager Impact on Pitcher Strikeout-to-Walk Ratio in Questec Parks

Manager	Impact
Bob Boone	-1.017
Ken Macha	-0.967
Tony La Russa	-0.966
Jim Tracy	-0.869
Larry Bowa	-0.743
Joe Torre	-0.639
Jimy Williams	-0.584
Clint Hurdle	-0.494
Hal McRae	-0.487
Mike Scioscia	-0.453
Bruce Bochy	-0.409
Lloyd McClendon	-0.406
Bobby Valentine	-0.387
Jerry Narron	-0.283
Bobby Cox	-0.275
Jack McKeon	-0.255
Lou Piniella	-0.23
Jerry Manuel	-0.156
Bob Melvin	-0.114
Felipe Alou	-0.085
Jeff Torborg	-0.084
Carlos Tosca	-0.024
Jerry Royster	0
Dusty Baker	0.024
Ned Yost	0.113
Art Howe	0.16
Grady Little	0.197
Tony Pena	0.215
Frank Robinson	0.271
Alan Trammell	0.289
Mike Hargrove	0.348
Eric Wedge	0.369
Luis Pujols	0.428
Buck Showalter	0.483
Ron Gardenhire	0.749
Bob Brenly	0.771

And then look at Bob Brenly, formerly the manager of the Arizona Diamondbacks and now a television commentator. Why is he so "bad"? First, it's not clear that he is bad at working the umpires. Although his impact is large, it's not statistically significant, which means we can't say that his improvement in Questec parks is outside the realm of random chance. I wonder if his arguing skills are so weak that he ends up hurting his pitchers. Or maybe other managers take advantage of him when Questec is not around and he can't counter with anything. But a more flattering possibility is that he protected his hitters to the extent that it hurt his pitchers. That wasn't such a bad strategy given the good pitching he had during these years in Arizona—Randy Johnson and Curt Schilling didn't need much help from the umpire. This indicates that maybe we need to look at manager influence on hitters as well as pitchers. Maybe a manager can argue to increase or shrink the strike zone, but it applies equally on both sides of the ball.

In order to examine this possibility, we can use the data to focus on the hitting side. I used the exact same sample and control variables, except I looked at the strikeout-to-walk ratio for the manager's players when they bat. Table 7 lists the impacts. This time a positive number is consistent with good lobbying for the manager's hitters. Batters want fewer strikeouts and more walks, and when the strikeout-to-walk ratio rises in Questec parks it indicates that hitters are losing that benefit. There doesn't seem to be any inverse relationship between arguing for pitchers and hitters, and only Ned Yost's impact was statistically significant.

However, the fact that a few managers might have a slight influence over umpires is not the real story here. Overall, it appears that most managers don't seem to have any real impact in arguing balls and strikes, which is consistent with rent-seeking outcomes. Everyone wastes energy arguing, but nothing is gained. I think the tables are instructive not in showing differences between managers, but that very few are different. Only three managers showed any statistically significant impacts (names in italic) in Questec parks.

The lesson for rent seeking in baseball is the same for rent seeking in society. Lobbying for special favors is something to be discouraged because, in the end, nothing is gained from the effort expended. Put Questec in every major-league ballpark to keep managers focused on the winning the game through baseball strategy rather than trying to

Table 7: Manager Impact on Hitter Strikeout-to-Walk Ratio in Questec Parks

Manager	Impact
Hal McRae	1.468
Bruce Bochy	0.741
Frank Robinson	0.472
Ken Macha	0.457
Felipe Alou	0.456
Luis Pujols	0.403
Jerry Narron	0.319
Bobby Cox	0.239
Jeff Torborg	0.14
Jimy Williams	0.073
Lloyd McClendon	0.015
Jack McKeon	0
Tony Pena	-0.039
Jim Tracy	-0.083
Clint Hurdle	-0.099
Alan Trammell	-0.139
Mike Scioscia	-0.162
Jerry Royster	-0.2
Bob Boone	-0.202
Tony La Russa	-0.204
Ron Gardenhire	-0.311
Joe Torre	-0.329
Carlos Tosca	-0.362
Mike Hargrove	-0.376
Lou Piniella	-0.379
Bob Melvin	-0.493
Jerry Manuel	-0.497
Grady Little	-0.536
Buck Showalter	-0.558
Eric Wedge	-0.623
Dusty Baker	-0.641
Art Howe	-0.646
Larry Bowa	-0.693
Bobby Valentine	-0.862
Bob Brenly	-0.996
Ned Yost	-1.92

manipulate the enforcement of the rules within the game. Maybe some fans will miss the elaborate tantrums of grumpy old men out there on the field, but I sure won't.

Part Two

ALMOST OFF THE FIELD

5

How Good Is Leo Mazzone?

Great pitchers make for good pitching coaches, and good pitching coaches don't mess up great pitchers.

—LEO MAZZONE[23]

URING THE 2004 OFF-SEASON the Braves said good-bye to resurrected pitching ace Jaret Wright, after he signed a large free agent deal with the New York Yankees. Many Braves fans were not worried. "Leo Mazzone can fix anyone," they said. "Bologna," I responded. "He's just been lucky, and we're focusing on the success stories and ignoring the failures. What we need is a study of all the players Leo has coached, and then we'll see he isn't so great." I soon found out how wrong I was.

Coaches and managers don't just throw tantrums on the field. Through coaching and training they help the players improve skills and give their best in the most important games. But how much do they help really? Assigning individual responsibility for success and failure is never simple in a team game. This is true not just in sports, but in all group activities. Is the success of a Fortune 500 company due to a brilliant CEO, an efficient workforce, or just dumb luck?

We like to celebrate not just the players on the field, but the managerial brains that organize and coach players to succeed. The question is, how much does the off-the-field part of the organization contribute? Everyone knows the famous managers—Connie Mack, Sparky Anderson, Leo Durocher, and Casey Stengel, just to name a few—maybe even a coach or two. But how good are they really? Unfortunately, win-loss records of coaches don't have much to say on the subject. Some coaches have the good fortune to coach several exceptionally talented athletes, while others are left to oversee near-minor-league teams. Determining the influence of any coach would require an experiment with coaches being randomly assigned players. Then we could compare the success of the coaches with different players. If one coach was better than the others, he should get more out of players when they are with him.

However, such an experiment isn't feasible. Major League Baseball isn't going to allow some young economist to shuffle coaches from team to team over the course of several seasons just to see which coaches are better than others. But we don't have to give up the quest to disentangle coaching and player contributions. What we can do is look at how individual players perform as they move from coach to coach. The frequent movement of players from team to team over their careers makes this possible. Using the right statistical tools, we can adjust for other factors that influence achievement, to see how players perform with and without a particular coach.

Specifically, I'm interested in charting the success of one man who has never even managed a major-league team: Leo Mazzone. The current pitching coach of the Baltimore Orioles made his name in baseball with my beloved Atlanta Braves during the mid-1990-through-2005 seasons. Though he never got higher than Double-A in the minor leagues as a pitcher, he was able to become a big-league pitching coach. Mazzone had the good fortune, as he sees it, to hook up with the legendary Johnny Sain.

Sain was a very good major-league pitcher who was the subject of a baseball poem about the 1948 Boston Braves:

> *First we'll use Spahn, then we'll use Sain.*
> *Then an off day, followed by rain.*
> *Back will come Spahn, followed by Sain.*
> *And followed, we hope, of two days of rain.*[24]

After finishing his successful eleven-year career as a player, he became a well-traveled pitching coach. Although his staffs were successful, he had a reputation for being a bit of a rebel, leading to his transient employment. When Leo had the opportunity to coach alongside Sain in the Braves' minor-league system, he listened and learned. Mazzone writes in his autobiography,

> He was so helpful to my thought process and approach. He was the smartest son of a gun and the nicest guy I'd ever talked to. He had all these things to offer. Believe it or not, there were some who wouldn't listen to him. I think sometimes he was so far ahead of his time that those other people feared his knowledge, so, therefore, they turned it off. Whatever their reason was, they were stupid. I went the exact opposite direction. I was going to jump all over it and listen to everything he had to say. . . .
>
> He didn't give the usual clichés when it came to what he was teaching me. He taught me everything from throwing programs to proper spins on a baseball to strategies of baseball to dealing with the front office. Everything he talked about and taught me, I've seen unfold from the top down. It was a tremendous education.[25]

Tom Glavine, a two-time Cy Young Award–winner who pitched twelve seasons for Mazzone, describes this unique approach:

> You get guys to throw as much as they want to, so they can develop feel on their pitches and understanding of their mechanics. In terms of getting guys to throw more often, I think a lot of people don't want to do that simply because they are scared to death somebody's going to get hurt. Coaches are going to err on the side of caution and not encourage guys to throw as much as Leo does.[26]

Four-time Cy Young–winner Greg Maddux elaborates:

There are no parachutes on your back, no cones to run around, no ten different meetings talking about something that doesn't concern you. All the other stuff, you don't partake in. So you spend less time doing nothing, and you spend all your time doing what it is you have to do to get better on the mound.[27]

Mazzone embraced a novel method others eschewed. He made his pitchers focus on pitching, with less concern for throwing and and general fitness drills. So if Mazzone's success with pitchers is more than a myth, then his pitchers should excel compared to other pitching coaches who rely on traditional methods.

Charting Mazzone's Success

As the Braves emerged from cellar-dwellers in the 1980s to perennial division champs in the early 1990s, Mazzone began to gain some notoriety for the consistently good pitching staffs he put together year after year. Clearly, the Braves' winning ways in the 1990s and 2000s had a lot to do with pitching. Table 8 lists the average league rank and ERA for each team in Major League Baseball since 1991, Mazzone's first full year as the Braves' pitching coach.

There is no doubt that the Braves had the best pitching staff in baseball during Mazzone's tenure as the organization's big-league coach. But early in his career, the media gave Mazzone little credit for the Braves' success. He was seen as an oddity: a little man who rocked back and forth on the bench as he nervously monitored his pitchers. Though the Braves pitching was always good, the praise went to the players. Leo Mazzone was just an unsuccessful minor leaguer who'd inherited some good players. Steve Avery, Tom Glavine, Greg Maddux, and John Smoltz were some of the best pitchers in the game. Even Mazzone has graciously acknowledged that he has been fortunate to work with some of the game's elite pitchers.

But after many of these pitchers moved on or missed time due to injuries, Mazzone continued to field good staffs. Soon people began

Table 8: Average League ERA Rank and ERA by Team (1991–2005)

Rank	Team	Mean League Rank	Mean ERA
1	Atlanta Braves	2.1	3.53
2	Los Angeles Dodgers	4.4	3.79
3	Boston Red Sox	5.0	4.28
4	New York Yankees	5.5	4.28
5	New York Mets	5.8	4.00
6	Chicago White Sox	6.1	4.40
7	Los Angeles Angels of Anaheim	6.3	4.40
8	St. Louis Cardinals	6.4	4.08
9	Houston Astros	6.5	3.99
10	Cleveland Indians	6.6	4.44
11	Oakland Athletics	6.7	4.43
12	Toronto Blue Jays	6.7	4.45
13	Washington Nationals/Expos	6.9	4.07
14	Seattle Mariners	7.1	4.49
15	Baltimore Orioles	7.2	4.56
16	Arizona Diamondbacks	7.6	4.28
17	San Francisco Giants	7.9	4.16
18	San Diego Padres	8.3	4.21
19	Minnesota Twins	8.3	4.64
20	Chicago Cubs	9.0	4.28
21	Kansas City Royals	9.1	4.77
22	Milwaukee Brewers	9.2	4.52
23	Florida Marlins	9.4	4.33
24	Cincinnati Reds	9.5	4.37
25	Philadelphia Phillies	9.7	4.31
26	Pittsburgh Pirates	9.7	4.37
27	Tampa Bay Devil Rays	10.1	4.95
28	Texas Rangers	10.3	4.93
29	Detroit Tigers	11.1	5.00
30	Colorado Rockies	15.0	5.31
League			4.38

to notice that the Braves had a habit of getting good seasons out of pitchers that no one else wanted. People began to discuss whether or not the coach deserved more credit.

John Burkett was waived by the Tampa Bay Devil Rays in 2000—a season in which they won sixty-nine games—when the Braves signed him. In the following two seasons with the Braves, coached by Mazzone, Burkett pitched 354 innings with an ERA of 3.74 and a strikeout-to-walk ratio of 2.45.

Chris Hammond was a career journeyman, having had two above-average seasons with the Florida Marlins in 1994 and 1995, but was otherwise unspectacular. His skills declining, Hammond retired from the game in 1998. In 2002, he returned to the majors with the Braves at the age of thirty-six, where he posted an ERA of 0.95 as a reliever. During that season, Hammond had two strikeouts for every batter he walked, while surrendering only one home run during seventy-six innings of work.

Mike Remlinger had bounced between starting and relief pitching roles, mostly with the Cincinnati Reds, when the Braves acquired him in a trade prior to the 1999 season. Before joining the Braves, he had a career ERA of 4.63 and a strikeout-to-walk ratio of 1.62. In his four seasons with the Braves as pure reliever he improved his ERA by two runs and his strikeout-to-walk ratio by one.

Jorge Sosa was acquired from the Tampa Bay Devil Rays for a light-hitting utility infielder, and then Sosa had a career year under Mazzone. As a fifth-starter/long-reliever, Sosa had a career ERA of 5.17 and a habit of giving up too many long balls (1.29 per nine innings). He began the 2005 season as the Braves' mop-up reliever, but soon became a starter, posting an ERA of 2.55 and cutting his home runs by approximately 40 percent (0.8 per nine innings).

Jaret Wright was once a promising young starter for the Cleveland Indians, but he was failing as reliever for the woeful San Diego Padres when the Braves picked him up off of waivers in 2003. In 2004, he became the number one starter in the Braves rotation, posting an ERA of 3.21 with a 2.27 strikeout-to-walk ratio.

After rebuilding their careers with a little help from Mazzone, these players, except for Sosa, left for new teams as big-name free agents. The Braves didn't have to hold on to these guys, because they could count on getting similar performances from pitchers whom the rest of the league found to be unworthy.

Mazzone's success is not without warts. Some pitchers who didn't pitch so well under Mazzone have had otherwise decent careers, like Jason Marquis, Odalis Perez, and Dan Kolb. Maybe we're just remembering the success stories, and some of the guys who were successful with the Braves just got a bit lucky during their tenure. Even if the tendency to succeed under Mazzone is real, there could be other contributing factors, such as age and defense. Hence, the success of Braves pitchers might be a product of selective memory or other factors that have nothing to do with coaching.

Isolating Individual Responsibility

Given the rate at which pitchers move on and off the Braves roster, we can take a large group of pitchers and analyze how much better (or worse) they were with Mazzone than without. All we need are the right statistical tools.

Let's look at pitchers who pitched regularly for Mazzone and for other pitching coaches in the league over their careers. The sample includes every pitcher who pitched at least one full year for Mazzone, and at least one full year for another pitching coach. Let's throw out pitchers who pitched for more than one team in a single season, to ensure the transition isn't affecting pitching performance. Also, the pitcher needs to throw a significant number of innings for the statistics to be useful. The cutoff for inclusion in the study is thirty innings pitched in a year. And because pitchers have various roles—starters throw many innings, while relievers pitch very few over the course of the season—I also compare performances according to pitching role.

We can compare seasonal pitching performances with and without Mazzone, but even with this suitable sample of pitchers, it is still complicated. Many other factors change as pitchers change teams; therefore, we need control for other potential factors. I employ multiple regression analysis to weight different influences, including Mazzone's oversight, on pitcher performance. What are they?

First, pitchers change over time. As pitchers mature they tend to get better, but then decline after a certain point—typically in their late twenties or early thirties. Including pitchers' ages when they post their performances allows us to adjust for this impact.

Another factor is that pitchers rely heavily on their defenses to help them, so we need to account for the quality of the defense on the team.

I use the percentage of balls hit into the field of play that the pitcher's team turned into outs to proxy defensive quality. Good defenses will have a higher percentage of outs on balls in play.

Also, the run environment in which the pitcher pitches can heavily influence his performance. Demographic and architectural features of ballparks can help or hurt pitchers. Atlanta, Mazzone's employer during this study, had two different ballparks during the sample. Until 1997, the Braves played in Atlanta-Fulton County Stadium, so loved by batters that it was nicknamed the "launching pad." Since 1997, the Braves have played in Turner Field, which slightly favors pitchers. We need to make sure that pitchers pitching for the Braves and for other teams are not punished or rewarded for playing in parks that favor or hinder hitters. Using a run-impact factor that measures the influence of a pitcher's home park on scoring, we can adjust the number of earned runs a pitcher gives up.[28]

Additionally, the era in which a pitcher plays influences the typical runs allowed. As I discuss in a later chapter, these differences can be quite extreme. Therefore, I look at the average ERA of the league for every year that a pitcher pitches, so that he will not be punished for pitching relatively well in a high run-scoring season, or rewarded for pitching relatively poorly in a low run-scoring season.

Finally, the quality of the pitcher himself is very important. If the Braves are simply bringing in very good pitchers, then noticing that Leo Mazzone's pitchers always pitch well doesn't tell us much about the coach. I include the career ERA of the pitcher—corrected for the run environment of all the parks in which he pitched—so that we can observe how well pitchers perform relative to the way that we expect them to perform. That is, we can see both good and bad pitchers improve or decline under Mazzone's guidance.

Defining a pitcher as a starter or a reliever is a bit tricky, because some pitchers do a little of both over the course of the season. After some toying around with the data, I settled on the following definitions. A starter is a pitcher who pitches at least seventy-five innings and starts 75 percent or more of the games played in that season. A reliever must pitch at least thirty innings and start in only 25 percent or less of

Table 9: Leo Mazzone's Impact on Pitcher ERA

Pitcher Classification	Impact on ERA
All	−0.64
Starters	−0.41
Relievers	−0.71

the games in which he played that season. I experimented with several other starter/reliever measures, but they yielded results that were not meaningfully different from the ones I present in this chapter.

Table 9 lists the impacts of Leo Mazzone on the ERAs for all pitchers' seasons in the sample.

Overall, Leo Mazzone's presence lowered a pitcher's ERA by about 0.64 ERA points. To put the effect in perspective, for the average 2005 National League pitcher (4.22 ERA), Leo's impact on earned runs is about 15 percent of the NL average. That is about the same as Coors Field in the opposite direction.

When separating pitchers into their defined roles, relievers appeared to benefit more from their time under Mazzone than starters did, though not by much. For starters, having Leo Mazzone as a pitching coach was worth about 0.41 earned runs per nine innings, or 1 earned run every twenty-two innings. For relievers, Mazzone was good for about a 0.71 reduction in earned runs per nine innings, or 1 run every twelve and two-thirds innings. It's pretty clear that he helps both classes of pitchers quite a bit.

One of the keys to Mazzone's success is a more frequent off-day throwing program for starters. At least so he believes:

> The general philosophy in baseball then was that pitchers should do one session of throwing off the mound in between starts. I wanted to do two. The reason for this is to close the gap between the four- and five-man rotation. The baseball world has now gone to a five-man rotation for health reasons. I've always felt you stayed sharper in four. So, I wanted to combine that, so they would stay sharp as though they were in a four yet healthy in a five.[29]

But if this were Mazzone's secret to success, we would expect his impact to be more pronounced for starters. At first glance, this does not appear to be the case, as relievers seem to benefit more from his coaching. On the other hand, just because the throwing program is designed for starters doesn't mean that relievers don't benefit from the philosophy. First, a good starting rotation means that relief pitchers can be used more sparingly. This ensures that relievers are not overworked, and allows the manager to save pitchers for spots in which they excel. Second, though it is not widely discussed, Mazzone also applies his frequent-throwing philosophy to his relievers. He states, "If a reliever goes more than two days without getting into a game, I try to really insist that they come over to a side session and throw a little bit."[30]

How does Mr. Mazzone work his magic? There are three main areas that pitchers have direct control over in preventing runs: strikeouts, walks, and home runs. Let's compare how the rates at which pitchers produce these outcomes with and without Mazzone.

Table 10 shows Leo's effectiveness in two areas: strikeouts and home runs. He does not seem to impact pitchers' walk rates versus what they were when he didn't coach them. Measured as a percent of the NL average of the statistics from 1991 to 2005, which are listed in the last row, the largest impact is in home runs. First, let's look at all of the players in the sample—this includes pitchers who did not meet the games started criterion to be classified as a starter or reliever. For a league-average home run pitcher, having Mazzone as

Table 10: Leo Mazzone's Impact on Strikeouts, Walks, and Home Runs

Pitcher Classification	Strikeout Rate Change		Walk Rate Change*		Home Run Rate Change	
	Actual	Percentage	Actual	Percentage	Actual	Percentage
All	+0.628	+ 9.54%	−0.133	−3.92%	−0.229	−22.90%
Starter	+0.852	+12.95%	−0.080	−2.36%	−0.152	−15.20%
Relievers	+0.347	+ 5.27%	−0.049	−1.45%	−0.229	−22.90%
NL Average		6.58		3.39		1.00

*None of the estimates of the effect on walks are statistically significant.

your pitching coach lowers your home run rate by about 23 percent from the average. In terms of strikeouts, a league-average strike-out pitcher under Mazzone increases his strikeout rate by about 10 percent.

The results mirror what Mazzone expresses as his advice to pitchers:

> Don't give in to the strike zone. This is about making pitches and trying to execute a good pitch. So forget about walks. And don't throw one down the middle just because you walked a guy. I'd rather you be off the plate a little than give up a three-run bomb.[31]

His effectiveness through areas of performance differs slightly be-tween starters and relievers. Starters improve on their strikeouts much more than relievers, while relievers experience a much stronger im-pact on home runs allowed than starters. However, both classifications of pitcher gain in each area. One reason for this change is that starters and relievers become what they are largely because of the way they pitch. Relievers tend to throw hard and fast—trying to get strikeouts—while starters must pace themselves. If a pitching coach is going to have an impact, he is going to have to improve in areas where pitchers have been less successful in the past.

Relievers tend to have high strikeout rates; therefore, there is less room for improvement here. A good pitching coach might say, "I know you can strike guys out with the heat, but let's be careful as to how you place the ball, so that when you make a mistake—and you will—it won't go over the fence." A starter who is pacing himself, and being careful not to give up the long ball, probably has more room to im-prove in getting strikeouts than a reliever. A good pitching coach might be able to help starters by pointing out strategies and methods for conserving energy so that pitchers can rear back for an extra strike-out when they get in tight spots. So it's not surprising to see different pitcher types improving differently.

Is There a Big Secret?

What about the ability of players to retain what they have learned from Leo? After all, many teams have hired away some of Mazzone's best performers. The above analysis tells us only how pitchers perform with and without Mazzone. Is he imparting secret knowledge of techniques or a workout regimen that was previously unknown, or is his presence important for suggesting immediate adjustments throughout the season? If it's some big secret, then we should see pitchers improve when they become his students, but also continue their success when they leave him. If the coach's everyday oversight is important, then a player should improve when he arrives, but revert to his prior form when he leaves.

The results in Table 11 indicate that pitchers of both classifications suffered when they left Mazzone. If Leo is just spotting problems and fixing them, pitchers should retain the advantage they received when they joined the team. It turns out that whatever inspiration Leo provides, you can't take it with you. Those coming to Mazzone increase their strikeout rates and lower their home run rates, thereby lowering their ERAs by about half a run per game. There is no identifiable difference in walks. However, when players leave, they typically pitch *worse* than they did before they pitched for Mazzone. Interestingly, the effect from joining Mazzone differs slightly by pitching classification. Starters don't benefit as much as relievers in terms of ERA and home runs, but all classes decline in strikeouts, home runs, and ERA upon their departure.

Table 11: Difference in Performance Before and After Pitching for Leo Mazzone

Pitcher Classification	ERA		Strikeout Rate		Home Run Rate	
	Before	After	Before	After	Before	After
All	+0.55	+0.78	−0.48	−0.80	+0.15	+0.33
Starter	+0.11*	+0.73	−0.70	−1.00	0.00*	+0.32
Relievers	+0.61	+0.90	−0.51	−0.12	+0.17	+0.33

*Not statistically significant

The fact that pitchers seem to lose the Leo magic when they leave the Braves indicates that part of the Mazzone method involves handling pitchers from day to day. This might seem surprising, but Leo describes correcting problems every year:

> It's amazing. I've been with [John] Smoltzie 13 years and I had Tommy [Glavine] for 12. And yet I had to restart it all over again whenever they started throwing. Their mechanics would be off. Usually, I'd have them pitch two days and then take one off. All we do is get on the mound and get some touch on the pitches. It's pretty much what we do in between starts in the regular season.[32]

Also, a potential downside of Mazzone's more-frequent throwing program is that pitchers may tire themselves out. Mazzone feels that his monitoring of these side sessions is key, as pitchers may have a tendency to throw too hard while practicing their pitches. But Mazzone says, "That's what the hell they pay you for, to regulate effort."[33] Because the Sain-Mazzone method is so unique, pitching coaches on other teams may not be able to replicate the in-season instruction required by the throwing program.

There is also the possibility that Mazzone and others on the Braves know when pitchers are about to lose it and, therefore, don't mind letting these players go. But, even if you ignore the decline, there is no doubt that pitchers improve when they arrive.

Mazzone for the Hall of Fame

Another problem in determining exactly who is responsible for the success of Braves pitching is that the team has had stable management during this era. The same general manager, John Schuerholz, and manager, Bobby Cox, have overseen the Braves pitchers throughout Mazzone's tenure. Isolating Mazzone's individual influence from the rest of the management is impossible with the data so far discussed.

But with Mazzone leaving to go to the Orioles for the 2006 season, we ought to be able to separate out his contribution after a few years with another set of coworkers.

However, Leo was in charge of the pitchers in Atlanta, and the rest of the management stuck by him for nearly two decades in the Braves organization. Surely we can attribute much of the pitching success to Mazzone even though other members of the Braves probably contributed to the consistent pitching success.

Though the data may not tell us exactly how important Mazzone is to his pitchers versus the rest of the organization, the pitchers themselves have quite a bit to say.

John Burkett, who had the best season of his fifteen-year career under Mazzone, said:

> I think the best thing about Leo is, he has this sternness and his belief in what he's doing. He's very convincing and he has the track record to back it up. When you look at some of the guys who were washed up when they came over—me being one of them, because I was done—maybe I was even starting to believe it at that time. But I remember throwing on the side one time when I first got over there and Leo told me, "You have the best control I've ever seen on the side, besides Greg Maddux." And then he said, "And your slider sucks. When you get behind in the count, quit throwing that thing. Throw your fastball down and away." And I did that. I mean, there were times when I was thinking, "Man, I can't throw this guy a fastball down and away. He's going to kill it." And I'd throw one and he'd take it for a strike. That went a long way for me. I kind of took off after that.[34]

Charlie Leibrandt, who pitched for Mazzone near the end of his career, said:

> He's able to communicate what he sees and kind of get you to throw the ball like you should be throwing. A lot of pitching coaches I had weren't able to do that. They'd always say, "Nice

pitch, nice pitch." That can't help me. One pitching coach I had, the relationship got so bad, I wanted to throw before he came to the park! I didn't want to hear that kind of stuff, because I knew it wasn't true. Leo would just say, "You can't get guys out with that." And we'd work on it, and we'd try to sharpen things up so that, when you go into a game, you'd have some confidence.[35]

Jason Marquis, who spent his first four years in the majors with Mazzone, said:

I know when a young guy comes in Leo tries to be a little harder on him because he wants to instill in him the values that he did with the Madduxes and the Smoltzes and the Glavines, when they were young. Some guys take it the wrong way. I tell you what, he's helped me a lot.[36]

Mike Remlinger, a middle-relief specialist, said:

Even he and I butted heads a couple of times. But the next day, he didn't hold things against you and it was time to get back to work. He helped me tremendously. A lot of guys don't want to hear the truth. Sometimes you need to hear, "You're not very good right now." Sometimes you have to face that reality and get things fixed.[37]

John Rocker, who needs no introduction, said:

The best thing he has going for him, as far as a teacher of pitching, is pitch selection. He's a big stickler on pitching away to hitters, coming in for effect, basically. Not a lot of pitching coaches or managers really teach that way. And it's really kind of funny that the Braves continue to have success year-in and year-out, no matter what kind of pitchers they seem to have, and a lot of it has to do with Leo's pitch-selection philosophy.[38]

Pete Smith, who had an unspectacular career, said:

Leo just seems to have every aspect covered. He can communi-
cate. He knows mechanics. As a pitching coach, I think he has a
pretty good case for the Hall of Fame. I'd put him in the Hall of
Fame.[39]

John Smoltz, who pitched for Mazzone in the minors and majors,
said:

He's had a lot of great pitchers. One would say that he's had an
easy job. I'd disagree with that. I'd say he hasn't screwed it up.
He's done a great job of not screwing it up. A lot of other people could have messed it up. Personalities sometimes get in the
way, but for the most part, everyone's who's been under the
system—myself, Glavine, Maddux, Charlie Leibrandt, Avery—
despite how much grief we give him personally, we all would acknowledge that he's helped us a lot in our career. What we were
able to accomplish, what we were able to do? It certainly can't
go unnoticed.[40]

Jorge Sosa, who had an ERA that was half his previous career average during his one season with Mazzone, said:

I am where I am today thanks to Leo, because he helped turn
me into the pitcher I am.[41]

And Jaret Wright went further in his praise than seems deserved,
but his enthusiasm is unassailable:

Physically, everything came together, and Leo's philosophy jelled
well with where I was at in my career. He definitely helped me,
and it's stuff I don't know if I would have figured out on my
own. But once you know it, you can move on and keep what he
taught you.[42]

Leo Mazzone's influence seems to extend beyond a simple training strategy or secret method for his pitchers, and both starters and relievers benefit from his oversight; furthermore, pitchers seem to lose the Leo magic when they leave Mazzone's guidance. If the powers that be ever decide to open the Hall doors to pitching coaches, Leo Mazzone has a very strong case.

6

The Big City vs.
Small City Problem

*The goal of a well-designed league is to produce adequate
competitive balance. By this standard, MLB is not now
well-designed. . . . Proper competitive balance will not exist
until every well-run club has a regularly recurring reasonable hope
of reaching postseason play.*

—FINAL REPORT OF THE BLUE RIBBON PANEL ON BASEBALL ECONOMICS[43]

IS THERE SOMETHING FLAWED in MLB's current structure that
leaves some teams always on top and others always on the bottom?
Commissioner Bud Selig, the former owner of the small-market
Milwaukee Brewers, has long argued that the fact that some cities are
bigger than others puts the smaller cities at a disadvantage. Does this
supposed competitive imbalance threaten the game?

All of the major professional sports teams in North America represent geographic areas. And though the geographic origins of sports
competition seem perfectly natural, the continued association of sports
teams with regions is not so obvious. For example, professional tennis,
golf, and auto racing all involve competition among participants who
represent only themselves. Couldn't team sports operate in the same
manner? Professional sports teams are composed of players from all
over the world, who may not even reside in the cities of the teams they
represent. Television allows fans to watch games from anywhere in the
world. Why couldn't the Atlanta Braves become the Coca-Cola Braves,
barnstorming the U.S. or just playing in front of cyberfans in Holly-
wood, garnering followers from all over the country? The economic
necessity for geographic organization of sports teams has passed, but

professional athletes continue to play as representatives of cities, states, or regions. Why does the geographic structure of all professional team sports leagues persist?

Local ties give fans like me something extra to cheer for. It is not easy for a Southerner to root for the Yankees, as my father found out when he moved from New York to Tennessee in his youth. While geographic proximity is no longer a prerequisite for watching a baseball game, the home team is easy to grab on to for fans who don't closely follow the game. Fans who reside outside of a metropolitan area with a baseball team don't have a home team to support, but those who do have a built-in reason to like the team. Win or lose, these teams evoke a sense of identity and pride that induces people to become fans. It is ordinary to hear sports fans say "we" in reference to a team they follow, and the logic is straightforward: the Reds play in Cincinnati; we live in Cincinnati; therefore, the Reds are *our* team.

Participants in sports without geographic representation sometimes have a hometown following; but when Bill Elliott wins a NASCAR race, no one in Dawsonville, Georgia, says, "We won," like baseball fans do when their team wins. These professional athletes have no home-field advantage because they have no home field. It's easy to see how such sentiments can lead to more fans and generate more revenue for owners. And if more fans mean more money, then owners will attempt to locate teams in the most populous cities. It is no surprise that MLB has at least one team in all but two (Portland and Sacramento) of the top twenty-six cities in the U.S. The greater the fan base is, the greater the revenue owners will receive.

However, this is where the problem starts. The Blue Ribbon Panel, which Commissioner Selig organized to study the impact of market size on competitive balance, identified the importance of fan-base size for the profitability of teams as a fundamental flaw in MLB's inherited league structure. The following is from their final report in 2000:

> Many observers of MLB believe that the root of the competitive balance problem is the fact that clubs located in smaller or less fertile markets are unable to generate sufficient revenues to

support the level of payroll necessary to be competitive on the field. The inability of a club to generate sufficient revenue in a particular market may be related to a lack of population, poor demographic composition, a lack of sufficient corporate presence and/or the proximity of other clubs.[44]

It just so happens that North America lacks thirty identically sized cities. Table 12 ranks the population of every metropolitan area with a major-league team. Extending the logic that geographic ties generate fan loyalty, this means that bigger cities ought to yield more revenue to owners than smaller cities. More people means more loyalty expressed

Table 12: Population by MLB City

Population Rank	Metropolitan Area	Team(s)	Population (millions)
1	New York	Mets, Yankees	18.323
2	Los Angeles	Angels, Dodgers	12.366
3	Chicago	Cubs, White Sox	9.098
4	Philadelphia	Phillies	5.687
5	Dallas–Ft. Worth	Rangers	5.162
6	Miami	Marlins	5.008
7	Houston	Astros	4.715
8	Toronto	Blue Jays	4.683
9	Detroit	Tigers	4.453
10	Boston	Red Sox	4.391
11	Atlanta	Braves	4.248
12	San Francisco–Oakland	Athletics, Giants	4.124
13	Montreal	Expos	3.426
14	Phoenix	Diamondbacks	3.252
15	Seattle	Mariners	3.044
16	Minneapolis–St. Paul	Twins	2.969
17	San Diego	Padres	2.814
18	St. Louis	Cardinals	2.699
19	Baltimore	Orioles	2.553
20	Pittsburgh	Pirates	2.431
21	Tampa Bay–St. Petersburg	Devil Rays	2.396
22	Denver	Rockies	2.179
23	Cleveland	Indians	2.148
24	Cincinnati	Reds	2.010
25	Kansas City	Royals	1.836
26	Milwaukee	Brewers	1.501

in fans purchasing tickets. Teams in large cities have a greater pool of fans to enjoy wins; therefore, wins ought to be more valuable to big-market teams than small-market teams. In an open market for players, the best players will gravitate toward the teams with the highest salary offers. This means trouble for teams in small cities, because the big cities will be able to pay higher salaries that teams in small markets cannot match. While an extra win per season in Kansas City may increase yearly attendance by 10,000, one more win for a New York team could generate a 100,000 more fans, as New York has the population of ten Kansas Cities.

So much for the notion that teams should have a near-equal shot at winning. The joy of competition is watching players on the field exploit all of their abilities to win the game. The uncertainty of the outcome is part of the thrill of witnessing sports events. If fans just wanted to watch good games, they could simply go to ESPN Classic Sports. The uncertainty of the outcome is important, if not critical, to the fun of watching. If certain teams have an advantage over other teams solely due to the population of their fan bases, the indeterminacy of competition disappears. The end result of competitive imbalance from the league's standpoint is that fans will stop watching the sport altogether.

At first glance, the recent history of baseball seems to confirm our suspicions that the population bases of teams influence the play of the game on the field. Over the past decade, the New York Yankees—representing a metropolitan area of 18 million—have been a dominant team, while several smaller markets—such as Milwaukee, Kansas City, and Pittsburgh—have been pushovers.

Although larger cities may have a revenue-generating advantage over smaller markets, it does not mean necessarily that small markets are doomed to perpetual failure. As long as the advantage is not too large, the league may possess a sufficient level of competitive balance. And any prolonged under/overperformance by small/big-market clubs does not prove market size to be the main culprit. Poor management and plain old bad luck may be contributing, if not dominating, factors.

Measuring Big-Market Advantage

In order to determine whether or not there exists a problem that needs correcting we must measure how market size translates into wins and losses. Do big-market teams have an insurmountable advantage over clubs in small markets? To find the answer, I use regression analysis to measure the effect of city size on wins. Using the metropolitan population of MLB cities as a proxy for the size of the fan base, the regression estimates the magnitude of the impact of population size on on-field success. The regression uses the data to identify how much differences in population are associated with differences in wins. With this information the regression procedure generates a predicted number of wins based on population size.[45]

The results from the analysis both confirm and reject some widely held beliefs regarding market size and winning. It is true that larger populations are associated with more wins than smaller markets; however, the magnitude of the impact explains only a minority of the difference in wins between the best and worst teams in recent history. Figure 2 maps population and average wins per season.

Each point in the figure plots the average wins by team from 1995 to 2004 and the population of the metropolitan area of the city as measured by the 2000 U.S. Census. The upward-sloping line shows the estimated relationship between wins and city size. The upward slope of the line matches the casual observation that for the past decade teams in big cities have won more games than teams in smaller cities. This is consistent with the theoretical prediction that big cities have more revenue than small cities to use on free agents, coaches, management, minor leagues, etc.

However, the story does not end here; the real question is *how large* is the big-city advantage? The regression estimates that every 1.58 million residents generates one extra win per season. For illustration, the largest market (New York) is expected to win 10.61 more games than the smallest market (Milwaukee) in terms of wins predicted solely by population. In this sample, the most successful of the New York teams

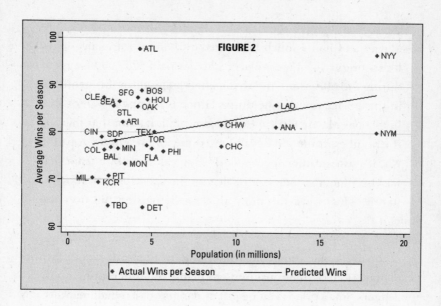

FIGURE 2

(the Yankees) won an average of 26.3 games more than the Milwaukee Brewers. This means the difference in market size explains about 40 percent of the difference in wins between the top and bottom markets. Forty percent isn't chump change, but what about the other 60 percent? These factors include the ineptitude and skill displayed by the front offices of these organizations.

On the ineptitude side, Joe Posnanski of the *Kansas City Star* recounts a story that points to an example of mismanagement of the Kansas City Royals—the second smallest MLB market and a perennial looser—that ran sabermetrics guru Bill James out of town and into the open arms of the Boston Red Sox:

It was Brent Mayne who finally broke Bill James. It's nothing personal. Mayne is a fine fellow. But he's also a 34-year-old catcher who hit .236 with no power, ran like he was a mime fighting the wind, guided the Royals pitchers to the second-worst ERA in baseball and got paid $2.5 million. This year, the financially strapped Royals will pay him $2.75 million. Meanwhile, catcher A. J. Hinch, who hit .298 the last two months of the season, banged the ball with significantly more power than Mayne and had a much better record behind the plate—plus, he's a bright, loyal team player who got paid $250,000—was cut during the offseason. And that's when James threw his hands up in the air. It's not that he thinks Hinch is Johnny Bench or that he blames Mayne for the Royals' downfall. It's not that this was the dumbest thing the Royals have done, or even in the top 100. No, it's just another spectacularly illogical move by a team that has become the new sports leader in spectacularly illogical moves. This is just the move that finally pushed Bill over the cliff.[46]

If you are looking to blame something for the woes of your favorite small-market club, don't just jump to blame the inherent inequities of the league. Small minds can be just as dangerous as small markets.

According to the Blue Ribbon Panel, the owners feel that it is important for every team to have "at least periodic opportunities for success," in order to keep maximum interest in the game. If some teams have inherent advantages due to the markets they serve, this standard may be in jeopardy. I can use the previous analysis to generate metrics that separate out the influence of market size on winning.

Using the estimate that every 1.58 million people in a city generate an additional win for the teams in that city, let's subtract the total number of wins due to the population from each team's actual average win total to create *population-adjusted wins* per season. Population-adjusted wins are the estimated wins of teams due to factors other than population size. I also calculate *predicted wins*, which is the number of wins a team should have based solely on the impact of market size. From this I calculate a third metric, *wins above predicted*, which is the difference between actual wins and predicted wins. This metric measures how well teams performed above/below the wins predicted by population size.

Table 13 lists MLB teams ranked according to population-adjusted wins and includes the other metrics and total postseason appearances from 1995 to 2004. It is as if each team played in a locality of equal size and, outside of luck, only the skill of the owners, managers, coaches,

Table 13: Average Wins Adjusted for Population, 1995–2004

Rank	Team	Average Wins	Population-Adjusted Wins	Predicted Wins	Wins Above Predicted	Postseason Appearances
1	Atlanta Braves	97.7	95.0	79.2	18.5	10
2	Cleveland Indians	87.4	86.0	77.9	9.5	6
3	Boston Red Sox	88.8	86.0	79.3	9.5	5
4	New York Yankees	96.6	85.0	88.1	8.5	10
5	San Francisco Giants	87.3	84.7	79.1	8.2	4
6	Seattle Mariners	86.5	84.6	78.5	8.0	4
7	Houston Astros	86.9	83.9	79.5	7.4	5
8	St. Louis Cardinals	85.6	83.9	78.2	7.4	5
9	Oakland Athletics	85.4	82.8	79.1	6.3	4
10	Arizona Diamondbacks	82.1	80.1	78.6	3.5	3
11	Los Angeles Dodgers	85.8	78.0	84.4	1.5	3
12	Cincinnati Reds	78.9	77.6	77.8	1.1	1
13	Texas Rangers	80.0	76.7	79.8	0.2	3
14	San Diego Padres	78.1	76.3	78.3	−0.2	2
15	Chicago White Sox	81.6	75.9	82.3	−0.7	1
16	Baltimore Orioles	76.7	75.1	78.2	−1.5	2
17	Colorado Rockies	76.2	74.8	77.9	−1.7	1
18	Minnesota Twins	76.5	74.6	78.4	−1.9	3
19	Toronto Blue Jays	77.2	74.2	79.5	−2.3	0
20	Anaheim Angels	81.2	73.4	84.4	−3.2	2
21	Florida Marlins	76.5	73.3	79.7	−3.2	2
22	Philadelphia Phillies	75.9	72.3	80.1	−4.2	0
23	Chicago Cubs	77.1	71.4	82.3	−5.2	2
24	Montreal Expos	73.3	71.1	78.7	−5.4	0
25	Milwaukee Brewers	70.3	69.4	77.5	−7.2	0
26	Pittsburgh Pirates	70.7	69.2	78.1	−7.4	0
27	New York Mets	80.1	68.5	88.1	−8.0	2
28	Kansas City Royals	69.3	68.1	77.7	−8.4	0
29	Tampa Bay Devil Rays	64.4	62.9	78.1	−13.6	0
30	Detroit Tigers	64.1	61.3	79.4	−15.3	0

and players determines the outcome. The Yankees cannot gain more population-adjusted wins than other teams because of a market-size advantage, only due to skill or luck.

Even without their big-market advantage, the Yankees are fourth. While the Yankees may be second in average total wins, it is clear that any big-market advantage is only a small part of the success of this organization in modern baseball history. The Bronx Bombers have won 8.5 more games than predicted given the population of New York. It's true that the Yankees operate in a big market, but they have done many other good things to attain success, just as the small-market Royals have done many bad things that have contributed to their failure. In contrast to the Yankees, the Royals have won 8.4 games below their population-predicted wins. In fact, the top and bottom clubs in population-adjusted wins, Atlanta and Detroit, have nearly equal predicted wins. And the eight clubs that never made the playoffs during the sample years are clustered at the bottom of population-adjusted wins.

Though the overall picture seems to indicate that market size had a very real but small impact on the performance of teams, small changes in wins can make huge differences in terms of making the playoffs. After all, baseball is a game of inches. Using the population-adjusted wins for every team in every season over the sample, we can see if any teams missed the playoffs due to differences in market size. When we look at each team's population-adjusted wins by season, it turns out that market size was a factor in keeping some teams out of the playoffs. Twelve times teams that missed the playoffs would have qualified if the cities were equally sized. Table 14 lists these teams along with their league, population ranks, and the number of post-season appearances over the sample period.

Again there is a counterintuitive story here. The losers are not necessarily the bottom-dwellers of the leagues or small-market clubs. Of these teams, only Montreal never made it to the postseason during this time period. And only the Braves and Yankees appeared more frequently in the playoffs than Cleveland, Houston, Oakland, San Francisco, and Seattle. Boston made five playoff appearances and won

Table 14: Post-Season Appearances Missed Due to Population Size, 1995–2004

Year	AL Team	AL Population Rank	Post-Season Appearances	NL Team	NL Population Rank	Postseason Appearances
1995	Texas	8	3	Houston	6	5
1996	Seattle	9	4	Montreal	9	0
1999	None	—	—	Cincinnati	15	1
2000	Cleveland	13	6	none	—	—
2000	Boston	7	5	none	—	—
2002	Seattle	9	4	none	—	—
2003	Seattle	9	4	Houston	6	5
2004	Oakland	8	4	San Francisco	8	4

the 2004 World Series. Cincinnati is a small-market team that has not been very successful compared to the others in this group; however, the Reds did win the World Series in 1990.

It is true that some clubs have missed the playoffs due to market size, but I am not sure that this is any more disheartening than teams that miss the playoffs due to playing in a strong division. It is quite common for the winner of a weak division to make the playoffs, while a team with more wins in a good division will be sent home. Over this time period four teams that did not make the playoffs had better records than at least one team in the playoffs. That is the structure of the game, and few complain about it. I am not sure that these teams missing the playoffs due to minor differences in market size merits any more complaints.

Another interesting aspect of the data presented in Table 13 is that it is hard to find much correlation between market size and "periodic success" in making the playoffs. The relationship between market size and postseason appearances is quite weak. Additionally, appearances in the postseason are not all that rare over these eight seasons. Eight teams (25 percent) did not make the playoffs over this span; but only once in these ten seasons did a club miss the playoffs because of its small population (Montreal in 1996). And even these poor teams have seen their share of success if we look a little further into the past. Montreal had the best record in baseball in 1994, but was not able to go to the playoffs because of the strike-shortened season. In 1992 and 1993 Toronto won back-to-back World Series, and they played the Philadelphia Phillies in the latter series. From 1990 to 1993 Pittsburgh played in three straight National League Championship Series. Even the real losers of the bunch had some share of success in the 1980s. Milwaukee played in the World Series in 1982, while Detroit and Kansas City were World Series champions in 1984 and 1985. Only the lowly Devil Rays failed to ever make the postseason, but the team has only existed since 1998.

"But," many will say, "what about the Yankees?" It is very true that the Yankees have had unprecedented success in the late-twentieth and early twenty-first centuries, not to mention the team's glorious past, but it is important to remember that the Yankees missed every one of thirteen playoffs held between their 1981 and 1995 postseason appearances. Where was the big-market dominance of that era? And we cannot blame the difference on free agency, where George Steinbrenner likes to spend big bucks, because free agency came into being in 1976.

While big-market teams may have an advantage over small-market teams, the advantage appears to be slight and virtually meaningless. The bigger problem appears to be inept management of a few clubs that happen to be small-market teams. Any attempt to improve the performance of these teams ought to focus first on creating incentives for owners of these teams to make better managerial decisions, before moving on to fixing any inequities that arise from differences in market size.

Why Don't Big Markets Dominate Small Markets?

But one question remains: why is it that large-market teams do not have much of an advantage over small-market teams? If bigger markets offer more potential fans to generate revenue for the teams in that area, why do these teams fail to further exploit this advantage?

First, there exist several rules that allow small-market teams to compete at a lower cost. The reverse order draft lets the worst teams pick new players first. The drafting team holds exclusive rights to any player it drafts, and therefore it does not have to compete with large-market teams who might be willing to pay more for the player for a short period of any player's career. After signing their initial contracts, these players are ineligible for arbitration for three years and free agency for six years. And small-market teams can also trade these players to big-market clubs for a more suitable bundle of players or cash to be used to hire free agents. Small-market teams that manage their rosters wisely can compete by identifying good talent early when it is relatively cheaper.

Second, the big-market advantage does not necessarily mean that the biggest market will always sign away all of the game's top free agents. Each player a team signs brings less value than the previous player (as a team improves, it values the additional player less); thus, are diminishing returns to signing additional free agents to the same team. For example, the two top free agents in the 2004 off-season were Carlos Beltran and Adrian Beltre. The Mets only signed Beltran, while Beltre signed with Seattle. Big-market teams may get the first crack at free agents, but there are plenty of good players to go around.

Third, we routinely overestimate the advantage big markets have over small markets. Though big cities hold more potential baseball fans than small cites, those people aren't necessarily freely available to watch baseball. Big cities also have more distractions. New York offers many more opportunities for entertainment than Milwaukee. Because New Yorkers have more to do, a win in New York may not generate as much fan interest as a win in Milwaukee. So, though wins may generate more revenue in big markets than small markets, the effect might not be as large as we think.

It's important to remember that attempts to limit the big-market advantage are not without risk. Revenue sharing, the most popular solution to the problem, while giving low-revenue teams more cash, also creates a disincentive for winning. Tying revenues to winning creates a strong incentive for management to put winning teams on the field. A small-market owner who receives a share of big-market earnings may prefer to live off this wealth transfer rather than put together a good team. Thus, proposals to minimize competitive imbalance must be crafted with caution, especially considering that competitive imbalance may not be the large problem many people suppose it is.

7

The Marlins and Indians? C'mon.

Baseball is too much of a sport to be called a business, and too much of a business to be called a sport.

—P. K. WRIGLEY, FORMER CHICAGO CUBS OWNER

WHICH TEAM has the best organization in baseball—not historically, but *right now*? It's a question that can rile up baseball fans whenever they meet. I might argue it's the Atlanta Braves, my favorite team. After all, the Braves won fourteen division titles, five NL pennants, and one World Series from 1991 to 2005. But New York Yankees fans could argue that eleven playoff appearances with four World Series titles from 1995 to 2005 is better. Furthermore, some fans of the low-budget Oakland Athletics and Minnesota Twins have a case that their combined seven postseason appearances from 2000 to 2005 on much smaller budgets is the more impressive feat. What might seem like a simple question isn't.

The answer to this question depends on what you want to know. I'm concerned with the present as opposed to the past, because I'm looking for something practical: a gauge of which franchises are likely to rise to the top in the coming years. A good organization ought to be able to generate sustained excellence for years to come. There is no doubt that the teams mentioned above have excelled in the past and may continue with some success in the future; however, maybe there are some organizations that are just getting things in order now and are primed to join or replace the reigning elite. How do we find them?

In this chapter, I'm going to evaluate organizational track records over the past three seasons (2003–2005). My approach provides several observations of each team, without digging too far into the historical record, and thus avoids contamination by past organizational structures no longer in place. It's reasonable to expect recent history to be a guide to the future. If an organization is doing things right, it will probably succeed in the near term as it continues doing the right things. Poorly managed organizations may also have some inertia, but they are not likely to plod along with the same failing methods. It's not surprising that seven of the nine teams that I identify as below-average organizations experienced front-office shakeups during the period of analysis.

Good baseball organizations should get the most out of their playing assets. To keep things simple, let's focus on these two relatively noncontroversial characteristics of well-managed baseball clubs to evaluate management:

1. A good organization puts a team on the field with a high potential for winning.
2. A good organization gets more value out of its players than it pays for them.

Winning Teams

An organization that expects to win must put a good team on the field. Good teams win, which brings fans to the park and generates revenue for owners. However, sometimes teams win and lose games not because of the way they are composed, but due to luck. Obviously, poorly constructed teams will typically win fewer games than well-constructed teams; but teams sometimes experience a series of good or bad bounces that give or take away a few victories over the course of the season. This is not management's fault, and therefore we shouldn't punish or reward teams for results beyond their control. To evaluate the quality of play, I use the total dollar value generated by the players of a team and listed in Appendix D. These values—generated using the method detailed in chapter 13—reflect the revenue that the players bring to the team through the number of wins that their performances generate. Good play brings in more money; bad play brings in less.

Table 15 ranks MLB organization according to the total value of play a team puts on the field. During this time frame, the top three teams reached the playoffs every year, while none of the bottom nine clubs reached the postseason even once. So, by the metric of overall

Table 15: Total Value of Team Play (2003–2005)

Rank	Team	Total Value
1	Boston Red Sox	$468.16
2	New York Yankees	$455.72
3	Atlanta Braves	$436.39
4	St. Louis Cardinals	$432.74
5	San Francisco Giants	$427.95
6	Florida Marlins	$423.73
7	Chicago Cubs	$419.23
8	Houston Astros	$417.40
9	Philadelphia Phillies	$411.69
10	Oakland Athletics	$405.49
11	Cleveland Indians	$401.92
12	Los Angeles Angels of Anaheim	$395.21
13	Texas Rangers	$394.78
14	Chicago White Sox	$392.51
15	Baltimore Orioles	$390.47
16	Minnesota Twins	$385.48
17	San Diego Padres	$385.37
18	Colorado Rockies	$383.67
19	Toronto Blue Jays	$380.71
20	Pittsburgh Pirates	$377.14
21	Los Angeles Dodgers	$376.11
22	Arizona Diamondbacks	$375.06
23	Milwaukee Brewers	$373.72
24	Seattle Mariners	$364.15
25	New York Mets	$364.00
26	Washington Nationals	$359.07
27	Detroit Tigers	$350.32
28	Cincinnati Reds	$350.18
29	Tampa Bay Devil Rays	$349.18
30	Kansas City Royals	$348.25

quality put on the field, the Red Sox, Yankees, and Braves have been the best, and the Royals, Devil Rays, and Reds have been the worst.

However, a team that puts the best players on the field isn't necessarily the best managed team. Imagine two office managers who both want to buy the best personal computers for their workers in order to maximize the work done in the office. They both look up the latest computer ratings in *Consumer Reports* and find the best-suited PCs for the job. One manager goes down to the local computer store and buys the machines for $5,000 a piece. He figures it's worth the expenditure since every computer will make each worker produce $10,000 more in revenue. His rival manager chooses a different strategy. She conducts a few Internet searches of computer sellers and negotiates a high-volume discount to acquire the very same computers for $2,500 a piece. It's obvious who the better manager is. Simply purchasing the inputs that everyone knows are valuable isn't the only component of a good management strategy. We ought to evaluate baseball teams according to the same standards on which we judge the office managers. Sure, you can purchase a winning team, making lots of fans happy, but there is more to it.

Efficient Teams

It's no secret that Alex Rodriguez (A-Rod) is one of the best players in the game. When he became a free agent in 2001, he was able to play for any team he wished, and he ultimately signed a ten-year $250 million deal with the Texas Rangers. Despite A-Rod's excellent play, the Rangers eventually dealt Rodriguez to the Yankees to free up some financial resources. According to his value listed in Appendix D, A-Rod's offense was worth nearly $16 million in 2005, about $9 million less than his average yearly salary. Even if his defense—and A-Rod is an excellent defensive player—and other winning qualities make up the difference, that is still a lot of money to pay for his production. Dontrelle Willis of the Florida Marlins contributed an almost identical value of play on the field as Rodriguez; however, he did so for a measly $380,000— generating more than forty times his salary in revenue.

The Marlins were able to get such a great deal by exploiting the league's collectively bargained reserve clause, which prevented Willis from offering his services to the highest bidder, like Rodriguez did in 2001. Willis could play for the team holding his reserve rights, or none at all. After acquiring Willis in a trade in 2000, the Marlins were able to pay "D-Train" any amount they wanted, subject to a minimum salary threshold. By identifying Willis as a soon-to-be star, which is quite a feat, the Marlins were able to get a $16 million pitcher for the salary of a washed-up utility infielder. The Rangers and Yankees, on the other hand, had to pay A-Rod a salary close to his expected value. Teams that have more Dontrelle Willises than Alex Rodriguezes are better managed teams. The next step in evaluating organizations is to identify the teams that are getting the most value from the financial resources they devote to player salaries.

Table 16 ranks MLB organizations by the average difference between total value produced and salaries paid out, and also lists the difference as a percent of each team's payroll. This ranking looks much different from the one in Table 15. The Cleveland Indians top the list as the franchise getting the most *net value* (total performance value minus total player salaries), with Willis's employer, the Florida Marlins, not far behind. The least efficient clubs were the Yankees, Mets, and Dodgers. The Yankees were so inefficient that the team actually paid its players more than the value they produced on the field. No one can accuse Mr. Steinbrenner being stingy.

But this list doesn't tell the whole story. The Tampa Bay Devil Rays may run an efficient organization, but they put the second worst team on the field over this period. While the team generates some revenue by simply existing as an MLB franchise, this cannot persist forever. A club that puts bad teams on the field year after year isn't going to be able to sustain itself, which may explain why the Devil Rays' owners replaced most of the front office following the 2005 season. And certainly, other teams won't be looking to follow their business model. Clearly, good management requires more than putting talent on the field that is worth more than you are paying for it.

Table 16: Net Value of Team Play (2003–2005)

Rank	Team	Net Value	% Difference
1	Cleveland Indians	$92.50	232%
2	Florida Marlins	$90.81	184%
3	Tampa Bay Devil Rays	$90.11	358%
4	Milwaukee Brewers	$88.54	256%
5	Pittsburgh Pirates	$83.99	216%
6	Oakland Athletics	$80.13	147%
7	Toronto Blue Jays	$77.90	159%
8	Kansas City Royals	$74.41	182%
9	San Diego Padres	$73.83	138%
10	Minnesota Twins	$73.40	134%
11	Washington Nationals	$72.45	155%
12	Colorado Rockies	$67.63	116%
13	Chicago White Sox	$67.04	112%
14	Houston Astros	$64.73	87%
15	Baltimore Orioles	$63.68	103%
16	Detroit Tigers	$61.74	119%
17	Cincinnati Reds	$60.77	112%
18	Texas Rangers	$60.13	102%
19	St. Louis Cardinals	$57.87	68%
20	San Francisco Giants	$57.63	69%
21	Arizona Diamondbacks	$54.10	78%
22	Chicago Cubs	$53.92	63%
23	Atlanta Braves	$51.17	55%
24	Philadelphia Phillies	$50.72	62%
25	Los Angeles Angels of Anaheim	$39.31	43%
26	Boston Red Sox	$39.14	35%
27	Seattle Mariners	$35.97	42%
28	Los Angeles Dodgers	$31.43	35%
29	New York Mets	$16.29	17%
30	New York Yankees	−$29.84	−15%

Winning Efficiently

To properly evaluate MLB organizations, we should consider the quality of the team and the efficiency with which it was constructed. Doing so is a bit tricky, but feasible. By adding the league ranks for total value and net value together, we combine each team's relative strengths in both areas to generate an overall ranking. This means that teams get credit for being both good and efficient, relative to the other organizations in the

league. Teams with lower summed ranks are both winning and generating bigger profits. Teams with higher summed ranks are losing and
earning less than other clubs.

Table 17 ranks the organizations according to the summed ranks of
both categories of value. The table includes five categories of organiza-

Table 17: Ranking the Best Organizations (2003–2005)

Overall Rank	Organization	Average Net Value	Total Performance Value	Net	Total	Sum	Organization Rating
1	Florida Marlins	$90.81	$423.73	2	6	8	Excellent
2	Cleveland Indians	$92.50	$401.92	1	11	12	Excellent
3	Oakland Athletics	$80.13	$405.49	6	10	16	Excellent
4	Houston Astros	$64.73	$417.40	14	8	22	Good
5	St. Louis Cardinals	$57.87	$432.74	19	4	23	Good
6	Pittsburgh Pirates	$83.99	$377.14	5	20	25	Good
7	San Francisco Giants	$57.63	$427.95	20	5	25	Good
8	Toronto Blue Jays	$77.90	$380.71	7	19	26	Average
9	San Diego Padres	$73.83	$385.37	9	17	26	Average
10	Minnesota Twins	$73.40	$385.48	10	16	26	Average
11	Atlanta Braves	$51.17	$436.39	23	3	26	Average
12	Milwaukee Brewers	$88.54	$373.72	4	23	27	Average
13	Chicago White Sox	$67.04	$392.51	13	14	27	Average
14	Boston Red Sox	$39.14	$468.16	26	1	27	Average
15	Chicago Cubs	$53.92	$419.23	22	7	29	Average
16	Colorado Rockies	$67.63	$383.67	12	18	30	Average
17	Baltimore Orioles	$63.68	$390.47	15	15	30	Average
18	Texas Rangers	$60.13	$394.78	18	13	31	Average
19	Tampa Bay Devil Rays	$90.11	$349.18	3	29	32	Average
20	New York Yankees	−$29.84	$455.72	30	2	32	Average
21	Philadelphia Phillies	$50.72	$411.69	24	9	33	Average
22	Washington Nationals	$72.45	$359.07	11	26	37	Mediocre
23	Los Angeles Angels of Anaheim	$39.31	$395.21	25	12	37	Mediocre
24	Kansas City Royals	$74.41	$348.25	8	30	38	Mediocre
25	Detroit Tigers	$61.74	$350.32	16	27	43	Mediocre
26	Arizona Diamondbacks	$54.10	$375.06	21	22	43	Mediocre
27	Cincinnati Reds	$60.77	$350.18	17	28	45	Mediocre
28	Los Angeles Dodgers	$31.43	$376.11	28	21	49	Poor
29	Seattle Mariners	$35.97	$364.15	27	24	51	Poor
30	New York Mets	$16.29	$364.00	29	25	54	Poor

tional ratings, ranging from Excellent to Poor. Three organizations stand out above the rest: Florida, Cleveland, and Oakland. All three of these clubs received much more value from their players than they paid out in salaries, while at the same time they put quality teams on the field. Let's look at how each club accomplished what it did.

The Florida Marlins averaged about eighty-six wins a year and won one World Series title from 2002 to 2005. Florida is often criticized for using its roster as a weapon to garner political support for a publicly financed stadium. It's an ugly strategy for which I have little sympathy, but that shouldn't distract us from what the organization has done on the field, which is quite impressive. The Marlins have done an excellent job of finding good players for cheap. For example, in 2005 the Marlins had five of the top 50 most valuable players in major-league baseball—four of the top 15. Only the NL champion Houston Astros had as many top 50 players. The Marlins were stocked with good players, while paying them only a fraction of their value.

As Table 18 shows, these five players generated just over $70 million in value, but the Marlins paid these players just under $11 million. That is quite a steal! Not only did the Marlins reap the rewards from these players' on-field accomplishments, but it freed up resources for the club to spend on other needs. One of the most interesting players on the list is Carlos Delgado, whom the Marlins signed to a four-year $52 million deal before the season. The team structured the contract so that it paid Delgado only $4 million in the first year of the contract, with higher salaries in the following seasons. Following the 2005 season, the Marlins traded Delgado to the Mets for three good prospects.

Table 18: Florida Marlins Player Value and Salary (2005) in Millions

Player	Value	Salary	Difference
Dontrelle Willis	$15.72	$0.38	$15.34
Miguel Cabrera	$14.57	$0.37	$14.20
A. J. Burnett	$14.52	$3.65	$10.87
Carlos Delgado	$14.51	$4.00	$10.51
Josh Beckett	$11.13	$2.40	$8.73
Total	$70.45	$10.80	$59.65

Even with the $7 million the Marlins sent along with Delgado to the Mets, the team still got much more out of Delgado than they had to pay for him. While the Marlins have done well at exploiting the reserve clause, they are also one of the most financial-savvy teams in the league.

The Cleveland Indians are the least successful of the top 3, having played .500 ball during the sample. However, the amount of money the Indians have spent on salaries over this span would make you think they'd played much worse. The Indians paid about $30 million a year less than organizations that put similar quality teams on the field. Furthermore, the Indians have been an improving team, winning sixty-eight, eighty, then ninety-three games from 2002 to 2005. In 2005, they missed the playoffs by one game after losing an exciting pennant race to the eventual World Series champion White Sox. They have a core of young talent that is relatively cheap, which should lead to a much better ball club in the near future. The general manager, Mark Shapiro, locked up many of his young players with long-term guaranteed contracts just before the 2006 season. By giving these players some long-run stability, the Indians will be paying less for them when they become eligible for arbitration and free agency. It's the same strategy the Indians' previous GM, John Hart, used to lock up Jim Thome and Manny Ramirez, who took the Indians to the playoffs for five straight years in the 1990s.

You may wonder why locking up players to long-term deals is a good idea. After all, there is no such thing as a costless choice. The potential pitfall is that if a player ends up playing worse than expected, the team will be stuck overpaying him. However, the strategy works because individuals tend to value stability more than organizations do, which allows teams to pay players less than their expected performance value. For example, let's say a player projects to generate $5 million a year for the next three seasons. He might play better or worse, but $5 million is the best guess. On a series of one-year contracts, when he plays better he gets more; when he plays worse, he gets less. Would you fault the player for signing a three-year $12 million deal even though he expects to be worth $3 million more than that over that span? Of course not, because the guaranteed contract gives the player some stability that a series of one-year $5 million contracts does not. If the player gets injured, or simply loses the ability to play, he'll still have plenty of money with the long-term contract. In this case, the team expects to get an extra $3 millon in value over what it pays out over the course of the contract. Furthermore, by signing several players to long-term deals, the team diversifies the risk of overpaying a player who under-performs. If the expectations about future performances are not bi-ased up or down, we should expect some players to exceed their expected value, while others will fall below it. In the long run, the per-formances above and below expectations ought to cancel each other out, leaving the team the financial benefits of signing players for less than their expected value.

Thanks to the book *Moneyball,* by Michael Lewis, we have a detailed portrait of things that the Oakland A's do to succeed. The A's rely heavily on statistical methods to evaluate players, in order to acquire undervalued players and trade away the overvalued. Though the team has only managed one playoff appearance from 2002 to 2005, it aver-aged nearly ninety-two wins a season. Lewis was right to claim that the Oakland A's have been one of the best managed teams in major-league baseball.

The teams at the bottom are a sad bunch. The Mets, Mariners, and Dodgers did not get much out of their players beyond what they paid for them, yet they still could not manage to put very good players on the field. The Dodgers did make the playoffs in 2004, but they were not very good in 2003 and 2005. These teams are full of expensive mis-takes, and it's unsurprising that all three of them recently experienced some turnover in front office leadership.

It may be tempting to view this as an evaluation of general managers—the person typically in charge of the franchise's baseball operations. Unlike players, general managers don't always play on the same field. The GM must navigate many unique obstacles besides putting talent on the team. Some organizations have intrusive owners that demand immediate solutions to intractable problems, keep relatives on staff, sign extravagantly expensive free agents, or refuse to sign free agents who are worth the price, to mention just a few of the venalities owners often commit. Other GMs may be saddled with the past mistakes of previous inept management. I'm not sure Billy Beane would act much differently than the Yankees general manager, Brian Cashman, if he had to answer to George Steinbrenner. The job has various responsibilities and political battles, so it doesn't seem fair to pin the entire credit and blame of a club on this one person. Moreover, GMs and their staffs come and go. The best organizations are those that can continue to function well even after a few key people leave. A good organization is built to get the right people who can make the right decisions.

The recent managerial excellence of the Marlins, Indians, and A's leads me to believe that these teams possess the ingenuity needed to put teams on the field better than the rest of the league. Billy Beane and the Oakland A's were a great subject for Michael Lewis to make the point that good management is the key ingredient to success. But let's not forget that the A's aren't the only well-managed team out there. The Marlins and Indians don't have that California flare, but they deserve some credit, if not more, than the A's. Now here come the pennants!

8

The Evolution of Baseball Talent

There were a lot of great players in my day, no doubt about it.
But there are a lot of great players today, too.

—AL BRIDWELL, CIRCA 1965 (MAJOR-LEAGUE CAREER: 1905–1925)[47]

W HEN WAS the "Golden Era" of baseball? Was it the era of
Ruth and Gehrig, DiMaggio and Williams, Mantle and Mays,
Aaron and Robinson, Boggs and Schmidt, or how about
A-Rod and Bonds? I am biased; I like baseball today the best. For some
reason, more people (mostly my elders) feel the best baseball was
played prior to my birth in 1973. How can I argue with these people? I
didn't watch much baseball until the 1980s. Was I deprived? Certainly,
I never got to watch Babe Ruth swat sixty home runs in a season; however, I also avoided the pain of watching the 1968 season, the worst offensive season in baseball's modern era. A lot of the bias in favor of the
past is plain nostalgia. It is the same thing that causes my parents to
tune in to 1950s radio stations and has me listening to music from the
1980s now. I am not sure if I really like eighties music—or if my parents
really like the "oldies"—but it seems to attract my attention out of some
longing to remember the past. That same feeling is sure to have some
effect on our judgment of baseball history.

What if we could identify an objective way to compare baseball
eras? To make this comparison, I developed a metric that can measure
the quality of competition. Judging the quality of today's game with
this tool takes nostalgia out of the process.

Furthermore, the analysis reveals some important information regarding the power surge in today's game. Many pundits claim that the modern era is tainted by steroids, which they see as the only explanation for the hitting achievements of a few great sluggers. These players may have used performance-enhancing drugs—only a handful of people know if they did—but it's not the case that their home run prowess could only come from "the juice." In fact, their great achievements in home run hitting are exactly what we would expect given the current distribution of talent in the league. The statistics don't convict them.

A General Theory of Quality

It is tempting to judge baseball quality according to absolute statistics, and to admire seasons with record statistics in different hitting and pitching categories. The problem with this analysis is that baseball players do not play games across generations, so such comparisons provide very little information about the quality of the game. Individuals generate these statistics relative to their peers. It was certainly a great feat that Roger Maris hit sixty-one home runs in 1961, but this in no way means that if we used a time machine to bring the 1961 Maris to face the pitchers in today's game he would perform at the same level. In fact, the idea is laughable. Athletic performance has improved drastically in all sports where we can observe absolute quality. For example, the world record marathon time has fallen by about 8 percent since Maris's glorious season. I expect that baseball players have improved similarly. Now, this does not say anything bad about Maris—he certainly cannot be held accountable for playing baseball when he did—but it does show the problem of using absolute statistics to judge the quality of a sport based on relative competition. As Figure 3 shows, the average offensive output has fluctuated quite a bit over baseball history. The runs-scored-per-game statistic reflects talent on both sides of the ball, because worse pitching must beget better hitting and vise versa.

If absolute statistics are not an appropriate metric to judge baseball

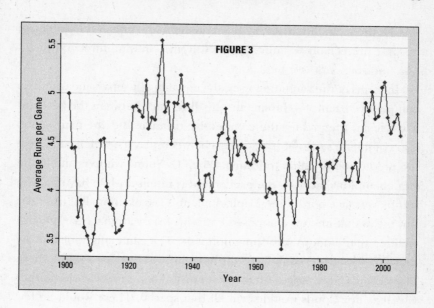

performance, what metric is appropriate? Well, what makes the game of baseball fun to watch? The drama, of course. Men at the highest end of the baseball talent spectrum bring forth their best in order to defeat one another in accordance with the rules of the game. These rules provide a roller coaster of action, from meetings on the mound to collisions at the plate. We tolerate the lows to see the highs, until one team emerges the victor. It is the drama along the way that makes the game interesting. But can we develop a statistic to measure drama? I think so.

The predictability of the outcome affects the drama of the game. With too much predictability the game is no longer very interesting. Baseball is a game of relative strengths. To win the game you do not have to be the best team in the league, just better than your opponent, plus or minus a little luck. A very good team playing a bad team is more likely to lead to a blowout than a game between closely matched talents. As the teams become more even, the uncertainty of the outcome will grow. But it is possible for the teams to be too even; predictability can result from extreme similarity as well as extreme differences. That "plus or minus a little luck" can put a damper on the enjoyment of the game. Luck will certainly play a role in many games, but I do not want it to be the main factor. As the teams become too equal, the game can become predictably boring as games will turn on wind direction, shadows, and rocks in the infield.

In terms of the wins and losses, the equality of teams is measured by competitive balance—the smaller the difference between the best and worst team, the greater the competitive balance. But the main game also contains a series of sub-contests between players, which can affect the predictability within the game. When Cy Young winners and home run champions face off, the excitement is intense, while having these star players face borderline Triple-A talent is less exciting. But this does not mean that lineups composed entirely of stars are necessarily more exciting than lineups with some non-stars. The game might be equally dull if the best batters only faced the best pitchers. Imagine a world where Barry Bonds faced Roger Clemens at every at-bat. In this world neither Clemens nor Bonds would seem all that special. There would be few automatic outs and few offensive outbursts. There would be strikeouts and home runs, but Clemens would never strike out twenty in a game, and Bonds would never hit seventy-three home runs in a season. In contrast, if Bonds faced pitchers in Single-A ball, the results would be spectacular, so spectacular you would hardly notice. Bonds would mash homers three and four a game. If Clemens faced only Single-A hitters, twenty strikeouts might be a bad game. In these worlds there would be no challenge, no competition, and little excitement. Clearly, the most desirable world is something in between. The best players in the game ought to be able to play well, but not to consistently dominate. Falling too far from this middle ground can make the game less interesting.

Evolutionary biologist Stephen Jay Gould first proposed the notion that altering the distribution of talent across the league can affect the level of competition between players.[48] He was attempting to explain why no player has hit .400 since Ted Williams in 1941. As the overall quality of players improves, extreme achievements should decline. Adding and subtracting players affects the distribution of talent in the league by including or excluding marginal major-league players. Over the years baseball has altered its talent pool on many occasions—mostly

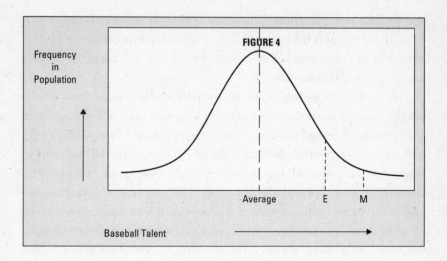

FIGURE 4

Frequency in Population

Baseball Talent

Average E M

increasing the size—but this seems to have had little effect on the average quality of play because the outcomes derive from *relative* competition. Theoretically, when MLB expands its size the league becomes worse in absolute terms, because those who were previously not deemed worthy to play in MLB become members of new MLB teams.

The histogram in Figure 4 represents the distribution of baseball talent across the entire population from which MLB can select its players. Most of the population has skills close to the average of the entire population. The best and worst players are much less numerous and are represented in the right and left tails of the distribution of baseball talent. MLB draws all of its players from the far right tail of the distribution. Line M, on the far right tail of ability, represents the cutoff for being a major-league player before an expansion. When the league expands, the cutoff shifts to the left to point E, thereby degrading the talent pool by filling the new roster spots with players who were previously unqualified to play in the majors. However, this decline will not show up in the average statistics that measure performance. The talent pool includes both offensive and defensive players; therefore, both offense and defense will suffer dilution. If the population distribution of quality for hitters and pitchers is the same, the effect of adding players should not affect the overall average performance of teams. Fringe hitters will hit the ball less, but fringe pitchers will give up hits more frequently; thus, there ought not be any change in the average measures of performance. The relative quality of play stays the same, as long as it is distributed equally across all clubs.[49]

However, the variability of performance will change, and this is where Gould's contribution begins. The good players will have very good years while bad players will be even worse, because good players will have more opportunities against bad players. Though the relative quality of the game will stay the same, its absolute quality will decline. Fans will endure a lower absolute quality of play as the difference between the player abilities widens. There is no doubt that a wider difference in abilities can create some exciting moments, but we certainly do not want the game to go too far in allowing the very best in the league to dominate the worst. The good news is that we are not anywhere near the extremes of excessive talent compression or dispersion—where the players are extremely similar or different in ability—but how close are we to some desired optimum?

Using Talent Dispersion to Compare Baseball Eras

Many things have changed in baseball since the birth of MLB at the turn of the century. With the emergence of the American League in 1901, the size of the major leagues remained relatively unchanged for its first half decade. However, in 1917 MLB did expand team rosters from twenty to twenty-five players, which was equivalent to adding four new teams to the overall talent pool. From 1901 to 1960, MLB consisted of sixteen teams, until the league expanded in 1961–1962 (four teams), 1969 (four teams), 1977 (two teams), 1993 (two teams), and 1998 (two teams). But, while the league has nearly doubled in size since its founding, the population of the United States has nearly quadrupled. In addition, MLB has since integrated, utilizing African-American talent that it shamefully neglected for a half century, and many teams now fill their rosters with players from Latin America and

Asia. If the population grows at a rate faster than baseball uses players, the number of high-quality players available to teams will rise. It stands to reason that if MLB draws its talent from an increased population base that the distribution of talent today must be smaller than in the past. This means that the absolute quality of play must be increasing.

Table 19 lists the population and league size by decade over the past eleven decades. It is true that the ratio of major-league players to the population was much higher when the league first started, but this ratio did not last for long. By 1940 the population-to-player ratio was greater than 330,000–to–1, which is higher than the sample average. From 1940 until the present, MLB seems to have done a good job expanding the league to keep this ratio constant through expansion. The current population-to-player ratio is very similar to the 1950 ratio; however, this does not mean that the talent dispersion today is equal to the dispersion of the 1950s. While racial integration was well on its way in 1950, following Jackie Robinson's entry into the National League in 1947, the number of black players did not reach a plateau until 1970. And though Latin Americans did play baseball, they were nowhere near the presence that they are today. Thus, if the population-to-player ratio has remained stable over the past fifty years, it is still possible that baseball

Table 19: Player/Population Ratio by Decade

Decade	United States Population	Total Teams	Roster Size	Total Baseball Players	Population/Player Ratio
1900	76,212,168	16	20	320	238,163
1910	92,228,496	16	20	320	288,214
1920	106,021,537	16	25	400	265,054
1930	123,202,624	16	25	400	308,007
1940	132,164,569	16	25	400	330,411
1950	151,325,798	16	25	400	378,314
1960	179,323,175	20	25	500	358,646
1970	203,211,926	24	25	600	338,687
1980	226,545,805	26	25	650	348,532
1990	248,709,873	26	25	650	382,631
2000	281,421,906	30	25	750	375,229
Sample Average	165,487,989	20	24	490	328,353
1940–2000 Average	203,243,293	23	25	564	358,921

team talent is drawn from a larger pool of talent that will compact talent dispersion.

However, there are several reasons why the simple population-to-player ratio may contain unreliable information about talent dispersion. First, there exists stronger competition in the labor market for players. Baseball is no longer the dominant professional sport available to athletes, as it was in the first half of the twentieth century. Professional football, basketball, hockey, soccer, and other sports all compete for athletic talent to some degree. Also, the growing U.S. economy provides many more nonathletic opportunities than in the past—if you don't believe me, consider your job opportunities compared to those of your grandparents—which can attract marginal major-league talent away from the game.

Second, the rising general population numbers do not necessarily mean that the age cohort for baseball players as a percent of the population has remained constant. Much of the nation's population growth is attributable to increasing life spans, not just increases in immigration and births. This is going to overstate the proportion of individuals available to play baseball over time. Whether or not these factors will have a measurable effect on using the population-to-player ratio as a proxy on talent dispersion is an empirical issue that we can investigate further. My bias is that the ratio is not really very informative with regard to the actual distribution of talent across the league.

The best way to analyze talent dispersion is not to hypothesize about the size of the labor pool, but to use Gould's theory of quality to examine the similarity of performance across players in different time periods using available statistics. To measure talent dispersion, I have chosen two statistics to measure variability across hitters and pitchers for players. For hitters I use the sabermetrician's shortcut for measuring the run—generation ability of any hitter, OPS. OPS is the sum of on-base percentage plus slugging percentage, and it is a good measure of individual hitter contributions toward offense. For pitchers, I use the earned run average, or ERA. To measure the dispersion of talent in the league—and this might sound complicated, but it isn't—I calculate the coefficient of variation of these statistics across players who engaged in one hundred or more batter-pitcher contests in a season. The coefficient of variation is a measure of the standard deviation relative to the mean value.[50]

The standard deviation is the average difference of the observations from the average value of the sample. Thus, the standard deviation of OPSs and ERAs of players tells us the typical talent spread from very worst to very best. A smaller standard deviation means that players are more uniform in ability, and a larger standard deviation means that players are more various in ability. The coefficient of variation normalizes the standard deviation as a percentage of the mean of the statistic, so that players can be compared no matter what era they came from or whether they are pitchers or hitters.[51] A greater coefficient of variation means a wider distribution of performance among all players. As the coefficient of variation decreases, the difference between the best and worst players shrinks. A greater talent dispersion on one side of the ball gives good players on the other side of the ball more opportunities to dominate bad players. For example, a wide dispersion among pitching talent gives hitters more plate appearances against exceptionally bad pitchers, and a greater dispersion of batters gives pitchers more chances against weak hitters.

Figure 5 shows the fluctuation of both statistics over time. The variation of both statistics is quite high until the 1920s. The population-to-player ratio is not much different from the previous decades, so it is likely that this is not the cause.

In 1920, something significant did happen in baseball that changed the game forever. Ray Chapman was hit by a pitch and killed. The pitcher that day, Carl Mays, blamed the incident on a slippery ball. Prior to the 1920s, the baseball was not the bright white ball of today, but a greasy, scuffed, tobacco-stained germ magnet. In response, baseball forced pitchers to throw with a clean ball, which eliminated one very special pitch known as the spitball. A few pitchers used only the spitball, which was a method distinct from the hard-throwing pitches still used in the modern game. Spitball pitchers were phased out of the

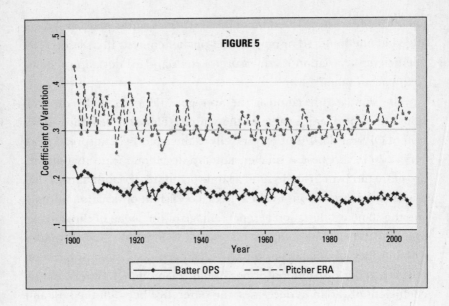

game over the following decade—many thought it was unfair to de-
prive pure spitballers of their livelihood. Removing this pitching
method likely reduced the variance of hitter and pitcher performance,
by making all pitchers more similar. Therefore, it is not surprising that
the deviation of pitcher and batter performances began to fluctuate
less with the spitball removed from play. Since the 1920s, the present
hitting and pitching dispersions have varied over time, but patterns are
difficult to identify from the yearly data.

For ease of interpretation, Figure 6 displays the average talent dispersion for pitchers and hitters of each decade to the average dispersion from 1920 until 2005. A higher bar on the graph means a greater
dispersion of player talent relative to the historical average, and a lower
bar means a greater similarity of players. Compared against baseball
history, the current era has a greater dispersion of pitching talent in
the entire decade, while batting talent is still quite compact. There is
also a distinct trend of dispersion increasing for batters and pitchers after the 1980s. In particular, the variation in the ability of batters in the
1980s was at an all-time low.[52] In any case, though the dispersion of talent began to widen some prior to the 1990s, the two rounds of expan-

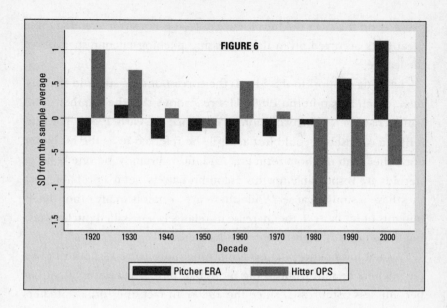

FIGURE 6

sion in this decade dramatically diluted the talent pool. This is a crucial factor in understanding the game today.

The Steroids Era?

What does this say about the current era of baseball history, especially given the intense public focus on steroids as the cause of the increased number of home runs? Pitching talent is more dispersed than it has ever been, while hitting talent is still quite concentrated. It means there are plenty of batters out there who are able to take advantage of bad pitchers. A more dispersed pitching talent pool gives the best hitters greater opportunities against weaker talent, which ought to lead them to perform extreme feats. Since the last round of expansion in 1998, Roger Maris's home run record of sixty-one has been surpassed six times by three men: Mark McGwire in 1998 (seventy) and 1999 (sixty-five); Sammy Sosa in 1998 (sixty-six), 1999 (sixty-three), and 2001 (sixty-four); and Barry Bonds in 2001 (seventy-three). While there has been much speculation that this outburst was aided by performance-enhancing drugs—and this does not mean it was not—it is not surprising that these great feats occurred given the increasing pitching talent-dispersion of the league.[53]

Lending support to this idea is the corresponding surge in hit batsmen, which began in the 1990s. Figure 7 shows that the number of hit batters has risen along with home runs since the early 1990s. The current era of baseball could just as easily be referred to as the hit batter era rather than the home run era. And most certainly, no one believes steroids are responsible for the rise in hit batters, yet it's probable that they have a similar cause. While there are certainly many other determinants of hit batters, the increase in relatively less-skilled pitchers taking the mound is likely a contributing factor.

Also, if low-quality pitchers are hitting more batters, shouldn't better pitchers benefit from facing more bad hitters as hitting talent has become less compressed since the 1980s? In fact, they do, as pitchers increased their strikeout rates over the same span (see Figure 8). Since 1993, a pitcher has struck out three hundred or more batters eleven times. Randy Johnson did it six times, Curt Schilling did it three times,

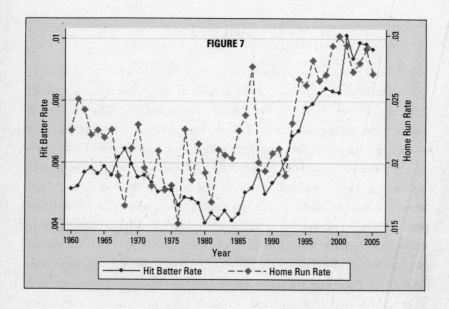

FIGURE 7

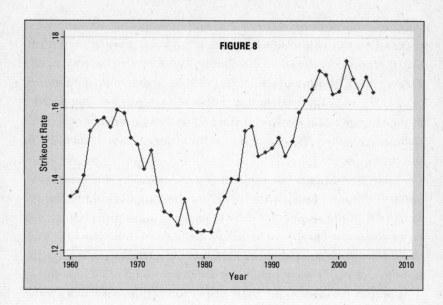

FIGURE 8

and Pedro Martinez did it twice. In the thirteen seasons prior to 1993, only two pitchers (Nolan Ryan and Mike Scott) reached the three-hundred-strikeout plateau. As we see with home runs for hitters, there are a few people at the extreme end of the talent spectrum reaching grand achievements.

The fact that talent dilution may be part of the cause for the great performances of players does not mean that steroids have not influenced the game. However, it's certainly incorrect to say that steroids, or other performance-enhancing drugs, are the only explanation.

Baseball's Golden Age

So what was the golden era of baseball? If the quality of baseball competition can be measured by talent dispersion, as I have argued, then we can use this information to roughly compare the competitiveness of baseball eras.[54] One thing that is clear from Figure 6 is that each decade of baseball has been unique. In some decades offense is fairly uniform, while defense varies widely, and in other decades the reverse occurs. In terms of individual seasons, it might be possible to find particular years where the talent distributions are similar to the current era. To generate a measure of similarity, I calculated the squared difference of pitching and hitting talent dispersions of each year and compared it to the average talent dispersion since since 2000. A smaller difference indicates that the year is more similar, in terms of talent dispersion, to the current era.

Table 20 ranks the talent dispersion of seasons by similarity to the baseball of today. Because the 1990s are similar and could be argued to be part of the same era, I did not compare these years. Of the top twenty years most similar to the current era, six of those years are from the 1980s, which is no surprise, because of its proximity in time to the present. Again, it is clear that talent dispersions tend to be unique.

Compared to today, the 1960s' dispersion of hitters is much greater and the dispersion of pitching is much lower. What if we wanted baseball today to be more like it was then? MLB could adjust rosters of pitcher/hitter compositions to alter the dispersion of talent playing the game. Increasing or decreasing the size of the league would not work in this instance, because while the dispersion of hitters would increase, so would the dispersion of pitchers. MLB would have to undertake a strategy that would treat each side of the game differently. For instance, if MLB wanted to dilute hitting talent only, it could expand rosters and limit the number of plate appearances any player can make in a season. More marginal hitters would enter the game while pitching talent would stay the same. I doubt anyone would want to do this; I'm throwing this out as theoretical possibility.

With a framework for measuring the competitiveness of baseball, comparing the league of today to any person's golden era is now possible. And not only is this information useful for bar bets, but MLB can use this information to alter the talent pool of MLB teams to provide the baseball that fans demand. I am not proposing that MLB do a fan survey to determine the public's favorite baseball decade and then manipulate rosters to do so. In fact, since the baseball of today is already at my social optimum, I have no incentive to push for any changes. What

Table 20: Seasons Ranked by Similarity to Current Era

Rank	Overall	Hitting	Pitching
1	1943	1987	1955
2	1958	1962	1943
3	1980	1959	1910
4	1953	1948	1958
5	1955	1926	1980
6	1989	1943	1915
7	1926	1952	1973
8	1946	1975	1953
9	1988	1974	1989
10	1973	1978	1967
11	1948	1958	1972
12	1985	1953	1923
13	1915	1980	1964
14	1981	1924	1985
15	1916	1988	1906
16	1987	1989	1912
17	1977	1976	1954
18	1935	1979	1920
19	1975	1945	1961
20	1964	1984	1913

Number of Top of 20 Similar Seasons per Decade

1900s	0	0	1
1910s	2	0	4
1920s	1	2	2
1930s	1	0	0
1940s	3	3	1
1950s	3	4	4
1960s	1	1	3
1970s	3	5	2
1980s	6	5	3

we have here is information about the quality of competition in baseball over the history of the game. Now, when owners, fans, and blue ribbon panels get together, they have an objective metric measure of the effect of competition quality as a result of hypothetical changes in the structure of the game.

9

The Steroids Game

Let me start by telling you this: I have never used steroids, period.
—RAFAEL PALMEIRO, TESTIMONY BEFORE CONGRESS, MARCH 17, 2005

ATELY IT SEEMS that if you want to ruin any discussion of base-ball, just bring up steroids. The S-word is a wild card that moves otherwise sober discussion of athletic achievements to wild spec-ulation. Players can be capable of everything with them, to nothing without them. In fact, we know very little about the potential impacts of anabolic steroid use on performance, but that has done little to curtail the discussions about threats to the "integrity" of the game. While steroids are very important drugs that help people who watch baseball, when players use them, the controversy starts. The same ben-eficial characteristics of steroids (strength building, increased heal-ing, etc.) that make them so valuable to the medical profession are also helpful for athletes who seek these qualities to enhance perfor-mance. It's when players use steroids as performance-enhancing drugs (PEDs) rather than to heal ailments that fans tend to view it as cheating.

Most certainly there are other non-steroid PEDs available to players (e.g., human growth hormone, amphetamines, cocaine, etc.) but for this chapter I'll use steroids as synonymous with PEDs, because these drugs are at the center of the PED controversy in MLB and have become a slang term for all PEDs. It's the role of the economist to evaluate the incentives that govern PED use rather than the particular drug of choice, and the incentives that apply to steroids will apply generally to other drugs as well. The furor in the public, as the media portrays it, is because using steroids to boost performance is considered cheating. The connections to steroids, alleged and documented use, has tainted many careers of recent MLB players. In his book, *Juiced,* former AL MVP Jose Canseco singled out several players—most notably his former teammates Mark McGwire and Rafael Palmeiro—of using steroids. Shortly after the publication of the book, both were called to testify before Congress regarding these claims.

At the time Canseco made his accusations, McGwire had retired from baseball. During the 1998 season, in which he hit seventy home runs for the St. Louis Cardinals to break Roger Maris's thirty-seven-year-old single-season record of sixty-one home runs, McGwire received much criticism for his acknowledged use of an androstenedione dietary supplement. At the time, "andro" was a perfectly legal over-the-counter supplement—which MLB has since banned—and when ingested, its performance-enhancing qualities are dubious. But the fact that McGwire's physique resembled a body builder's raised suspicion that his unprecedented home run hitting was aided by steroids. At the hearing, McGwire refused to address Canseco's allegations, and this was enough to taint all of his accomplishments for many fans.

Palmeiro, who was still an active player for the Baltimore Orioles, did not back down from his former teammate. He addressed Canseco's allegations head-on by shaking his finger and declaring his innocence of all charges. Soon after amassing his three thousandth hit in the season after the hearing, Palmeiro failed a drug test that showed he had used the anabolic steroid stanolozol. The test result, and Palmeiro's subsequent denials, became such a distraction that the Orioles dismissed him from the team at the end of the 2005 season. Though he did not retire, no team would sign him for the 2006 season.

The sagas of McGwire and Palmeiro tell us quite a bit about the feelings of the fans, media, and even former players regarding steroids. Two men who were once cheered by everyone as all-time greats are now stains on the game to some observers. It will be interesting to see how Hall of Fame voters treat these men when they become eligible for election. McGwire would have been a lock, and Palmeiro would certainly have had a good chance if not for the steroid controversy. My guess is that McGwire will make it because of his spectacular career and the fact that there are only allegations, and no positive drug tests, to pin any perceived steroid misdeeds on him. Palmeiro, on the other hand, will probably have a very tough time due to his somewhat lesser accomplishments—I'm not belittling his over three thousand hits and five hundred home runs, but he's still no McGwire—and a positive drug test soon after his public finger-wagging. It's clear that the S-word is distracting fans from the fun of the game.

Barry Bonds is another figure at the center of the steroid controversy. After already compiling a Hall of Fame career, Bonds raised his game to new heights in the twenty-first century. At the age of thirty-six, a time when many players' skills are in steep decline, Bonds hit seventy-three home runs. In the following three seasons Bonds would belt forty-five or more homers in each. Bonds's new muscular physique led to whispers of steroid use. And soon the whispers grew into serious accusations when a federal investigation into the BALCO sports nutrition company found records of steroid use among many athletes, including Bonds. The book *Game of Shadows,* by two *San Francisco Chronicle* reporters, reveals secret grand jury testimony of several sources who fingered Bonds for use of steroids. Bonds claims that he's innocent. The media and Congress placed pressure on Major League Baseball to "clean up" the game, and Commissioner Bud Selig immediately launched an investigation. Many sportswriters proclaimed that Bonds should not be in the Hall of Fame, despite his spectacular numbers. Ultimately, I think Bonds's Hall of Fame chances will be determined in the courtroom. If Bonds is found guilty, I suspect he will not get into the Hall. Anything short of a conviction, and he'll get in because of how good a player he was.

Should We Care About Steroids?

Steroid use infuriates fans and sportswriters. The phenomenon almost always provokes an especially emotional response. Why? For the sake of argument, let's assume steroids do improve performance, even though there is not a lot of evidence on the subject. Steroids are then simply a way to improve performance, just like eating right, getting plenty of rest, and working out. These are qualities that we normally appreciate. Why do we view steroids so differently?

No one would contest that the nonsteroid methods of enhancing performance are morally illegitimate. One possible objection to steroids is that they are "unnatural." If we're purging the unnatural, let's include a few other unnatural procedures in the game to see how we view them, following the logic that unnatural is bad.

First up is surgery, especially of the "Tommy John" variety. I don't think anyone would argue there is anything natural about cutting off a piece of the body (tendon from the foot, forearm, or hamstring) and placing it on another part of the body (elbow). And some players come back from the procedure throwing harder than before the surgery. If your arm blows out, that should just be one of those breaks.

Also, Curt Schilling's bloody sock performances in two games of the Red Sox's 2004 World Championship postseason should be a cause for condemnation, not celebration. Before the games he had a torn tendon surgically stabilized so that he could delay the proper surgical repair until after the season. This is hardly natural.

What about cortisone shots? Players often receive shots of cortisone to affected parts of the body, which reduce inflammation and allow a player to play. Cortisone is actually a steroid hormone. It naturally occurs in the body, which makes it somewhat "natural"; however, delivering a high dose directly to an affected part of an athlete's body to improve performance certainly is not natural. It was a cortisone shot that allowed Kirk Gibson to hit his game-winning pinch-hit home run for the Dodgers in the 1988 World Series.

Next, let's get rid of laser eye surgery. Optometrists have corrected the vision of many players, including Greg Maddux, Bernie Williams, and Kenny Rogers. If God didn't give you 20/20 vision, well that's tough. Improving the vision of a player gives him an unnatural advantage over players with naturally good vision. In the past, players who suffered vision deterioration had to retire early. Why should things be any different now?

Maybe we don't like steroids because ingesting performance-enhancers is something everyday people don't do. What about caffeine, sugar, and nicotine? All are stimulants that can improve performance. NBA player Darrell Armstrong used to fuel his spastic play with coffee and chocolate. Do you complain to your boss that the guy in the neighboring cubicle is cheating because his reports are coffee-enhanced?

The general public tolerates these practices, which are clearly non-natural; therefore, unnaturalness of steroids is not the sole reason their use is deemed cheating.

Maybe we are concerned that steroids are bad for players' health. While all of the adverse health effects of steroids are not known, some include: acne, aggressive personality tendencies (sometimes known as "roid rage"), enlarged heart, and increased cancer risk. However, some people argue, like Jose Canseco, that with proper supervision the health impacts can be minimized. These risks are no different from ones that Americans take every day. Many people engage in risky activities and occupations that we celebrate. For example, automobile racing is very dangerous, yet these athletes fill 100,000-seat raceways weekly. And standing sixty feet and six inches away from a man hurling a baseball in your direction at around a hundred miles per hour is, well, risky.

If fans are concerned about the health of baseball players and that is the reason they want to get steroids out of the game, banning tobacco and alcohol—certainly not performance-enhancers in the long run—would be a more effective strategy. So I'm not convinced that the health effects alone create the negative impression of steroids.

If it's not the performance-enhancing element or the health effects, then maybe it's a combination of the two. Alone, neither of these seem to matter much to fans. Players do a lot of unnatural things to their bodies to improve their performance besides using steroids, as well as do things detrimental to their health. But the fact that players might trade their health for performance, which is something that many players might not want to do, then creates a problem. Why do players use steroids even when there are health risks to doing so? Having Tommy John surgery might help a player get back in the big leagues, but it's not going to cause many healthy players to opt for the surgery. Steroid use choices, however, influence other players, which means it's no longer just a personal freedom issue for individual players. The decision to take steroids is dependent on other players' steroid decisions.

Steroids and Strategic Behavior

Whenever an individual takes into account the behavior of other individuals before acting, economists classify the behavior as "strategic." We see players making strategic decisions frequently on the field. For example, consider the strategic interaction between a base runner and a pitcher. If the base runner sees that the pitcher has a slow delivery, he may attempt to steal. Fearing a steal, the pitcher may speed up his delivery and throw a fastball to the catcher to prevent a steal. Each player is making a strategic response to the other. Similarly, players may make strategic decisions off the field based on the behavior of their colleagues.

Because many choices in life involve strategic behavior, economists have developed models to explain decisions governed by strategic incentives. Consider two players of equal ability in a world in which they are only two baseball players. In the labor market for players, each of these players will command the same salary, equal to half of the total sum of money owners are willing to pay players. However, if one player becomes better than the other, the better player will garner more of that sum, in proportion to the improvement in his performance. Each player's performance affects the income of his colleague. If they both sit around drinking beer and eating doughnuts, they will earn the same amount of income as if they both worked out every day. The only way to earn more money is to be *relatively* better than the other player. Harvard economist Robert Barro describes why this is the case:

> To a considerable extent, a team's or athlete's output is measured not so much by absolute skill—how far a ball is hit or how fast a race is run—but by comparisons with the skills of other performers. How much difference would it make if the longest home run went 600 feet or 300 or whether 100 meters could be run in 8 or 10 seconds? These numbers matter mainly in relation to what other athletes can do (now and in the past).[55]

Given the monetary incentive to be relatively better than other players, both players will work as hard as they can only to find themselves earning the same amount before they exhibited the effort. The incentives encourage the players to bring the best possible quality of baseball to fans.

Assuming that steroids improve performance, introducing steroids as an option for improvement changes the contest. If one player starts using steroids and his performance improves, not only will his income rise, but the income of the other player will fall. In order to keep up—because otherwise the labor market will value his natural services less—the formerly clean player must begin taking steroids too. Using steroids creates an externality because the actions of a player spill over onto other players. However, both players end up back where they started: even in skill and income. Except, if steroids have negative health consequences, then both players will be worse off than in a world without steroids. How is this possible?

The incentives of this strategic game lead both players to make decisions that are sub-optimal—meaning the situation could be improved—and neither party can improve the outcome by unilaterally choosing not to take steroids. This is a curious outcome that results from the fact that if one player decides not to take steroids, it is in the best interest of the opposing player to take them, because doing so will increase his income. Also, if the other player chooses to take steroids, the competing player must also take steroids to avoid losing income. A common tool economists use to predict human behavior reveals why this happens.

It is called *game theory*. Each player in the game makes choices based on payoffs that are affected by the behavior of the other. A matrix of payoffs, such as those illustrated in Figure 9, models the incentives for action. The numbers in the boxes make it easy to see the consequences of a choice given what the other party chooses. The payoffs below represent hypothetical monetary rewards (in millions of dollars) to both players for the four possible outcomes of the steroid game:

This is a symmetric game, which means that both players receive the same payoffs for the same choices. This is a realistic assumption for two players with similar skills: each ought to suffer and gain equally from the other's steroid use. In a world without steroids, both will receive $2 million on the labor market. If one player decides to use, but the other does not, the using party will gain from superior perfor-

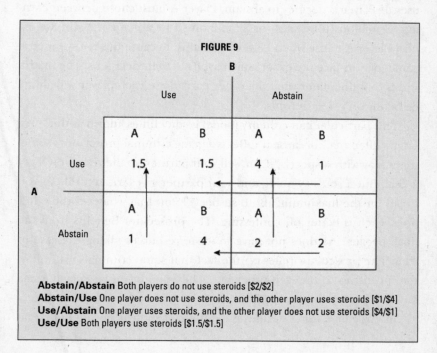

FIGURE 9

Abstain/Abstain Both players do not use steroids [$2/$2]
Abstain/Use One player does not use steroids, and the other player uses steroids [$1/$4]
Use/Abstain One player uses steroids, and the other player does not use steroids [$4/$1]
Use/Use Both players use steroids [$1.5/$1.5]

mance, while the abstaining player will lose income. If both use steroids, neither player will be better than the other, thus their salaries
will be the same as in the world without steroids ($2 million). However,
the difference between the Use/Use and Abstain/Abstain outcomes is
that the players will suffer health consequences of using the drugs that
may include minor discomfort, future medical bills, and shortened life
span. For this example, I'm guessing the cost to be $500,000. If there
are costs to using steroids, then both players would be worse off in a
world with steroids than in one without, even though they end up receiving the same salary from their teams.

The payoff matrix is an easy way to observe the incentives for use
based on what the other player chooses. The arrows in the matrix point
toward the optimal choice for each player given what the other player
chooses. Player A's choices are represented vertically. Player B's choices
are represented horizontally. If Player B decides to use steroids, Player
A must choose between earning $1.5 million (if he uses) or $1 million
(if he abstains). Therefore, we expect Player A to use when Player B
uses. If Player B decides to abstain, Player A must chose between earning $4 million (if he uses) or $2 million (if he abstains). Again, we expect Player A to use when Player B abstains. Because this is a symmetric
game, players face the exact same payoffs to their decisions. The matrix
shows that no matter what the other party does, each player will always
be better off using steroids.

This particular game theory model is sometimes known as the "pris-
oner's dilemma," because it reflects a game criminal prosecutors sometimes play with suspects. "If you sell your partner up the river, you'll get
a deal. But if you stay quiet, and your partner gives you up, I'll put you
in jail for the maximum." Both suspects know that whatever the other
does, each is better off confessing. The prosecutor benefits from the
deal, because he does not have to waste resources taking the case to
trial. The prosecutor relies on the fact that some criminals will follow
the incentives to rat each other out. The same incentives may induce
baseball players to use steroids.

In this game, using steroids is a dominant strategy, meaning that no matter what the other player chooses to do, using steroids is the best strategy. This strategy is also a stable outcome, or equilibrium, from which no player has a reason to deviate. This particular state is a *Nash equilibrium*—named for the Nobel Prize–winning mathematician/ economist John Nash, who is the subject of the book and movie *A Beautiful Mind*—which occurs if no party has any reason to deviate from a strategy as long as other parties do not deviate. It just so happens that both of the parties in the game would prefer the no-steroid outcome to the steroid outcome, because of the health consequences of the latter choice.

Expanding the model to include many players worsens the situation. If better players earn more income and fame than worse players, then all players have an incentive to take steroids. Even the very best players may have to use steroids to prevent the next-best group of players from outcompeting them. If there is a fixed pot of fame and income to go around, this is a suboptimal system. Marginal players can become good, good players can become stars, and stars can become superstars; yet, relative to one another, players are still the same and will be rewarded according to their relative abilities. Players suffer the negative health consequences of steroids and receive nothing in return. All players have an incentive to sacrifice their health to improve performance, but players are not rewarded for their improvements. Even players who abstain from steroids lose, because they suffer lower incomes as steroid-aided players with less talent improve.

Another interesting result of this model is that players have an incentive to violate informal agreements not to cheat. If two players realize the harm of this game, then the players may reach an "I'll quit if you quit" deal. However, the incentives of the game are such that if one player agrees to abstain, then the other player has an incentive to cheat. The abstaining player is then left with what economists often call "sucker's payoff." By getting your competitor to think you are cooperating, you can win big. The big gains from cheating, and the fear that the other party may hurt you by cheating, cause informal agreements to cooperate to break down. The more parties involved in the agreement—over a thousand different players play in the major leagues every year—the more likely it is that parties will cheat. This is why an externally enforced ban on steroids that includes testing and punishment seems to be the only solution.

Why Have Players Resisted Testing?

If banning steroids is a good thing for the players, why has the MLB Players Association fought so hard to limit testing? From the analysis above, it is clear that players ought to want to stop the use of steroids. And strict testing with sanctions seems to be the only practical way to police their use. However, in the media, the players have ended up bearing most of the blame for the whole steroids mess. I think the case against the players is a little overblown. First, the owners have an incentive to keep steroids in the game, which gives them a reason not to push hard for testing. Second, players may be resisting testing for reasons other than wanting to keep steroids in the game.

Though the relative salary differences between players ought to be roughly the same—with superior players making more than inferior players—the overall play of the game can improve with the ratcheting up of individual performances. When the athletic abilities of all players improve, there will be more spectacular plays in the game: diving catches, hard-hit balls, faster pitches, and close plays on the base paths. If the overall level of the game rises, then this ought to create more fan interest, which generates financial gain to owners.

It is possible that owners, who plead that it's the players who have fought off testing programs, have been covertly hesitant to institute an effective steroid testing program. There is a strong positive correlation between winning and revenue. An owner who can convince his players to take steroids can reap the returns from winning extra games. For most of baseball history, owners have been in a great position. Steroids have been prohibited in baseball, but with toothless punishment and weak detection. An owner certainly could not openly encourage his players to take steroids, but he could set a precedent for players who visit the right "doctors" by giving implicit bonuses, such as avoiding salary arbitration—the process by which owners and players agree on salaries for the upcoming season—more frequently. Marvin Miller, the famed MLBPA leader who opposes testing, indicates that this was the owners' attitude toward amphetamines in the 1970s:

> In most locker rooms, most clubhouses, amphetamines, red ones, green ones, etc., were lying out there in the open, in a bowl, as if they were jellybeans. . . . They were not put there by the players, so of course there was no pressure to test. They were being distributed by ownership. I can't remember ever having a proposal from the owners, that we're going to have random testing or testing of any kind.[56]

But this leads to the obvious question of why the owners seem to be for testing and the players against it. Are owners looking out for the integrity of the game? Yeah right, the same guys who threaten contraction and want to put Spider-Man on the base paths. (I actually find nothing objectionable in either of these proposals, but I am clearly in the minority on this.) Are the owners concerned about the health of the players? Especially considering that the positive effects of steroids occur in the present, and the negative effects occur in the long run?

The owners ought to bear a larger share of the public blame than they have received for the lack of testing, but the player resistance is not just owner propaganda. The MLBPA has publicly opposed drug testing for most of its existence. Maybe the players are principled civil libertarians taking a stand, but I doubt it.

One possible reason for players' reluctance to allow drug testing has gone largely undiscussed in the midst of the steroid debate. A urine specimen given over to test for steroids can be used for other purposes. Urine contains not just information on the use of steroids, but also other health-related information. Players would prefer to keep some of this information to themselves. I suspect there is a higher than average incidence of THC—the intoxicating chemical in marijuana—in the bodies of major-league players. This is a cohort of men in their twenties and thirties who spend large amounts of time on the road trying to kill time where there is a lot of partying going on. It may not be quite rock star level—these guys do have to play baseball—but I bet it's way higher than the average American's. Players most certainly like to keep their partying levels a secret from owners. Pot is not performance-enhancing, but it probably makes being on the Devil Rays at least funny. With the knowledge from tests for performance-enhancers, owners can learn about the bad stuff too.

While the league is prohibited from testing for drugs of abuse—the classification of marijuana—under the current collective bargaining agreement, the information is still there. Vials can go missing and lab technicians can be bribed; as long as the information is available, there is the risk of exposure of information players wish to keep private. In 2004, federal agents seized urine samples of players, matching names with samples, that both owners and players had agreed to keep anonymous. I don't blame the players for being suspicious. Would you want a potential employer to be the keeper of personal information, at which he promised not to peek?

Players have an incentive to support the availability of drugs that harm performance for the same reason they want to prevent performance-enhancers. The spillovers from performance-inhibiting drugs work in a similar way, except using drugs lowers the income of users and raises the income of abstainers. It is interesting to note that the incentives facing owners and players is diametrically opposite. Many players probably feel that the value of protecting recreational drug users is greater than that of identifying cheaters.

Ultimately, the opposition to testing may come from simple concerns over personal privacy. I think that players are predisposed to oppose testing because the testing procedure itself is costly in terms of the discomfort it causes. I would certainly prefer less salary if it meant that I didn't have to stand naked in a room to urinate into a cup held by a stranger. Rafael Palmeiro's positive test probably did more to motivate players to seek testing from a practical point of view than a political one. Here was a very good player who was taking steroids, even with all of his success. While players would prefer not to incur the embarrassment of testing, if it means sacrificing hundreds of thousands of dollars in free agency because a few players use them, it's an inconvenience that many can learn to live with.

A Possible Remedy

There is a solution to all of this that can make the players happy without giving in to the potential ulterior motives of owners. The MLBPA should adopt its own testing policy. As a requirement for membership, players would be subject to fines—not suspension, since owners would not like this—for using drugs deemed to be performance-enhancing. The fine revenue would be distributed equally across players of similar quality. This fine would act like a tax on the incomes of players who choose to take steroids along with a corresponding subsidy to cover the costs of those who suffer lower incomes because they choose not to use steroids. I suspect the players could find the right penalty to make the returns from steroids sufficient to offset incomes from steroid-enhanced performance. Of course, the owners will hate it and can preach from the altar about how the MLBPA cannot be trusted. But I think the MLBPA has a much better chance of keeping steroids out of the game than any joint solution between the parties.

The tough steroid policy instituted in 2005, which included random tests and fines, did seem to be effective at deterring steroid use. Less than 1 percent of major-league players tested positive during its first year. However, the gains from using steroids don't disappear with testing. In fact, there is a greater opportunity for gains. Wherever profits exist, human beings will find a way to get them. Some players will surely figure out ways to beat the test. These leaks will eventually be discovered and closed, but there will always be new ones. I have more confidence in the players than the owners to close them, because incentives matter.

Part Three

WAY OFF THE FIELD

10

Innovating to Win

Baseball people generally are allergic to new ideas.
We are slow to change.

—BRANCH RICKEY[57]

I F YOU WANT a fun but practical exercise in constrained maximization, join a fantasy baseball league. In most leagues, each owner has a budget to spend on teams of real major-league players. Not only must you be careful with the money you spend, but you have to compete for talent with the other owners in the league. Owning a fantasy team is similar to being a real major-league general manager, which probably explains the game's popularity. But if you've ever played in a league, you also know how frustrating it can be. Every other owner seems to know the exact same things about players that you do. Even that tip about your ace reliever favoring his elbow after the game on your pay-for-access roto-website seems to have made its rounds on the Internet before you palm him off on one of your competitors. Everyone wants the players you do and doesn't want the ones you want to get rid of. In the end, you realize you can't win by just reading the Internet. You have to learn something new about evaluating the players in order to win, which most people don't have the time or skill to do. For most of us, we just hold out hope that everyone else in the league will lose his best players to injury.

Major-league GMs aren't allowed to give up or hope for the best. Either they win or get fired. So maybe fantasy baseball isn't all that similar to the real thing, but you gain an appreciation for what it takes to win. To succeed, a GM has to be able to innovate, to find new ideas before his competitors do. And once new ideas proliferate, they must be replaced by newer ones. In short, the good GM is an entrepreneur.

Pinning down an exact meaning of entrepreneurship gets a bit tricky. And I've seen economists go to war over the most trivial aspects of the definition. I don't want to get caught up in all of this, so I'll just keep it simple. An entrepreneur is a person who develops a new method for earning extra profits—taking in more revenue than is spent on costs. The entrepreneur might find an untapped market, develop a new technology to produce a product more cheaply, or invent a new product altogether. And it is in this quest for profits that he serves a valuable function for society. New and cheap products only survive in the market if they bring customers what they want. The entrepreneur is finding ways to help citizens get more of what they want.

To function and grow, market economies need entrepreneurs, which is why economists often stress their importance. This explains why Michael Lewis's *Moneyball* generated a buzz among economists following its publication in 2003. *Moneyball* chronicles the entrepreneurial quest of the Oakland A's general manager, Billy Beane. The A's new ownership group gave Beane a task that is given to thousands of CEOs across the country every year: do as much as you can on a fixed budget. But the sum the A's ownership group gave Beane to work with was quite small compared to what other owners had given their teams. Beane had two choices: give up, or find a way to win within his current constraints. It's a simple economic problem of constrained maximization, and a seemingly unfair one. Many other owners didn't constrain their front offices as much as the A's did theirs.

But Beane's story is not unique. All owners place limits on what their GMs can do, and expect them to win with what they have. And it's not necessarily the whims of owners that restrict the financial resources that the GM has to do his job. Important determinants of budgets include the size of the fan base, the wealth of the fans, the appetite for winning, and even the generosity of the owner. It doesn't really matter. The point is that these things do differ from team to team, meaning that some teams have fewer resources at their disposal than other teams, and there is not much that can be done about it unless the structure of the league is radically altered. A GM who is asked to win with less can't afford to play with the same methods other teams use. And even if teams were equally constrained, as most fantasy owners are, the only way a GM can get a leg up is to discover new methods for winning that others GMs have missed. Success requires innovation. One source of innovation is to find *inefficiencies*—meaning incorrectly priced commodities—in the input market for wins. By winning more games, the team will bring in more revenue. The main input to winning is players; therefore, a good place to find inefficiencies is in the market for players.

When inputs sell for prices equal to the returns they generate, economists say that the market is *efficient*. We can view the returns-to-inputs ratio in many different ways. For example, in a competitive labor market, a worker who generates $10 an hour for the labor he provides to the employer generally earns $10 an hour. Why? Because, if the employer pays him less (say $7 an hour), an alternate employer will hire him away, because he knows that input is more valuable than $7. Paying the worker more than the value he produces would be inefficient as well. An employer who pays the same worker $15 an hour will not be returning enough on the output produced by the worker to cover the cost of his employment. Firms that overpay for inputs will spend more money than they take in, and that will lead to losses, and eventually bankruptcy. Therefore, in a competitive market for inputs, we expect the price of all inputs to be equal to the amount of revenue they generate.

Without innovation, this proves to be a huge problem for the general manger. If everyone knows Joe Blow is worth five extra wins a year, which generates an extra $12 million in revenue, the GM has no choice but to pay the market price for Joe Blow's skills. And with a small budget, a GM won't be able to field a team of players who could win a lot of games. He would run out of money before he had assembled his team. Winning within his constraints requires finding mistakes in the market, a frequent pursuit of entrepreneurs. This might involve using statistical methods to find hidden talent, sending scouts to foreign countries to find neglected talent, or developing new training methods.

Let's say a GM wants to find inefficiencies in the market for baseball talent. The first step is to find out what every action on the field is worth. Hitting, pitching, fielding, and possibly even leadership have quantitative values. How much do the things players do in these areas affect winning? Once the question is answered, the GM can sift through the players themselves to find whose skills were mis-priced in the market. Joe Blow might be worth $12 million in the current players market, but maybe there is another player who can produce those same five wins for a fraction of the price. Entrepreneurship is about finding bargains.

But finding bargains isn't all that easy. There isn't a coupon section in the back of *Baseball Weekly* that GMs can clip. Finding cheaper players requires technological innovation. Technology is not just some fancy new gadget with wires, it is also ideas that lead to new ways of doing things. The gadgets we often refer to as technology are just junk without a human mind to turn the pile of raw materials into something useful. Take, for example, the growing use of computers in scouting players through statistical analysis. What is important about the numbers that come out of the computers is not the product of that computer. The numbers are a product of discoveries of mathematical truths and statistical properties. These things existed long before the invention of computers; they are just difficult to employ without them. Every statistical procedure done on a computer can be done by a human being with a pencil and paper. Yes, the computer and the computer programs used are also products of technological innovation and make these calculations much easier, but without the ideas to create the need for computing help, the computer is useless.

New technologies help teams in their quest to get more from less. Every instance of finding a new way to win for less frees up more of the budget to hire better players. How is it that these new ideas generate wins? Let's assume that teams can buy wins by purchasing players. Consistent with the law of demand, teams are willing to purchase more wins the cheaper each win is. By finding cheaper methods for acquiring the things that lead to wins—an undervalued player, a coach who motivates his players, or a new training regimen—a team can purchase more wins on the same budget. Or by finding a new way to market the team—better concessions, a new start time for games, or adding seats—a GM can generate more revenue to purchase more wins.

Finding new ways to win baseball games is easier said than done, particularly when it comes to identifying undervalued talent. The wealth of stats produced by the game makes following talent from a distance simpler than most business activities. Compare a player posting a stat-line in a box score to a résumé on Monster.com. Baseball teams can identify and find talent quickly. Innovation can be tough, especially when it involves finding new information in the stats that passed in front of every GM's eyes.

Great Innovators

Branch Rickey is the man all general managers aspire to be. Rickey made his mark on the baseball world by bringing several innovations to the game. His first notable invention was the modern minor-league farm system, which he employed with the St. Louis Cardinals to win six NL pennants and four World Series for the previously inept franchise. He is also known for trading star players before age caused their play to decline, employing a statistician, and attempting to start a third major league. But his most famous innovation was the integration of Major League Baseball, with the signing of Jackie Robinson to the Brooklyn Dodgers in 1947. This was not just an important ethical move and the beginning of the correction of gross social injustice. Rickey certainly realized the political importance of this moment, but even from a baseball management standpoint this was a fantastic move. It took advantage of an untapped talent pool that was ignored out of racial prejudice. The Negro Leagues contained many players who could not only play major-league-quality baseball, but would excel at it. Robinson exploded into the National League, winning "Rookie of the Year" in 1947, a batting title (1949), and MVP (1949), while taking the Dodgers to six World Series over his career.

Rickey didn't just get lucky. He knew the Negro Leagues contained a gold mine of big-league players, and the only thing holding them back was an irrational prejudice. After signing Robinson to a minor-league deal in 1946, Rickey announced to the world what he was doing. "The greatest untapped reservoir of raw material in the history of our game is the black race," he said. Rickey also signed other Negro League standouts, who would become National League All-Stars, such as Roy Campanella and Don Newcombe.

Rickey saw an inefficiency in the market and exploited it at the expense of his competitors. And it didn't take long for other teams to see what a bargain Branch Rickey had found. Eleven weeks after Robinson joined the Dodgers, the Cleveland Indians signed Larry Doby to be the first black player in the American League. In his first full season in the majors (1948) he helped the Indians win the World Series. In fact, the teams that were quick to integrate were reaping huge rewards in wins. By exploiting the inefficient use—or nonuse—of black talent, teams were able to win more games.

Eventually, black talent spread throughout the major leagues, with the best Negro League talent jumping to the AL and NL, until there were no more gains to be had by adding additional talent. This demonstrates one of the other characteristics of innovation: successful innovative practices will spread. Once the rest of baseball realized the success of black athletes, the inefficiency went away. Players who were once cheap and untouchable became caught in bidding wars between teams. The price of talent again rose to its old level, where black and white players of equal talent cost teams the same. The market for baseball talent was no longer inefficient when it came to race.

The great lesson in the reversion of rewards from innovation is that inefficiencies in markets don't persist for long. To win by innovation one must be adept at finding inefficiencies and swift at acting on them once they're found. No organization can build a baseball dynasty off one lucky strike. Only the continued pursuit of inefficiencies will lead to perpetual success. Which brings us back to the A's in *Moneyball*.

As I mentioned above, in *Moneyball*, Michael Lewis recounts Billy Beane's entrepreneurial skill. Billy Beane didn't have a huge untapped talent pool to draw from. Many teams in the 1990s and 2000s were scouring the globe for talent. To find new ways to win on their small budget, the A's needed to develop new ways for finding talent that was hiding just beneath the nose of every scout across the country. The answer lay in the complexity of the data. Baseball generates many quantifiable results with every play, so many that it's hard for even a group of people to generate meaning from these numbers. Everyone can look at what Barry Bonds does and see that the things Bonds does well cause his teams to win. He hits for average and power, draws walks, and doesn't strike out.

There's no way the A's could afford to pay Bonds to come across the Bay from San Francisco to play in the Oakland Coliseum, so the A's needed to find something like Bonds to win. But one player who resembled Bonds would still be too expensive. Gary Sheffield could have been considered a Bonds-lite at the time, but he too commanded a huge salary in the market for baseball talent. Instead, the A's found several players who did things important to Bonds's success just enough better than the average player to be valuable, but not well enough for the rest of baseball to know it.

The first step in building a Frankenstein Bonds from several players was to find out what it was about Bonds that made his teams win. Then they had to figure out the going rate for those qualities in the open market and, finally, check out the options of baseball talent packaged in individual human beings. Once these steps were completed, the A's could snatch up any mis-priced players who would yield the wins that everyone else was missing.

While Bonds has many noble qualities, I'll focus on the offensive stats of on-base percentage and slugging average. Bonds is very good in both of these areas, but that does not mean they are equally important. Winning baseball games requires scoring more runs than the other teams you play. Therefore, to discover the importance of each of these metrics in scoring runs, Beane's assistant, Paul DePodesta—an economics major from Harvard who would become the general manager of the Dodgers for a short time—used statistical methods to estimate how much each statistic impacted run scoring in recent history. To the surprise of many, DePodesta found something that everyone else was missing: each point of on-base percentage was worth about three times each slugging percentage point in producing runs. And this finding just happened to coincide some very favorable conditions in the market for baseball talent:

> In major league baseball . . . Paul's argument was practically heresy. . . . Heresy was good: heresy meant opportunity. A player's ability to get on base—especially when he got on base in unspectacular ways—tended to be dramatically underpriced in relation to other abilities. . . . The one attribute most critical to the success of a baseball team was an attribute they could afford to buy.[58]

In this passage, Michael Lewis captures the essence of entrepreneurship. DePodesta had just stumbled upon a market inefficiency, a tool that would allow the A's to purchase wins at a price less than what other teams had to pay for those wins.

Economists Jahn Hakes and Skip Sauer have verified the underpricing of on-base percentage and overpricing of slugging percentage at the time *Moneyball* was written—during the 2002 season. And this is just one innovation that would allow the A's to purchase wins at a lower cost than the rest of the league. However, the success the A's would have with on-base percentage is something that would not even last until the book hit the best-seller lists. Hakes and Sauer find that the inefficiency did not last for long:

> This diffusion of statistical knowledge across a handful of decision-making units in baseball was apparently sufficient to correct the mispricing of skill. The underpayment of the ability to get on base was substantially if not completely eroded within a year of *Moneyball's* publication.[59]

Innovation is a process, and though its returns are positive and real, they are short-lived. Just as the wins from integration evaporated, so did the wins from exploiting the underpricing of on-base percentage. To stay on top, the A's would have to do new things. While the A's had the third highest on-base percentage in the AL by 2000 and 2001, in 2002 they would fall to fifth and in 2003—the year *Moneyball* was released—the A's were a woeful tenth in on-base percentage. How did the A's manage to win ninety-six games in 2003 if on-base percentage is so important? The A's found new inefficiencies to exploit. Having a good on-base percentage isn't the only way to win. Beane didn't reveal all his secrets in *Moneyball*. Maybe this was partly to hold on to some trade secrets to use against his rivals, but I think it's more likely that those secrets just hadn't been discovered and employed yet.

It was probably not a single magic bullet that propelled the A's' success; instead, it was an intellectual infrastructure put in place by Beane's predecessor, Sandy Alderson. Beane, who worked closely with Alderson until he left the club, continued to modify the organization so that it could adapt to new information and the baseball market. By 2005, Beane had lost or traded away nearly all of the players that had been a part of the A's recent success, yet the A's kept on winning. An important lesson of this story is not just that an inefficiency can be exploited, but that these moments of inefficiencies are fleeting. The market acts fast to correct for its mistakes, so if you want to exploit them, you have to develop a method to always be looking for them and ready to act.

One of the misunderstandings of *Moneyball* is that Billy Beane had found a honey hole of success that twenty-nine other intelligent GMs chose to ignore. Nor was Beane the only GM stumbling on to new and innovative ideas that helped his team win. He is just one example of a successful entrepreneur. Economists refer to the pursuit of new innovative ways of doing things at the cost of discarding outdated methods as *creative destruction*—a term coined by economist Joseph Schumpeter. Creative destruction is a natural function of the competitive process, which is as old as humanity. Just as the wheel replaced dragging and the CD replaced the vinyl record, so too have many inferior practices been replaced through the process of creative destruction in baseball. Integration forced many marginal white players to leave the game, and the use of statistical tools may replace some of the work of traveling scouts. In the short run, this process seems unfriendly and mean; but the end result is unquestionably good: we get to consume more and better baseball for less.

Unlike creative destruction in the product market, new technologies do not lead to ever increasing wins for a team. For example, if someone invents a new method to produce corn, the price and quantity of corn will change permanently. The extra effort and money used to produce and purchase corn can now be devoted to producing and purchasing other goods and services. However, in baseball, wins and losses are a zero-sum game. One team's wins necessitate other teams' losses. As one innovation spreads from one team to the league, the innovative edge simply disappears. So how does creative destruction benefit baseball as a whole? If teams can identify and use all the best talent available, the outcome will be a more interesting game. Younger players may be identified earlier, struggling teams regenerate faster, plays become closer and more spectacular as everyone improves together, etc. Off the field, those resources that used to fund old methods can be devoted to making the ballpark experience better. Fans welcome cheaper tickets, more comfortable seats, and bigger, clearer scoreboards. These are just a sample of the benefits that result from managerial innovation. It is often overlooked that fans benefit substantially from such innovation.

11

Scouts vs. Stat-Heads

"Performance scouting," in scouting circles, is an insult. It directly contradicts the baseball man's view that a young player is what you can see him doing in your mind's eye. It argues that most of what's important about a baseball player, maybe even including his character, can be found in his statistics.

—MICHAEL LEWIS, *MONEYBALL*[60]

A GENERAL MANAGER must be efficient with his operation. In economic terms, being efficient means the GM attempts to put all of his resources to their most highly valued uses. If the market overvalues a particular baseball talent, such as saves, you liquidate your assets in this area. If the market undervalues a talent, such as on-base percentage, you acquire it while it's cheap. It's all very simple in theory, but difficult in practice. And to continue winning, a team must continue to innovate, as the profits returned from new inventions will disappear.

Finding new ways to win is a goal that all GMs aspire to. Whether it's hitting, pitching, fielding, aging, speed, intelligence, or fan popularity, it's the GM's job to put a value on it. Once the values are in place, he can do the wheeling and dealing the fans love to analyze. All of this translates into winning. One of the newer ways for GMs to evaluate talent is to use statistical methods to scout players. Thanks to *Moneyball*, we know it's something that the Oakland A's use heavily, but they're not the only team doing so.

The proper role for statistical methods is a sensitive issue in baseball these days. *Moneyball* made the debate public, but it was already happening. The backlash came from the traditionalists within the game, but not the same traditionalists who think the DH and lights in Wrigley are travesties. It came from those who believe in the traditional method of identifying talent by "scouting," by putting a pair of human eyes on potential players. How can anyone learn more about what's happening on the field by staring at numbers or charts on a computer screen?

Traditional scouting isn't all that different in its approach from "performance scouting," the subject of the opening quote, in terms of identifying future major-league ballplayers. The goal of both approaches is to predict the future production of major-league talent from a vast pool of prospects. It's the method of prediction that divides these schools of thought. These two philosophies are often thought of as extreme stereotypes. Scouts are old men armed with radar guns and Skoal, who spend their time on the road scouring the high school and college ranks. Performance scouts, or "stat-heads" as they are more commonly known, are computer geeks who took *The Matrix* a little too seriously. It's the numbers that matter to them, and not just any numbers. Stat-heads often use nontraditional stats, some developed and tested with sophisticated empirical techniques.

The Stat-Head Method

Stat-heads don't just stare at numbers or combine numbers at random to judge players, and they certainly aren't ignoring the human element of the game. The bias against statistics isn't something unique to the baseball establishment; it's something pervasive in society. Using statistics requires computers and numbers, very impersonal things, but they are tools that can help us see things that our eyes miss on the field. And in many cases, numbers are more honest than our eyes.

But the idea that you can evaluate players using statistics alone just cuts against everything the old scouts are about. There's no gut instinct or personal experience from watching hundreds of games a year. Rather than viewing players in person, the performance scouts look for specific markers of future success as predicted in statistical models. These markers were chosen because many models involving hypothetical simulations, regression analysis, or just thought experiments said they were the best. While judging human beings solely on numbers is a little unsettling, think about all the transactions in life that are made without personal contact. Banks make loans based on credit scores, insurance agencies set premiums based on the number of speeding tickets you've had in the past five years, and eBay auction winners feel safe sending money to a stranger because he has a 97.4 percent positive feedback score.

This is not to say that the any team could succeed without putting some eyes on players, but in order to beat the competition they're also looking for the things that the old methods might have missed.

It's not that numbers don't matter to scouts; they do. But over the years scouts have learned, correctly, that numbers can be deceiving. With the baseball talent spread so thin in amateur ball, it's hard to know what those numbers mean. High batting averages, home runs, and strikeouts may be a product of poor competition, not major-league skills. These statistics can have very little to say as raw metrics, a problem that stat-heads are aware of. Scouting involves putting a pair of eyes on the players to try and pick out the guys who are going to play pro ball.

Perception is a funny thing. Small differences that are real and important are often very hard to perceive, even when you pay close attention. Bill James made the point quite clearly in his *1977 Baseball Abstract*. What is the difference between hitters with batting averages of .275 and .300? These batting averages range from decent to good. But, how many hits does a good hitter have compared to a decent hitter over a two-week period? One. That's right, a mere two hits a month separates the wheat from the chaff among hitters. If we assume the batters average twenty at-bats per week, over a two-week span the good hitter will have twelve hits and the decent hitter will have eleven. Over the course of the season, that translates to twelve extra hits for the good player. Even if you watched every game, it would be hard to know who was the better player. And if you stepped out to the bathroom at inopportune times over the year, you could easily gain the wrong impression of each player's ability.

But, because the numbers generated at low levels of competition can't tell us much about the professional baseball career of teenagers, even when aggregated, we have to look to something else. Scouts developed some rules—tall is better than short, skinny is better than fat, etc.—and tried to quantify tools that were measurable—radar-gun fastballs, speed around the base path, the mechanics of a swing, or an arm motion. They might even conduct interviews to find out the unquantifiable: competitive drive, the heart of a champion, sanity, etc. For most of the history of baseball, this is all the scout had to go on, and this information was better than no information at all. Teams that scouted prospects instead of randomly selecting talent tended to win more games.

It's common to hear stat-heads emphasize the bias of psychological factors that can cause scouts to develop irrational likes or dislikes for certain types of players. Using numbers removes such biases. But we don't even need to consider these biases to show why stat-head scouting can have advantages over the traditional methods. I think these biases do exist, but certainly there are good scouts out there who have learned to avoid the obvious pitfalls. Consider the scouting of a player like Barry Zito. Zito is known for his deceptive curveball and changeup, with a fastball in the high-80s.[61] Many teams refused to give him a chance because he couldn't break 90 on the radar gun. While speed tells the scout something, speed just isn't everything. The failure to identify Zito as a future Cy Young winner wasn't a product of human scouting, just bad scouting. Relying on a radar gun, rather than examining deceptive ability, could cause a scout to conclude Zito would be a dud. But a good scout would not be stuck on this particular metric. The failure of scouting in this instance had to do with individuals, not the process.

This is a very simple discovery to make, and most people in baseball, including scouts, are probably aware of the weaknesses of the gun. But what about some other weaknesses in scouting that are yet undiscovered? How does a GM find those? Statistical methods offer insights as to the things scouts are missing. Maybe college pitchers who always pitch the second half of Sunday doubleheaders face weaker competition, which artificially inflates their strikeout rates. I have no idea if my conjecture is true, but certainly such quirks exist, which might take a long time to find out without statistical analysis. And even if you figure out that these stats ought to be discounted, how much should you discount them? A couple of scouts sitting around talking may eventually realize such a phenomenon, but it's something a stats-geek with a spreadsheet can pick up in an hour of goofing around with data. And imagine if you're the first team to figure this out. You get a huge jump on the competition for new talent.

The process is important to avoid mistakes, but not because statistics avoid the biases of human perception. How did the Oakland A's figure out Zito was worthy of being drafted in the first round? From the stats. When you look at major-league players, you can see that many succeed in different ways. There are many young guys who have fastballs near the century mark but can't make it out of Double-A. Other pitchers with much lower velocity have great success in the major-leagues, like Greg Maddux with his mid-80s fastball. But a common trait among major-league pitchers is throwing hard, and very few players in the big leagues get away with fastballs under 90 miles per hour. How can you figure out which of these pitchers are more likely to succeed? What if we had a spreadsheet—like the popular Microsoft Excel—with a list of characteristics for every twenty-year-old college pitcher? Table 21 shows a hypothetical short list of stats for three pitchers.

How can we know which of these metrics gives us the most information about the future success of a pitcher? Certainly, all scouts will have their ideas, which are mostly correct. Speed is good, walks are

Table 21: Spreadsheet of Pitcher Prospects

Name	Pitch Speed	Ks per 9	BBs per 9	HR per 9	Conference
Hank Dunn	95	5.6	2.5	0.5	ACC
Joe Smith	89	9.2	4.3	1.1	SEC
Fred Taylor	93	6.6	5.1	0.7	PAC-10

bad, etc.; but how can we determine what is most important among a sea of data? Some guys have low walk rates but no speed, or vice versa. We can see any number of combinations across players. Over time, a group of scouts may be able to figure out what is the most important, how to discount the bad or inflate the good, but these are all guesses. If you are lucky, your team will have some of the better guessers. Statistics give us a method to sort through the data to spot trends and according to different factors. A better understanding of what characteristics are important for predicting the future performance of a player adds some certainty to predictions. Statistical methods also present guesses, but they are much more precise guesses. Here is how this works for projecting baseball players.

Statisticians have developed methods to quantify the impact of individual factors on outcomes when many factors are involved. As long as we have a large group of players, the statistical methods identify when the individual characteristics of pitchers differ and how these differences in college translate to differences in the future. We can then identify what each factor is worth in terms of predicting the future. When one goes up, we see the quality of the player go up, when another goes down, the player's success falls. Each factor receives a weight based on the importance of affecting the outcome.

$$\text{Predicted ERA}_{\text{Age 27}} = (\text{Weight}_{PS} \times \text{Pitch Speed}) + (\text{Weight}_K \times \text{Strike-outs}) + (\text{Weight}_{BB} \times \text{Walks}) + (\text{Weight}_{HR} \times \text{Home Runs}) + (\text{Weight}_{ACC} \times \text{ACC}) + (\text{Weight}_{SEC} \times \text{SEC}) + (\text{Weight}_{PAC} \times \text{PAC-10})$$

The formula above is a simple linear model that tells us how much each of these important characteristics predicts the ERA of any player at the age of twenty-seven. Certainly some players will do better, and some worse, but knowing these factors can tell use more about what that player's true performance will be by the time he is twenty-seven than just guessing the average ERA of all twenty-seven-year-old pitchers. How can we possibly *know* this? Well, the laws of statistics give us certain insights about the likelihood of events occurring based on other events. A particularly useful tool of applied statisticians, multiple regression analysis, can be a big help. Appendix A provides further description of this method.

What does multiple regression tell us? Multiple regression can spot patterns in the data, even when the data seem quite confusing. But when we observe statistical metrics of a large number of individuals, we can identify differences in some of these predicting factors (strikeouts, walks, etc.) that move with or against the predicted metric (ERA). In fact, human eyes really don't view these changes all at once. It would be too hard. Multiple regression involves using mathematics to measure the changes in multiple factors. It identifies when movements in predicting factors and the predicted metric change from player to player and how big those movements are. With history as our guide—that is looking at what college players did in the past—a performance scout can see what these factors reveal about their future performances. Thus, the multiple regression analysis of the past data provides information on how to value performance in the present as it relates to the future. We might learn that a pitcher who strikes out a lot of batters will be expected to have a lower ERA at twenty-seven, while a pitcher who walks a lot of batters ought to have a higher ERA. Maybe pitcher ERAs in the ACC and SEC need to be valued differently.[62] If a scout wanted to see how Sunday doubleheaders affect the prediction, he could add a variable that counted for the number of Sunday doubleheaders pitched to weight the effect. In the end, these estimates are not just educated guesses, but based on objective past performance, which generates weights from a history of events. And if the data set used is of a certain size and accurate in its information, we can feel reasonably confident in the estimated weights.

These estimates will not be perfect, but they can identify and correct unseen errors that human scouts miss in some areas. The human mind is just not equipped to process such a wealth of information all at once. Just as a metal detector helps a beachcomber find coins buried in the sand, statistical analysis helps general managers find players buried among sweaty teenagers.

Efficient Efficiency

The use of statistical methods to enhance scouting represents another type of efficiency. Efficiency is also a term statisticians use to judge what are known as *estimators*. Estimators are theoretical tools for predicting a numerical estimate from a sample of data. Rather than being a number, an estimator is a method for generating predicted estimates. There are lots of different methods we could choose to predict estimates from a group data.[63]

For example, let's say I was asked to predict the SAT score of a randomly selected student at a university. I would have many options to educate my guess. I could ask the next student who walked down the street what his score was and go with that score. Or I could go with the mean (total scores divided by total students), the median (the middle score), or the mode (the most common score) of the student population. These choices represent methods, or estimators, that will generate an estimate that we can use to predict. Statisticians try to determine properties of competing estimators that will minimize the mistakes, in size and frequency, of estimates. The "stat-heads versus scouts" debate is an argument over estimators, except that the estimators are not necessarily purely known mathematical functions of the data, like the mean or median, which statisticians use. Each camp makes predictions about the same population of players, based on different sets of estimators.

Statistical estimators are judged on two properties: bias and consistency. First, we want our estimator to be unbiased, that is, not consistently above or below the true value we are estimating. We don't want to choose a method that will regularly over- or underpredict how good a player will become. Second, we want to minimize the size of the predicting mistake, a quality known as consistency. We would prefer that the mistakes that we make about a player's future performance be small and infrequent. When we choose from several unbiased estimators to predict a true outcome from population, we want the one that minimizes the errors of the prediction. Fewer and smaller mistakes are preferred to more and larger mistakes, right? In the language of statistics, an estimator with the greater consistency, or smaller variance, is said to be *more efficient* than a less consistent estimator. In this sense, being efficient means making fewer and smaller mistakes in predicting the future. This, in turn, increases the economic efficiency of the organization, because it now needs fewer resources to devote to scouting talent. By adopting a new technology, the A's became more "efficient" in their evaluation of talent.

Hobbyist stat-heads that I know tend to have a bias toward college players when it comes to the draft. Indeed, in *Moneyball*, Lewis touts the A's focus on college players over high school talent as an edge. But the edge isn't because college players are better. The A's focused on college players because they are more predictable from the statistical tools the A's favor. A technological innovation in performance scouting, such as the DIPS ERA—a modified ERA heavily based on strikeouts, walks, and home runs—can increase the efficiency in evaluating talent. You can use a DIPS ERA to better predict a college player because of the quantity and quality of the observations, but probably not a high school player. And if a technology can be employed with a higher confidence in one area than in another, it's no surprise that the A's would concentrate on a talent pool where this new technology is useful. Just as the cotton gin caused Southern farmers to switch to cotton farming in the late eighteenth century, where this technological innovation was relevant, so too did the A's turn to the college talent pool where their inventions were useful. The reason for this choice is well documented in the book:

> From Paul's point of view, that was the great thing about college players: they had meaningful stats. They played a lot more games, against stiffer competition, than high school players. The sample size of their relevant statistics was larger, and therefore a more accurate reflection of some underlying reality. You could project college players with greater certainty than you could project high school players.[64]

Sophisticated statistical analysis of baseball data is a new technology, and a technology that is superior to the old technology. Yes, it is possible to build a successful ball club solely with scouts instead of spreadsheets, but why would any GM choose to do this? It requires a much larger operation to compensate for the greater errors in prediction. It just so happens that the performance methods are a cheap operation to run if you do it right. Rather than deploying an army of scouts across the globe to report back on thousands of personal observations, from which personal impressions can be quantified, why not target those who exhibit qualities of successful ballplayers? And the more you can afford to limit the talent pool you draw from, the more efficient you can be at evaluating it.

The End of Traditional Scouting?

The personal observations from the past are not useful in the same way that they once were. Yes, this type of scouting can be used to put a winning team on the field. But just as a train can still get you from New York to Los Angeles, why would you want to take Amtrak when you can fly much cheaper in a fraction of the time? Statistical analysis is a tool that was no different a discovery than the radar gun that many scouts can't live without. It reveals new information that was once hidden behind the millions of factors that influence the game.

Am I predicting an end to traditional scouting? I sincerely doubt that any baseball team, including any team run by Billy Beane, will ever abandon personal scouting. No matter how far the knowledge of predicting talent progresses, there will always be things that the stats will miss. Teams can learn from statistics what information they really need from scouts, and statistics can make the scouts more effective. For example, teams might notice that pitchers with high strikeout rates from Mid-State Junior College sometimes flame out while others are dominant in the pros. On a spreadsheet, these guys might have similar stats in every way. With a scout on hand to chart pitches, the team may learn that the pitching coach teaches some of his pitchers a dinky knuckle-curve that kills the junior college hitters just as badly as the guys with real talent on the team. When all of the guys are drafted the guys with natural movement, speed, and deception succeed; the knuckle-curve guys learn how to hit or move on. Statistical analysis does not eliminate the need for on-site scouting, but the role of the scout may be reduced and modified to focus on different things.

Also, other organizations that have been successful in evaluating talent through traditional methods have made their own innovations for evaluating talent that have caused them to be successful on a small budget, too. *Moneyball* speaks to the success of the implementation of one methodology, a method that happened to come to baseball from the outside, which makes it more interesting. It's tempting to say the method the A's employ—in which sabermetrics play a large role—is superior to all other methods and that's why the A's have been winning as of late. This upsets a lot of people. After all, haven't teams been successful without employing sabermetric methods? There is no arguing that Beane used a sabermetric mind-set to stay ahead of his competitors. I'm going to resist the temptation to call the A's' method superior. We don't know that other teams don't employ similar methods, and other organizations have been just as successful as the A's, if not more so, in winning with cheap talent.

In looking at the performance of baseball teams during Oakland's recent run of success, the A's clearly aren't the only team that's been winning, even in terms of their limited budget. This is a point that Clark Medal–winning economist Steven Levitt brought to light on his *Freakonomics* weblog. Table 22 ranks teams on total budget as a percent above or below the league-average payroll, and the number of playoff appearances by team from 2000 to 2005.

While the big-budget teams at the bottom of the table dominate the playoff appearances, the A's are not the only members of the winning paupers club. The most noted comparable to Oakland is the Twins, with three postseason appearances over this span. Also, the Marlins and the White Sox have posted some success on smaller-than-average budgets, each with a World Series trophy. None of these teams are known to be performance scouting clubs—or at least they are not declaring

Table 22: MLB Team Payroll Ranks and Playoff Appearances (2000–2005)

Rank	Team	Payroll Difference from League Average	Playoff Appearances
1	Kansas City Royals	−42.82 percent	0
2	Milwaukee Brewers	−40.12 percent	0
3	*Minnesota Twins*	−40.09 percent	3
4	Tampa Bay Devil Rays	−39.61 percent	0
5	*Florida Marlins*	−38.95 percent	1
6	Washington Nationals	−38.40 percent	0
7	Pittsburgh Pirates	−36.76 percent	0
8	*Oakland Athletics*	−33.08 percent	4
9	San Diego Padres	−24.87 percent	1
10	Cincinnati Reds	−22.97 percent	0
11	Detroit Tigers	−16.65 percent	0
12	*Chicago White Sox*	−14.92 percent	2
13	Toronto Blue Jays	−13.38 percent	0
14	Colorado Rockies	−6.86 percent	0
15	Cleveland Indians	−4.80 percent	1
16	Houston Astros	−1.04 percent	3
17	Philadelphia Phillies	0.03 percent	0
18	Baltimore Orioles	3.33 percent	0
19	Los Angeles Angels of Anaheim	7.33 percent	3
20	San Francisco Giants	11.48 percent	3
21	Chicago Cubs	13.88 percent	1
22	Seattle Mariners	16.73 percent	2
23	St. Louis Cardinals	17.74 percent	5
24	Texas Rangers	20.28 percent	0
25	Arizona Diamondbacks	21.45 percent	2
26	Atlanta Braves	38.24 percent	6
27	Los Angeles Dodgers	43.85 percent	1
28	New York Mets	44.94 percent	1
29	Boston Red Sox	60.65 percent	3
30	New York Yankees	115.40 percent	6

Note: Italics highlight the teams discussed in the text.

themselves to be using similar methods. We think of these franchises as successes of traditional scouting and good overall management, which allow them to win on a tight budget. And just as traditional scouting organizations would be wise to adopt innovations from sabermetric organizations, so too can stat-savvy clubs learn from the innovations in traditional scouting. Innovations are innovations. And clubs that wish to win will shift their resources to take advantage of these new methods.

Again, this is just the process of creative destruction at work. Old ways and old scouting methods may disappear, but the end result is a good one for the fan: better and cheaper baseball. While we might bemoan the loss of scouting jobs, we must remember that the old-school scouting ways are just as much a part of the process. The guys who took the train to watch games lost out to guys that had cars, the full-time day scouts lost out when part-time scouts could scout night games, and the Negro Leagues scouts replaced some of the guys with an expertise in the low-level white-only minor leagues. Someday a new technology will come along to sweep away the current wave of scouts. Maybe it's a new statistical method or a computer that simultaneously records every baseball play in the world through computer chips placed in the ball. In any event, I'm glad for this change, because it brings us better baseball.

If statistical methods are just a new technology that contributes to the production of a winning ballclub, why does the creeping use of statistical analysis upset so many people inside the game? The fierce resistance to technological change is much older than baseball. Just as certain frightened seventeenth-century English textile workers known as Luddites vandalized machines that could do their jobs, those within the baseball establishment are scared of essentially the same thing.

12

How to Judge a Hitter
or a Pitcher

Do not judge by appearances, but judge with right judgment.

—JOHN 7:24

THERE'S NOTHING SUBTLE about the Cincinnati Reds' Adam Dunn. The six-feet six-inch, 275-pound left fielder was slated to play football at the University of Texas before he turned his attention to baseball. In 2004, Dunn became the owner of a dubious record: he struck out more times in a single season (195) than any other player in the history of baseball. While many were quick to chastise Dunn for his tendency to strike out, few noticed that Dunn was the eleventh best run producer in the National League that year. In 2003, the Atlanta Braves' Russ Ortiz led the National League in wins with twenty-one, while being only the fiftieth best run preventer. By 2006, Ortiz's deficiencies had become so obvious that the Arizona Diamondbacks cut him in mid-season, eating the remainder of his $22 million contract—the largest amount any team has ever paid to waive a player.[65]

Evaluating players is a contentious issue among fans. But rigorous answers to the arguments in bars and managerial offices can be established. That is, with a little help from sabermetrics and an economic perspective. I often hear fans bash or praise the same player for the right reasons. "He hit thirty home runs and had 120 RBI, how can you complain about that?" one fan says. Another responds, "He strikes out all the time and rarely gets on base when he doesn't hit." We ought to be concerned with viewing the complete player. The key to evaluating players is not to focus on the good and the bad independently; it's to focus on all the things a player does and *weigh* the good and the bad. Sometimes the answers are surprising. Some .300 hitters aren't as good as players who hit .240. Some pitchers with a lot of wins aren't as good as those with very few wins.

One thing that we need to be careful of is to not let our evaluations be biased by our memories, particularly when it comes to grand events. In 1993, Joe Carter won the World Series for the Toronto Blue Jays with a walk-off home run, and few people will forget that. He had plenty of home runs and RBI in his career—he's forty-fifth on the all-time home runs list with 396 and fifty-second in RBI with 1445—which is why we tend to think of him as a very good player. But actually, Carter was very average. When he wasn't hitting home runs, he was making a lot of outs. Nearly 70 percent of his trips to the plate resulted in an out for his team, compared to the league average of 67 percent. As fans, we find it easy to remember the home runs and runs batted in. They are visible good events that we recall fondly, because they directly produce runs. In a game where an out is the most common outcome, outs do not have the same visible impact on run production as hits and they don't stick in our memories. However, nineteenth-century French economist Frédéric Bastiat pointed out that just because something is less noticed doesn't mean it's less important than things that are obvious:

> In the department of economy, an act, a habit, an institution, a law, gives birth not only to an effect, but to a series of effects. Of these effects, the first only is immediate; it manifests itself simultaneously with its cause—it is seen. The others unfold in succession—they are not seen: it is well for us, if they are foreseen. Between a good and a bad economist this constitutes the whole difference—the one takes account of the visible effect; the other takes account both of the effects which are seen, and also of those which it is necessary to foresee. Now this difference is

enormous, for it almost always happens that when the immediate consequence is favorable, the ultimate consequences are fatal, and the converse.[66]

How to Judge a Hitter

Hitters have long been recognized as especially complicated to evaluate. Unlike pitchers, who can be more closely evaluated based on their direct impact on run prevention (but do have their own complexities), batters do lots of things than indirectly impact run production for their teams. Ichiro Suzuki of the Seattle Mariners hits for a high average, but has little power. While Adam Dunn of the Cincinnati Reds hits for a low average, but he has a lot of power and walks quite a bit. It's easy to see how fans can disagree about who is a more valuable contributor in terms of producing runs.

Most of these arguments are rarely resolved, despite the fact that we have the capability to do so. Using certain analytical techniques, the sabermetrics community has done quite a good job of weighing the values of the different skills that hitters have. In fact, this analysis can get quite complicated and detailed. In his book *Baseball's All-Time Best Sluggers,* Michael Schell (a biostatistician at the University of North Carolina) goes so far as to measure the specific impacts of different eras and parks for nearly every possible batting outcome in the entire history of baseball. More modestly it is possible to demonstrate simple rules of thumb that are useful for evaluating players based on a few readily available statistics. Certain things are definitely worth noting in hitting performance—for example, Coors Field inflates and Dodger Stadium deflates hitting success—but even without these corrections we can judge the general hitting contributions of players. There are more complex and accurate measures of hitters, but those few simple numbers flashed under a player's name on the scoreboard before a batter steps to the plate contain quite a bit of information.

The Big 3

A batter steps to the plate and leaves it with an out or a nonout. He could strike out, put himself out, or give the fielder a choice: put out an existing base runner or put the batter out. For a batter, the best nonouts are hits: singles, doubles, triples, and home runs. The batter can reach base without making an out by a walk, being hit by a pitch, through a fielding error, and a few other trivial ways, including catcher interference and a strikeout combined with a wild pitch. Given these events, we judge batters by three main statistics: on-base percentage, batting average, and slugging percentage. In total, these stats measure players' abilities to reach base in any manner, to hit safely, and to advance many bases per hit.

On-Base Percentage (OBP)

The on-base percentage (OBP), sometimes known as the on-base average (OBA), is the number of times a player reaches base safely without making an out. It's sort of a fancy batting average.

$$OBP = \frac{\text{Hits} + \text{Walks} + \text{Hit by Pitch}}{\text{At-bats} + \text{Walks} + \text{Hit by Pitch} + \text{Sacrifice Flies}}$$

OBP does not discriminate between the walks and hits or singles and home runs. All it counts is how many times a player reaches base without making an out. It is measured as a rate, in terms of the number of opportunities a player has to make an out. Sacrifice flies are added to the denominator, because although the player may give himself up to advance a base runner, it's not clear that was his intention. Sacrifice bunts are ignored, because the hitter clearly is not trying to reach base in this situation.

On-base percentage is one of the most underrated statistics in the game. It's often ignored, because it has no flash. A guy who gets on base by walking is not nearly as interesting as someone who reaches base by hitting the ball on the field or over the fence for a home run. There seems to be a mentality that there is something cheap about getting on base via a base on balls. In fact, a walk does not have as much of an impact on scoring runs as a single, because a single can advance existing runners beyond a single base. However, not making outs is an important skill, because a team's opportunities to score runs are constrained by its outs. In a nine-inning game a team only gets twenty-seven outs, three outs per inning, to put up more runs than the opposing team. Every out brings the end of the inning and game closer, thereby lowering the team's opportunity to score runs. Also, getting on base, at the minimum, puts your team one base closer to scoring a run.

Batting Average (AVG)

The batting average is the gold standard of baseball hitting statistics. Almost all fans accept AVG as the benchmark for comparing hitters, and it's normally the first statistic you see next to a player's name. In fact, the "batting title" for the best hitter in the game is awarded to the player with the highest AVG.

$$AVG = \frac{\text{Hits}}{\text{At-bats}}$$

AVG measures the rate at which a batter reaches base by hitting the ball relative to the opportunities the player has to hit the ball. At-bats are the total number of times a player steps to the plate when he does not walk, get hit by a pitch, or sacrifice himself to advance a runner via a bunt or fly ball. Unlike with OBP, batters are not punished for sacrifice flies. This exclusion creates opportunity for a player to have an AVG higher than his OBP, which seems to indicate the mathematical impossibility of a batter reaching base from hitting more than he reached in total. In fact, it's just the result of the different denominators of the two statistics. Having an AVG greater than one's OBP is still a rare feat, yet Billy Beane—the OBP-loving protagonist of *Moneyball*—did just this in 1989. AVG rewards players for hitting their way on base, it is neutral toward walks and being hit by a pitch, and it punishes nonsacrificial outmaking. Like OBP, it weights all hit types the same.

Slugging Percentage (SLG)

The slugging percentage (SLG) is a batting average that accounts for hitting power. Each hit type is weighted by the number of bases the hitter advances.

$$SLG = \frac{(1 \times 1B) + (2 \times 2B) + (3 \times 3B) + (4 \times HR)}{\text{At-bats}}$$

SLG quantifies the power punch per at-bat. Certainly, a player who hits lots of doubles and home runs is more valuable to the team than a singles hitter with an identical AVG. And at some point, the team might even prefer a player with a lower AVG if his SLG is high enough, because he can push himself and his teammates farther around the bases when he does hit the ball. While SLG certainly tells us more about a player's value to the team than AVG, it's not perfect. First, the arbitrary weighting of bases from one through four, though intuitively appealing, is wrong. Using some sophisticated techniques to estimate the run values of the different types of hits, we know that doubles, triples, and homers are not two, three, and four times more valuable than singles in producing runs. But for a rough approximation of hitting power, SLG has the benefit of being very simple to calculate.

A second deficiency of SLG is that it captures more than just hitting power. Because its denominator is at-bats, it also captures hit frequency. For example, take two hitters with one hundred at-bats. Steve Single hits forty singles, and Donny Double his twenty doubles.

$$SLG_{\text{Steve}} = \frac{(1 \times 40\ 1B) + (2 \times 0\ 2B) + (3 \times 0\ 3B) + (4 \times 0\ HR)}{100} = .400$$

$$SLG_{\text{Donny}} = \frac{(0 \times 0\ 1B) + (2 \times 20\ 2B) + (3 \times 0\ 3B) + (4 \times 0\ HR)}{100} = .400$$

Clearly, Donny has more power than Steve, but their slugging percentages are identical. One way to remedy this problem is to look at only the extra-base hits. The metric known as "isolated power" (or iso-power) weights only extra-base hits, and does not count singles.

$$\text{Isolated Power} = \text{SLG} - \text{AVG}$$

Using isolated power, it's easy to see Donny is the player with greater hitting power, with an iso-power of .200 compared to Steve's .000. Again, no metric is perfect, but it's always good to know the strengths and weaknesses.

Some Old Favorites That Don't Say Much

Runs batted in (RBI) is the second category in the "triple crown" of batting competitions—the AVG and home runs are the first and third. It measures the number of times a player drives in runners, except when he hits into a double-play, because even a run isn't worth two outs. The RBI is a stat that we often judge a player by, but probably should not. Why? Well, RBI totals depend on not just the quality of the player, but several outside factors. A player who bats clean-up, behind three excellent players with high OBPs, will generate a lot more RBI than a lead-off man, who often bats with no players on base. For reasons other than hitting ability, we would expect very different RBI totals from these players. It's possible that the lead-off hitter does many things that if he were given the opportunity, would generate more RBIs than the man in the four-hole. It's just very hard to know.

For this reason, the RBI is a nearly useless statistic to judge baseball players. Certainly, to have a high RBI total, you have to be a good baseball player. But there are lots of good baseball players, so it's not a good idea to compare players on this statistic. If you want to judge a player's ability to knock players in, certainly a worthy goal of a team, SLG is a far better measure of this ability. SLG is not dependent on the base-runner configurations that a batter normally faces over a season.

Baseball is about scoring runs, right? Thus, a player who scores more runs is preferred to a player that does not. However, runs (RS), like RBI, are largely dependent on the play of teammates. There is only one case in which a player does all of the work to score a run, when he hits a home run. However, rarely do home run hitters lead the league in runs. Don't get me wrong, producing runs is valuable, but the run total of any player is largely determined by the players who bat behind him in the lineup. Lead-off hitters typically lead the RS category, because they precede good hitters in the lineup. Certainly, a player with a lot of runs has to be good at reaching base and can enhance his scoring ability with speed. But the run totals largely reflect things that other players do.

A batter's batting average with runners in scoring position (RISP AVG) is a commentator classic: "You know, Johnny's had a tough time keeping his average above the Mendoza line, but when it matters most, he's been a real clutch hitter, batting .425 with runners in scoring position." RISP AVG is simply a batting average calculated only when a player bats with at least one runner on second base or beyond. There is no doubt that hits in these situations are more valuable than hits with no men on base. Certainly, a manager loves for his players to get hits in these situations. But I wouldn't advise any manager to bench a .300 hitter with a .200 RISP AVG for a .200-hitter with a .400 RISP AVG. The problem is that hitting with RISP is not a skill, or at least not much of one that we can identify, but a statistical anomaly.[67]

Just because we can observe a number does not mean it contains useful information regarding a skill that a player has. Take early season batting averages. Everyone understands that regular batting averages for players can be absurdly high or low early in the season, simply because bad or good luck has not had time to even out. With few opportunities and a couple of odd bounces, in early May a player can have an AVG that is far from his norm. This is also what is going on with RISP

AVGs, as well as other situational statsistics. Players don't have as many RISP opportunities over the season, for some of these statistics to fall back or rise to a player's normal AVG.

Is it really such a good thing for a player to have a RISP AVG higher than his regular AVG? If I were the manager, my question to the player in question would be, "What the heck are you doing not hitting when there's no one on base? We need base runners, and it's awfully selfish of you to hold back unless there's some potential RBI out there!" If hitting with RISP is something a hitter can purposely alter, I have a hard time believing he is holding something back in non-RISP situations. It might be possible that some hitters hit the ball in ways that are more likely to succeed with runners on due to a common defensive configuration, but there has been little evidence of this.

Using the Big 3 to Evaluate Offense

Now, the next obvious step is to evaluate what these statistics tell us about run production. The goal of the offense is to score more runs. Which statistics tell us the most about a team's ability to produce runs? To do this, let's analyze team-level statistics using a simple statistical method to predict team run scoring.[68] We observe teams instead of players, because individuals can only contribute to runs scoring. Only in the case of a home run does the offense of a single player cause a run to occur. Players need the help of their teammates to score runs; therefore, looking at teams will tell us something about the value of these stats in predicting runs. We'll exclude a few of the statistics discussed above for obvious reasons. Runs are out, because, at the team level, the sum of runs scored will obviously be equal to the runs scored. RBI suffers from almost the same problem, although some runs can score without an RBI being awarded. Let's ignore RISP AVG since it contains a lot of luck. A team with a good RISP AVG will obviously score more runs than a team with a poor average. Getting hits in key spots is a good thing, but not largely controlled by players or teams.

The stats I'm interested are the Big 3: AVG, OBP, and SLG. When evaluating players, it's important to know which characteristics matter the more than others. As I've discussed, properly valuing skills, when other teams do not, can pay big returns. In evaluating the run-producing impact of these metrics using linear regression analysis, my time period of analysis is the era following the most recent expansion (1998–2004). This is so we are evaluating players playing in the same level of competition. Regression analysis tells us many things, but initially we ought to be concerned with how close each metric predicts the runs per game. We can then attribute the difference in runs per game across teams based on differences in the values of the different metrics. Figure 10 plots the relationship between the AVG, OBP, and SLG and runs per game by team. Each point represents the runs per game scored by a team and the associated value of the statistic in question. The slope of the regression line represents the estimated relationship between the metrics and runs that minimized the squared error of the prediction.

An obvious trend reflected in all of these graphs is a strong positive correlation between the offensive statistics and runs scored per game. A positive correlation means the metrics move in the same direction—when AVG goes up, runs go up; when AVG falls, runs go down—and a negative correlation means the metrics move in opposite directions. The higher a team's AVG, OBP, or SLG, the more runs the team is expected to score, which is not surprising. What is surprising is the proximity of the predicted runs of the regression lines to the actual runs scored by teams. Notice that the actual data points are farther away from the regression line for AVG than for OBP and SLG. The closer the points are to the prediction, the better the "fit" of the data to the prediction, yielded by the offensive stat.

While the graphs provide a nice guide, we can quantify exactly how much better OBP and SLG are at predicting run scoring from the regression estimates. Table 23 reports the difference in runs scored by teams that is explained by difference in the offensive metrics by league. We need to generate estimates for both leagues, because the use of the designated hitter in the AL may cause the estimates to differ. The

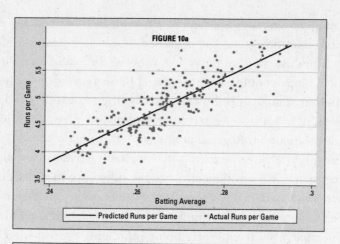

FIGURE 10a

Runs per Game (y-axis)
Batting Average (x-axis)

— Predicted Runs per Game   • Actual Runs per Game

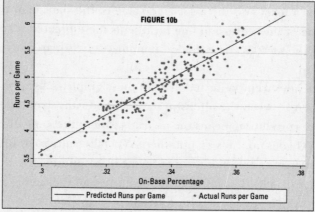

FIGURE 10b

Runs per Game (y-axis)
On-Base Percentage (x-axis)

— Predicted Runs per Game   • Actual Runs per Game

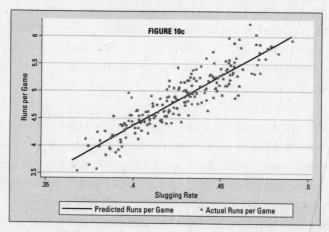

FIGURE 10c

Runs per Game (y-axis)
Slugging Rate (x-axis)

— Predicted Runs per Game   • Actual Runs per Game

Table 23: Explained Variance from Individual Batting Statistics

Statistic	National League Explained Variance	American League Explained Variance
AVG	72 percent	64 percent
OBP	81 percent	85 percent
SLG	82 percent	80 percent

differences in AVG across teams explain between 64 percent and 72 percent of the difference in runs scored per game, while OBP and SLG explain 80–85 percent. In other words, AVG tells us 8–21 percent less about a team's run scoring ability than OBP or SLG. This means that OBP and SLG are better predictors of run scoring than AVG.

In one sense, this is not surprising; OBP captures a team's ability to get on base via hits (like AVG), *plus* walks, and getting hit by pitches. SLG is just a batting average that weights the power of the hits; it's an AVG with kick. The reason one might consider it surprising is that the one statistic that everyone in baseball seems to focus on to judge offensive prowess is the batting average. But it's still too early to give up the search. Maybe AVG does tell us something important beyond OBP and SLG. What if we looked at all of the metrics at the same time for each team? It's possible that AVG could have an a greater *marginal* impact on generating runs—the impact of each additional batting average "point" being more valuable to run production than additional points of OBP and SLG.

Using the same sample of teams, we can estimate the impact of all of the metrics on runs per game at the same time with multiple regression analysis, which has some distinct advantages over the single variable regressions discussed above. Figure 11 shows a much tighter relationship between the predicted runs and actual runs than any of the metrics on their own, explaining approximately 92 percent of the variance in runs scored. But the story doesn't end here. The results indicate that the statistics have different impacts on run scoring.

Table 24 lists two types of measured impact of each statistic on runs per game: the direct marginal impact and the elasticity. Because all of

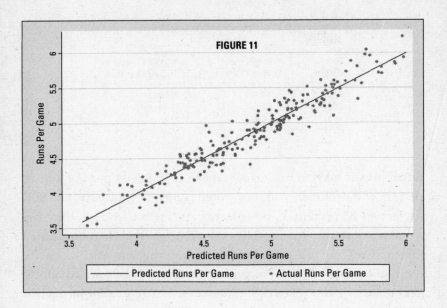

FIGURE 11

the statistics are included in the same regression model, we can calculate the added impact of each additional point of AVG, OBP, and SLG. *Elasticity* is also a marginal impact measure, but it interprets the effect in percentage terms at the average value for runs per game and the statistic. For example, the elasticity of 1.22 percent for NL OBP when all of the metrics are included means that a 1 percent increase in OBP is associated with a 1.22 percent increase in runs per game. This metric is useful for comparing the sensitivity of the impacts in the same terms.

The results are even more striking than before. AVG has a very small impact on runs per game compared to OBP and SLG. And in the case of the American League the impact is actually negative, meaning additional points of AVG are associated with lower runs scored. But note two things. First, the estimate of AVG is not "statistically significant," which means we cannot say with a high level of confidence that the AVG has any effect on scoring runs beyond the information we gather from OBP and SLG. Second, AVG seems to have zero explanatory power in predicting runs. Table 25 lists the variance explained with all of the metrics in the regression model and with only OBP and SLG and not AVG. The inclusion of AVG does not impact the variance

Table 24: Predicting Runs from Multiple Batting Statistics

Statistic	Marginal Impact		Elasticity		Marginal Impact		Elasticity	
	NL	AL	NL	AL	NL	AL	NL	AL
AVG	3.51	−0.32	0.20 percent	−0.02 percent	—	—	—	—
OBP	17.25	21.14	1.22 percent	1.43 percent	18.47	20.97	1.31 percent	1.41 percent
SLG	9.27	9.01	0.83 percent	0.78 percent	10.00	8.99	0.92 percent	0.78 percent

explained in a regression model, which means it doesn't add any more predictive power than OBP and SLG alone. So it would be very wrong to interpret higher batting averages as lowering offense. Instead, the regression tells us that AVG adds no more information once we know the OBP and SLG of a team.

These numbers also identify an anomaly that the A's exploited, which *Moneyball* documents. At the time, the conventional wisdom was that each point of OBP was worth between 1.5 and 1.8 times more than each point of SLG. The A's found that, in fact, each point of OBP was about three times more valuable than each point of SLG. The marginal impact numbers from Table 25 for the American League, in which the A's play, indicate that OBP is 2.33 times more important than SLG ($21/9 = 2.33$) in producing runs over this time period. While it's not quite as large for this sample as what Lewis reported, when I exclude the 2003–2004 seasons, which occurred after *Moneyball* was written, the marginal effect of OBP is almost exactly three times that of SLG.

Despite the fact that OBP and SLG tell us more about a player's offensive contribution, television commentators continue to post AVG at the bottom of the screen as each batter steps to the plate. OBP and SLG often make appearances, but they are secondary. Why? Habit.

Table 25: Explained Variance from Multiple Batting Statistics

Statistic	National League Explained Variance	American League Explained Variance
AVG, OBP, SLG	91 percent	93 percent
OBP, SLG	91 percent	93 percent
OBP + SLG = OPS	90 percent	91 percent

Calculating AVG is very simple, and without the help of computers, generating an OBP and SLG was quite a taxing affair. The inertia of tradition can be strong, especially in baseball.

But if you want to buck tradition and look to statistics with more to say about producing, there are plenty of options. OBP and SLG are just the beginning of metrics sabermetricians have developed to predict offense. Some examples include runs created and linear weights. The list of new statistics is very long, and most of the metrics out there are quite good and accurate in their attempts to measure player contributions to producing runs. However, these metrics require several sophisticated calculations or a trip to several baseball statistics websites. If you're watching a game, by the time you look up a player's stats online, you've missed the whole half inning. Most of these stats are not "couch worthy"—I can't calculate them without leaving the couch. But there does exist a simple shortcut for gauging the ability of a player. The solution is to add OBP and SLG together to create a metric conveniently known as OPS (on-base plus slugging), developed by John Thorn and Pete Palmer.[69] While it may seem odd and intuitively it doesn't make much sense, OPS does a fantastic job at predicting runs per game. Compare the graph of OPS in Figure 12 to the graph of the Big 3 in Figure 11 in terms of predicting runs. They are nearly identical. Table 25 shows that the explained variance of OPS is about 90 percent, which is quite high. OPS is the sabermetricians shortcut, and I find it quite handy on the couch and at the ballpark.

These metrics may be nothing more than the product of human beings playing baseball, but each number has a story to tell. Between two players, I can predict that the player with the higher AVG will produce more runs and I'll be right most of the time. OBP and SLG have more to say in different ways, and I'd listen to these guys over AVG. A player who has an OBP of .285 is an out machine. A player with a SLG greater than .500 has a lot of pop in his bat; and the larger the difference between SLG and AVG, the greater the power. A guy with an OPS of .975, well he's a stud. Some other stats we hear about contain much less information. RISP AVG, runs, and RBI get a lot of attention, but they're just fluff.

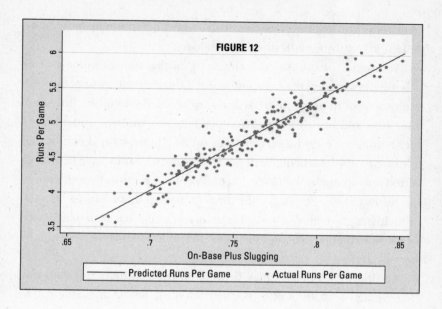

FIGURE 12

The Pitcher Puzzle

Evaluating individual player contributions on defense in baseball is a tricky thing, compared to the offensive side of the game. Hitters face a defense alone, posting hitting statistics largely independent of teammates. Batters with good statistics in these areas can be credited with producing runs for their teams, and players with better statistics in these areas obviously deserve more credit than those with worse statistics. A general manger can be reasonably confident that a batting order composed of batters with good statistics will produce more runs than one with poor statistics. Although some teammate spillovers may occur from batter to batter, the spillovers on defense are much more problematic.

It is the joint responsibility of the pitcher and his fielders to prevent runs that make judging each party's contribution complicated, though this difference is not widely recognized. At the end of a season, game, or even an inning, we can view the jointly produced results, but we may be unsure of how much each contributed. To evaluate pitchers, most analysts and fans use the earned run average (ERA) as a measure of run prevention. However, ERA differs from offensive statistics because of its joint production. A pitcher with a good defense may have an excellent ERA substantially due to his fielders.

Adding to the confusion is the fact that the metrics we have available to measure defense are quite poor. Errors are the most commonly used statistics to judge fielders, and it's the third line in the box score after runs and hits. But the difference between an error and a hit is a highly subjective decision, which an official game scorekeeper determines. Should a particular ball put in play by the batter have been converted into an out by the fielder? Scorekeepers have to believe their eyes, but they can be deceiving. A line drive to the gap that bounces off a fast outfielder's glove may be scored as an error, while that same ball played by a slow outfielder, who doesn't come within ten feet of the ball, may be scored a hit.

Additionally, pitchers may bear some responsibility for their batting average on balls in play (BABIP). After all, he did allow the ball to be put in play, and the type of ball hit may affect the probability that an error occurs. High fly balls result in fewer hits and errors, since fielders have plenty of time to get under the balls. Ground balls and line drives travel at fast speeds, making these balls much harder to field.

While the responsibility for balls in play is a bit murky, separating the player contributions for some events is easy. When a pitcher throws the ball to the catcher, several outcomes may follow. The most common outcomes are a strike, a ball, a ball in play, or a home run—I'll exclude rare events such as hit batters, balks, and catcher interference. Of these events, three do not involve a fielder other than the catcher. From the defensive end, balls, strikes, and home runs are solely the responsibility of the pitcher. Whether you have Ozzie Smith or John Kruk at shortstop, it doesn't matter one way or the other when one of these events occurs. Balls and strikes pass harmlessly to the catcher, and home runs—excepting the ultra-rare inside-the-park home run—pass over the helpless fielders below. Only the hit ball in play requires that the pitcher receive help from his fielders. His fielders may convert the balls in play into outs or they may fall in for hits.

Wouldn't it be smart to start in an evaluation of pitchers where we can determine responsibility? Well, luckily someone had the idea to do

Table 26: ERAs for Randy Johnson and Roger Clemens (Careers Through 2005)

Pitcher	Average	Minimum	Maximum	Standard Deviation
Randy Johnson	3.32	2.28	4.82	0.76
Roger Clemens	3.22	1.87	4.60	0.84

this. Voros McCracken—a former paralegal who, while looking for new ways to win his rotisserie baseball league, ended up earning a World Series ring in the front office of the Boston Red Sox—is generally credited with being the first person to do this type of analysis. McCracken, who plays a small hero in *Moneyball*, developed a new metric known as DIPS ERA. DIPS stands for defense-independent pitching statistics. McCracken noticed an interesting phenomenon among major-league pitchers: ERAs are not very predictable from year to year. Sure, you can expect Randy Johnson and Roger Clemens to have better ERAs than a team's typical fifth starter, but even these hallmarks of consistency have had ERAs that fluctuate quite a bit. This observation was the key to finding the responsibility in the prevention of runs.

Table 26 shows that Johnson and Clemens have been very good over their careers, but they have had up and down seasons. The last column contains the standard deviation of their ERAs, which quantifies the average yearly difference from each player's career average in terms of earned runs. This difference is just under a full earned run per game for each pitcher, which is quite a large margin. If these consistent superstars suffer from fluctuations in their performances, then how does the rest of the league fare? Well, for pitchers who averaged one hundred or more innings over twenty-five seasons from 1980 through 2004, the standard deviation was about 0.9 earned runs. With the average ERA for these pitchers at about 4.04, this means an average pitcher's ERA is expected to fluctuate by about 22 percent, again a sizable fluctuation. There is a good chance that an average pitcher will post an ERA of somewhere between 3.00 and 5.00, which means it's quite easy for an average pitcher to look very good or very bad.

If these statistics fluctuate quite a bit, how are we to know how much of a pitcher's performance is due to skill and how much is a product of luck? Skill should persist over time, while luck should not. If we observe a pitcher performing similarly from year to year in certain areas, then it is likely that he has some control over this area. By looking at different areas of performances over time, we should be able to find metrics that correlate from year to year. Those metrics that remain similar from year to year—past good (bad) performance begets future good (bad) performance—are metrics that capture pitcher skill. Those with little relationship over time are probably just capturing luck.

Figure 13 plots the relationship between pitcher ERAs in a current season and the previous season for every season in which the pitcher threw more than one hundred innings from 1980 to 2004. The ERAs discussed in this chapter are corrected for the typical influences of their home parks. Pitchers that play in hitter-friendly and pitcher-friendly parks have this factored into their ERAs. The current season is measured on the vertical axis and the previous season on the horizontal axis. The dots are quite dispersed, with only a slightly upward, or positive, trend—measured by the regression line. This means that the higher the ERA in the previous season, the higher we expect it to be the following year, and the lower the ERA, the lower we expect it to be the following year. But

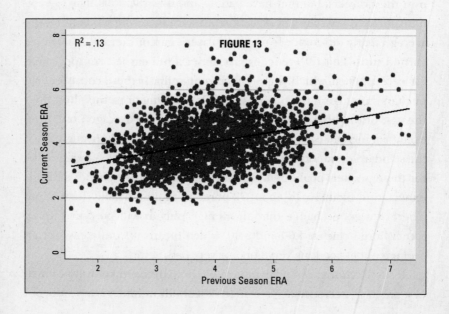

the fact that the points are so widespread indicates that the relationship between ERA of the past and present is not very strong. The R^2 is a statistical measure of the strength of the correlation in explaining the observed events, where 1 means the previous year's ERA explains 100 percent of the present seasons's ERA and 0 means it explains 0 percent. The R^2 of 0.13 means that only 13 percent of the variance in this year's ERA can be explained by the previous year's ERA. This is not a tight relationship.

Well, so what? Baseball fans know that players have good years and bad years. The fact is that the fluctuation in ERAs may reflect more than just a deviation in a pitcher's performance. It turns out there are factors beyond the pitcher's control that have a huge impact on pitcher ERAs.

McCracken set out to remove the impact of fielders, to examine pitchers only in the areas of the game where fielders are not used: walks, strikeouts, hit batters, and home runs. He was actually not the first person to engage in this type of analysis. In his 1987 *Baseball Abstract*, Bill James developed a similar metric he named *Indicated ERA*. Indicated ERA looked only at walks and home runs allowed by pitchers. As James puts it, he was looking to develop "a meaningful indicator of the pitcher's self-destructive tendencies."[70] And this is where he left his analysis. Just over a decade later McCracken noticed that there was something more to these defense-independent metrics than just being defense independent. Not only could you tell a lot about how good a pitcher was by looking only at DIPS, but looking at non-DIPS stats— that is, statistics that include fielder involvement on balls in play—tells us very little about pitchers. "Heresy!" was the responsive cry of the baseball establishment. "Everyone knows that Greg Maddux is so good because his pitches produce easily fielded balls." But when McCracken looked at Maddux's numbers, he found that Maddux's hits on balls in play, as measured by BABIP, fluctuated widely from year to year. And the same was true for all pitchers.

Figure 14 shows the relationship between the previous and current seasons' performances on the three main DIPS metrics—strikeouts, walks, and home runs. If a pitcher has a skill in any area, he should

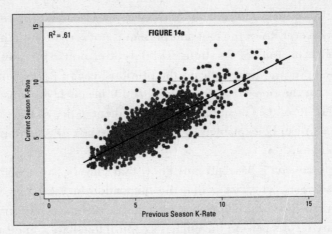

FIGURE 14a

$R^2 = .61$

Current Season K-Rate

Previous Season K-Rate

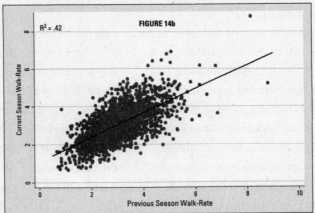

FIGURE 14b

$R^2 = .42$

Current Season Walk-Rate

Previous Season Walk-Rate

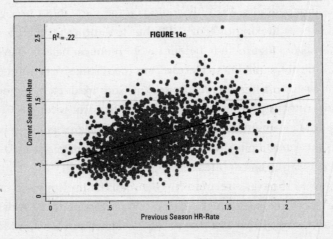

FIGURE 14c

$R^2 = .22$

Current Season HR-Rate

Previous Season HR-Rate

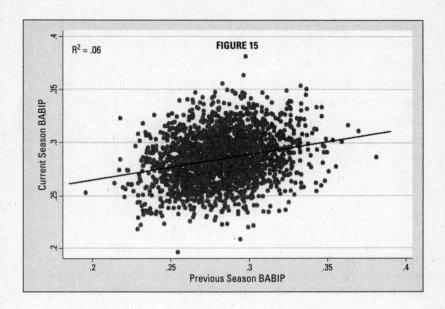

perform similarly in that skill from year to year. If pitchers tend to re-peat their performances in an area, reflected by a strong correlation from season to season, then we can reasonably assume that pitchers have a skill in that area. There is an extremely strong relationship for the strikeouts and a moderately strong relationship for walk rates and hit batters, with R^2s of 0.61 and 0.42. And while the relationship is weaker for home runs, the R^2 of .22 is much stronger than the correlations of ERAs from season to season.

The other way in which pitchers can prevent runs is to prevent hits on balls in play. Figure 15 shows that there is almost no correlation be-tween a pitcher's ability to prevent hits on balls in play, with an R^2 of .06, indicating pitchers have little skill in this area. If fluctuations in ERA are heavily influenced by BABIP, which pitchers appear to have little control over, then ERA contains quite a bit of misleading infor-mation regarding a pitcher's skill.

Because strikeouts, walks, and home runs seemed to be much more stable from year to year than hits on balls in play, McCracken attempted to use these three metrics on their own to predict pitcher ERAs in the following season. In fact, he found that a pitcher's preceding season's

DIPS are better predictors than that pitcher's overall ERA from the preceding season. The noise of earned runs generated on balls put in play, which were randomly turned into hits or outs by fielders, actually hindered the identification of the pitcher's true ability. In turns out that the real reason Greg Maddux is so good is that, though he is not an overpowering strikeout pitcher, he rarely walks batters or gives up home runs. This makes DIPS a valuable tool for disentangling responsibility for preventing runs.

Using DIPS to Predict Pitcher Performance

Strikeout rates may be strongly correlated from season to season, but how do well these stats predict pitcher ERAs?

In order to find the answer, we need to establish how accurately DIPS predict pitcher ERAs in the season in which pitchers are playing. Using multiple regression analysis, I estimated the impact of different pitching statistics on ERA. The metrics that most concerned me were strikeouts, walks, homers, hit batters, and batting average on balls in play. At the same time, I included measures of team defense, the age of the pitcher, the league of the pitcher, and the season, to control for these possible outside influences in the predictive model. Table 27 reports the unit and percentage impacts of the variables on a pitcher's ERA.[71]

The unit impact quantifies the effect of a one-unit change in the pitching statistic on ERA. For example, an increase of one strikeout per nine innings lowers a pitcher's ERA by about 0.17. The percentage impact (or elasticity) tells us the percentage change of ERA in response to a 1 percent change in the statistic calculated at the average. So a 1 percent increase in the strikeout rate lowers a pitcher's ERA by approximately 0.24 percent. The percentage impact helps us judge the impact of the different metrics relative to their normal values. For example, the unit impact of every walk (0.30) is nearly twice that of a strikeout (0.17); however, in terms of the average number of walks and strikeouts,

Table 27: The Impact of Current Season's Stats on Current ERA

Statistic	Unit	Percentage
Strikeouts	−0.17	−0.24 percent
Walks	0.30	0.23 percent
Home Runs	1.42	0.32 percent
Hit Batters	0.34	0.02 percent
BABIP	18.16	1.28 percent
R^2		0.77

their percentage impacts on ERA are nearly identical (0.23 percent and 0.24 percent).

Differences in the variables included in the regression explained 77 percent of the variance of pitcher ERAs, which is quite good. All of the estimated impacts were statistically significant, meaning there is less than a 5 percent chance that the true impact of a statistic has no effect on ERA. The large impact of BABIP is quite interesting. A one-standard-deviation increase in BABIP (0.023) raised a pitcher's ERA by about 0.42 (approximately 10 percent of the average ERA for the sample). If pitchers have little effect over balls in play, then a random fluctuation of BABIP can influence a pitcher's ERA quite a bit. These estimates provide a good baseline to evaluate how well the DIPS predict future run prevention.

Using DIPS to Predict ERA in the Future

Predicting an ERA based on a pitcher's statistics from the prior season is not much different from the exercise above. Table 28 shows the estimated impacts of these characteristics in the preceding season on the following season's ERA, controlling for the defense, age, and league of the pitcher. To account for the impact of the defense playing behind the pitcher, I included the team's batting average on balls in play for *all* pitchers on the team.

Again, all of the estimates are statistically significant, except for hit

Table 28: The Impact of Pitchers' Previous Season's Performance on the Following Season's ERA

Statistic	Unit	Percentage
Strikeouts	−0.18	−0.26 percent
Walks	0.14	0.10 percent
Home Runs	0.20	0.04 percent
BABIP	−1.63	−0.11 percent
R^2		0.28

batters.[72] The result for strikeouts is quite interesting. The previous year's strikeout rate impacts the following season's ERA (0.18) about as much as the season's strikeout rate affects that same season's ERA (0.17)—see Table 27 for comparison. This is not totally surprising, because strikeouts are strongly correlated from year to year. While walks and homers are important, they are not as consistent predictors of ERA as strikeouts.

BABIP has a real impact on ERA, but the effect is small and in the opposite direction than one would expect: a higher BABIP is associated with a lower ERA in the following year. Rather than there being some inverse relationship between BABIP from year to year, this is more likely derived from a few extremely high and low BABIP seasons that typically regress to the mean the following year.

But how does the DIPS prediction stand up to a prediction based on the previous season's ERA? It fares much better, just as McCracken found. Table 29 shows the very weak relationship between the previous year's ERA and the ERA in the following year. In reality, the effect is nothing, since the estimate is not statistically different from zero. The R^2 is not quite half of the DIPS-only model. Knowing a pitcher's defense independent stats, sometimes referred to as "peripherals," does tell us

Table 29: The Impact of Previous Season's ERA on Current ERA

Statistic	Unit	Percentage
Previous ERA	0.011	0.01 percent
R^2		0.16

more about a pitcher's future ERA than his current ERA. To judge a pitcher solely by his ERA might give him credit or blame for something he's not able to control. But I'm not sure if these findings necessarily mean pitchers do not have control over balls in play.

Pitcher's Control of Hits on Balls in Play

Is it possible that pitchers do have the ability to affect hits on balls in play, but that this influence is so strongly correlated with the DIPS that it is masked? Multiple regression analysis identifies a correlation between the predicting and predicted variables included in the model, but it does not tell us why. If a pitcher strikes out a lot of batters, it does not mean necessarily that the corresponding effect on ERA comes solely through the direct impact of strikeouts. The correlation between strikeouts and ERA could reflect a pitcher's ability to affect hits on balls in play in addition to the direct effect on limiting balls in play. If strikeout pitchers cause weak ground-outs and walk-prone pitchers serve up more line drives, these factors will be captured in the weights assigned to strikeouts and walks in a multiple regression estimation.

For all practical purposes, this possibility is irrelevant—if DIPS tells us all we need to know about run prevention, it doesn't matter why— but let's see if it is true. Maybe the previous year's BABIP doesn't give us much information about the following year's BABIP, but the DIPS do, because they are correlated with a pitcher's ability to affect hits on balls in play. If this is the case, then it's possible for a pitcher to control BABIP through his DIPS. And in a regression on ERA, the effect would

Table 30: The Impact of the Previous Season's DIPS on Current BABIP

Statistic	Unit	Percentage
Strikeouts	−0.00184	−0.038 percent
Walks	0.00007	0.001 percent
Home Runs	−0.002	−0.011 percent
BABIP	−0.05842	−0.058 percent
R^2	.14	

be captured by the DIPS variables. Table 30 reports that estimated impact of the previous year's pitching statistics on the following season's BABIP.

The results confirm something startling in the magnitude and statistical significance of the predicting variables: differences in pitcher control over hits on balls in play are somewhat predictable from past performance. But that information is not in the statistic we would think to look at first, BABIP. This ability has been hidden due to its correlation with DIPS metrics. It turns out that, in fact, the strikeout rates are inversely related to BABIP in the following season. Though it's not widely discussed, Voros McCracken also found correlations between both strikeouts with a pitcher's future BABIP. The effect for strikeouts seems a bit obvious. The fear of strikeouts possibly induces hitters to take weaker protective swings to stay alive, and thus yields softer hits that are more likely to result in outs.

But just because something is statistically significant does not mean it is practically significant. Using the estimate of the impact of the predicting variables reported in Table 30 and the earlier estimate of the impact of BABIP on ERA (18.16) in Table 29, I am able to assign an earned run value to strikeout prevention through its effect on balls in play. For every one strikeout increase per game, the BABIP decreases by 0.00172. Multiply that by 18.16 and every strikeout saves 0.03 earned runs per game through reducing hits on balls in play, which is not meaningless but small. Why doesn't BABIP correlate very well from year to year when strikeouts do? Well, there's just a lot more noise generated by random bounces from year to year in BABIP than there is in strikeouts; therefore, it's hard to directly observe pitcher control over this metric.

Although it turns out that pitchers do seem to have some minor ability to prevent hits on balls in play, it does not alter the predictive element of DIPS theory one bit. Why not? Because that ability is captured in DIPS statistics.

DIPS theory is a powerful tool in evaluating pitchers independent of their fielders. More importantly, the story of DIPS is a triumph of intellect over an intractable problem. Michael Lewis quotes McCracken, responding to the claim that separating the pitching and fielding contributions in run prevention was impossible: "That's a stupid attitude. Can't you do *something*? It didn't make any sense to me that the way to approach the problem was to give up."[73] The joint prevention of runs would be quite complicated to sort out if not for this imaginative invention. Alfred Marshall—the father of modern neoclassical economics, wrote

> The economist needs the three great intellectual faculties, perception, imagination, and reason: and most of all he needs imagination, to put him on the track of those causes of visible events which are remote or lie below the surface.[74]

He would applaud the inspired work of Voros McCracken.

13

What Is a Ballplayer Worth?

How you play the game is for college ball. When you're playing for money, winning is the only thing that matters.

—LEO DUROCHER, FORMER MANAGER

GOOD THINGS tend to be scarce, thanks to the finite nature of our world, which means we must make trade-offs when consuming resources. Economists refer to the process of getting the most out of what you have as *constrained maximization,* and managing a baseball team is an exercise in precisely this process. Imagine that just this instant you are hired as the GM of your favorite baseball team. It is now your job to take all that you have—your players, staff, facilities, etc.—to earn as much money as possible for the owner. It's not your fault that the previous GM raided the farm system and signed washed-up veterans to hefty long-term contracts, but it is your job to take your lot and win as many games as possible. To improve, how should you best rearrange what you already have? Should you hire or fire coaches, trade away players, or sign free agents? Constrained maximization is what it is all about.

This is not a simple task, which makes it fun. In fact, millions of rotisserie league fans simulate the act of baseball general managers—choosing players on a limited budget—every year. While money is involved in the exercise, it is primarily useful as a tool to measure value. To properly allocate resources, you need to value the trade-offs of resources, and money makes the task simpler.

• • •

Economists operate on the assumption that humans prefer more money to less. And since owners are human beings, it's probably not a bad assumption to make when evaluating team decisions. There are plenty of goals other than wealth that motivate owners—public relations, ego, and altruism are a few—but there is no doubt that money plays a large part. Even though most owners don't have a direct hand in baseball decisions, a GM seeking something other than financial reward for the owner cannot expect to keep his or her job for too long. Therefore, in order to value players, I'm going to assume that owners are profit maximizers.

However, if owners only care about profits, this might take the fun out of evaluating players. Attempting to value their ability to give rich men more money is about as fun as trying to find an additional product endorsement for Donald Trump. Luckily, this is not going to be a problem. The fans who spend their incomes on baseball tend to value wins; hence, the financial success of a team is directly linked to its success on the field. Certainly, there are other factors involved, but owners concerned about maximizing profits can do so through winning; therefore, we are justified in valuing players according to their abilities to generate wins.

In order to win baseball games, you have to build an organization that is equipped for the job, and the things that lead to wins vary in price. A general manager needs to purchase many inputs—facilities, equipment, coaches, and, most importantly, players—to put a winning team on the field. Subpar inputs can lead to bad outcomes, so a GM is always going to want to buy the best. The cheaper you can purchase any one factor, the more financial resources will be available to purchase other items that contribute to winning.

Unfortunately for any one GM, but fortunate for players, twenty-nine other GMs want to purchase the same inputs, forcing GMs to bid against one another for available resources. Some factors, like bats, helmets, and medical equipment, are not auctioned; one team purchasing a video camera to record performances doesn't prevent another team from purchasing another camera just like it. But some players, managers, coaches, scouts, and trainers are better than others, and hiring one of these people prevents another team from getting that individual. Better personnel will earn higher salaries than inferior personnel because teams will bid higher wages for people who contribute more to winning. Underbidding for a potentially valuable employee will generally cause the individual to move to a new team. Leo Mazzone's excellent performance as a pitching coach eventually caused him to leave the Atlanta Braves for the Baltimore Orioles, who were willing to nearly double his annual salary.

Evaluating off-the-field inputs such as coaching are difficult, because we do not have a good idea of what all these people do to help/hinder winning. Players are much easier to value, because we can directly observe their contribution. The two biggest contributors to winning are hitting and pitching. Using factors that predict how many runs hitters and pitchers generate, we can measure individual player contributions in dollars.

Converting Wins into Dollars

The basic method for converting player performance into dollar values was developed by economist Gerald Scully in 1974.[75] At the time Scully wrote his landmark paper, the organization of MLB, with respect to paying players, was much different. All players were bound by the "reserve clause," which gave teams exclusive rights to their players, and thus prevented players from seeking employment on other teams. Consequently, team owners didn't feel any pressure to pay players much more than a fraction of their monetary contributions to winning, because players could play for the team that held their reserve rights or not at all.

Economists value an input into production according to its marginal revenue product (MRP). The MRP of any input is the added dollar value that the input brings to generating output. Thus, the MRP of a player is the value he adds to a team's revenue through his individual contributions. In a free market for labor, which professional baseball lacked when Scully conducted his study, players ought to earn wages equal to their MRPs. This occurs because teams bidding against one another for talent are willing to pay a player up to the revenue value he generates for the team. For example, a player who is expected to produce an additional $2 million for a team could not be hired for less than $2 million. Why not? There is still profit generated by hiring the player at a wage of less than his MRP. Just as a pedestrian is willing to expend the effort to bend over and pick up a $100 bill blowing down the sidewalk, any team would certainly be willing to pay a player a wage below his production value. But if one team offers a player less than his MRP, other teams will be willing to offer higher bids to capture the added value that the player brings. But once a player receives an offer equal to his MRP, the bidding should stop, because no team wants to pay a player more than he brings to the team.

Because the reserve clause did not allow a competitive bidding process to take place, it was unlikely that players earned their MRPs. Scully wanted to know how much of their value players earned under the reserve system. To find out, he developed a three-step method for estimating a player's MRP to compare to player wages.

Step 1: Estimate the dollar value of a win to a team.
Step 2: Estimate the contribution of a player to winning, accounting for the quality and quantity of play.
Step 3: Convert the player contribution to wins from Step 2 into dollars using the estimates from Step 1, which should approximate a player's MRP.

Scully found that reserved players earned between 80 and 90 percent less than their MRP values, which meant major-league owners were extracting excess value from their players. In 1976, soon after Scully's study, the right of "free agency" was added to the collective bargaining agreement (CBA) between players and owners. While the rules are a bit complicated, and have changed some over time, the CBA now permits a player with six years of major-league service to become a free agent and sign with any team willing to offer him a contract. Interestingly, free agent players' wages rose to levels similar to the MRP estimates of Scully soon after free agency came to baseball.

While Scully's method is useful as a policy tool, it can also help the armchair general manager. Using Scully's method as a guide, we can build a similar model to estimate player values in the present era. We are going to have to change a few things, but the overall process is the same.

Step 1: What Is a Win Worth?

Estimating the value of a win requires connecting a few pieces of information. First, we need to know the revenues of all MLB clubs. By looking at how team revenues differ according to relevant factors, we can weight each factor's impact on revenue. Wins and the size of the local fan base are obviously important determinants of revenue. Winning teams generate more fan interest than losing teams, which results in more dollars to the team. Bigger cities benefit from a larger population of potential fans who are likely to spend their incomes on the local baseball club.

There is not much that any owner can do about the size of the city in which he hosts the team; thus, the GM need not worry much about this. However, because city size does influence revenue, it is important to take its influence into account to ensure that the estimated impact of wins on revenue is not picking up any biases from city size. It turns out that every person in a city is worth about $3.88 to team revenue. For example, the city of Atlanta, with approximately 4.1 million people, generates approximately $15.9 million to the Braves (4.1 × $3.88 = $15.9). While controlling for city size, a win for a .500 team is worth about $1.34 million.[76]

A slight modification to the Scully method is necessary. For Step 2, we are going to need to know how much each player contributes to winning. The things that pitchers and hitters contribute to winning are independent of each other. If we were to estimate the impact of the

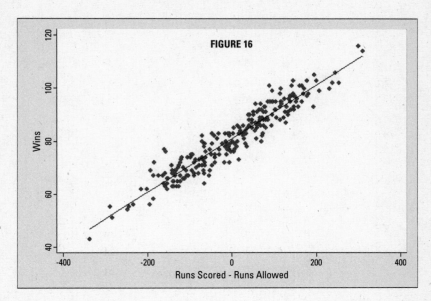

sum total of pitcher and hitter performances on winning, rather than preventing and producing runs independently, the estimates could be biased. For example, if a few teams have excellent pitching and horrible hitting, or vice versa, the estimated individual impact of player contributions to winning may be distorted. What we would like is know how much *runs* are worth to teams as they produce wins, since both pitchers and hitters affect runs.

Not surprisingly, there is a very strong relationship between the runs-scored-versus-runs-allowed difference and winning. Bill James even developed a technique, which he dubbed the Pythagorean method, for estimating wins from a team's difference in runs scored and runs allowed. Figure 16 shows the tight relationship between a team's run differential and winning [from 1998–2005], with the run differential explaining more than 90 percent of the difference in wins across teams. Therefore, instead of estimating the impact of wins on revenue, we can use the difference between runs scored and runs allowed. This enables us to use the estimates of individual player contributions to run production and prevention to value their individual impact on revenue.

Figure 17 maps the relationship between the run differential and

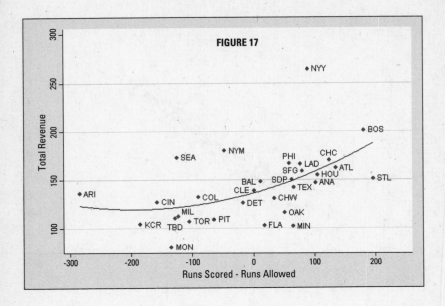

FIGURE 17

revenue in 2004. The relationship is positive and nonlinear, with each run scored or prevented adding a little more to revenue than the previous run. It turns out that the first run scored or prevented that pushes a team's record above .500 adds approximately $127,000 to team revenue. However, additional runs beyond .500 are worth a little more. What does this mean? Being a little above average brings in more fans, but being a good bit better than average draws in increasingly more fans.[77]

A few teams earned far more (e.g., Yankees, Mets, and Mariners) and far less (e.g., Expos, Marlins, and Twins) than the amount estimated by run differential. That is to be expected, considering that other factors may determine revenue. For example, we expect some of these divergences because of differences in market size. But recall that the estimate of the run differential on revenue takes into account differences in city size, so New York teams don't get extra credit for winning just because of their larger population base. While other factors besides winning and population may influence revenue, there are no obvious factors that should bias the estimate of the impact of the run differential on winning.

Step 2: What Do Players Contribute to Wins?

The next step requires measuring how the things that players do on the field contribute to winning, by determining how many runs hitters produce and pitchers prevent. Chapter 12 reveals some simple but good metrics we can use for estimating players' contributions to run production and prevention. The on-base percentage (OBP) and slugging percentage (SLG) do an excellent job of measuring the run production of hitters. Strikeouts, walks, and home runs are factors that pitchers control and that measure their contributions to run prevention. Using these factors, we can estimate how many runs a player contributed—scored or allowed—based on his on-field performance and playing time. To get a recent but large sample, I use four seasons of team data (2002–2005) to estimate the impact of the performance metrics on runs.

Recent history reveals that for hitters each "point"—every 1/1000th—of OBP is worth about 3.013 runs, and each point of SLG is worth about 1.688 runs to a team's total runs scored in a season.[78] By multiplying each player's statistics by these weights, we generate a prediction of how many runs a lineup composed of only this player would score over an entire season. I then adjust the number of runs scored to account for the run impact of the home park of the hitter. This is necessary because some parks are more friendly to offense—like Coors Field in Colorado—while others hurt offense—like Dodger Stadium in Los Angeles. It would be incorrect to credit or punish players for producing something that is beyond their control, and this method puts all players on equal footing.

While this calculation is useful for our exercise of estimating player values, it is also fun to see which player would produce the most runs as a team all by himself. Table 31 lists the top 10 run producers by league in 2005 if the player had taken 100 percent of his team's plate appearances. Not surprisingly, the list includes some of the more prominent sluggers in the game.

Table 31: Top-10 Run Producers by League (2005)*

	American League			National League		
Rank	Player	Team	Season RS	Player	Team	Season RS
1	Travis Hafner	Cleveland Indians	1380	Derrek Lee	Chicago Cubs	1397
2	Alex Rodriguez	New York Yankees	1321	Albert Pujols	St. Louis Cardinals	1331
3	David Ortiz	Boston Red Sox	1266	Carlos Delgado	Florida Marlins	1297
4	Jason Giambi	New York Yankees	1255	Brian Giles	San Diego Padres	1247
5	Vladimir Guerrero	Los Angeles Angels of Anaheim	1255	Miguel Cabrera	Florida Marlins	1215
6	Manny Ramirez	Boston Red Sox	1221	J. D. Drew	Los Angeles Dodgers	1212
7	Brian Roberts	Baltimore Orioles	1170	Lance Berkman	Houston Astros	1178
8	Mark Teixeira	Texas Rangers	1131	Jason Bay	Pittsburgh Pirates	1176
9	Jhonny Peralta	Cleveland Indians	1108	Chipper Jones	Atlanta Braves	1167
10	Richie Sexson	Seattle Mariners	1099	Morgan Ensberg	Houston Astros	1166

*Minimum 5 percent of team's plate appearances.

For pitchers, every strikeout per nine innings lowers runs allowed by 25.8 runs. Every walk and home run allowed per nine innings increases runs allowed by 60.7 and 249.5 runs.[79] Just as we did for hitters, we multiply the weights times the pitchers' statistics to generate a prediction of the number of runs a pitcher would allow if he pitched every inning for his team over an entire season. One slight modification is necessary because defense plays a large role in preventing runs, even though pitchers cannot do much to help their defense prevent hits on balls hit into play—the central result of the DIPS theory already discussed. To view pitchers on equal footing, I assign pitchers the average rate at which defenses convert balls hit in play into outs (70 percent) and multiply this value times the regression-predicted impact for fielders generating outs in balls in play—every one-tenth of a percent increase on outs on balls in play lowers a team's runs allowed by about 4.2 runs a season. This gives all pitchers the same defense to help them prevent runs so that no pitcher receives credit or blame in run prevention from luck or defensive quality. Again, the estimates are adjusted for the run environment of the home park. Table 32 lists the top 10 pitchers by league in preventing runs over the course of the 2005 season.

These leaders are a little more interesting than batting leaders, because the list includes many players who make their living as part-time

Table 32: Top 10 Run Preventers by League (2005)*

	American League			National League		
Rank	Player	Team	Season RA	Player	Team	Season RA
1	Mariano Rivera	New York Yankees	408.47	Todd Jones	Florida Marlins	435.19
2	Juan Rincon	Minnesota Twins	483.87	Billy Wagner	Philadelphia Phillies	465.66
3	Mike Timlin	Boston Red Sox	487.51	Chris Reitsma	Atlanta Braves	488.09
4	Huston Street	Oakland Athletics	509.54	Zach Duke	Pittsburgh Pirates	508.15
5	Roy Halladay	Toronto Blue Jays	527.21	Chris Carpenter	St. Louis Cardinals	517.02
6	Justin Duchscherer	Oakland Athletics	529.27	Brian Fuentes	Colorado Rockies	527.72
7	Rich Harden	Oakland Athletics	541.47	Roger Clemens	Houston Astros	528.76
8	Johan Santana	Minnesota Twins	546.26	Aaron Heilman	New York Mets	533.59
9	Felix Hernandez	Seattle Mariners	546.54	Dontrelle Willis	Florida Marlins	535.78
10	Doug Brocail	Texas Rangers	575.06	Pedro Martinez	New York Mets	542.08

*Minimum 5 percent of team's plate appearances.

players. Only nine players on the list are full-time starters. The relief pitcher used to be the role for pitchers deemed not good enough to start. Now the reliever is a pitcher used for getting outs in key spots during the game. The closer, who often pitches late in a game when a win is on the line, has grown into one of the most prestigious members of the team.

A reliever normally pitches differently than a starter: he may have only one or two pitches and normally throws at a high velocity for short stints. He is less concerned with in-game endurance than a starter, so he can expend more energy. There is no way Mariano Rivera, possibly the best closer in the history of baseball, could sustain his usual level of pitching excellence as a starter, pitching more than twice as many innings. We can see how this is true from the example of John Smoltz of the Atlanta Braves. Smoltz spent several years as both a reliever and a starter, making the All-Star team in both roles. In 2004, he struck out 9.37 batters and walked only 1.83 per nine innings while pitching nearly 82 innings as a closer. When he returned to the starting rotation in 2005, Smoltz struck out 6.62 and walked 2.08 per nine innings over 230 innings. These are good numbers, but not as good as his reliever numbers. Clearly, Smoltz adjusted the way he pitched according to his role. Keep this bias in mind when comparing pitcher statistics that are normalized for playing time, and remember that generally all pitchers can pitch better in short relief stints than as starters.

We can now calculate the difference in runs that a player contributes compared to a player who would produce the average number of runs in the same amount of playing time in the same league—AL teams score more runs than NL teams because of the designated hitter. Better-than-average hitters will produce more runs than average hitters, and above-average pitchers will produce less runs than average pitchers. This step is especially important for evaluating pitchers, because even the best pitcher will always yield runs to opposing teams. The average provides a useful baseline for comparison, as pitcher contributions ought to be valued according to the runs they prevent, not the few they produce.

Finally, to account for playing time, we multiply the percent of a team's total plate appearances or innings pitched times the difference in runs scored/allowed from the average. A player's runs scored above average (RSAA) or runs allowed below average (RABA) reports how much better the player is than the average player with the same playing time in terms of producing/preventing runs. For example, let's look at the top hitter and pitcher in 2005 in terms of RSAA and RABA. Derrek Lee of the Chicago Cubs produced 74.30 runs more than an average player taking 11.22 percent of his team's plate appearances. Chris Carpenter of the St. Louis Cardinals saved 35.51 more runs than the average pitcher throwing 16.72 percent of his teams innings. This does not mean that Lee is necessarily more valuable than Carpenter. To determine the overall value of the player, we need to value playing time.

Step 3: What Are Players Worth?

We have the basic ingredients to calculate what players are worth in dollar terms: we know what players contribute to winning through runs, and what runs are worth to team revenue. The first step is to calculate the dollar value of runs scored/allowed above/below average by multiplying the dollar value of runs, estimated in Step 1, times the run contribution above or below average, generated in Step 2. The relationship between the run difference and revenue is increasing, which means each additional run produced/prevented is more valuable than the previous run. This result is the dollar value above average ($ValAA), which measures the value over what the average player would produce given the same playing time.

Next, we need to establish a baseline dollar value for the average player, to add to the value above average, which will give us the MRP of a player. The average hitter would produce the league-average amount of runs if he took 100 percent of his team's plate appearances, and the average pitcher would produce the league-average amount of runs if he pitched 100 percent of his team's innings. I estimate that an average team—a team that is predicted to win eighty-one games based on runs scored and runs allowed—will earn approximately $109 million in revenue. Assigning an equal weight to the run contributions of offense and defense, each side is responsible for half of that value, $54.5 million each. Therefore, the average player will produce a percentage of $54.5 million equal to the percentage of his team's plate appearances or innings pitched. For example, a player who generates the average run production, like rookie shortstop Ronny Cedeno of the 2005 Chicago Cubs, would be worth exactly his percentage of playing time multiplied by $54.5 million. Ronny Cedeno took 1.45 percent of the Cubs' plate appearances in 2005, which was worth approximately $790,000 ($54.5 × 0.0145 = $790,000) in terms of the revenue he generated to the Cubs.

We then add the dollar value that players generate above/below average to the baseline average dollar value. Let's look at two of Cedeno's Cubs teammates who contribute value above and below average, Nomar Garciaparra and Neifi Perez. Garciaparra produced 0.75 runs above what the average player, taking 4.01 percent of the Cubs' plate appearances, would produce, thereby generating a value of $100,000 more than the average player. An average player taking 4.01 percent of his team's plate appearances generates \$2.18 million (\$54.5 × 0.0401) for his team. Adding Garciaparra's \$100,000 to the average raises his total hitting value to \$2.28 million. Perez is a below-average hitter; hence, we must subtract his contribution from the average to calculate his worth. Perez took 9.89 percent of the Cubs' plate appearances in 2005, costing the Cubs \$1.85 million versus the average player with the same playing time (\$54.5 × 0.0989 = \$5.39). Therefore, Perez generated \$3.54 million (\$5.59 − \$1.85) in revenue for the Cubs from his hitting.

It is important to note that these estimates value *only hitting* contributions, just as the estimates for pitchers value only pitching contributions. Why did Cubs manager Dusty Baker put Perez on the field for so many plate appearances if he was worse than the average Ronny Cedeno, who logged most of his defensive time at shortstop when Perez was out of the lineup? Some would say Baker is a stubborn man with an irrational preference for a "proven veteran" like Perez. I think that a manager with thirteen years of experience and three NL Manager of the Year awards (1993, 1997, and 2000) probably has a decent idea of what he is doing. It is more likely that Baker went with Perez because he brings something to the team other than his offense. Perez is a noted defensive specialist, who is an out-machine, not just as a hitter, but as a defender. I can't say how much Perez's defensive contribution is worth, but I suspect his contribution with the glove makes it worthwhile to keep his poor bat in the lineup.[80] In fact, many shortstops and catchers, which are primarily defense-first positions, earn less \$ValAA with the bat than most of the other position players. Cedeno was a twenty-two-year-old rookie in 2005, who was still learning the game. It is certainly possible that Cedeno deserved more playing time than Perez, but Baker's decision is defendable.

In addition to defense, the MRP calculations do not account for base running, leadership, community goodwill, etc. All of these characteristics are valuable to teams. If I were the GM of the team, I would need to figure these things out using a similar, but more complicated, set of calculations. For simplicity, I'm going to stick with valuing batting and pitching.

Who is the MRP MVP?

Fans love to argue every year over who is worthy of the Most Valuable Player awards (MVP); however, the word *value* means different things to different people. Many fans believe the award should go to the best player in the league. Others think it should go to the best player on a contending team—the idea is that a good player on a bad team isn't adding value toward getting the team to the postseason. Another argument is that pitchers should not be eligible, because the best pitcher in the league wins the Cy Young Award. I cannot say that any of these criteria are wrong, but what if we took *value* to mean value in dollars, meaning the MVP ought to be the player with the highest MRP.

Who was the most valuable player in MLB in 2005 according to estimated MRPs? Table 33 lists the top 50 "most valuable" players in the majors in 2005. The table also notes the MVP and Cy Young award winners for the season. Because the official definition of the MVP award is open to interpretation, it is not surprising to see that the player who generated the greatest dollar returns to his team, Derrek Lee of the Chicago Cubs, did not win the award. I suspect that play-

Table 33: Top 50 Most Valuable Players (2005)

Rank	Player	Team	% IP or % PA	RABA or RSAA	$ValAA	MRP	Position
1	Derrek Lee	Chicago Cubs	11.22%	74.30	$13.06	$19.18	Hitter
2	Albert Pujols MVP_{NL}	St. Louis Cardinals	11.21%	66.85	$11.42	$17.53	Hitter
3	Alex Rodriguez MVP_{AL}	New York Yankees	11.16%	59.65	$9.90	$15.99	Hitter
4	Brian Giles	San Diego Padres	10.75%	55.09	$8.98	$14.84	Hitter
5	David Ortiz	Boston Red Sox	11.14%	53.32	$8.63	$14.70	Hitter
6	Chris Carpenter CY_{NL}	St. Louis Cardinals	16.72%	35.51	$5.33	$14.59	Pitcher
7	Miguel Cabrera	Florida Marlins	11.03%	53.00	$8.56	$14.57	Hitter
8	Carlos Delgado	Florida Marlins	9.91%	55.72	$9.11	$14.51	Hitter
9	Johan Santana	Minnesota Twins	15.82%	37.22	$5.63	$14.40	Pitcher
10	Jason Bay	Pittsburgh Pirates	11.36%	50.22	$8.02	$14.22	Hitter
11	Travis Hafner	Cleveland Indians	9.24%	54.78	$8.92	$13.96	Hitter
12	Dontrelle Willis	Florida Marlins	16.38%	36.96	$5.58	$13.75	Pitcher

(continued)

Table 33 (continued)

Rank	Player	Team	% IP or % PA	RABA or RSAA	$ValAA	MRP	Position
13	Roy Oswalt	Houston Astros	16.75%	32.04	$4.73	$13.55	Pitcher
14	Mark Buehrle	Chicago White Sox	16.04%	28.89	$4.21	$13.27	Pitcher
15	John Smoltz	Atlanta Braves	15.91%	25.31	$3.62	$12.87	Pitcher
16	Andy Pettitte	Houston Astros	15.41%	30.25	$4.43	$12.55	Pitcher
17	Pedro Martinez	New York Mets	15.12%	29.92	$4.38	$12.48	Pitcher
18	Mark Teixeira	Texas Rangers	11.59%	39.85	$6.09	$12.41	Hitter
19	Roger Clemens	Houston Astros	14.64%	31.69	$4.67	$12.40	Pitcher
20	Manny Ramirez	Boston Red Sox	10.15%	44.10	$6.87	$12.40	Hitter
21	Morgan Ensberg	Houston Astros	10.16%	43.85	$6.82	$12.36	Hitter
22	Vladimir Guerrero	Los Angeles Angels of Anaheim	9.61%	44.92	$7.02	$12.26	Hitter
23	Brian Roberts	Baltimore Orioles	10.43%	39.97	$6.11	$11.80	Hitter
24	David Wright	New York Mets	10.69%	38.84	$5.91	$11.74	Hitter
25	Brandon Webb	Arizona Diamondbacks	15.72%	18.56	$2.57	$11.72	Pitcher
26	John Lackey	Los Angeles Angels of Anaheim	14.27%	30.25	$4.43	$11.65	Pitcher
27	Todd Helton	Colorado Rockies	10.04%	39.61	$6.05	$11.52	Hitter
28	Lance Berkman	Houston Astros	9.20%	40.84	$6.27	$11.29	Hitter
29	Jeff Kent	Los Angeles Dodgers	10.39%	36.64	$5.52	$11.19	Hitter
30	Randy Johnson	New York Yankees	15.78%	15.94	$2.18	$11.10	Pitcher
31	Richie Sexson	Seattle Mariners	10.76%	33.59	$5.00	$10.86	Hitter
32	A. J. Burnett	Florida Marlins	14.49%	25.35	$3.63	$10.86	Pitcher
33	Aaron Harang	Cincinnati Reds	14.77%	15.38	$2.10	$10.82	Pitcher
34	Michael Young	Texas Rangers	11.62%	30.39	$4.45	$10.79	Hitter
35	Adam Dunn	Cincinnati Reds	10.62%	33.41	$4.96	$10.75	Hitter
36	Jason Giambi	New York Yankees	8.51%	39.81	$6.08	$10.72	Hitter
37	Miguel Tejada	Baltimore Orioles	11.48%	30.03	$4.39	$10.65	Hitter
38	Jake Peavy	San Diego Padres	13.95%	28.41	$4.13	$10.56	Pitcher
39	Nick Johnson	Washington Nationals	8.91%	37.12	$5.61	$10.46	Hitter
40	Esteban Loaiza	Washington Nationals	14.89%	22.43	$3.17	$10.44	Pitcher
41	Danny Haren	Oakland Athletics	14.96%	13.17	$1.78	$10.38	Pitcher
42	Tom Glavine	New York Mets	14.72%	17.72	$2.45	$10.33	Pitcher
43	Andruw Jones	Atlanta Braves	10.86%	29.81	$4.36	$10.28	Hitter
44	Josh Towers	Toronto Blue Jays	14.42%	15.35	$2.10	$10.24	Pitcher
45	Carlos Zambrano	Chicago Cubs	15.51%	12.23	$1.64	$10.24	Pitcher
46	Paul Konerko	Chicago White Sox	10.81%	29.75	$4.35	$10.24	Hitter
47	Bobby Abreu	Philadelphia Phillies	11.33%	27.37	$3.96	$10.13	Hitter
48	Freddy Garcia	Chicago White Sox	15.45%	10.03	$1.33	$10.07	Pitcher
49	Bartolo Colon CY_{AL}	Los Angeles Angels of Anaheim	15.21%	17.04	$2.35	$10.01	Pitcher
50	Geoff Jenkins	Milwaukee Brewers	10.04%	29.75	$4.35	$9.82	Hitter

ing on a bad team really hurt him in the eyes of the Baseball Writers' Association of America, who vote for the award. However, the writers certainly didn't give the MVP awards to undeserving candidates. In the AL, the actual 2005 MVP, Alex Rodriguez, was the MRP MVP as well, and the NL MVP, Albert Pujols, had the second highest MRP in both leagues.

The NL Cy Young winner, Chris Carpenter, was the sixth most valuable player in all of baseball in 2005. The writers got this one right, despite blowing the AL award on Bartolo Colon of the Los Angeles Angels of Anaheim—the 49th most valuable player. Despite the fact that starting pitchers only take the field once every fifth day, they still make up nearly half (44 percent) of the top 50. While the number of games in which starting pitchers play is less than hitters, when they do play, they play a lot more. In 2005, pitchers who appeared only as starters and pitched in more than twenty games faced an average of a little more than twenty-six batters a game for thirty games— approximately 780 batter-pitcher contests in a season. A good batter normally steps to the plate a little more than 4 times a game in 150 games—approximately 640 batter-pitcher contests in a season. This gives good pitchers more opportunities to contribute to winning than good hitters, who bat only when their lineup position comes up. Of the pitchers in the top 50, players threw an average of 15 percent of their teams' innings, while batters took an average of 10.5 percent of their teams' plate appearances.

Another interesting finding for pitchers is that the top relievers do not tend to be as valuable as you might think. Mariano Rivera had the highest MRP among pure closers, generating $5.89 million for the New York Yankees. That is a mere $39,000 more than his rookie teammate, Chien-Ming Wang, who played part of the 2005 season in Triple-A. The reason for the closeness in their values, despite Wang's decent but inferior stats, is that he pitched more innings. Do we put too much weight on the value of closers? It's not clear. The runs that Rivera prevents are very likely important to winning a game. As a closer, Rivera enters the game when giving up runs likely leads to a loss and preventing runs preserves a win. The runs Rivera saved actually had more value than the average run scored against the Yankees, because they occurred in specific spots that would tilt the game one way or the other. However, Rivera pitched less than 6 percent of the Yankees' innings, nearly a third of what the Yankees' top starter, Randy Johnson, provided. Still, I suspect the top closers are more valuable than their estimates. Unfortunately, weighting the MRPs for this additional value is quite difficult, and requires some very specific information about performance, so I will not do so here. Just be aware that closers may be a little more valuable than the MRPs estimates.

How Does the Labor Market Value Players?

A complete list of players and their estimated dollar contributions to hitting and pitching in 2005 and 2006 is available in Appendix D. In a free market for baseball talent, teams ought to bid up the wage of a player until it equals his MRP. How out of line are the estimates with what the market is actually paying for talent?

Figure 18 shows the correlations between a player's actual dollar salary in 2005 and his MRP, for hitters and pitchers separately. It only includes players with more than seven years of major-league "service"—to guarantee their free agent status—and who played more than 2 percent of their teams' total playing time. The names of players with salaries or MRPs of greater than $10 million are listed. The regression lines map the positive relationships, which are statistically significant. For hitters, differences in player MRPs explain about 27 percent of the difference in actual salaries. For pitchers, MRPs explain about 23 percent. Given some of the limitations we face, that MRPs explain only 23–27 percent of player salaries is not that surprising.

First, even among free agents, valuing what a contract is worth to a player in any given year is difficult, because structures of long-term

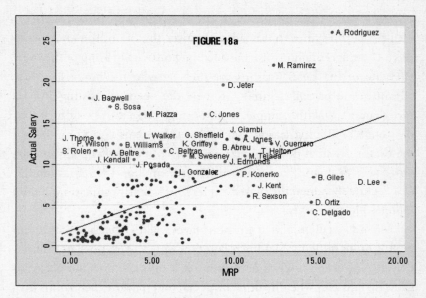

FIGURE 18a

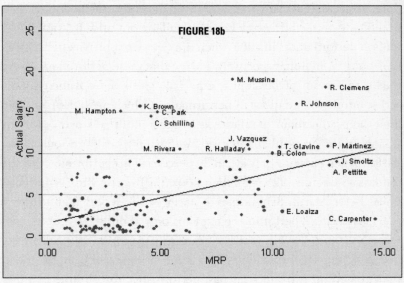

FIGURE 18b

contracts vary. A player's salary in any one year may not be consistent with his performance, but it might be over the life of the entire contract. Contracts often involve back-loading or front-loading of the overall value of the deal. Reasons for such agreements range from tax advantages to payroll flexibility to meet the needs of existing and future teammates. For example, a player might sign a five-year deal that pays out $5 million a season for the first three years and $15 million a season for the final two years. If he performs at a level equal to the average yearly value of the total contract of $9 million ($45/5), then the GM accurately valued the player, even though yearly estimates will miss high and low every year.

Second, predicting what any one player will do from one year to the next is quite difficult. Signing a contract with a team does not bind a player to a certain level of performance; it only requires the player to show up and play when healthy. Both GM and player expectations may differ from what actually transpires over the course of a contract. Few would have predicted Derrek Lee's $19 million or Carlos Beltran's $5.75 million performances in 2005, when they earned approximately $8 million and $17 million respectively. It's not that these performances were out of the realm of possibility, especially given the possibility of injuries, but these deviations in performances, which are quite common, limit the predictability of salaries as a function of performance for any season. In the previous chapter we saw that a pitcher's previous season performance explains only about 30 percent of his performance in the following season. Similarly, in their book *The Wages of Wins*, economists David Berri, Martin Schmidt, and Stacey Brook report that a hitter's previous season's performance explains only about a third of his performance the following year.[81] A team or player may have been justified in signing a contract that pays a value far different from his added value, based on expecting his past performance to continue in a predictable manner, but the performance of players varies widely.

Comparing salaries to MRPs by salary class is interesting. Because teams have the sole right to employ their own players during any player's fist six years of service, we should expect salaries to be below MRPs during this indenture. For his first three years in the league, a player makes what the team says he makes, subject only to some minimum salary constraint. After a player's third year of service, he becomes eligible to negotiate his salary subject to the opinion of an arbitrator. While the player's negotiating leverage is somewhat limited, we should expect his salary to tick upward. Finally, upon becoming a free agent, a player should earn his MRP as teams bid for his services.

Table 34 lists the median salary differences from estimated MRPs as a percentage by salary class. As expected, reserved players earn less of their MRPs than the other classes. The extracted value for purely reserved players, approximately 90 percent less, is nearly the same level that Scully estimated before the introduction of free agency.

Arbitration-eligible players earn a little more than the reserved class, but still earn far less than their MRPs. While arbitration gives some power to players, the rules of the process require the arbitrator to judge appropriate compensation based on comparisons to players with similar levels of service. Because low-service players tend to earn less, arbitrators continue to favor salary proposals that are far lower than a player's MRP.

If young players are generating more value than they are being paid, then why do players continue to allow this "exploitation" of their abilities? As puzzling as this might seem, I don't think it is all that exploitive. In order to become a good player, you need plenty of training. Most players make stops at five levels of the minor-league system during their careers—rookie ball, Low-A, High-A, Double-A, and Triple-A. Along the way, the players do much more than give fans in towns without major-league teams some live baseball to watch. Players receive

Table 34: Difference in Salary and MRP Estimates (2005)

Salary Class**	Median Difference from MRP*	
	Hitters	Pitchers
Reserved	− 89 percent	− 90 percent
Arbitration Eligible	− 77 percent	− 79 percent
Free Agents	− 8 percent	− 19 percent
Total	− 45 percent	− 57 percent

*Percentage difference from MRP estimates for players with greater than 2 percent of team playing time.
**Service estimated from years since MLB debut.

heavy monitoring and instruction. Each organization has personnel in place to evaluate and guide players through the minors. Most of the players won't see a day on a major-league roster. And as good as organizations are at identifying talent, many first-round draft picks flame out, and some undrafted roster fillers become All-Stars. But in order to train those who will succeed, you have to train all players to succeed, for many years. The cost of producing a major-league player is not cheap.

If all players became free agents after every season, teams would have very little incentive to train players to succeed over their careers. Why spend resources to improve a player who will become more expensive to hire the following year—the better he gets, the more money he will command on the free agent market—and possibly employ his skills against you if he's hired away?

This is similar to the problem private companies face with research and development of new technologies. To develop a cure for cancer, which would be a very valuable thing to discover, drug companies spend billions of dollars every year to get close. All of these companies are willing to spend resources searching for a cure, because a cure will earn them a patent—a time-limited legal monopoly on the cure—that should generate more than enough revenue to cover the costs of development. What would happen if other companies could copy a successfully designed cure and sell it for a fraction of the cost? Then no company would expend the effort to develop the cure in the first place. We would be stuck with a bunch of companies waiting to copy a cure that would never come.

This is the same dilemma faced by teams. Players need teams to spend resources to develop their raw talent into major-league ballplayers. If players are free to bolt upon development, teams aren't going to be willing to supply the needed grooming. Players and organizations could agree on other payment plans to get them to the majors, such as each player paying to join a private development league, but the players and owners settled on the reserved method through the collective bargaining process. It's likely that both sides favor the limited reserved-time arrangement because players have unique skills that MLB teams want to groom, and teams have access to specific training that future players want. The arrangement still might be exploitive, but it is not necessarily the case.

While the results for reserved and arbitration classes are expected, the result for free agents seems a little puzzling. In a free labor market, shouldn't players earn their MRPs? Well yes, but not necessarily the same number we just estimated. The MRP we estimated is a gross estimate, which includes the total value of what the player contributed without taking into account any additional costs, borne by the team, that allow the player to do the things that generate wins. If a team spends $200,000 on a player to produce $1 million in value on the field, his value is equal to $800,000 in additional revenue to the team, which is the net MRP that his salary should equal. That $200,000 may include things such as coaching, weight training, medical attention, video equipment, advanced scouting reports, etc., which teams often provide to players. Without the help of these inputs, for which the team often picks up the tab, players would not be effective on the field. These items represent additional costs of hiring a player beyond his salary. If teams are willing to pay player salaries equal to the value produced on the field minus other training costs, then our gross MRP estimates should be above actual player salaries.

Why not compare net MRP estimates to player salaries? This would be ideal, but these additional costs are difficult to estimate, especially for individual players. Some players require more complementary inputs than others. For example, a pitcher with arm problems that require regular expensive medical treatment, is going to cost more than a naturally healthy teammate. Assuming the players produce equal value to the team on the field, we expect that the player who needs the expensive medical care will earn a lower salary even though they have identical on-field gross MRPs. But it would be very hard to identify the difference between the players without access to hard-to-get information.

Not only is it difficult to identify costs by player, but even to know how much teams spend on players beyond salary in general. However, the MRP estimates may provide a guide to the answer. After all, these players are hired on an open market by owners who want to win. They are as unlikely to forgo profit opportunities as pedestrians are unwilling to leave $100 bills lying on the sidewalk.

The median difference between actual salary and MRP estimates is about 19 percent for pitchers and 8 percent for hitters; therefore, it's likely that teams spend around 19 percent and 8 percent of the salaries of pitchers and hitters on complementary inputs. The fact that pitchers receive less of their gross MRP than hitters does not surprise me considering the resources needed to support pitchers. Teams appear to spend more on coaching and medical treatment for pitchers than hitters, with pitching and bullpen coaches, video analysis, and Tommy John surgery. The fact that pitchers report earlier to spring training than the rest of the team is a good indicator that pitchers are more costly to maintain than hitters.

As distasteful as reducing a player's athletic accomplishments down to a dollar amount may seem, it's a task every general manager in baseball must do. With dollar-value estimates of players—based on the things players contribute to wins—the GM is equipped to make decisions for the franchise. Identifying potential problems in performance due to injury, psychology, the team social dynamics, and media pressure are huge challenges. GMs must deal with human beings, whose tempers and egos are the stuff of legend. So it's more than just crunching the numbers. However, a GM who can help a player through a messy divorce but can't tell a fourth outfielder from a rising star won't succeed either.

Part Four

WHAT FIELD?

14

Is Major League Baseball a Monopoly?

Gentlemen, we have the only legal monopoly in the country and we're f***ing it up.

—TED TURNER[82]

THIS IS A SILLY QUESTION, right? Major League Baseball (MLB) is, after all, the only professional sports league in North America providing "major league" level baseball. Many leagues have tried to compete with it, but all have fallen short in their noble quest. And don't forget about the infamous exemption that gives MLB protection from the antitrust laws responsible for preventing monopolies in other American industries. On top of all of this, MLB seems to fit the monopoly stereotype perfectly with its gentlemen's club of billionaire owners, headed by a real-life version of C. Montgomery Burns, Allan H. "Bud" Selig. Even the organization in question admits it is a monopoly. A silly question? It's outright preposterous!

But I'm not sure MLB is a monopoly. This is one of those cases where most economists—or at least the economists who choose to write on the subject—agree with the conventional wisdom. But I don't.

A monopolist is not some old white guy with a bushy mustache and sporting a top hat, like that cartoon fellow on the board game by Parker Brothers. A monopoly is a market institution that sells a product without threat of competition from outside rivals. And this lack of competition causes the monopolist to behave in a manner that is quite predictable and easily identifiable. This absence of competition allows the monopolist to increase its revenues by doing something other than providing better products at cheaper prices. By selling output to those customers willing to pay higher prices for the product, the monopolist earns profits. In a competitive environment this behavior will not work; restricting output and raising prices sends customers running to competitors. Trying to act like a monopolist when you are not one is a good way to kill your business.

While the league is not completely competitive, I think that the places it isn't are harmless. Several other major sports leagues do not share baseball's antitrust exemption. It turns out that baseball seems to be the best behaved of the bunch in terms of responding to market forces. Maybe MLB is a special kind of monopolist, one which can hide the most egregious sins of the typical monopolist. However, this sort of monopolist is benign—it provides baseball fans with the baseball they want. But why does MLB act as if it is governed by competitive market forces without any competitors? History shows that when the league has ignored the wishes of the fans, competitors have sprung up to challenge MLB. As an organization, MLB is constantly on the lookout for new competitors. These virtual competitors stop it from acting like a monopolist. Is this really true? Moreover, is it a stable arrangement?

Since 1903, when the American League (AL) and National League (NL) agreed to collude, for all but two years MLB has been the only producer of major-league-level baseball in North America. The exception occurred from 1914 to 1915, when the Federal League (FL) operated in direct competition with MLB as a major professional baseball league. Its brief existence ended when MLB agreed to expand, but more importantly, the FL is the prime evidence of baseball's pernicious monopolist character.

One disgruntled FL team decided to sue MLB rather than accept the settlement with MLB that forced the end of the FL. Baltimore formally accused MLB of violating the Sherman Antitrust Act in *Federal League v. Major League Baseball.* But the unfortunate event of this case was the "Landis decision," which was the first step in creating baseball's infamous exemption from antitrust laws—the rules designed to protect against monopoly. The motivation for this decision was an odd one; simply, baseball is not interstate commerce, and therefore it is not subject to federal antitrust laws. Despite this strange ruling, which has never applied to other sports leagues, the Supreme Court has upheld the Landis Decision on several occasions. To many, these series of legal precedents have created MLB's "antitrust exemption," and this means that baseball can act as a monopolist without fear of legal intervention to stop its behavior.

A monopoly faces no competitors in providing the goods or services it sells. In the standard model of monopoly—known as the "single price" model because the monopolist charges the same price to all consumers—the monopolist manipulates the price of the product it sells by adjusting the output it produces. By producing less of a product, the monopolist artificially raises the price of the product by selling fewer units. The higher price of the product generates additional revenue to produce monopoly profits—the gain from artificially raising the price of the product. In a competitive market, producers cannot affect the price of a product to earn monopoly profits, because competitors can capture consumers by selling additional units at lower prices. But, by definition, a monopolist faces no competitors; therefore, it does not have to worry about rival companies entering and charging a lower price. What could this mean for baseball fans? MLB produces less baseball—in the form of fewer games, shorter games, or fewer teams—and fans pay a higher price for baseball than they would in a competitive atmosphere.

The Real Problem with Single-Price Monopolists

If there is $1 of revenue to be gained, the monopolist firm, indeed any firm, will spend up to $1 to gain that dollar. If the firm takes in an amount of revenue that is more than the cost of producing a unit, the firm will be all the richer.

Table 35 shows hypothetical costs and revenues faced by a monopolist at differing levels of output. For simplicity, I set the cost of producing

Table 35: Hypothetical Costs and Revenues Faced by a Monopolist

Price (P)	Quantity (Q)	Total Revenue (P × Q)	Marginal Revenue (MR)	Marginal Cost (MC)	Total Cost (Q × Cost)	Profit (TR − TC)
12	1	12	12	2	2	10
11	2	22	10	2	4	18
10	3	30	8	2	6	24
9	4	36	6	2	8	28
8	5	40	4	2	10	30
7	**6**	**42**	**2**	**2**	**12**	**30**
6	7	42	0	2	14	28
5	8	40	2	2	16	24
4	9	36	4	2	18	18
3	10	30	6	2	20	10
2	11	22	8	2	22	0
1	12	12	10	2	24	12

every unit to be the same. According to the law of demand, the higher the price the fewer the units sold, and the lower the price the greater the number of units sold. The total revenue earned by any firm is determined by the number of units sold times the price of each unit. The total cost equals the number of units sold times the cost of producing each unit. We see that as the price falls, the quantity sold rises. Initially, the total revenue begins to rise, but as the price continues to fall, further profits will also begin to decline. In this example, we can see that the maximum amount of profit earned occurs at the quantity where the marginal cost, the cost of producing an extra unit of product, equals the marginal revenue, the additional revenue generated. Let me assure you that this is a mathematical necessity.

The figure that follows shows this hypothetical market graphically. The demand curve (D) is downward sloping, because the firm can expect consumers to purchase more of the product at a lower price and less of the product at a higher price. For simplicity, the marginal cost (MC) is flat at $2; however, this does not have to be so. The quantity at which the MR = MC is 6, which means each of these units sells for $7. The firm earns $42 in revenue (6 × $7) and expends $12 in costs (6 × $2) for a maximum profit of $30. Box A represents the monopoly profit ($5 × $6). We can see that producing units beyond 6 would generate profits for the firm until the firm reached 11 units, because the price per

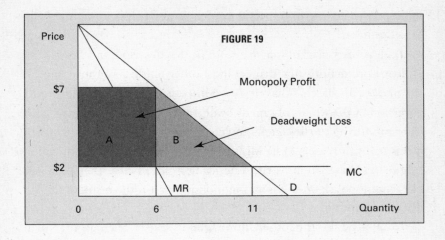

unit would still exceed the cost per unit. Triangle B under the demand curve represents the lost gains to both the seller and the consumer. The monopolist loses the revenue and consumers lose the goods. Economists refer to the loss of the underproduction as *deadweight loss*, because sellers and consumers would gain if the additional units were produced.

The single-price monopolist maximizes profits by restricting output. An unfortunate side effect is that the monopolist cannot sell units it would like to sell to consumers willing to pay a price greater than the cost of producing those extra units. It is the lack of competition that allows the monopolist to do this. Competitive pressure would cause the market to provide the output where price equals the marginal cost.

At the heart of the argument that MLB acts like a monopolist is the existence of the antitrust exemption. Beginning with the Sherman Antitrust Act of 1890 the federal government has been empowered to fight the monopoly abuses of the marketplace to protect consumers. Antitrust laws are designed to preserve the competitive process that satisfies consumer desires when businesses might prefer to do otherwise. To the general public, and even some economists, antitrust laws are a safety feature like brakes on a car, that keep the economy from running off the road. A car without brakes can turn an invaluable tool into a deadly weapon. Similarly, a market without antitrust might be doomed to control by hungry monopolists, itching to restrict output and raise prices to sap the help-less consumer.

Baseball is a market that seems to fit this description. Without the antitrust protections that protect most other markets in the economy, the market for baseball has devolved into a single monopolistic entity governed by the whims of greedy owners who conspire to raise its prof-its by producing too few teams and charging fans exorbitant prices. But is this really the case? While MLB is clearly the sole producer of major-league-level baseball in North America, it is not so clear that MLB acts like a monopolist; or, if it is a monopolist, that it is the result of the an-titrust exemption.

Compared to the other three major sports leagues in North America—professional basketball, football, and hockey—the baseball market looks very similar. Each market is controlled by a single league: the National Basketball Association (NBA), the National Foot-ball League (NFL), and the National Hockey League (NHL). Although each of these leagues enjoys some antitrust exemptions for collective bargaining with labor unions and negotiating television contracts, the antitrust exemption put forth in the Landis decision applies only to baseball. All of these leagues can be and have been sued and found guilty of violating antitrust laws. Though the courts have reviewed some baseball cases involving the antitrust decision, the judiciary has made it clear that Congress must legislate the exemption away, which it often threatens to do but never does.

Given that baseball is the only major sports product in the United States not protected by antitrust laws, it stands to reason that MLB's out-put and pricing ought to differ from the other professional sports leagues. Table 36 compares the price and output of the four major sports leagues. According to the standard analysis of monopoly, with-out competition a monopolist producer will choose to restrict output and raise prices. Leagues can restrict output through several means, but the most obvious way is to limit the number of teams per league, the games per season played by each team, and the temporal length of the season. As the data in Table 36 indicates, MLB produces more of its product at a lower price than any major sports league in the country.

Table 36: Comparison of the Four Major North American Sports Leagues[83]

Sports League	Number of Teams per League	Regular Season Games per Season	Length of Regular Season (months)	Average Ticket Price*	Adjusted Average Ticket Price*
NBA	30	82	6	$43.60	$35.75
NFL	32	16	4	$50.02	$ 8.00
NHL	30	82	6	$41.56	$34.08
MLB	30	162	6	$18.30	$29.65
Average	30.5	85.25	5.5	$38.37	$26.87

*Prices from 2002 or the 2002–2003 season.

In terms of teams, only the NFL has more than MLB, while MLB, the NHL, and the NBA all have thirty teams. Baseball certainly does not seem to be using its antitrust exemption to restrict output to fewer markets in comparison to the leagues that have no exemption.

MLB could restrict output in the number of regular season games. Baseball is the clear leader, with almost twice as many games as produced by the NBA and NHL and ten times more than the NFL. However, this might result from another factor: baseball is a less physical game than the other major sports. Baseball is not a contact sport; it is played at a slow pace, and involves a lot of sitting down. It is no accident that the only professional athletes that use tobacco during athletic contests are baseball players. As former Philadelphia Phillies All-Star John Kruk once said in response to a fan who questioned his tobacco and alcohol vices, "I ain't an athlete, lady. I'm a professional baseball player." The less physically demanding nature of baseball, relative to other sports, allows its participants to play more games. Therefore, maybe the nature of the game allows baseball to produce more games than other sports but still produce fewer games than it could.

However, it is hard to imagine baseball adding more games to its schedule given the constraints of the game. Baseball is primarily an outdoor sport, unlike basketball and hockey, which makes it vulnerable to the weather, particularly seasonal weather. Football is also an outdoor sport, although a larger fraction of the teams play in indoor domed stadiums. Also, football is played with constant motion and players covered in safety pads, which keeps them warm. The intermittent and often slow pace of baseball makes it ill-suited for play in the cold. The regular season begins in early April and ends in late September, six full months. Out of the 181 days available for baseball, a player can expect to have twenty-one days off during the regular season (this is not taking into account doubleheaders). A typical five-day-a-week worker gets forty-eight days off just for weekends over this same span. And that is not all. Spring training begins in mid-February, when teams travel south to warmer American locales ranging from Florida to Arizona, to ensure maximum preparedness for the upcoming season. Also, the postseason playoffs can extend into November, giving the possibility of nine months of player effort. In sum, it is hard to imagine baseball extending its season any more than it currently plays. If baseball is restricting its output, it is not in terms of games played.

On price, baseball is cheaper to fans than any of the major sports. In terms of the average regular season ticket, baseball fans pay about 40 percent of the price for NBA basketball and NHL hockey games and 50 percent less than for NFL football. However, baseball games are of a different character than these other sports, which might push the profit-maximizing price downward. A single game in an NFL season represents 6.25 percent of the football played by a team in that season, while a game in baseball represents 0.62 percent of the baseball played by a team. Each game represents a smaller slice of the total season in baseball, therefore fans may be less willing to pay for the single game experience than they would in other sports. To account for this, I adjust the average ticket price relative to the total amount of the regular season observed with a single ticket purchase, listed in the last column of Table 36. For example, you would have to attend ten regular season MLB games to see the same percentage of the regular season as you would if you attended one NFL game. By this metric NFL football has the cheapest price as a percent of the regular season seen per dollar paid, but MLB still has a lower adjusted price than the NBA and NHL. It is hard to find evidence of the antitrust exemption altering the output of MLB in the price relative to the other leagues.

There is no strong evidence that the antitrust exemption provides any monopoly privileges to MLB other than protecting it from expensive lawsuits. These lawsuits, which the NFL, NBA, and NHL all endure due to the scrutiny of antitrust laws, do not seemed to have fostered any more competition in these sports. And the output of these leagues indicates that the threat of antitrust sanctions has not led the leagues to produce a greater output than MLB, which does not face such legal regulation. Perhaps the fear of losing the antitrust exemption keeps MLB honest, not wanting to look too different from its sister leagues. But, if this is the case, then the antitrust exemption is benign.

MLB's similarity to the other major sports leagues in output and prices does not necessarily mean that baseball is not a bad monopolist, ultimately destined to give customers a bad deal. The price and quantity differences may reflect something unique about fans' willingness to pay for baseball. And this outcome is also consistent with the failure of antitrust laws to enforce competitive environments in the other sports leagues. In fact, baseball may be acting just like the other leagues exactly because they all behave as monopolistic producers. We need to investigate further to determine if competitive behavior is responsible for the similar price and output of the leagues. But what is clear from the analysis is that calls to reform the competitiveness of baseball that focus on removing the antitrust exemption are misguided. As best we can tell, the antitrust exemption does very little to make MLB more monopolistic than any other major professional sports league.

15

Bud the Benevolent

It is not from the benevolence of the butcher, the brewer, or the baker, that we expect our dinner, but from their regard to their own interest. We address ourselves, not to their humanity but to their self-love, and never talk to them of our necessities but of their advantages.

—ADAM SMITH[84]

THOUGH THE STRENGTH of baseball's monopoly power is overblown, we shouldn't ignore it. Let's apply a different model of monopoly to MLB. Even if baseball is a monopoly, it is an unusual one.

The standard single-priced monopolist I discussed above produces an output lower than a perfectly competitive market would provide. This is harmful because some consumers are willing to pay a price that is high enough to cover the cost of producing additional units, but no trade takes place. If there is only one thing that economists agree on, it's that trade is good. Two parties will exchange their wares only if each party values what the other party has more than what he has. Therefore, trading must be mutually beneficial, and the world is a happier place after every voluntary exchange. Trades that should take place but don't are bad, because trades are a benefit both to buyers and sellers.

It is the desire to maximize profits that forces the monopolist to underserve its market. It's the same motivation that causes firms in competitive markets to provide the products consumers want. When a monopolist can only charge one price to all customers, it must make a trade-off between selling many units at a lower price or fewer units at

a higher price. If the monopolist tries to sell products to everyone willing to pay a price greater than the cost of production, the monopoly
forgoes some higher-priced sales to consumers who are willing to pay
more for the product. But, if it sells only to customers willing to pay a
very high price, it forgoes selling some units to individuals who value
the product less. Which method yields more profits? It turns out that a
monopolist earns more revenue from selling fewer products at a higher
price than it would in a competitive market.

To judge whether or not this model is appropriate for baseball, we
must identify what quantity baseball is restricting and the price that
baseball is charging. The price of baseball is very easy to measure. It is
the ticket price fans pay for games plus the implicit price fans pay in
the form of watched advertising during broadcast games. As shown in
Table 36, baseball's average ticket prices are not higher than in other
sports leagues. The quantity is a bit more complicated. The quantity of
baseball provided to fans can be expanded or contracted along two
metrics: the quantity of games played by all teams or the quantity of
baseball teams. We know that the former is pretty much fixed, but the
latter is a metric that MLB often discusses adjusting. MLB began with
the eight original teams of the NL and has continued to expand until it
reached its current thirty teams.

While expansion has been the general trend in baseball output,
there has been much recent talk about contracting the league. In 2002,
Commissioner Bud Selig announced the MLB was considering contracting two teams related to financial problems; however, the storm of
contraction blew over, and as part of the 2002 labor agreement, contraction decisions were to be postponed. Certainly, contraction is consistent with monopoly behavior. Monopolies restrict output, MLB was
trying to restrict output; hence, MLB wants to restrict output to earn
monopoly profits.

I believe the contraction threat was a noncredible bargaining chip
wielded by the commissioner in his negotiations with the players union. It
seems odd that baseball would expand by two teams in 1998 and then reverse course only a few years later. The owners are not that shortsighted.
When MLB decided to move the Montreal Expos to Washington, DC,

there were numerous suitors. Why would MLB want to neglect the revenue from cities willing to cough it up? No wonder Commissioner Selig has announced that contraction is no longer on the table. In a single-price monopoly, contraction makes sense, but MLB faces some conditions very different from most single-priced monopolists.

Different Prices for Different People

If MLB is a monopolist, it is a multi-price monopolist. A multi-price monopolist can sell its output to different consumers at differing prices. This detail changes everything. The multi-price monopolist does not face the price-quantity trade-off of the single-price monopolist. Selling output at a low price to individuals with a low willingness to pay does not force the monopolist to trade off high-price sales to individuals with a high willingness to pay. This monopolist can *price discriminate*, which sure sounds bad. Price discrimination is simply the selling of the same goods at different prices to different consumers. Now, again, some readers may balk. How is selling the same product at different prices morally acceptable? I will get to that in a moment. First, let's see why MLB is more likely to act as a price-discriminating monopolist than a single-price monopolist.

The ability to price discriminate is not as common as you might think. A firm must meet three very stringent conditions for price discrimination to be a sustainable business practice.

First the producer must be a monopolist in the market. In a competitive market, if a firm tries to price goods above the price of the production costs, a competitor will enter the market and steal away that business. Whether or not baseball has monopoly power is up for debate. While I think MLB's monopoly strength is much less than many people believe, I think that MLB does have a small cushion—sometimes known as "market power"—to engage in monopolistic practices without encouraging entry from competitors.

Second, the monopolist must be able to accurately identify what different individuals are willing to pay for a product. For example, if wealthy people all wore top hats and walked with canes, while poor people wore barrels held up by straps, it would be easy to identify, and separate out, the high- and low-paying customers. If such detection is not possible, the monopolist will not be able to know whom to sell to at what price. If the monopolist offers the wrong price to the wrong market segment, the low-valuing consumers of the product will not purchase the product at the high price and high-valuing customers will receive the product for less than they are willing to pay for it.

MLB adjusts its output by the number of teams in the league. We know the league would be hard-pressed to provide more games played per team. Right now, thirty teams serve twenty-five metropolitan statistical areas. If baseball were to expand to a new market, and it is a multi-price monopolist, it could charge a franchise fee to the new owner equal to his/her willingness-to-pay to put a team in the area. Because an owner's willingness-to-pay for a team will be governed by the potential revenue stream of baseball sales in the new market, the price that the league can charge for the team is easy to determine. Using demographic data to identify the new community's demand for a baseball team, the league can estimate the value of the new team and then demand the maximum from any owner in that area. Simple measures of consumer preference for baseball, population, wealth, and other demographic factors are readily available to owners as they try to determine their expansion price. There is little danger of MLB owners failing to extract the maximum price for any new team; therefore, MLB clearly meets the second condition.

The third condition necessary for price discrimination is the ability to prevent resale of the product. If resale is possible, the low-price purchasers of the product can compete with the producing firm. A low-price consumer may be willing to sell his product to a high-price customer at a price less than what the monopolist would charge. If the monopolist cannot prevent this type of sale, then its price discrimination strategy will fail, because high-price customers will simply purchase their products from low-price consumers.

MLB can, and does, charge different franchise fees for expansion franchises. But what if there is a city that values a new team more than an expansion city? It is possible in this situation that a higher-valuing city might induce the owner of the new team to move to that city, and MLB teams have been known to move cities. However, this movement is rare, as only one MLB team has switched cities since 1971—the Expos moved from Montreal to Washington, DC, to become the Nationals. Also, it is highly unlikely that MLB would approve the move of a team they had just created so that this new owner could capture extra profits. All moves require at least two-thirds approval from the owners. It would be odd that the owners would approve a sale to a low-demand city, if another city was willing to pay more for a new baseball team. The owners can generate more revenue by putting the team in the more valuable market.

It seems that MLB meets all of the conditions necessary for it to price discriminate, if it is a monopoly. Therefore, when judging the harm done from any monopoly power, we ought to view MLB as a multi-price monopolist, which is not nearly as bad as the traditional single-price monopolist.

A multi-price monopolist lessens the most undesirable feature of single-price monopoly: the underproduction of a product valued by consumers. The profits earned by monopolists are not undesirable. While some people who purchase the product pay a higher price for the product than they would under a perfectly competitive market structure, every consumer is paying a price equal to or less than their willingness-to-pay for the product. The additional revenue gained by the monopolist is not a net loss to society, since consumers who do consume the product at a higher price value the consumption of that product at the higher price. These consumers would be better off if they could purchase the product at a lower price, but the happiness lost to the consumer is gained by the producer. The consumers' loss exactly equals the gain to the producer; thus, society is no better or worse off from this transfer.

The important distinction between the two models of monopoly lies with the underproduction of the desired product. When the single-price monopolist fails to supply consumers who are willing to pay a price greater than the additional cost of production, the firm is producing too few goods. This represents deadweight loss; consumers who would gladly pay for a product are not able to consume it, but no one captures the potential gains from trade. Everyone loses from the nonproduction of these additional units, but no one gains. This is simply the by-product of the monopolist's decision to earn higher profits by concentrating on high-price customers.

The single-price monopolist must pick one price, and the point at which it will maximize profits will leave some willing customers empty-handed. The multi-price monopolist does not have to choose between selling to a few high-price customers or many low-price customers; it can sell to both types of consumers at different prices. It may not seem perfectly fair, but the multi-price system does fundamentally serve customers.[85]

That is to say, a multi-price monopolist maximizes profits in a way that enables him to help society as he helps himself, in a way the single-price monopolist cannot achieve. With perfect price discrimination, each unit sells for the price the consumer is willing for pay for each unit; a model followed by certain online airfare agents. The multi-price monopolist does not have to restrict quantity to maximize profits as the single-price monopolist must do. The only difference in outcomes between perfect competition and a *perfectly* price-discriminating monopolist is that the former generates no profits for producers while the latter eliminates consumer gains from purchasing the product at a bargain price. Economists do not pick winners and losers in terms of who gets revenue, just allocation of outcomes; and the perfectly price-discriminating monopolist outcome is just as desirable at the perfectly competitive option that economists treasure so dearly.

If MLB is a monopolist, it is a price discriminating monopolist. Assuming that self-interested owners who are interested in maximizing profits— I think few will deny the appropriateness of this assumption—run MLB, they ought to be engaging in price discrimination in their provision of baseball.

It seems that the quantity of teams is the only way MLB can adjust its output. In this case MLB will expand its teams into markets as long as the revenues from running a team in the town exceed the cost, and MLB will set its expansion fee according to each locale's profitability. Each team prices its product according to the local demand for baseball, as evidenced by the differing ticket prices across baseball teams. In 2005 the average ticket price was about $22, with a range of $14 in Kansas City to $46 in Boston.[86] MLB can set expansion fees based on the estimated revenues according to the potential demand. The Kansas Cities of the country would pay lower fees while Bostons would pay a much higher fee. Given that MLB has the ability to price discriminate, it has no incentive to restrict its output of baseball below the competitive optimum; because doing so would require ignoring uncaptured revenue. This is not what owners tend to do.

If MLB has some monopoly power, this does not mean baseball fans necessarily suffer from the typical abuses associated with monopoly. The most commonly applied model of monopoly, the single-price monopolist, is associated with the underproduction of its product. However, the single-price model doesn't fit MLB. MLB can easily sell baseball to different markets at different prices. Price discrimination by multi-price monopolists leads to higher profits for owners, but also more games at acceptable prices for fans. In fact, the output of baseball should not differ considerably from the economist's benchmark of perfectly competitive output. Contrary to our country's great prejudice against monopolies, the extent to which MLB is one turns out not to be problem at all.

16

Expansion and the Invisible Hand

The position of a single seller can in general be conquered—and retained for decades—only on the condition that he does not behave like a monopolist.

—Joseph Schumpeter[87]

MLB is the only league providing top-level baseball to fans in the U.S., so it is easy to begin the analysis of MLB using standard microeconomic models of monopoly that I have discussed. However, monopolies simply do not pop up into existence to impose their wrath on society in market economies. A business cannot become a monopoly by declaring itself to be one. Any firm that attempts to act like a monopoly will fail without some help from outside forces or strange internal forces inherent to that particular industry. Acting like a monopolist—raising prices and restricting output—encourages rival firms to enter the market, cut prices, and steal customers, and they will do so as long as they can.

Given the openness of the American economy, how is it possible that MLB is the only producer for major-league-level baseball in America? Is there some artificial or natural barrier to entering the baseball market? Or is baseball not acting like a monopolist, thereby creating no room for entry by potential competitors? One of these outcomes must be true. The answer lies in the history of MLB expansion.

Let us take a moment on what competition really is. The economic theory of *perfect competition* is based on three simple conditions:

- There are many sellers and buyers in the market.
- All firms in the market sell highly substitutable (if not identical) products.
- There is free entry and exit into and out of the market by potential rival firms not currently in the market.

If these conditions prevail in a market, that market will guide self-interested sellers to produce the output consumers desire at the lowest sustainable price. In contrast to the perfectly competitive model a monopoly results from these three conditions:

- The market has a single seller.
- There exist no close substitute products.
- There exists a barrier to entry in the market.

The first two assumptions of perfectly competitive markets are clearly not met in the American baseball market. Though we have many buyers, there is only one seller (MLB), and there are no competing baseball leagues. If MLB is the only producer of baseball, how can the baseball market provide fans with the baseball they want? There is no competition in the baseball market to restrain MLB from acting like a monopolist. So, again, there is a barrier to entering the baseball market—and we have more inferior baseball than we would otherwise—or some competitive pressure exists that forces MLB to produce good baseball.

Barriers to entry take two forms: artificial and natural. Artificial barriers, the most common, typically come from the government. Government actions by the legislature, judiciary, and executive branch can limit competitive pressures in a market. The most blatant example of artificial monopoly protection in the United States is the U.S. Postal Service. Since the mid-nineteenth century the post office has been the sole provider of everyday mail in the United States. Companies that seek to compete in everyday mail delivery are barred from doing so by law. This permits the post office to operate with the efficiency of . . . well, the post office—slow, expensive, and unreliable. While numerous providers of express mail such as FedEx and United Parcel Service would gladly compete with the post office in the distribution of mail, they are barred from doing so. Most artificial protections are a bit subtler. Tariffs on imported goods prevent foreign producers from competing with domestic producers not subject to the tariff. Like the post office, the tariffs limit the competitive pressures from outside producers.

The baseball antitrust exemption is not a barrier to entry into the baseball market. Any group of individuals may legally provide baseball to consumers without violating the antitrust exemption. The antitrust exemption merely gives legal protection to MLB if someone decides to sue the league for violating antitrust laws. MLB cannot seek legal remedies to protect it from competitors.

Perhaps the public subsidy of ballparks by localities is an artificial barrier to entry into baseball markets. Most MLB stadiums receive substantial public funds, and similar funding might not be available for competing teams. While the city of New York might support building new stadiums for the Yankees and Mets, New Yorkers would likely be less sympathetic, if not hostile, to subsidizing a new team in a new league. To survive, the teams in the new league would have to earn revenues sufficient to cover the costs of operation, and the league would have to put a product of similar quality on the field. The revenues needed to cover the cost of operation for a new team would include the everyday costs of running the team plus the rent on a new stadium. Taxpayer-subsidized stadiums would give MLB teams an advantage in signing talent over teams without subsidized facilities. The profits from running a baseball team, or revenues earned beyond the costs of operation, would be less to potential competitors, who would have to spend a portion of their earnings on facilities. MLB teams would therefore have more earnings available to sign talent. In this case, the profit motive would not be sufficient to induce entry by competitors.

This argument has two problems. First, it does not apply to cities without current MLB teams. Teams in competing leagues may be just as successful at extracting public subsides as MLB if they promise to bring major-league-level baseball to town. Plus, even if the costs of operating a team are higher in a city without an MLB team, the new team doesn't have to worry about its fans migrating to a crosstown MLB rival.

A slightly inferior product may still yield sufficient revenue for the owner to purchase major-league talent. This puts these teams in a rival league on competitive footing with MLB teams.

Second, the history of competing leagues does not reveal any public bias toward the public funding of stadiums for new leagues. Many of the teams in the United States Football League (USFL), which competed with the NFL in the mid-1980s, played in publicly financed stadiums. In fact, many USFL teams shared stadiums with NFL teams. History shows that the public's willingness to subsidize teams extends beyond the dominant league brand. The point here is not that MLB teams could share stadiums with rival league teams—I think this would be highly unlikely—but that the public does not seem averse to subsidizing major sports teams from leagues other than the dominant existing league. It seems as long as a new league promises to pursue top-level talent, as the USFL did in football, citizens will subsidize the new teams. So public subsidization of stadiums doesn't seem to be much of a barrier to entry in the baseball market.

So if there is no artificial barrier, perhaps there is a natural one. A natural monopoly arises as a result of the declining cost structure of an industry, which experiences extreme "economies of scale" in production. This means a producer can produce additional units of the product more cheaply than any other potential producer. Baseball, like the other major sports, fits this model quite well.

Starting a league is quite an expensive endeavor that requires heavy up-front investment to have any chance of success. Adding the first few teams is much more expensive than the last few teams, due to the high start-up costs. Therefore, the cost for the new league of supplying teams to meet the unmet market demand is greater than the cost of adding teams to the current league. Say the market could bear ten more teams. While a new league could enter the market to fill this gap, the incumbent league could easily counter by adding ten new teams to its league at a lower cost, thereby bankrupting any potential entrants. The rival league's teams cost more than the existing league's teams. If potential rivals have knowledge of the market, no firm will enter the market, and the incumbent league can act as a monopolist. So, in this special case, a monopoly can exist naturally in the market without aid of any artificial entry barriers.

This model has its problems. A natural monopoly model of MLB does not discount the possibility of a rival league entering the market all at once with the optimal number of teams, thereby taking advantage of the economies of scale in baseball production and replacing MLB altogether. If baseball is a natural monopoly and the optimal number of teams in the league is forty, while MLB produces only thirty, then why can't a new league enter as a natural monopoly, provide a superior product to baseball fans for a cheaper price, and put MLB out of business altogether? According to the theory of contestable markets, this is a completely plausible possibility.

Contestable market theory maintains that as long as the cost of entry and exit are low, merely the threat of entry by potential competitors is sufficient to induce a single producer to generate the socially optimal output of the product. Like the theories of perfectly competitive and monopoly markets discussed above, the market must meet several conditions for the threat of competition to produce the optimal output with only a single producer:

- Potential rival firms must have access to the same production technology, input prices, and information about the market as the current sole producer.
- Firms must be able to resell any inputs at a price equal to the cost of purchasing the inputs (minus depreciation) if the firm chooses to exit the market, such that exit from the industry is costless.

How does the baseball market fit the assumptions of contestable markets? The first assumption is certainly true. There are many potential team owners inside and outside of MLB who have the knowledge and skill to operate baseball franchises. Also, the labor would be drawn from the same pool as MLB, and therefore labor prices would be identical in both leagues. Current MLB players are not bound to play within MLB. If a new league rose up, any player could jump from the majors or minors to a team in a competing league. Just as the owners tried to open the 1995 season with replacement players, players could just as easily jump to a replacement league. The easiest targets for a rogue league would be players who are not eligible for free agency. According to MLB's reserve agreement with the player's union, these players are restricted to one team that owns their rights to play in MLB for their first six years in the big leagues. This allows teams to pay these players substantially less than the revenue they generate for their teams.

The second assumption is a bit more complicated. Simply put, the threat of entry is credible to an existing firm as long as entry and exit are low-cost. This does not mean that firms do not bear start-up costs or risks from entering markets, only that if a firm is not directly prohibited from entering a market and it decides to leave, it can liquidate its capital assets for a price equal to the cost of purchase minus any wear on the capital. For example, a firm that builds a T-shirt factory must be able to sell the machines that make T-shirts on the open market to another buyer at a prices equal to the depreciated value of the machines used in making T-shirts while the factory was in operation. If the industry meets these entry/exit capability criteria, this industry is subject to competitive entry pressures.

The physical capital owned by a baseball team includes office equipment, office space, and tools for skilled labor, for the most part like any other business. The biggest capital asset of interest is the stadium where the game it played. The unique stadium required for baseball is a potential barrier to entry by any rival league. Any new team wishing to compete with MLB must provide a stadium of quality and capacity similar to MLB facilities. If the league fails, the stadium owners can receive some value for the stadium, but probably less than they would receive from selling it for use as a baseball stadium.

One obvious solution to this problem is to use one of the many existing baseball stadiums that are not currently hosting a team, until the league gains a sense of permanency. Some of these parks include minor-league facilities. Most potential major-league cities host Triple-A minor-league teams, which draw decent-sized crowds. Almost all of these stadiums could be expanded quickly to accommodate a larger audience. Also, public stadiums previously occupied by MLB teams could provide potential new homes to new teams. For example, Olympic Stadium in Montreal, Candlestick Park in San Francisco, and the Astrodome in Houston are all operable sports stadiums that could host a professional baseball team. Even if the stadiums of the new teams were not quite as nice as current MLB facilities, owners could compensate fans in other ways, such as offering better baseball, cheaper concessions, etc. And recall from above the success of the USFL in finding stadiums for its football games to compete with the NFL. Finding a place to play the game is not a huge obstacle for a league. Baseball has been played for too long and too widely to make finding a place to play a real problem.

So Is Baseball a Contestable Market?

It seems that economic theories can only give us competition predictions without absolute answers. Unfortunately there is no way to know which one is right. But history sheds light on the subject. Economist James Quirk compiles an excellent economic history of rival leagues in baseball in his book with Rodney Fort, *Pay Dirt.*

In the history of American professional baseball six leagues have challenged the dominant league to sell major-league baseball, including the AL, which was started as a competing league before it agreed to join forces with the NL in 1903. The American Association (1882–1891, 12 teams), the Players League (1890, 8 teams), the Union Association (1884, 8 teams), the Federal League (1914–1915, 8 teams), and the Continental League (1960s, 8 teams) have all attempted to meet the demand of baseball fans that was not met by the dominant league.

The American Association was the first baseball league to challenge the NL, which began play in 1876. For several reasons 1882 was a good time to enter the baseball business. After a gambling scandal caused several NL teams to fold, seven of the ten most populous cities in America lacked major-league teams. On top of this, the NL decided to cease Sunday games and remove beer from concessions to clean up its reputation. But this was not what fans like Homer Simpson, who believes baseball too boring to be watched without beer, wanted. The American Association brought teams to cities that the NL had abandoned, served beer and liquor, played Sunday games, and charged half the NL ticket price. In the first year of American Association operation, the new league and the NL raided each other's rosters; however, the leagues eventually enforced some agreements to prevent this. For most of the 1880s the leagues coexisted rather peacefully as the majority of their teams played in different cities.

The Union Association joined the competition in 1884, though its main competition was the American Association, not the NL. In response to the Union Association's entry to its turf, the American Association expanded from eight to twelve teams. When the Union Association could not compete, it folded after a year, and the American Association then dropped back to eight teams.

The American Association and the NL coexisted as rival leagues until 1890, when the Players League came into existence. Seven of the eight Players League teams played in cities already supported by the NL or the American Association. In an attempt to survive, the Players League raided the best talent of the incumbent leagues, which resulted in its teams attracting more fans than their hometown rivals in both incumbent leagues. All of the leagues suffered losses, and there was no way the baseball market could support all three. The leaders of the Players League reached agreements with both the American Association and the NL that ended the new league, with its rivals purchasing most of the Players League player contracts. But the 1890 season also signaled the beginning of the end of the American Association, with several of its teams folding after the season. Following the 1891 season, the NL purchased all of the American Association's assets and accepted its four strongest franchises, expanding to a twelve-team league. From 1882 to 1889 the NL continued to operate with twelve teams, but for the 1900 season the owners bought out four teams and the league returned to its original eight-team size—dropping Baltimore, Cleveland, Louisville, and Washington.

Once again, the NL would pay for its failure to offer baseball to areas that could support a team. The American League was originally just a minor league that decided to step up to the major-league level. Not surprisingly, three of its eight teams played in cities dropped by the NL, although Baltimore did move to New York in 1903 to become the team that would one day be known as the Yankees. The AL stocked 60 percent of its players from NL clubs during its inaugural year as a major league, and it drew more fans than the NL during its first two years of existence. It was particularly successful in cities where it competed directly with the NL. The AL ultimately succeeded. In 1903 the AL and NL became the organization we know today as Major League Baseball, with a merger that kept the leagues separate, but in which each would agree to honor player contracts.

The Federal League is the most famous of the rogue leagues, for its role in creating the antitrust exemption in baseball. In 1914 the Federal League opened as a major league with eight teams and eighty players from AL and NL rosters. In its first year of operation, attendance in the NL and AL dropped by 40 percent and 23 percent respectively. This is even more astonishing considering the Federal League competed with AL or NL teams in only four cities. But after the 1915 season the Federal League was suffering financially—two teams went bankrupt—and the NL and AL bought it out. However, the owner of the Baltimore Terrapins refused to agree to the settlement and went ahead with a previously filed antitrust lawsuit against the MLB.

But the most influential of these leagues may have actually been the one that never played a single game. The Continental League was founded at a time when many baseball fans felt neglected by existing leagues. From the end of the Federal League, in 1915, until 1961, there were no new major-league clubs added to either league, even though the U.S. was undergoing a dramatic demographic shift in population size and location. During the 1950s the Boston Braves, Brooklyn Dodgers, and New York Giants all moved west, to Milwaukee, Los Angeles, and San Francisco. This was particularly upsetting to New York City Mayor Robert Wagner, who wanted the NL to put a team in New York, which had suddenly dropped from hosting three teams to one. Wagner hired lawyer William Shea—the namesake of the Mets stadium—who then brought in baseball's entrepreneur extraordinaire, Branch Rickey, to oversee the formation of a new league. The Continental League would include eight teams, in Atlanta, Buffalo, Dallas, Denver, Houston, Minneapolis, New York, and Toronto. The goal of the Continental League was to expand into markets that MLB was neglecting; only New York hosted a major-league team at the time. Branch Rickey put a real scare into the dominant league, especially when he threatened to stock his rosters with its players. Rickey had been told he was wrong before, but he was proven right over and over again. MLB decided it was in its best interest to seek a deal with the Continental League, and the leagues expanded into four cites, three of which were hosting Continental League teams (New York, Houston, Minneapolis, plus Los Angeles).

Since its challenges, Major League Baseball seems to have learned its lesson; as the country has grown, so have the leagues. Baseball continued its expansion in 1969, 1977, 1993, and 1998, to reach its current size of thirty teams. Unlike its past expansions, no explicit external threat of entry was necessary to force the leagues to act. Although a few new leagues have been formed on paper, none have been taken seriously. MLB's failure to provide baseball to areas that could support it has proved to be costly to owners. Though only one of the leagues survived intact (AL), the rival leagues had a significant impact on the league we know today. Four current MLB franchises were once members of the American Association: Dodgers, Pirates, Reds, and Cardinals. Three cities gained major-league teams after pressure from the Federal League, and four cities gained teams due to pressure from the Continental League. In each instance where a league entered to compete with MLB, MLB revenues suffered. The lesson learned by the owners is that they must supply what the baseball fans want, or someone else will. And although MLB can weather the storm, it would prefer not to. The only way to prevent this pain is to respond quickly to provide baseball to fans willing to pay for it.

Because no rival league has put teams on the field since the Federal League folded in 1915, it seems hard for current fans to imagine the hidden competition MLB must address. But MLB's actions are consistent with the economic model of a contestable market, in which the threat of competition is sufficient to cause a single entity to properly supply the market. MLB has tried to act like a monopolist several times by shrinking its size or ignoring important markets, but in each instance a competing league has threatened to enter the market, inflicting financial losses on MLB owners. And MLB has always countered such a threat with expansion to meet unsatisfied consumer demand. Since the near entry of Branch Rickey's Continental League in 1960, MLB has actively sought potential markets to prevent any room for entry.

This buying up of baseball markets to prevent rival league entry may seem like monopoly behavior; however, what is harmful about monopoly behavior is not that competitors beat up on one another, but that a dominant supplier restricts the provision of its product to consumers. If MLB wants to hurt rival leagues by providing more baseball, then I am all for it! It is the ends, not the means, that economists care about in the allocation of goods and services from the competitive process. The same competitive pressures that drive competitive markets are still in place in contestable industries. Has the competitive pressure that fueled interleague baseball competition in the past evaporated, or does that competitive pressure lurk in the minds of owners, who fear the entry by a new outlaw league? The fear probably still lurks. We have plenty of rich men and women looking to be loved by baseball fans across the continent. I doubt that our current stock of eccentric wealthy egomaniacs could leave large quantities of money and public adoration alone. If MLB is acting as a monopoly, there is still a lot of money and love available for the taking. And I have a feeling that the current stock of owners who are members of this crowd are far more familiar with this threat than the average baseball fan realizes. Government intervention in the baseball market is unnecessary and might possibly do more harm than good.

As an economist, I marvel every day at the power of market forces in allocating resources in all kinds of markets. I can find no reason to believe that these market forces are doing anything but bringing fans the baseball we deserve . . . and we must have been awfully good.

Epilogue

*Under normal conditions the research scientist is not an innovator
but a solver of puzzles, and the puzzles upon which he concentrates
are just those which he believes can both be stated and solved within
the existing scientific tradition.*

—THOMAS KUHN

I CONSIDERED calling this book *An Economist Ruins Baseball*. After all, many people feel that economics really is dismal. However, I hope I have offered useful methods for understanding baseball on and off the field and demonstrated how satisfying and fun economics can be.

Applying my professional training to the game that I love has taught me new, unexpected lessons. Notions that I held about the game turned out to be false. I thought Leo Mazzone was overrated as a pitching coach and that batters protected one another in the lineup. I'm happy to have eliminated some of my ignorance.

One of my former professors once expressed to me his admiration for a book in which he disagreed with almost every single one of the author's conclusions. Why was he so fond of the book? The methods used by the author were right, so, because the conclusions reached were unsatisfying, my professor thought about the subject in new ways. The book forced him to examine why he thought the author was wrong and so helped him better understand the subject. Unsatisfying answers provide opportunities to expand knowledge. I hope that if you find any of my conclusions to be unsatisfying, this will motivate your search for better ones.

If you ever find yourself next to an economist at a social function,

ask what his or her hobbies are. I guarantee, within five minutes of discussing the topic, you'll learn about a puzzle or two and some satisfying, intriguing solutions. Whatever you do, don't ask about how to
invest your money, unless you want the economist to notice his drink
needs refilling. Economics furthers our understanding of important
topics in so many areas. But really, what could be more important than
baseball?

Acknowledgments

FIRST, I want to thank the many readers of my blog, *Sabernomics*, who have encouraged and challenged me over the past two years. Darren Viola at BaseballThinkFactory.com, David Pinto at BaseballMusings.com, and Mac Thomason at BravesJournal.com have provided other Internet forums to discuss and guide people to my work. The feedback has been helpful and kept me going.

This book would have been much more difficult without the availability of baseball data. The Lahman Baseball Archive (maintained by Sean Lahman) provides seasonal baseball statistics in a database format. The Retrosheet Project, which is maintained by David Smith but is the product of many volunteers, provided the historical play-by-play, game-by-game, and box score information. I think there are few people who have visited Baseball-Reference.com more than I have in the past two years. The site administrator, Sean Forman, has created the best baseball site on the web. I am grateful for Sean's efforts, and I can't wait to see what he has in store for the future as he sets his sights on making the site even better. Furthermore, Sean read parts of the manuscript and gave me several good suggestions.

I want to acknowledge and thank all of those people who helped me with this project in other ways. Some gave a lot, others a little, but I

appreciate all of the contributions. Jim Albert, Dave Berri, Andy Brad-
bury, Dennis Coates, Tom Coker, Tyler Cowen, Mark Crain, Craig
Depken, Heather Fain, David Gassko, Jahn Hakes, James Hall, Charlie
Hallman, Elizabeth Hamilton, Jill Hendrickson, Kevin Holman, Brad
Humphreys, Charles Israel, Dave Laband, Rich Lederer, Robert May-
hew, Chris McDonough, Jeff Merron, Jim Porter, Skip Sauer, Alan
Schwarz, Johnny Shoaf, Clay Shonkwiler, Bill Shughart, Frank Stephen-
son, Dave Studenmund, Greg Tamer, Todd Thrasher, and Bob Tollison.
Also, seminar participants with Clemson University, Wofford College,
Southern Economic Association, Western Economic Association, and
American Mathematical Society provided many helpful suggestions. I
thank John McArthur for his economic inspiration and for encouraging his sports economics students to find errors in the first edition of
this book.

I owe a huge debt of gratitude to Stephen Morrow, my editor. He
convinced me to write this book for Dutton, improved the manuscript
in ways that I never would have seen on my own, and handled the bu-
reaucratic tasks to make life much simpler for me. It's been an absolute
pleasure to work with him. I also want to thank my publicist, Beth
Parker, and the rest of the folks at Dutton who contributed to the book.

This project would not have happened without my crossing paths
with Doug Drinen five years ago, when we both joined the faculty at the
University of the South. Though Doug is a mathematician, he's a natural economist and an avid sports fan. He runs the best football statistics
site on the web (Pro-Football-Reference.com) and happens to own a
complete collection of *The Bill James Baseball Abstracts.* We spent many
lunches discussing sports, politics, and life. I didn't know how many
undiscovered questions existed in sports until we met. We challenged
each other's ideas, and he corrected many of my mistaken notions. He
helped me develop the ideas in the book, and several of the chapters
are the product of joint research projects. Though he has not read the
entire manuscript, no idea here is new to him. Additionally, he taught
me several useful computer skills for organizing data, and in some instances he did the computer work for me. Doug is also a good friend,
and I miss our weekly lunches, summer research projects, and Sunday

football watching now that I have moved to Kennesaw State University. Though our research continues at a distance, it is not as enjoyable.

There is no way I could have completed this project without my loving wife, Rachael, who gave time so that I could write. She also provided plenty of encouragement and offered many valuable suggestions. Our three-year-old daughter, Rebekah, continues to be a constant source of inspiration. My in-laws contributed good advice and encouragement.

My mother and father, both former journalists, gave me plenty of suggestions, though their moral support was much more important. They spent many hours taking me to Little League practices and games, which helped build my passion for baseball. My father shared his childhood stories of going to Yankee Stadium to watch Yogi Berra and Mickey Mantle. And, most importantly, he sympathized with the pain felt by a ten-year-old who struck out at every trip to the plate; he made time for extra practice to teach me how to hit well enough to make the All-Star team. We tend to like the things we are good at; if it were not for my father's persistence, I don't think I'd care much for baseball today, which is why I dedicate this book to him.

A Simple Guide to
Multiple Regression Analysis

WHAT DO YOU do if you want to know the impact of one event on an observed outcome, but the factor to be explained results from several potential explanatory factors? Disentangling the responsibility of different factors in the real world is virtually impossible without the aid of certain statistical tools. In the physical sciences, holding constant, or controlling for, the influence of factors is often done in a laboratory. For example, a physicist who wants to know how a baseball behaves absent the friction of the atmosphere could place a baseball inside a vacuum—thereby removing the atmosphere entirely—and run experiments. The economist who studies human behavior doesn't normally have the opportunity to run such controlled experiments. We have to observe individuals going about their daily lives and attempt to make them comparable through statistical tools. Multiple regression analysis is one such tool. A spreadsheet program like Microsoft Excel can run a basic regression.[88]

Let's assume that we want to figure out the impact of years of schooling on the annual income of workers. We take an unbiased sample of workers, meaning we don't want to accidently pick workers of a certain type, and look at the education and incomes of these individuals. Figure 20 maps the income and years of schooling of a sample of fifteen workers in a scatterplot. Fifteen is a far smaller sample than we would like—typically, samples of thirty or larger are best, with more observations preferred to fewer—but lowering the number for this example makes the analysis easier to see graphically. Each point represents an individual according to these two characteristics. We often refer to the

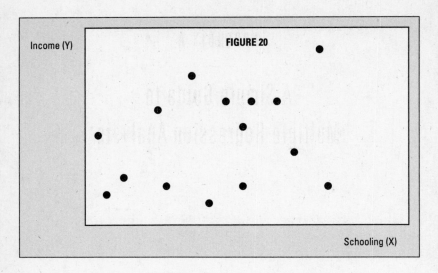

characteristics of observations as *variables,* because the characteristics vary among those in the sample.

From eyeballing the figure, there appears to be a slight upward trend in the relationship between education and income, but the relationship is far from perfect. There are plenty of wealthy people without high school diplomas, just as there are many Ph.D.s living on modest means. However, the characteristics tend to move in the same direction. If more educated individuals tended to earn less income than those with less education, this would be a negative, or inverse, correlation. In that case, the points would form a pattern that would slope down toward the southeast corner of the diagram.

Knowing that there is a positive correlation between two variables is useful, but it doesn't really provide much information. We would like to know two further bits of information: magnitude and certainty. How big an effect does an additional year of education have on schooling? $100, $1,000, $10,000, or some other amount? And once we estimate a magnitude, how confident are we in this estimate given the range of other possible estimates? For example, should we give or take $50 or $500? What we can do to answer this question is to estimate a *regression line* through the points to predict an average impact of education on earnings. A common technique for generating a regression line from the data is *ordinary least squares* (OLS). The method calculates the average distance from the observed values to many hypothetical predicted relationships between variables and then "picks" the line that minimizes the sum of the squared errors in prediction.

Figure 21 adds an OLS estimated regression line to the scatterplot of worker income and schooling. The vertical distance between the line and the actual points shows the individual prediction mistakes, or *residuals.* Squaring the pre-

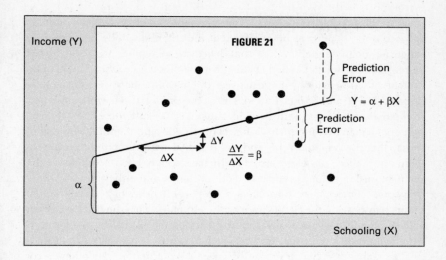

diction errors of all observations and adding them together will yield a number lower than any other hypothetical line drawn through these points. Squaring the errors serves two valuable functions: it counts positive and negative errors equally, and bigger errors receive greater weight. Because this is a linear function, it can be expressed in a simple formula, which many of us probably remember from middle school: $Y = mX + b;$ where m is the slope of the line— remember rise-over-run $(\Delta Y/\Delta X)$—and b is the Y-intercept. In this example, the Y-variable, or the explained variable, is income, and the X-variable is schooling, which is an explanatory variable. Econometricians typically use a different notation—replacing the slope m with β and the Y-intercept b with α— so that $Y = \alpha + \beta X$.

The slope of the line, β, is the estimated magnitude of the effect of schooling on income. Every one-unit increase in X is associated with a β-unit change in Y. Thus, for this example, every additional year of schooling is associated with a $\$\beta$ increase in income. The Y-intercept, α, accounts for all of the factors that are not included in the regression equation. In a properly specified regression model, the factors are random and will cancel out.

The magnitude of the β estimate—also known as a regression coefficient— is important, but so is the confidence we have in it. Regression procedures, such as OLS, pick the intercept and slope that minimize prediction mistakes from a range of possible β values; but, given the dispersion of the data, the estimates may not be precise. Therefore, we also want information on the spread of the range of estimates, known as a confidence interval. Even though a β coefficient is positive or negative, there might not be a relationship between education and income; therefore, the β we observe is just an artifact of random fluctuations in the data. For example, if we estimate $\beta = \$2,500$, what is the range of this possible relationship? The commonly preferred range of estimates is based on a 95 percent probability that the true magnitude lies within the range; although, higher levels of confidence are sometimes preferred. For example, if there is a 95 percent chance that the range lies within $1,000 of the estimate, then we can say that each year of education increases education by between $1,500 and $3,500. Can we say for certain that this correlation is positive? No, but we have a pretty good idea that it is. Because there is less than a 5 percent chance that the relationship between education and income is zero, we say that the relationship is positive. If the 95 percent confidence interval lies entirely above or below zero, then we have a high level of confidence that the relationship is not a product of random chance and is therefore *statistically significant*.[89] Oftentimes, researchers will report t-statistics or z-statistics so that others may observe the significance of the estimates. These metrics are generated from the coefficient's standard errors of the estimates. As a rule of thumb, t-statistics and z-statistics greater than two are statistically significant.

The main advantage of regression analysis is not that we can generate correlations between two variables. The most useful aspect of this method to the social scientist is its ability to accommodate more than one explanatory factor. By including other important determinants of an explained variable, we can know the added, or marginal, impact that each explanatory variable has on the value of the explained variable. This impact is separate, or in addition to, the other factors included in the analysis.

In the analysis of income and education, we implicitly assume that all other possible explanatory influences are random and cancel out, but do they? Obviously, there are more factors than years of education that determine the incomes of workers, such as natural intelligence (IQ), work ethic, field of study, location, and physical attractiveness—just to name a few. The problem is that some excluded characteristics may, in fact, be correlated with education. For example, we expect people with high intelligence to continue to get more education than those who are not so gifted. If this occurs, then the β estimate of education may actually be picking up a correlation between income and intelligence. Education might actually not be as important as natural ability, but because we did not include a measure of worker intelligence in the model, it will look like education is a greater determinant of income than it actually is.

This problem is known as *omitted variable bias*, and it occurs when non-random outside factors not included in the regression estimation are correlated with explanatory variables that are included in the regression estimation. This can create serious problems; therefore the empirical researcher must be very careful to include all relevant factors in the regression. OLS allows us to control for the influence of other factors by including many relevant factors in the model. For example, if we had an IQ test score of every worker in the sample, we could estimate the marginal impacts of both factors on income. Our equation would be: Income $= \alpha + \beta_1$Schooling $+ \beta_2$IQ. β_1 and β_2 are individual estimated magnitudes for each factor, and each factor's weight takes into account the impact of the other factor.

How does this work? It involves a complicated mathematical procedure—which, thankfully, computers can do in a matter of seconds—that examines how *all* of the explained and explanatory variables differ across the sample. But it's easier to understand if you think about it like this: Let's say we were able to group every worker in our sample by number of years of schooling. We could then look at the income of the members of each group (e.g., twelve years, thirteen years, etc.) as their IQs differed. Because the education level remains constant, we can assign a weight to the importance of IQ without having the education level confuse our estimate. Similarly, we could group every worker in the sample by IQ. Then we could look at whether each additional year of schooling impacted income while holding IQ constant. OLS, and other multiple regression analysis procedures are able to hold constant numerous factors and assign marginal impacts to each.

Another useful result from multiple regression analysis is that we can see how much the explanatory factors influence the explained factors. When OLS minimizes the sum of squared errors, it generates useful information that tells us how well the model "fits" the data. The smaller the errors in prediction, the more the difference in the explained variable is explained by the explanatory variables. The measure of fit generated by OLS is the R^2, or "R-squared." The R^2 ranges from 0 to 1 and can be understood as a percentage. As the R^2 approaches 1, the fit of the model improves. For example, assume that our hypothetical model estimating income from schooling and IQ has an R^2 of 0.75. This means that 75 percent percent of the differences in incomes across these workers is explained by difference in education and IQ.

Multiple regression analysis allows the empirical researcher to control for, or hold constant, many possible influences on an observed outcome. This is valuable because is enables the researcher to isolate individual impacts among many concurrent determinants. The multiple regression analysis estimator OLS is just one of many possible estimators; however, it is the estimator most commonly employed by economists. But all of the alternative procedures share the ability to hold multiple factors constant.

This appendix is only an introduction to the subject. Using regression analysis requires understanding issues beyond what can be provided in this mini-primer.

Baseball Statistics Glossary

Batting Average (AVG): Number of hits divided by number of at-bats.

Batting Average on Balls in Play (BABIP): The number of hits less the number of home runs divided by the number of at-bats less the number of home runs less the number of strikeouts.

Earned Run Average (ERA): Earned runs allowed divided by innings pitched multiplied by nine.

ERA+: A measure of ERA expressed in terms of the run production of the league and the home park in which the pitcher pitches. A league-average pitcher has an ERA+ of 100. A better (worse) pitcher has an ERA+ above (below) 100. *The metric is available for all players at Baseball-Reference.com.*

Fielding Independent Pitching (FIP): Thirteen times home runs, plus three times walks minus two times strikeouts, all divided by innings pitched, and add 3.2. *A metric that generates an ERA using only defense independent statistics. Some versions exclude hit batters and use a different constant. It is a simplified version of Voros McCracken's DIPS ERA developed by Tom Tango.*

Home Runs per 9 Innings (HR9): Home runs divided by innings pitched multiplied by nine.

Isolated Power (Iso-Power): Slugging percentage minus batting average.

Linear Weights (LWTS): $(0.46 \times \text{Singles}) + (0.8 \times \text{Doubles}) + (1.02 \times \text{Triples}) + (1.4 \times \text{Home Runs}) + (0.33 \times \text{Walks}) + (0.33 \times \text{Hit by Pitch}) + (0.3 \times \text{Stolen Bases}) - (0.6 \times \text{Caught Stealing}) - (0.25 \times (\text{At-Bats} - \text{Hits}))$. *A metric developed by John Thorn and Pete Palmer that weights each offensive event according to its run production value.*

On-Base Percentage (OBP): The sum of hits, walks, and hit by pitches divided by the sum of at-bats, walks, hit by pitches, and sacrifice flies.

OPS: The sum of on-base percentage and slugging percentage. *A metric developed by John Thorn and Pete Palmer that correlates well with Linear Weights but is much simpler to calculate.*

OPS+: A measure of OPS expressed in terms of the run production of the league and the home park in which the hitter plays. A league-average hitter has an OPS+ of 100. A better (worse) hitter has an OPS+ above (below) 100. *The metric is available for all players at Baseball-Reference.com.*

PrOPS: PrOPS is an OPS predicted by how a player hits the ball. It includes a player's drive percentage, groundball-to-flyball ratio, strikeout rate, walk rate, hit batter rate, and home run rate. A player with a PrOPS greater (less) than his OPS is likely to improve (decline). *The author developed this metric in conjunction with* The Hardball Times, *and it is available on their website (hardballtimes.com).*

Pythagorean Winning Percentage: The square of runs scored divided by the sum of the squares of runs scored and runs allowed. *A hypothetical winning percentage based on the runs scored and allowed by a team. The original metric was developed by Bill James, and several slight modifications to the formula exist.*

Slugging Percentage (SLG): Singles plus two times doubles, plus three times triples, plus four times home runs, divided by at-bats. *A batting average that weights each hit equal to the number of bases the hitter advances.*

Strikeouts per 9 Innings (K9): Strikeouts divided by innings pitched multiplied by nine.

Strikeout-to-Walk Ratio (K/BB): Strikeouts divided by walks.

Walks per 9 Innings (BB9): Walks divided by innings pitched multiplied by nine.

APPENDIX C

—

Useful Websites

Statistics

The Baseball Cube: TheBaseballCube.com

Baseball-Reference: Baseball-Reference.com

First Inning: FirstInning.com

The Hardball Times: HardballTimes.com

The Lahman Baseball Database: Baseball1.com

Retrosheet: Retrosheet.org

Analysis

Baseball Analysts: BaseballAnalysts.com

Baseball Musings: BaseballMusings.com

Baseball Prospectus: BaseballProspectus.com

The Hardball Times: HardballTimes.com

Sabernomics.com (my favorite!): Sabernomics.com

The Sports Economist: thesportseconomist.com

Player Values

Season RS: Runs scored by the team if the player had 100 percent of the plate appearances for the team in the season.

Season RA: Runs allowed by the team if the player had 100 percent of the innings pitched for the team in the season.

%PA: The percentage of the team's plate appearances made by the player.

%IP: The percentage of the team's innings pitched made by the player.

RSAA: Runs scored above what the average player with the same percentage of plate appearances would have produced.

RABA: Runs scored below what the average player with the same percentage of innings pitched would have produced.

$ValAA: Dollar value above what the average player would have produced given the same %PA or %IP.

MRP: The gross marginal revenue product of the player, which is the dollar value (in millions) of what the player is worth to the team in generating revenue. In a competitive market for talent, player wages should equal the gross MRP minus the marginal resource cost of putting the player on the field (i.e., training and equipment costs). The 2006 and 2007 values are based on an estimated 10 percent annual growth rate in revenue from 2005.

MRP Estimates for Hitters (2005)

ARIZONA DIAMONDBACKS

Player	Season RS	%PA	RSAA	$ValAA	MRP
Troy Glaus	969.79	10.02%	23.57	$3.35	$8.81
Chad Tracy	1007.28	8.74%	23.83	$3.39	$8.15
Luis Gonzalez	877.24	10.62%	15.15	$2.07	$7.86
Shawn Green	873.87	10.37%	14.44	$1.96	$7.62
Tony Clark	1165.04	6.21%	26.74	$3.85	$7.24
Craig Counsell	695.24	10.59%	-4.17	-$0.52	$5.26
Royce Clayton	566.30	9.06%	-15.24	-$1.77	$3.17
Jose Cruz	783.24	3.87%	1.88	$0.24	$2.35
Alex Cintron	607.31	5.50%	-7.00	-$0.85	$2.15
Chris Snyder	420.26	5.90%	-18.53	-$2.11	$1.10
Kelly Stinnett	668.57	2.26%	-1.49	-$0.19	$1.04
Luis Terrero	553.01	2.91%	-5.28	-$0.65	$0.94
Quinton McCracken	459.53	3.89%	-10.69	-$1.28	$0.84
Conor Jackson	445.42	1.56%	-4.52	-$0.56	$0.29
Koyie Hill	420.24	1.44%	-4.52	-$0.56	$0.23
Andy Green	529.85	0.62%	-1.26	-$0.16	$0.18
Matt Kata	479.84	0.60%	-1.53	-$0.19	$0.14
Scott Hairston	-395.73	0.32%	-3.57	-$0.44	-$0.27

ATLANTA BRAVES

Player	Season RS	%PA	RSAA	$ValAA	MRP
Andruw Jones	1008.97	10.86%	29.81	$4.36	$10.28
Chipper Jones	1166.96	6.98%	30.19	$4.42	$8.23
Marcus Giles	875.61	10.57%	14.91	$2.03	$7.79
Rafael Furcal	774.70	11.14%	4.47	$0.58	$6.65
Adam LaRoche	735.89	8.12%	0.11	$0.01	$4.44
Jeff Francoeur	934.29	4.43%	8.85	$1.17	$3.58
Ryan Langerhans	770.43	6.03%	2.16	$0.28	$3.56
Wilson Betemit	817.82	4.43%	3.69	$0.47	$2.89
Julio Franco	812.07	4.28%	3.32	$0.43	$2.76
Kelly Johnson	683.28	5.40%	-2.77	-$0.34	$2.60
Johnny Estrada	544.08	6.19%	-11.80	-$1.40	$1.98
Brian McCann	719.77	3.30%	-0.49	-$0.06	$1.74
Pete Orr	658.18	2.62%	-2.00	-$0.25	$1.18
Brian Jordan	473.22	4.06%	-10.61	-$1.27	$0.95
Raul Mondesi	439.02	2.51%	-7.41	-$0.90	$0.47
Eddie Perez	423.05	0.63%	-1.96	-$0.25	$0.10
Todd Hollandsworth	285.11	0.65%	-2.91	-$0.36	-$0.01
Brayan Pena	25.05	0.65%	-4.59	-$0.57	-$0.21
Andy Marte	71.19	1.07%	-7.08	-$0.86	-$0.28

BALTIMORE ORIOLES

Player	Season RS	%PA	RSAA	$ValAA	MRP
Brian Roberts	1170.08	10.43%	39.97	$6.11	$11.80
Miguel Tejada	1048.64	11.48%	30.03	$4.39	$10.65
Melvin Mora	968.24	10.82%	19.62	$2.73	$8.64
Jay Gibbons	945.41	8.44%	13.38	$1.81	$6.41
Rafael Palmeiro	892.40	6.88%	7.25	$0.95	$4.70
Javy Lopez	856.68	6.90%	4.80	$0.62	$4.38
Luis Matos	760.93	7.06%	-1.84	-$0.23	$3.62
Sammy Sosa	624.00	6.91%	-11.27	-$1.34	$2.43
Chris Gomez	768.51	4.14%	-0.77	-$0.10	$2.16
Sal Fasano	851.01	2.84%	1.82	$0.23	$1.78
Larry Bigbie	682.27	3.81%	-4.00	-$0.49	$1.59
B. J. Surhoff	547.66	5.23%	-12.53	-$1.48	$1.37
Bernie Castro	784.22	1.45%	-0.04	-$0.01	$0.79
David Newhan	456.69	4.06%	-13.41	-$1.57	$0.64
Eli Marrero	831.58	0.91%	0.41	$0.05	$0.55
Walter Young	977.89	0.60%	1.15	$0.15	$0.48
Alejandro Freire	634.96	1.17%	-1.78	-$0.22	$0.42
Eddie Rogers	9391.88	0.02%	1.40	$0.18	$0.19
Jeff Fiorentino	542.85	0.77%	-1.87	-$0.23	$0.18
Ramon Nivar	700.52	0.24%	-0.21	-$0.03	$0.11
Eric Byrnes	328.83	2.95%	-13.52	-$1.59	$0.02
Keith Reed	430.81	0.10%	-0.35	-$0.04	$0.01
Eli Whiteside	253.54	0.20%	-1.04	-$0.13	-$0.02
Napoleon Calzado	3.50	0.08%	-0.64	-$0.08	-$0.04
Midre Cummings	-996.65	0.03%	-0.58	-$0.07	-$0.06
Geronimo Gil	267.77	2.18%	-11.34	-$1.35	-$0.16

BOSTON RED SOX

Player	Season RS	%PA	RSAA	$ValAA	MRP
David Ortiz	1265.85	11.14%	53.32	$8.63	$14.70
Manny Ramirez	1221.41	10.15%	44.10	$6.87	$12.40
Johnny Damon	898.87	10.74%	12.02	$1.61	$7.47
Jason Varitek	982.55	8.42%	16.46	$2.26	$6.85
Bill Mueller	892.69	9.21%	9.74	$1.29	$6.32
Edgar Renteria	716.36	10.81%	-7.64	-$0.93	$4.97
Trot Nixon	884.18	7.34%	7.13	$0.94	$4.94
Kevin Millar	796.23	8.11%	0.75	$0.09	$4.51
Tony Graffanino	895.89	3.12%	3.40	$0.44	$2.14
Mark Bellhorn	654.25	5.23%	-6.95	-$0.85	$2.01
John Olerud	851.33	3.00%	1.93	$0.25	$1.88
Kevin Youkilis	942.55	1.48%	2.31	$0.30	$1.10
Jay Payton	720.86	2.25%	-1.49	-$0.19	$1.04
Doug Mirabelli	682.95	2.37%	-2.47	-$0.31	$0.99

(continued)

MRP Estimates for Hitters (2005) (continued)

Player	Season RS	%PA	RSAA	$ValAA	MRP
Alex Cora	655.21	1.81%	-2.39	-$0.30	$0.69
Roberto Petagine	880.77	0.56%	0.53	$0.07	$0.37
AGabe Kapler	498.09	1.62%	-4.69	-$0.58	$0.31
David McCarty	1896.63	0.09%	1.04	$0.13	$0.18
Adam Hyzdu	588.99	0.28%	-0.56	-$0.07	$0.08
Jose Cruz	547.33	0.20%	-0.49	-$0.06	$0.05
Alejandro Machado	735.24	0.09%	-0.05	-$0.01	$0.04
Shawn Wooten	-927.58	0.02%	-0.27	-$0.03	-$0.03
Hanley Ramirez	-927.58	0.03%	-0.54	-$0.07	-$0.05
Adam Stern	188.83	0.25%	-1.49	-$0.19	-$0.05
Ramon Vazquez	155.11	1.03%	-6.51	-$0.79	-$0.23
Kelly Shoppach	-741.16	0.25%	-3.82	-$0.47	-$0.34

CHICAGO CUBS

Player	Season RS	%PA	RSAA	$ValAA	MRP
Derrek Lee	1396.86	11.22%	74.30	$13.06	$19.18
Aramis Ramirez	1059.91	8.22%	26.73	$3.85	$8.33
Jeromy Burnitz	731.72	10.89%	-0.31	-$0.04	$5.90
Michael Barrett	873.60	7.74%	10.77	$1.44	$5.66
Todd Walker	893.88	7.03%	11.20	$1.50	$5.33
Neifi Perez	572.79	9.89%	-16.00	-$1.85	$3.54
Jerry Hairston	660.62	6.98%	-5.16	-$0.63	$3.17
Matt Murton	1066.63	2.60%	8.63	$1.14	$2.56
Nomar Garciaparra	753.30	4.01%	0.75	$0.10	$2.28
Todd Hollandsworth	590.06	4.71%	-6.81	-$0.83	$1.74
Corey Patterson	383.60	7.81%	-27.41	-$2.96	$1.29
Jason Dubois	695.59	2.47%	-0.96	-$0.12	$1.22
Henry Blanco	554.68	2.89%	-5.20	-$0.64	$0.94
Ronny Cedeno	733.13	1.45%	-0.02	$0.00	$0.79
Jose Macias	390.19	3.08%	-10.62	-$1.27	$0.41
Matt Lawton	420.29	1.35%	-4.24	-$0.52	$0.21
Ben Grieve	654.48	0.41%	-0.33	-$0.04	$0.18
Mike Fontenot	833.16	0.08%	0.08	$0.01	$0.05
Geovany Soto	-956.47	0.02%	-0.27	-$0.03	-$0.03
Scott McClain	147.37	0.26%	-1.53	-$0.19	-$0.05
Ryan Theriot	68.40	0.23%	-1.51	-$0.19	-$0.07
Enrique Wilson	139.25	0.41%	-2.42	-$0.30	-$0.08
Jody Gerut	-158.43	0.26%	-2.32	-$0.29	-$0.15

CHICAGO WHITE SOX

Player	Season RS	%PA	RSAA	$ValAA	MRP
Paul Konerko	1062.32	10.81%	29.75	$4.35	$10.24
Jermaine Dye	905.00	9.42%	11.12	$1.49	$6.62
Tadahito Iguchi	809.49	9.45%	2.12	$0.27	$5.43
Aaron Rowand	719.46	10.41%	-7.04	-$0.86	$4.82
Carl Everett	711.88	8.90%	-6.69	-$0.82	$4.04
Scott Podsednik	687.87	9.24%	-9.16	-$1.10	$3.94
Joe Crede	719.60	7.66%	-5.17	-$0.64	$3.54
A. J. Pierzynski	680.31	8.09%	-8.63	-$1.04	$3.37
Juan Uribe	644.21	8.79%	-12.55	-$1.48	$3.31
Frank Thomas	978.12	2.02%	3.86	$0.50	$1.60
Pablo Ozuna	547.09	3.53%	-8.47	-$1.02	$0.90
Chris Widger	584.03	2.51%	-5.09	-$0.63	$0.74
Willie Harris	580.09	2.26%	-4.68	-$0.58	$0.66
Joe Borchard	1265.18	0.20%	0.93	$0.12	$0.23
Timo Perez	352.62	3.19%	-13.86	-$1.62	$0.12
Pedro Lopez	394.38	0.13%	-0.51	-$0.06	$0.01
Jamie Burke	-909.57	0.02%	-0.28	-$0.03	-$0.03
Raul Casanova	3.19	0.08%	-0.64	-$0.08	-$0.04
Brian N. Anderson	233.25	0.57%	-3.15	-$0.39	-$0.08
Geoff Blum	218.50	1.61%	-9.16	-$1.10	-$0.22
Ross Gload	39.90	0.72%	-5.35	-$0.66	-$0.27

CINCINNATI REDS

Player	Season RS	%PA	RSAA	$ValAA	MRP
Adam Dunn	1049.24	10.62%	33.41	$4.96	$10.75
Ken Griffey	1056.34	8.78%	28.25	$4.10	$8.89
Felipe Lopez	863.20	10.25%	13.19	$1.78	$7.37
Sean Casey	818.49	9.29%	7.79	$1.02	$6.09
Jason LaRue	816.42	6.68%	5.46	$0.71	$4.35
Joe Randa	882.26	5.82%	8.60	$1.14	$4.31
Rich Aurilia	756.77	7.41%	1.64	$0.21	$4.25
Austin Kearns	754.04	7.09%	1.38	$0.18	$4.04
Ryan Freel	735.74	6.82%	0.08	$0.01	$3.73
Javier Valentin	946.77	4.02%	8.53	$1.13	$3.32
Wily Mo Pena	737.48	5.30%	0.15	$0.02	$2.91
Edwin Encarnacion	657.52	3.70%	-2.85	-$0.36	$1.66
Jacob Cruz	661.94	2.29%	-1.67	-$0.21	$1.04
Chris Denorfia	792.68	0.70%	0.40	$0.05	$0.43
D'Angelo Jimenez	466.38	1.88%	-5.05	-$0.62	$0.41
Jason Romano	781.84	0.54%	0.25	$0.03	$0.33
Ray Olmedo	428.86	1.39%	-4.26	-$0.53	$0.23
Aaron Holbert	444.62	0.51%	-1.47	-$0.18	$0.09
Kenny Kelly	566.85	0.14%	-0.24	-$0.03	$0.05

(continued)

MRP Estimates for Hitters (2005) (*continued*)

Player	Season RS	%PA	RSAA	$ValAA	MRP
Luis Lopez	330.02	0.44%	-1.79	-$0.22	$0.02
Andy Machado	-911.36	0.03%	-0.52	-$0.07	-$0.05
Dane Sardinha	-911.36	0.05%	-0.78	-$0.10	-$0.07
Miguel Perez	-911.36	0.05%	-0.78	-$0.10	-$0.07
William Bergolla	-327.85	0.60%	-6.39	-$0.78	-$0.45

CLEVELAND INDIANS

Player	Season RS	%PA	RSAA	$ValAA	MRP
Travis Hafner	1379.84	9.24%	54.78	$8.92	$13.96
Victor Martinez	1067.81	9.94%	27.92	$4.05	$9.47
Grady Sizemore	988.77	11.29%	22.77	$3.22	$9.37
Jhonny Peralta	1108.48	9.11%	29.29	$4.27	$9.24
Coco Crisp	944.31	10.49%	16.50	$2.27	$7.98
Ron Belliard	851.44	9.38%	6.05	$0.79	$5.90
Casey Blake	777.08	9.32%	-0.93	-$0.12	$4.96
Ben Broussard	819.45	8.07%	2.62	$0.34	$4.74
Aaron Boone	641.39	9.03%	-13.15	-$1.55	$3.38
Jody Gerut	823.20	2.51%	0.91	$0.12	$1.48
Jose Hernandez	496.38	4.09%	-11.90	-$1.41	$0.82
Ryan Ludwick	991.49	0.77%	1.57	$0.20	$0.62
Jason Dubois	603.35	0.80%	-1.47	-$0.18	$0.25
Ramon Vazquez	662.92	0.42%	-0.52	-$0.06	$0.16
Josh Bard	353.36	1.52%	-6.59	-$0.80	$0.02
Franklin Gutierrez	605.76	0.03%	-0.06	-$0.01	$0.01
Alex Cora	321.19	2.51%	-11.69	-$1.39	-$0.02
Ryan Garko	-996.65	0.02%	-0.29	-$0.04	-$0.03
Juan Gonzalez	-996.65	0.02%	-0.29	-$0.04	-$0.03
Jeff Liefer	191.17	0.91%	-5.43	-$0.67	-$0.17
Brandon Phillips	-996.65	0.14%	-2.57	-$0.32	-$0.24

COLORADO ROCKIES

Player	Season RS	%PA	RSAA	$ValAA	MRP
Todd Helton	1129.26	10.04%	39.61	$6.05	$11.52
Matt Holliday	862.87	8.43%	10.82	$1.44	$6.04
Garrett Atkins	707.13	9.19%	-2.52	-$0.31	$4.69
Luis A. Gonzalez	660.35	7.07%	-5.25	-$0.64	$3.21
Cory Sullivan	636.54	6.80%	-6.67	-$0.81	$2.89
Clint Barmes	673.03	6.04%	-3.72	-$0.46	$2.83
Brad Hawpe	681.81	5.63%	-2.97	-$0.37	$2.70
Preston Wilson	736.62	4.75%	0.10	$0.01	$2.60
Dustan Mohr	587.64	4.70%	-6.90	-$0.84	$1.72

(*continued*)

MRP Estimates for Hitters (2005) (*continued*)

Player	Season RS	%PA	RSAA	$ValAA	MRP
Jorge Piedra	974.44	1.99%	4.77	$0.62	$1.70
Aaron Miles	490.18	5.56%	-13.60	-$1.60	$1.44
Ryan Shealy	953.31	1.67%	3.65	$0.47	$1.38
J. D. Closser	542.31	4.36%	-8.39	-$1.01	$1.36
Danny Ardoin	537.55	3.98%	-7.83	-$0.95	$1.22
Eddy Garabito	762.59	1.64%	0.46	$0.06	$0.95
Todd Greene	616.75	2.15%	-2.53	-$0.32	$0.86
Desi Relaford	442.90	3.82%	-11.13	-$1.32	$0.76
Michael Restovich	760.72	0.55%	0.14	$0.02	$0.32
Jeff Baker	540.81	0.69%	-1.34	-$0.17	$0.21
Choo Freeman	483.34	0.35%	-0.89	-$0.11	$0.08
Ryan Spilborghs	1225.06	0.06%	0.31	$0.04	$0.07
Alfredo Amezaga	531.74	0.05%	-0.10	-$0.01	$0.01
Tim Olson	33.75	0.05%	-0.34	-$0.04	-$0.02
Eric Byrnes	238.71	0.96%	-4.77	-$0.59	-$0.06
Larry Bigbie	215.44	1.12%	-5.83	-$0.71	-$0.10
Omar Quintanilla	226.92	2.29%	-11.64	-$1.38	-$0.13
Andy Machado	-444.75	0.21%	-2.46	-$0.31	-$0.19

DETROIT TIGERS

Player	Season RS	%PA	RSAA	$ValAA	MRP
Chris Shelton	1028.60	7.03%	16.97	$2.34	$6.17
Brandon Inge	779.76	11.31%	-0.82	-$0.10	$6.06
Craig Monroe	801.11	10.15%	1.43	$0.18	$5.72
Placido Polanco	1023.00	6.16%	14.54	$1.98	$5.34
Dmitri Young	854.20	8.28%	5.56	$0.72	$5.24
Rondell White	955.14	6.52%	10.96	$1.46	$5.02
Carlos Guillen	924.41	5.88%	8.08	$1.06	$4.27
Magglio Ordonez	897.55	5.59%	6.18	$0.81	$3.85
Ivan Rodriguez	701.34	8.56%	-7.33	-$0.89	$3.77
Carlos Pena	865.94	4.81%	3.80	$0.49	$3.11
Curtis Granderson	859.80	2.84%	2.06	$0.26	$1.81
Nook Logan	560.09	5.80%	-13.17	-$1.55	$1.61
Omar Infante	455.55	7.07%	-23.45	-$2.60	$1.26
Marcus Thames	559.98	1.92%	-4.37	-$0.54	$0.51
John McDonald	556.22	1.27%	-2.93	-$0.37	$0.33
Vance Wilson	376.25	2.82%	-11.58	-$1.37	$0.16
Ramon Martinez	458.41	1.01%	-3.32	-$0.41	$0.14
Alexis Gomez	220.91	0.29%	-1.66	-$0.21	-$0.05
Kevin Hooper	3.36	0.11%	-0.89	-$0.11	-$0.05
Tony Giarratano	132.61	0.77%	-5.01	-$0.62	-$0.20
Jason Smith	144.46	1.03%	-6.60	-$0.80	-$0.24
Bobby Higginson	-481.91	0.44%	-5.58	-$0.68	-$0.44

FLORIDA MARLINS

Player	Season RS	%PA	RSAA	$ValAA	MRP
Miguel Cabrera	1215.27	11.03%	53.00	$8.56	$14.57
Carlos Delgado	1296.61	9.91%	55.72	$9.11	$14.51
Juan Encarnacion	892.40	9.06%	14.30	$1.94	$6.88
Luis Castillo	897.28	8.43%	13.72	$1.86	$6.46
Juan Pierre	653.09	11.56%	-9.42	-$1.13	$5.17
Jeff Conine	895.75	6.18%	9.96	$1.32	$4.69
Paul Lo Duca	724.80	7.98%	-0.78	-$0.10	$4.25
Alex Gonzalez	653.82	7.69%	-6.21	-$0.76	$3.43
Mike Lowell	573.95	8.98%	-14.43	-$1.68	$3.21
Damion Easley	726.49	4.89%	-0.40	-$0.05	$2.62
Lenny Harris	948.95	1.26%	2.69	$0.34	$1.03
Jeremy Hermida	1338.56	0.76%	4.57	$0.59	$1.00
Matt Treanor	404.93	2.48%	-8.17	-$0.99	$0.36
Josh Willingham	902.64	0.45%	0.76	$0.10	$0.34
Chris Aguila	349.29	1.30%	-5.02	-$0.62	$0.09
Mike Mordecai	-1027.70	0.03%	-0.57	-$0.07	-$0.05
Josh Wilson	-85.82	0.18%	-1.45	-$0.18	-$0.09
Robert Andino	206.14	0.80%	-4.25	-$0.53	-$0.09
Ryan Jorgensen	-1027.70	0.06%	-1.13	-$0.14	-$0.11
Joe Dillon	145.87	0.63%	-3.70	-$0.46	-$0.12

HOUSTON ASTROS

Player	Season RS	%PA	RSAA	$ValAA	MRP
Morgan Ensberg	1165.98	10.16%	43.85	$6.82	$12.36
Lance Berkman	1178.30	9.20%	40.84	$6.27	$11.29
Craig Biggio	817.83	10.60%	8.83	$1.17	$6.95
Jason Lane	843.77	9.14%	9.98	$1.33	$6.31
Willy Taveras	600.60	10.34%	-13.86	-$1.62	$4.02
Brad Ausmus	664.07	7.35%	-5.18	-$0.64	$3.37
Adam Everett	532.06	9.69%	-19.63	-$2.22	$3.06
Orlando Palmeiro	804.68	3.76%	2.64	$0.34	$2.39
Mike Lamb	608.46	5.68%	-7.17	-$0.87	$2.23
Chris Burke	596.60	5.85%	-8.07	-$0.98	$2.21
Jeff Bagwell	768.49	2.00%	0.68	$0.09	$1.18
Jose Vizcaino	513.79	3.34%	-7.37	-$0.90	$0.92
Eric Bruntlett	622.01	1.97%	-2.22	-$0.28	$0.80
Luke Scott	338.45	1.45%	-5.74	-$0.70	$0.09
Todd Self	318.68	0.80%	-3.32	-$0.41	$0.02
Charles Gipson	252.56	0.23%	-1.10	-$0.14	-$0.01
Humberto Quintero	75.66	0.93%	-6.12	-$0.75	-$0.24
Raul Chavez	110.73	1.71%	-10.67	-$1.27	-$0.34

KANSAS CITY ROYALS

Player	Season RS	%PA	RSAA	$ValAA	MRP
Mike Sweeney	991.16	8.45%	17.24	$2.38	$6.98
Emil Brown	890.67	10.01%	10.37	$1.38	$6.84
David DeJesus	904.62	8.59%	10.11	$1.34	$6.03
Matt Stairs	947.78	7.66%	12.31	$1.66	$5.83
Angel Berroa	622.15	10.71%	-17.66	-$2.02	$3.82
Terrence Long	675.28	8.03%	-8.98	-$1.08	$3.30
Mark Teahen	634.22	8.07%	-12.33	-$1.46	$2.94
Tony Graffanino	869.69	3.57%	2.95	$0.38	$2.32
John Buck	589.52	7.07%	-13.95	-$1.63	$2.22
Aaron Guiel	901.64	1.99%	2.28	$0.29	$1.38
Ruben Gotay	515.21	5.21%	-14.16	-$1.66	$1.18
Chip Ambres	683.89	2.74%	-2.83	-$0.35	$1.14
Matt Diaz	726.06	1.59%	-0.97	-$0.12	$0.75
Dennis Hocking	667.08	1.17%	-1.40	-$0.18	$0.46
Alberto Castillo	470.96	1.87%	-5.92	-$0.72	$0.30
Paul Phillips	558.38	1.10%	-2.52	-$0.31	$0.29
Shane Costa	496.51	1.45%	-4.20	-$0.52	$0.27
Ken Harvey	484.12	0.79%	-2.39	-$0.30	$0.13
Joe McEwing	357.42	3.14%	-13.48	-$1.58	$0.13
Justin Huber	314.31	1.40%	-6.60	-$0.81	-$0.04
Eli Marrero	311.22	1.64%	-7.82	-$0.95	-$0.05
Calvin Pickering	182.90	0.51%	-3.08	-$0.38	-$0.10
Donnie Murphy	231.11	1.45%	-8.04	-$0.97	-$0.18
Andres Blanco	131.77	1.41%	-9.26	-$1.11	-$0.34

LOS ANGELES ANGELS OF ANAHEIM

Player	Season RS	%PA	RSAA	$ValAA	MRP
Vladimir Guerrero	1254.55	9.61%	44.92	$7.02	$12.26
Chone Figgins	825.98	11.65%	4.54	$0.59	$6.94
Garret Anderson	756.64	9.75%	-2.96	-$0.37	$4.95
Darin Erstad	695.73	10.72%	-9.79	-$1.17	$4.67
Bengie Molina	862.10	7.26%	5.45	$0.71	$4.67
Adam Kennedy	785.49	7.44%	-0.11	-$0.01	$4.04
Juan Rivera	813.06	6.08%	1.58	$0.20	$3.52
Orlando Cabrera	634.51	9.50%	-14.48	-$1.69	$3.49
Casey Kotchman	980.40	2.31%	4.47	$0.58	$1.84
Steve Finley	533.11	7.12%	-18.07	-$2.07	$1.81
Dallas McPherson	740.45	3.56%	-1.66	-$0.21	$1.73
Jeff Davanon	660.16	4.38%	-5.56	-$0.68	$1.71
Maicer Izturis	592.70	3.40%	-6.60	-$0.81	$1.05
Jose Molina	534.61	3.28%	-8.29	-$1.00	$0.79
Robb Quinlan	588.60	2.31%	-4.59	-$0.57	$0.70
Josh Paul	413.66	0.65%	-2.42	-$0.30	$0.05

(continued)

MRP Estimates for Hitters (2005) (*continued*)

Player	Season RS	%PA	RSAA	$ValAA	MRP
Jeff Mathis	656.30	0.05%	-0.06	-$0.01	$0.02
Dave Matranga	-975.89	0.02%	-0.29	-$0.04	-$0.03
Chris Prieto	-975.89	0.05%	-0.86	-$0.11	-$0.08
Zach Sorensen	-13.25	0.21%	-1.68	-$0.21	-$0.10
Lou Merloni	-527.59	0.11%	-1.49	-$0.19	-$0.12
Curtis Pride	-370.88	0.18%	-2.06	-$0.26	-$0.16

LOS ANGELES DODGERS

Player	Season RS	%PA	RSAA	$ValAA	MRP
Jeff Kent	1087.28	10.39%	36.64	$5.52	$11.19
J. D. Drew	1212.03	5.07%	24.22	$3.45	$6.22
Milton Bradley	954.79	5.14%	11.31	$1.51	$4.32
Hee Seop Choi	854.03	6.00%	7.17	$0.94	$4.21
Olmedo Saenz	865.35	5.73%	7.49	$0.98	$4.10
Jayson Werth	717.97	6.44%	-1.07	-$0.13	$3.38
Jose Cruz	1168.68	2.92%	12.67	$1.71	$3.30
Oscar Robles	689.02	6.51%	-2.97	-$0.37	$3.18
Antonio Perez	831.85	4.68%	4.55	$0.59	$3.14
Ricky Ledee	831.41	4.34%	4.20	$0.54	$2.91
Cesar Izturis	512.13	7.80%	-17.34	-$1.99	$2.26
Jason Phillips	539.12	7.08%	-13.84	-$1.62	$2.24
Willy Aybar	1208.42	1.71%	8.11	$1.07	$2.00
Dioner Navarro	770.60	3.25%	1.17	$0.15	$1.92
Jason Repko	556.47	4.91%	-8.74	-$1.05	$1.62
Mike Edwards	535.47	4.21%	-8.38	-$1.01	$1.28
Jose Valentin	488.63	3.00%	-7.38	-$0.90	$0.74
Paul Bako	663.22	0.77%	-0.55	-$0.07	$0.35
Brian Myrow	568.97	0.41%	-0.68	-$0.09	$0.14
Mike Rose	388.93	0.75%	-2.59	-$0.32	$0.09
Chin-Feng Chen	220.15	0.13%	-0.67	-$0.08	-$0.01
Cody Ross	-51.65	0.42%	-3.33	-$0.41	-$0.18
Jason Grabowski	180.98	2.01%	-11.11	-$1.32	-$0.23
Norihiro Nakamura	-156.52	0.67%	-5.96	-$0.73	-$0.36

MILWAUKEE BREWERS

Player	Season RS	%PA	RSAA	$ValAA	MRP
Geoff Jenkins	1030.93	10.04%	29.75	$4.35	$9.82
Brady Clark	874.42	10.95%	15.31	$2.09	$8.06
Lyle Overbay	897.65	10.10%	16.48	$2.26	$7.77
Carlos Lee	832.64	11.18%	10.96	$1.46	$7.56
Bill Hall	899.65	8.87%	14.64	$1.99	$6.83
Damian Miller	756.40	7.00%	1.53	$0.19	$4.01
Russell Branyan	998.85	3.93%	10.39	$1.38	$3.53

(continued)

MRP Estimates for Hitters (2005) (*continued*)

Player	Season RS	%PA	RSAA	$ValAA	MRP
Rickie Weeks	701.59	6.73%	-2.22	-$0.28	$3.39
J. J. Hardy	667.92	6.94%	-4.62	-$0.57	$3.21
Jeff Cirillo	877.45	3.56%	5.08	$0.66	$2.60
Wes Helms	881.33	3.05%	4.48	$0.58	$2.24
Junior Spivey	593.95	3.28%	-4.62	-$0.57	$1.22
Chad Moeller	427.49	3.51%	-10.78	-$1.28	$0.63
Prince Fielder	729.71	1.01%	-0.05	-$0.01	$0.54
Chris Magruder	358.01	2.52%	-9.48	-$1.14	$0.23
Corey Hart	468.83	1.02%	-2.72	-$0.34	$0.22
Nelson Cruz	1000.32	0.11%	0.30	$0.04	$0.10
Trent Durrington	319.64	0.29%	-1.21	-$0.15	$0.01
Julio Mosquera	-966.04	0.02%	-0.28	-$0.03	-$0.03
Dave Krynzel	-966.04	0.11%	-1.93	-$0.24	-$0.18

MINNESOTA TWINS

Player	Season RS	%PA	RSAA	$ValAA	MRP
Joe Mauer	868.56	8.95%	7.30	$0.96	$5.83
Jacque Jones	755.89	9.45%	-2.94	-$0.37	$4.78
Lew Ford	712.68	9.53%	-7.08	-$0.86	$4.33
Shannon Stewart	684.24	9.67%	-9.94	-$1.19	$4.08
Torii Hunter	831.07	6.72%	2.96	$0.38	$4.04
Justin Morneau	708.75	8.77%	-6.86	-$0.84	$3.94
Michael Cuddyer	763.20	7.59%	-1.81	-$0.23	$3.91
Matt LeCroy	871.41	5.65%	4.77	$0.62	$3.70
Nick Punto	529.98	7.09%	-18.22	-$2.08	$1.78
Luis Rodriguez	711.64	3.28%	-2.47	-$0.31	$1.48
Mike Redmond	772.35	2.57%	-0.38	-$0.05	$1.35
Juan Castro	550.28	4.72%	-11.16	-$1.33	$1.24
Jason Bartlett	574.60	4.07%	-8.64	-$1.04	$1.18
Glenn Williams	1173.90	0.69%	2.69	$0.34	$0.72
Luis Rivas	527.96	2.39%	-6.19	-$0.76	$0.55
Jason Tyner	792.88	0.97%	0.06	$0.01	$0.54
Michael Ryan	460.78	2.12%	-6.90	-$0.84	$0.31
Brent Abernathy	513.27	1.28%	-3.49	-$0.43	$0.26
Chris Heintz	295.61	0.42%	-2.06	-$0.26	-$0.03
Terry Tiffee	294.32	2.57%	-12.65	-$1.49	-$0.09
Bret Boone	76.22	0.94%	-6.66	-$0.81	-$0.30
Corky Miller	-927.58	0.19%	-3.32	-$0.41	-$0.31

NEW YORK METS

Player	Season RS	%PA	RSAA	$ValAA	MRP
David Wright	1097.91	10.69%	38.84	$5.91	$11.74
Cliff Floyd	974.98	10.19%	24.48	$3.49	$9.04

(*continued*)

MRP Estimates for Hitters (2005) (*continued*)

Player	Season RS	%PA	RSAA	$ValAA	MRP
Carlos Beltran	733.65	10.58%	-0.10	-$0.01	$5.75
Jose Reyes	597.41	11.93%	-16.36	-$1.89	$4.61
Mike Piazza	786.79	7.19%	3.75	$0.48	$4.40
Mike Cameron	879.08	5.58%	8.06	$1.06	$4.10
Victor Diaz	823.37	5.09%	4.52	$0.58	$3.36
Mike Jacobs	1376.03	1.82%	11.69	$1.57	$2.56
Doug Mientkiewicz	697.14	5.09%	-1.91	-$0.24	$2.54
Ramon Castro	742.47	3.90%	0.31	$0.04	$2.17
Marlon Anderson	654.60	4.23%	-3.38	-$0.42	$1.89
Chris Woodward	719.47	3.12%	-0.47	-$0.06	$1.64
Kazuo Matsui	537.44	4.80%	-9.46	-$1.14	$1.48
Miguel Cairo	477.00	5.97%	-15.38	-$1.79	$1.47
Jose Offerman	531.89	1.30%	-2.64	-$0.33	$0.38
Brian Daubach	554.37	0.55%	-1.00	-$0.13	$0.18
Gerald Williams	491.58	0.52%	-1.27	-$0.16	$0.13
Eric Valent	373.32	0.81%	-2.94	-$0.37	$0.08
Mike Difelice	-134.56	0.31%	-2.69	-$0.33	-$0.17
Anderson Hernandez	-560.75	0.31%	-4.00	-$0.50	-$0.33

NEW YORK YANKEES

Player	Season RS	%PA	RSAA	$ValAA	MRP
Alex Rodriguez	1321.37	11.16%	59.65	$9.90	$15.99
Jason Giambi	1254.91	8.51%	39.81	$6.08	$10.72
Gary Sheffield	1038.83	10.54%	26.54	$3.82	$9.57
Derek Jeter	965.74	11.74%	20.98	$2.94	$9.34
Hideki Matsui	976.82	10.98%	20.83	$2.92	$8.90
Jorge Posada	824.33	8.52%	3.18	$0.41	$5.06
Robinson Cano	776.36	8.60%	-0.92	-$0.12	$4.57
Bernie Williams	631.12	8.52%	-13.29	-$1.56	$3.09
Tino Martinez	767.99	5.43%	-1.03	-$0.13	$2.83
Ruben Sierra	473.46	2.83%	-8.86	-$1.07	$0.47
Tony Womack	356.48	5.48%	-23.59	-$2.61	$0.38
Bubba Crosby	514.53	1.61%	-4.38	-$0.54	$0.34
Rey Sanchez	539.68	0.75%	-1.85	-$0.23	$0.18
Felix Escalona	772.59	0.27%	-0.04	$0.00	$0.14
Russ Johnson	514.21	0.31%	-0.85	-$0.11	$0.06
Kevin Reese	552.83	0.03%	-0.07	-$0.01	$0.01
Mark Bellhorn	303.69	0.31%	-1.51	-$0.19	-$0.02
Mike Vento	-909.57	0.03%	-0.53	-$0.07	-$0.05
Matt Lawton	269.87	0.89%	-4.60	-$0.57	-$0.08
Wil Nieves	-909.57	0.06%	-1.06	-$0.13	-$0.10
Melky Cabrera	51.23	0.30%	-2.18	-$0.27	-$0.11
Andy Phillips	122.46	0.64%	-4.25	-$0.53	-$0.18
John Flaherty	105.57	2.15%	-14.68	-$1.71	-$0.54

OAKLAND ATHLETICS

Player	Season RS	%PA	RSAA	$ValAA	MRP
Mark Ellis	994.76	7.75%	16.09	$2.21	$6.43
Eric Chavez	814.44	11.06%	3.03	$0.39	$6.42
Mark Kotsay	732.00	10.02%	-5.52	-$0.68	$4.79
Dan Johnson	866.91	6.92%	5.53	$0.72	$4.49
Nick Swisher	762.56	8.32%	-2.03	-$0.25	$4.28
Jason Kendall	624.87	10.77%	-17.47	-$2.00	$3.87
Bobby Crosby	850.39	5.91%	3.75	$0.48	$3.71
Bobby Kielty	762.90	6.90%	-1.66	-$0.21	$3.55
Scott Hatteberg	628.88	8.33%	-13.18	-$1.55	$2.99
Marco Scutaro	638.86	6.74%	-9.99	-$1.20	$2.48
Eric Byrnes	851.29	3.43%	2.20	$0.28	$2.15
Jay Payton	713.95	4.64%	-3.39	-$0.42	$2.11
Erubiel Durazo	587.48	2.66%	-5.31	-$0.65	$0.80
Adam Melhuse	547.18	1.63%	-3.90	-$0.48	$0.40
Freddie Bynum	628.52	0.11%	-0.18	-$0.02	$0.04
Alberto Castillo	-909.57	0.02%	-0.27	-$0.03	-$0.03
Matt Watson	143.64	0.80%	-5.13	-$0.63	-$0.20
Hiram Bocachica	-429.17	0.30%	-3.68	-$0.46	-$0.29
Keith Ginter	204.84	2.49%	-14.47	-$1.69	-$0.33
Charles Thomas	13.08	0.88%	-6.78	-$0.83	-$0.35

PHILADELPHIA PHILLIES

Player	Season RS	%PA	RSAA	$ValAA	MRP
Bobby Abreu	976.15	11.33%	27.37	$3.96	$10.13
Pat Burrell	976.71	10.54%	25.53	$3.66	$9.41
Chase Utley	997.21	9.90%	25.99	$3.73	$9.13
Jimmy Rollins	723.52	11.54%	-1.28	-$0.16	$6.13
Ryan Howard	986.21	5.48%	13.80	$1.87	$4.86
Kenny Lofton	853.54	6.40%	7.61	$1.00	$4.49
Jason Michaels	867.05	5.41%	7.16	$0.94	$3.89
Mike Lieberthal	697.67	6.98%	-2.58	-$0.32	$3.48
David Bell	534.17	9.72%	-19.49	-$2.21	$3.09
Placido Polanco	806.51	2.73%	1.96	$0.25	$1.74
Jim Thome	659.05	3.81%	-2.88	-$0.36	$1.72
Todd Pratt	646.89	3.09%	-2.71	-$0.34	$1.35
Ramon Martinez	577.21	1.02%	-1.61	-$0.20	$0.36
Tomas Perez	344.26	2.77%	-10.83	-$1.29	$0.22
Shane Victorino	851.00	0.30%	0.35	$0.04	$0.21
Jose Offerman	481.38	0.60%	-1.52	-$0.19	$0.14
Marlon Byrd	702.24	0.24%	-0.08	-$0.01	$0.12
Michael Tucker	382.68	0.33%	-1.16	-$0.15	$0.03
Danny Sandoval	-894.48	0.03%	-0.51	-$0.06	-$0.05
Matt Kata	-169.06	0.09%	-0.85	-$0.11	-$0.06
Endy Chavez	251.50	1.86%	-8.98	-$1.08	-$0.07

PITTSBURGH PIRATES

Player	Season RS	%PA	RSAA	$ValAA	MRP
Jason Bay	1176.46	11.36%	50.22	$8.02	$14.22
Matt Lawton	900.29	7.15%	11.85	$1.59	$5.49
Rob Mackowiak	699.27	8.23%	-2.91	-$0.36	$4.12
Freddy Sanchez	713.76	7.91%	-1.65	-$0.21	$4.10
Daryle Ward	669.29	7.28%	-4.76	-$0.59	$3.38
Jack Wilson	542.95	10.27%	-19.69	-$2.23	$3.37
Craig Wilson	900.73	3.83%	6.36	$0.83	$2.92
Jose Castillo	655.82	6.40%	-5.04	-$0.62	$2.87
Ryan Doumit	676.27	4.13%	-2.41	-$0.30	$1.95
Chris Duffy	908.76	2.19%	3.81	$0.49	$1.68
Ty Wigginton	784.94	2.75%	1.38	$0.18	$1.67
Humberto Cota	541.59	5.14%	-9.93	-$1.19	$1.62
Brad Eldred	640.60	3.34%	-3.14	-$0.39	$1.43
Tike Redman	471.07	5.53%	-14.57	-$1.70	$1.31
Nate McLouth	704.90	1.93%	-0.57	-$0.07	$0.98
Bobby Hill	623.32	1.69%	-1.88	-$0.23	$0.69
Dave Ross	461.66	1.91%	-5.22	-$0.64	$0.40
Michael Restovich	463.52	1.48%	-4.01	-$0.50	$0.31
Ronny Paulino	1668.88	0.08%	0.75	$0.10	$0.14
J. J. Furmaniak	452.64	0.48%	-1.36	-$0.17	$0.09
Ray Sadler	833.86	0.13%	0.13	$0.02	$0.09
Benito Santiago	475.67	0.37%	-0.96	-$0.12	$0.08
Alfredo Amezaga	-210.79	0.06%	-0.61	-$0.08	-$0.04
Jody Gerut	170.65	0.29%	-1.63	-$0.20	-$0.05
Jose Bautista	15.52	0.50%	-3.58	-$0.44	-$0.17

SAN DIEGO PADRES

Player	Season RS	%PA	RSAA	$ValAA	MRP
Brian Giles	1247.19	10.75%	55.09	$8.98	$14.84
Ryan Klesko	907.24	8.29%	14.32	$1.95	$6.47
Dave Roberts	921.75	7.65%	14.33	$1.95	$6.12
Mark Sweeney	1122.13	4.26%	16.50	$2.27	$4.59
Mark Loretta	781.94	7.38%	3.50	$0.45	$4.47
Ramon Hernandez	849.11	6.25%	7.16	$0.94	$4.35
Khalil Greene	726.17	7.59%	-0.64	-$0.08	$4.06
Xavier Nady	824.32	5.68%	5.09	$0.66	$3.76
Damian Jackson	690.74	4.99%	-2.19	-$0.27	$2.45
Robert Fick	748.97	4.15%	0.60	$0.08	$2.34
Phil Nevin	680.62	4.88%	-2.63	-$0.33	$2.33
Geoff Blum	705.94	4.02%	-1.15	-$0.14	$2.05
Joe Randa	680.73	3.84%	-2.07	-$0.26	$1.84
Eric Young	832.40	2.60%	2.54	$0.33	$1.74
Miguel Olivo	983.00	1.98%	4.91	$0.64	$1.71
Sean Burroughs	554.04	5.06%	-9.13	-$1.10	$1.66

(*continued*)

MRP Estimates for Hitters (2005) (*continued*)

Player	Season RS	%PA	RSAA	$ValAA	MRP
Ben Johnson	840.78	1.40%	1.49	$0.19	$0.95
Dave Ross	1111.04	0.30%	1.14	$0.14	$0.31
Wilson Valdez	763.82	0.24%	0.07	$0.01	$0.14
Paul McAnulty	393.31	0.46%	-1.58	-$0.20	$0.05
Jesse Garcia	324.32	0.62%	-2.55	-$0.32	$0.02
Adam Hyzdu	138.59	0.40%	-2.38	-$0.30	-$0.08
Manny Alexander	36.22	0.33%	-2.34	-$0.29	-$0.11
Miguel Ojeda	87.64	1.32%	-8.56	-$1.03	-$0.31

SAN FRANCISCO GIANTS

Player	Season RS	%PA	RSAA	$ValAA	MRP
Moises Alou	1135.42	8.06%	32.32	$4.78	$9.17
Ray Durham	846.84	9.22%	10.34	$1.38	$6.40
Randy Winn	1386.81	4.06%	26.51	$3.82	$6.03
Omar Vizquel	665.18	10.71%	-7.44	-$0.90	$4.94
Pedro Feliz	647.02	10.12%	-8.86	-$1.07	$4.45
J. T. Snow	698.03	6.75%	-2.47	-$0.31	$3.37
Mike Matheny	619.81	7.98%	-9.16	-$1.10	$3.25
Edgardo Alfonzo	612.97	6.62%	-8.05	-$0.97	$2.63
Lance Niekro	713.32	4.97%	-1.06	-$0.13	$2.58
Jason Ellison	606.51	6.35%	-8.14	-$0.98	$2.48
Michael Tucker	629.22	4.71%	-4.96	-$0.61	$1.96
Deivi Cruz	624.77	3.64%	-3.99	-$0.49	$1.49
Barry Bonds	1404.09	0.86%	5.73	$0.75	$1.21
Todd Linden	447.86	3.08%	-8.82	-$1.06	$0.61
Yorvit Torrealba	532.17	1.73%	-3.50	-$0.43	$0.51
Alex Sanchez	463.15	0.77%	-2.10	-$0.26	$0.16
Tony Torcato	508.73	0.20%	-0.45	-$0.06	$0.05
Angel Chavez	367.19	0.33%	-1.21	-$0.15	$0.03
Julio Ramirez	213.41	0.07%	-0.34	-$0.04	-$0.01
Marquis Grissom	267.83	2.42%	-11.29	-$1.34	-$0.02
Brian Dallimore	-54.43	0.12%	-0.91	-$0.11	-$0.05
Adam Shabala	82.07	0.30%	-1.93	-$0.24	-$0.08
Doug Clark	-473.42	0.10%	-1.19	-$0.15	-$0.10
Dan Ortmeier	76.77	0.43%	-2.81	-$0.35	-$0.12
Justin Knoedler	-254.58	0.18%	-1.79	-$0.22	-$0.13
Yamid Haad	-320.87	0.53%	-5.56	-$0.68	-$0.39

SEATTLE MARINERS

Player	Season RS	%PA	RSAA	$ValAA	MRP
Richie Sexson	1099.14	10.76%	33.59	$5.00	$10.86
Ichiro Suzuki	862.30	12.12%	9.13	$1.21	$7.82

(*continued*)

MRP Estimates for Hitters (2005) (*continued*)

Player	Season RS	%PA	RSAA	$ValAA	MRP
Raul Ibanez	878.46	11.32%	10.35	$1.38	$7.55
Adrian Beltre	680.08	10.66%	-11.40	-$1.35	$4.46
Randy Winn	761.02	7.15%	-1.86	-$0.23	$3.67
Jeremy Reed	635.22	8.93%	-13.55	-$1.59	$3.28
Mike Morse	745.38	4.23%	-1.76	-$0.22	$2.09
Bret Boone	619.40	4.95%	-8.31	-$1.00	$1.70
Yuniesky Betancourt	586.17	3.74%	-7.51	-$0.91	$1.13
Willie Bloomquist	501.43	4.38%	-12.51	-$1.48	$0.91
Jose Lopez	558.53	3.33%	-7.61	-$0.92	$0.89
Rene Rivera	1183.85	0.82%	3.26	$0.42	$0.87
Greg Dobbs	493.19	2.53%	-7.42	-$0.90	$0.48
Chris Snelling	981.58	0.57%	1.12	$0.14	$0.46
Yorvit Torrealba	514.00	1.95%	-5.33	-$0.65	$0.41
Wiki Gonzalez	604.29	0.77%	-1.41	-$0.18	$0.24
Jamal Strong	664.83	0.39%	-0.48	-$0.06	$0.15
Miguel Ojeda	480.45	0.61%	-1.86	-$0.23	$0.10
Ramon Santiago	534.74	0.21%	-0.54	-$0.07	$0.05
Dave Hansen	264.11	1.44%	-7.55	-$0.92	-$0.13
Dan Wilson	21.53	0.46%	-3.52	-$0.44	-$0.19
Shin-Soo Choo	-271.97	0.34%	-3.65	-$0.45	-$0.26
Jaime Bubela	-310.37	0.33%	-3.60	-$0.45	-$0.27
Pat Borders	198.20	2.05%	-12.08	-$1.43	-$0.31
Wilson Valdez	201.39	2.18%	-12.78	-$1.51	-$0.32
Scott Spiezio	-274.69	0.84%	-8.88	-$1.07	-$0.61
Miguel Olivo	48.18	2.58%	-19.03	-$2.16	-$0.76

ST. LOUIS CARDINALS

Player	Season RS	%PA	RSAA	$ValAA	MRP
Albert Pujols	1331.06	11.21%	66.85	$11.42	$17.53
Jim Edmonds	1072.93	9.08%	30.71	$4.51	$9.46
David Eckstein	779.52	11.42%	5.13	$0.67	$6.89
Larry Walker	1017.78	5.88%	16.64	$2.29	$5.49
Mark Grudzielanek	713.08	9.01%	-1.94	-$0.24	$4.67
Reggie Sanders	961.62	5.27%	11.96	$1.61	$4.48
Abraham Nunez	662.89	7.48%	-5.36	-$0.66	$3.42
So Taguchi	685.99	6.79%	-3.30	-$0.41	$3.29
John Rodriguez	901.67	2.82%	4.71	$0.61	$2.15
Yadier Molina	518.60	6.74%	-14.56	-$1.70	$1.98
John Mabry	596.31	4.39%	-6.07	-$0.74	$1.65
Scott Rolen	639.81	3.57%	-3.38	-$0.42	$1.53
Hector Luna	746.52	2.45%	0.29	$0.04	$1.37
John Gall	735.83	0.62%	0.01	$0.00	$0.34

(*continued*)

MRP Estimates for Hitters (2005) (*continued*)

Player	Season RS	%PA	RSAA	$ValAA	MRP
Scott Seabol	344.68	1.83%	-7.12	-$0.87	$0.13
Skip Schumaker	444.39	0.42%	-1.21	-$0.15	$0.08
Chris Duncan	636.64	0.16%	-0.16	-$0.02	$0.07
Einar Diaz	244.21	2.23%	-10.91	-$1.30	-$0.09
Mike Mahoney	57.01	1.20%	-8.14	-$0.98	-$0.33
Roger Cedeno	-75.72	0.98%	-7.91	-$0.96	-$0.43

TAMPA BAY DEVIL RAYS

Player	Season RS	%PA	RSAA	$ValAA	MRP
Carl Crawford	861.71	11.23%	8.39	$1.11	$7.23
Julio Lugo	843.11	11.28%	6.33	$0.83	$6.97
Jonny Gomes	1096.84	6.65%	20.61	$2.89	$6.51
Jorge Cantu	847.29	10.30%	6.21	$0.81	$6.42
Aubrey Huff	759.27	10.40%	-2.88	-$0.36	$5.31
Travis Lee	787.09	7.21%	0.01	$0.00	$3.93
Alex Gonzalez	734.76	6.26%	-3.27	-$0.41	$3.01
Toby Hall	640.50	7.57%	-11.09	-$1.32	$2.81
Eduardo Perez	1022.09	3.11%	7.30	$0.96	$2.65
Damon Hollins	668.00	6.03%	-7.18	-$0.87	$2.42
Nick Green	643.97	6.13%	-8.77	-$1.06	$2.28
Alex Sanchez	984.36	2.37%	4.68	$0.61	$1.90
Josh Phelps	773.92	2.89%	-0.38	-$0.05	$1.53
Joey Gathright	595.72	3.56%	-6.82	-$0.83	$1.11
Chris Singleton	721.06	1.10%	-0.72	-$0.09	$0.51
Charles Johnson	531.47	0.90%	-2.30	-$0.29	$0.20
Eric Munson	446.94	0.39%	-1.33	-$0.17	$0.05
Kevin Cash	359.25	0.54%	-2.31	-$0.29	$0.01
Tim Laker	-946.32	0.02%	-0.28	-$0.04	-$0.03
Reggie Taylor	279.49	0.39%	-1.99	-$0.25	-$0.04
Pete LaForest	245.64	1.14%	-6.19	-$0.76	-$0.13
Fernando Cortez	-380.44	0.23%	-2.67	-$0.33	-$0.21

TEXAS RANGERS

Player	Season RS	%PA	RSAA	$ValAA	MRP
Mark Teixeira	1130.93	11.59%	39.85	$6.09	$12.41
Michael Young	1048.60	11.62%	30.39	$4.45	$10.79
David Dellucci	993.81	8.22%	17.00	$2.34	$6.82
Alfonso Soriano	826.10	10.83%	4.23	$0.55	$6.45
Kevin Mench	811.23	9.76%	2.36	$0.30	$5.62
Hank Blalock	719.52	11.19%	-7.55	-$0.92	$5.18
Gary Matthews	733.51	8.35%	-4.47	-$0.55	$4.00
Rod Barajas	740.65	7.13%	-3.30	-$0.41	$3.47

(*continued*)

MRP Estimates for Hitters (2005) (*continued*)

Player	Season RS	%PA	RSAA	$ValAA	MRP
Richard Hidalgo	611.16	5.38%	-9.46	-$1.14	$1.80
Mark DeRosa	754.38	2.63%	-0.86	-$0.11	$1.33
Laynce Nix	516.67	3.81%	-10.30	-$1.23	$0.85
Adrian Gonzalez	546.05	2.57%	-6.20	-$0.76	$0.64
Sandy Alomar	518.10	2.17%	-5.85	-$0.72	$0.47
Chad Allen	545.80	0.89%	-2.14	-$0.27	$0.22
Esteban German	2894.92	0.06%	1.34	$0.17	$0.20
Jason Botts	642.25	0.48%	-0.69	-$0.09	$0.17
Gerald Laird	425.97	0.67%	-2.41	-$0.30	$0.06
Phil Nevin	348.03	1.71%	-7.53	-$0.91	$0.02
Marshall McDougall	-57.32	0.29%	-2.41	-$0.30	-$0.15
Andres Torres	-7.34	0.33%	-2.65	-$0.33	-$0.15

TORONTO BLUE JAYS

Player	Season RS	%PA	RSAA	$ValAA	MRP
Shea Hillenbrand	837.43	10.35%	5.22	$0.68	$6.32
Vernon Wells	792.94	10.88%	0.64	$0.08	$6.01
Frank Catalanotto	912.89	7.62%	9.59	$1.27	$5.43
Eric Hinske	777.30	8.62%	-0.84	-$0.11	$4.59
Gregg Zaun	749.17	8.21%	-3.11	-$0.39	$4.09
Russ Adams	673.70	8.74%	-9.91	-$1.19	$3.58
Orlando Hudson	695.08	8.04%	-7.39	-$0.90	$3.48
Reed Johnson	743.49	7.04%	-3.07	-$0.38	$3.46
Alexis Rios	643.55	8.33%	-11.95	-$1.41	$3.12
Corey Koskie	734.98	6.48%	-3.37	-$0.42	$3.11
Aaron Hill	727.64	6.53%	-3.88	-$0.48	$3.08
Frank Menechino	691.33	2.89%	-2.76	-$0.34	$1.23
John McDonald	619.02	1.70%	-2.86	-$0.36	$0.57
Gabe Gross	612.73	1.64%	-2.85	-$0.35	$0.54
John-Ford Griffin	1136.09	0.21%	0.73	$0.09	$0.21
Andy Dominique	66.01	0.05%	-0.35	-$0.04	-$0.02
Guillermo Quiroz	252.58	0.63%	-3.34	-$0.42	-$0.07
Greg Myers	-326.18	0.21%	-2.32	-$0.29	-$0.18
Ken Huckaby	238.41	1.54%	-8.45	-$1.02	-$0.18

WASHINGTON NATIONALS

Player	Season RS	%PA	RSAA	$ValAA	MRP
Nick Johnson	1151.39	8.91%	37.12	$5.61	$10.46
Jose Guillen	924.91	9.95%	18.93	$2.63	$8.05
Brad Wilkerson	834.18	10.76%	10.72	$1.43	$7.30

(continued)

MRP Estimates for Hitters (2005) (*continued*)

Player	Season RS	%PA	RSAA	$ValAA	MRP
Vinny Castilla	726.93	8.94%	-0.68	-$0.09	$4.79
Ryan Church	952.46	4.90%	10.68	$1.42	$4.10
Brian Schneider	773.20	6.64%	2.56	$0.33	$3.95
Jose Vidro	829.36	5.65%	5.35	$0.70	$3.78
Preston Wilson	829.17	4.56%	4.31	$0.56	$3.04
Jamey Carroll	556.23	5.83%	-10.40	-$1.24	$1.94
Marlon Byrd	680.43	3.97%	-2.15	-$0.27	$1.90
Ryan Zimmerman	1352.47	1.01%	6.24	$0.81	$1.36
Cristian Guzman	373.79	8.01%	-28.90	-$3.10	$1.27
Carlos Baerga	599.99	2.83%	-3.81	-$0.47	$1.07
Junior Spivey	736.38	1.48%	0.03	$0.00	$0.81
Rick Short	2179.84	0.28%	4.00	$0.52	$0.67
Gary Bennett	418.42	3.71%	-11.74	-$1.39	$0.63
Terrmel Sledge	774.81	0.75%	0.30	$0.04	$0.45
Brendan Harris	1668.82	0.16%	1.52	$0.19	$0.28
Endy Chavez	916.03	0.20%	0.35	$0.04	$0.15
Matt Cepicky	486.85	0.42%	-1.05	-$0.13	$0.10
Kenny Kelly	1164.58	0.08%	0.35	$0.04	$0.09
Deivi Cruz	376.33	0.88%	-3.15	-$0.39	$0.09
Brandon Watson	361.02	0.78%	-2.92	-$0.36	$0.06
Jeffrey Hammonds	340.57	0.60%	-2.37	-$0.30	$0.03
Henry Mateo	580.90	0.03%	-0.05	-$0.01	$0.01
J.J. Davis	305.66	0.46%	-1.96	-$0.24	$0.00
Tyrell Godwin	-1038.75	0.05%	-0.87	-$0.11	-$0.08
Keith Osik	-1038.75	0.07%	-1.15	-$0.15	-$0.11
Tony Blanco	156.67	1.06%	-6.12	-$0.75	-$0.17
Wil Cordero	-233.41	0.91%	-8.83	-$1.06	-$0.57

MRP Estimates for Pitchers (2005)

ARIZONA DIAMONDBACKS

Player	Season RA	%IP	RABA	$ValAA	MRP
Brandon Webb	592.87	15.72%	18.56	$2.57	$11.72
Javier Vazquez	690.82	14.81%	2.39	$0.31	$8.92
Brad Halsey	710.79	10.99%	-0.51	-$0.06	$6.32
Shawn Estes	766.43	8.49%	-5.31	-$0.65	$4.29
Jose Valverde	495.85	4.55%	9.97	$1.33	$3.93
Claudio Vargas	813.62	8.22%	-9.17	-$1.10	$3.69
Lance Cormier	725.15	5.45%	-1.07	-$0.13	$3.03
Russ Ortiz	972.70	7.90%	-21.88	-$2.45	$2.16
Mike Koplove	773.46	3.41%	-2.38	-$0.30	$1.69
Brandon Medders	531.92	2.08%	3.77	$0.49	$1.68
Tim Worrell	693.85	2.18%	0.28	$0.04	$1.30

(*continued*)

MRP Estimates for Pitchers (2005) (*continued*)

Player	Season RA	%IP	RABA	$ValAA	MRP
Brian Bruney	860.68	3.16%	-5.07	-$0.62	$1.23
Mike Gosling	773.09	2.22%	-1.54	-$0.19	$1.10
Brandon Lyon	919.07	2.01%	-4.45	-$0.55	$0.64
Greg Aquino	952.62	2.15%	-5.51	-$0.68	$0.59
Buddy Groom	779.01	1.05%	-0.79	-$0.10	$0.51
Jason Bulger	704.70	0.69%	0.01	$0.00	$0.40
Dustin Nippert	871.32	1.01%	-1.73	-$0.22	$0.38
Oscar Villarreal	890.99	0.94%	-1.81	-$0.23	$0.33
Randy Choate	674.74	0.48%	0.16	$0.02	$0.30
Javier Lopez	961.29	0.98%	-2.60	-$0.32	$0.26
Armando Almanza	1249.13	0.27%	-1.55	-$0.19	-$0.03
Kerry Ligtenberg	1418.98	0.67%	-4.94	-$0.61	-$0.20
Edgar Gonzalez	10377.37	0.02%	-2.07	-$0.26	-$0.24
Matt Herges	1751.15	0.55%	-5.97	-$0.73	-$0.39

ATLANTA BRAVES

Player	Season RA	%IP	RABA	$ValAA	MRP
John Smoltz	553.38	15.91%	25.31	$3.62	$12.87
Tim Hudson	696.24	13.30%	1.40	$0.18	$7.91
Horacio Ramirez	843.80	14.01%	-20.03	-$2.26	$5.86
John Thomson	569.55	6.84%	9.73	$1.29	$5.24
Jorge Sosa	729.78	9.28%	-2.26	-$0.28	$5.12
Chris Reitsma	488.09	5.08%	11.53	$1.54	$4.45
Mike Hampton	632.56	4.80%	3.68	$0.47	$3.25
Kyle Davies	759.72	6.08%	-3.37	-$0.42	$3.12
Adam Bernero	615.26	3.26%	3.08	$0.40	$2.28
Danny Kolb	727.35	4.00%	-0.87	-$0.11	$2.22
Blaine Boyer	525.85	2.61%	4.90	$0.64	$2.13
John Foster	695.46	2.40%	0.27	$0.03	$1.43
Kyle Farnsworth	616.45	1.89%	1.77	$0.23	$1.32
Macay McBride	338.76	0.97%	3.71	$0.48	$1.02
Kevin Gryboski	639.30	1.48%	1.03	$0.13	$0.98
Roman Colon	929.37	3.07%	-7.12	-$0.87	$0.94
Jim Brower	948.12	2.08%	-5.23	-$0.64	$0.59
Chuck James	507.74	0.39%	0.82	$0.10	$0.33
Anthony Lerew	885.74	0.55%	-1.03	-$0.13	$0.20
Jorge Vasquez	975.36	0.62%	-1.74	-$0.22	$0.15
Seth Greisinger	874.87	0.35%	-0.61	-$0.08	$0.13
Jay Powell	996.02	0.23%	-0.69	-$0.09	$0.05
Frank Brooks	427.56	0.02%	0.06	$0.01	$0.02
Matt Childers	1249.13	0.28%	-1.56	-$0.20	-$0.03
Tom Martin	1822.53	0.16%	-1.85	-$0.23	-$0.13
Joey Devine	1681.80	0.35%	-3.51	-$0.44	-$0.22

BALTIMORE ORIOLES

Player	Season RA	%IP	RABA	$ValAA	MRP
Rodrigo Lopez	847.26	14.66%	-2.62	-$0.33	$6.93
Erik Bedard	678.17	9.93%	14.17	$1.92	$6.85
Daniel Cabrera	772.98	11.30%	5.95	$0.78	$6.36
Bruce Chen	909.91	13.82%	-10.70	-$1.28	$5.58
B. J. Ryan	495.03	4.92%	15.60	$2.13	$4.64
Sidney Ponson	870.27	9.13%	-3.63	-$0.45	$4.05
Todd Williams	724.91	5.35%	5.26	$0.68	$3.34
Jorge Julio	951.95	5.02%	-5.89	-$0.72	$1.74
Chris Ray	782.04	2.85%	1.26	$0.16	$1.57
James Baldwin	803.84	2.75%	0.64	$0.08	$1.44
Tim Byrdak	752.45	1.87%	1.35	$0.17	$1.10
Steve Kline	1060.44	4.27%	-9.42	-$1.13	$0.94
Steve Reed	938.50	2.29%	-2.40	-$0.30	$0.82
John Parrish	843.74	1.21%	-0.18	-$0.02	$0.57
Hayden Penn	1066.38	2.68%	-6.06	-$0.74	$0.55
Eric DuBose	1049.36	2.05%	-4.31	-$0.53	$0.46
Aaron Rakers	942.97	0.96%	-1.04	-$0.13	$0.34
John Maine	1166.69	2.80%	-9.00	-$1.08	$0.26
Jason Grimsley	1157.04	1.54%	-4.81	-$0.59	$0.14
Rick Bauer	1195.07	0.58%	-2.03	-$0.25	$0.02

BOSTON RED SOX

Player	Season RA	%IP	RABA	$ValAA	MRP
David Wells	648.18	12.88%	17.04	$2.35	$9.49
Matt Clement	692.61	13.37%	11.69	$1.57	$8.99
Bronson Arroyo	734.89	14.37%	6.43	$0.84	$8.82
Tim Wakefield	820.82	15.77%	-6.62	-$0.81	$7.94
Mike Timlin	487.51	5.62%	16.56	$2.27	$5.38
Curt Schilling	665.36	6.53%	7.51	$0.99	$4.60
Wade Miller	779.32	6.37%	-0.01	$0.00	$3.53
Geremi Gonzalez	783.83	3.92%	-0.18	-$0.02	$2.15
John Halama	695.34	3.06%	2.59	$0.33	$2.03
Mike Myers	704.20	2.61%	1.98	$0.25	$1.70
Chad Bradford	556.04	1.63%	3.68	$0.47	$1.37
Jonathan Papelbon	768.23	2.38%	0.26	$0.03	$1.35
Keith Foulke	897.40	3.20%	-3.82	-$0.47	$1.31
Alan Embree	912.88	2.64%	-3.56	-$0.44	$1.03
Matt Mantei	851.82	1.84%	-1.35	-$0.17	$0.85
Lenny DiNardo	566.83	1.03%	2.21	$0.28	$0.85
Manny Delcarmen	656.84	0.63%	0.78	$0.10	$0.45
Chad Harville	917.17	0.49%	-0.68	-$0.09	$0.19
Mike Stanton	236.49	0.07%	0.38	$0.05	$0.09
Blaine Neal	1138.71	0.56%	-2.03	-$0.25	$0.06

(continued)

MRP Estimates for Pitchers (2005) (*continued*)

Player	Season RA	%IP	RABA	$ValAA	MRP
Scott Cassidy	466.63	0.05%	0.15	$0.02	$0.05
Craig Hansen	1157.59	0.21%	-0.80	-$0.10	$0.02
Abe Alvarez	1333.03	0.16%	-0.90	-$0.11	-$0.02
Mike Remlinger	1361.74	0.47%	-2.76	-$0.34	-$0.08
Cla Meredith	2373.00	0.16%	-2.59	-$0.32	-$0.23

CHICAGO CUBS

Player	Season RA	%IP	RABA	$ValAA	MRP
Carlos Zambrano	649.25	15.51%	12.23	$1.64	$10.24
Greg Maddux	674.12	15.63%	8.40	$1.11	$9.77
Mark Prior	705.35	11.58%	2.57	$0.33	$6.75
Glendon Rusch	675.75	10.09%	5.26	$0.68	$6.27
Ryan Dempster	602.11	6.39%	8.08	$1.06	$4.60
Michael Wuertz	631.44	5.26%	5.09	$0.66	$3.57
Jerome Williams	793.24	7.36%	-4.90	-$0.60	$3.48
Roberto Novoa	699.45	3.10%	0.87	$0.11	$1.83
Kerry Wood	856.17	4.58%	-5.96	-$0.73	$1.81
Sergio Mitre	910.68	4.19%	-7.75	-$0.94	$1.39
Will Ohman	808.65	3.01%	-2.47	-$0.31	$1.36
Mike Remlinger	764.36	2.29%	-0.86	-$0.11	$1.16
Rich Hill	905.37	1.65%	-2.96	-$0.37	$0.55
Scott Williamson	763.19	0.99%	-0.36	-$0.05	$0.51
John Koronka	852.22	1.09%	-1.38	-$0.17	$0.43
LaTroy Hawkins	949.87	1.32%	-2.97	-$0.37	$0.37
Todd Wellemeyer	1062.09	2.24%	-7.58	-$0.92	$0.33
Jermaine Van Buren	1135.85	0.42%	-1.72	-$0.22	$0.02
Chad Fox	1219.97	0.56%	-2.76	-$0.34	-$0.03
Joe Borowski	1269.63	0.76%	-4.18	-$0.52	-$0.09
Jon Leicester	1295.67	0.63%	-3.59	-$0.44	-$0.09
Cliff Bartosh	1356.64	1.37%	-8.70	-$1.05	-$0.28

CHICAGO WHITE SOX

Player	Season RA	%IP	RABA	$ValAA	MRP
Mark Buehrle	595.02	16.04%	28.89	$4.21	$13.27
Freddy Garcia	707.96	15.45%	10.03	$1.33	$10.07
Jon Garland	716.23	14.98%	8.46	$1.12	$9.58
Jose Contreras	734.00	13.87%	5.32	$0.69	$8.53
Orlando Hernandez	817.78	8.70%	-4.10	-$0.51	$4.41
Neal Cotts	536.73	4.09%	9.79	$1.30	$3.59
Cliff Politte	664.97	4.56%	4.96	$0.64	$3.21
Dustin Hermanson	643.24	3.88%	5.08	$0.66	$2.84

(*continued*)

MRP Estimates for Pitchers (2005) (*continued*)

Player	Season RA	%IP	RABA	$ValAA	MRP
Luis Vizcaino	795.32	4.74%	-1.15	-$0.14	$2.54
Bobby Jenks	544.40	2.66%	6.17	$0.81	$2.30
Brandon McCarthy	861.65	4.54%	-4.17	-$0.52	$2.05
Damaso Marte	823.19	3.07%	-1.62	-$0.20	$1.53
Jon Adkins	692.50	0.56%	0.45	$0.06	$0.37
Kevin Walker	995.97	0.47%	-1.09	-$0.14	$0.13
Shingo Takatsu	1196.54	1.95%	-8.43	-$1.02	$0.10
Jeff Bajenaru	1326.82	0.29%	-1.65	-$0.21	-$0.04
David Sanders	1716.22	0.14%	-1.31	-$0.16	-$0.08

CINCINNATI REDS

Player	Season RA	%IP	RABA	$ValAA	MRP
Aaron Harang	600.47	14.77%	15.38	$2.10	$10.82
Brandon Claussen	748.39	11.63%	-5.96	-$0.73	$6.14
Eric Milton	881.51	13.00%	-24.83	-$2.73	$4.92
Ramon Ortiz	878.58	11.95%	-22.46	-$2.50	$4.54
Dave Weathers	636.34	5.42%	3.60	$0.46	$3.65
Matt Belisle	703.24	5.98%	-0.23	-$0.03	$3.50
Todd Coffey	607.17	4.05%	3.93	$0.51	$2.88
Kent Mercker	699.35	4.31%	0.01	$0.00	$2.54
Ryan Wagner	615.10	3.19%	2.83	$0.36	$2.23
Luke Hudson	945.26	5.91%	-15.24	-$1.77	$1.75
Brian Shackelford	598.29	2.07%	2.20	$0.28	$1.49
Randy Keisler	895.25	3.91%	-8.03	-$0.97	$1.36
Jason Standridge	777.32	2.16%	-1.76	-$0.22	$1.06
Paul Wilson	932.73	3.23%	-7.91	-$0.96	$0.98
Josh Hancock	534.28	0.98%	1.70	$0.22	$0.78
Ben Weber	659.88	0.86%	0.36	$0.05	$0.55
Ricky Stone	991.03	2.14%	-6.55	-$0.80	$0.49
Elizardo Ramirez	1046.67	1.56%	-5.67	-$0.70	$0.25
Allan Simpson	932.32	0.47%	-1.14	-$0.14	$0.14
Danny Graves	1134.96	1.28%	-5.84	-$0.71	$0.07
Joe Valentine	1282.14	1.00%	-6.10	-$0.75	-$0.13
Chris Booker	3380.00	0.14%	-3.93	-$0.49	-$0.38

CLEVELAND INDIANS

Player	Season RA	%IP	RABA	$ValAA	MRP
Jake Westbrook	731.43	14.50%	14.43	$1.96	$8.97
C. C. Sabathia	712.72	13.54%	15.85	$2.17	$8.72
Cliff Lee	735.93	13.90%	13.24	$1.79	$8.51
Kevin Millwood	719.41	13.21%	14.64	$1.99	$8.39
Scott Elarton	935.24	12.51%	-11.52	-$1.37	$4.70

(*continued*)

MRP Estimates for Pitchers (2005) (*continued*)

Player	Season RA	%IP	RABA	$ValAA	MRP
Bobby Howry	596.93	5.02%	11.35	$1.52	$4.01
Rafael Betancourt	556.95	4.66%	12.28	$1.65	$3.97
Arthur Rhodes	527.06	2.98%	8.69	$1.15	$2.64
David Riske	819.31	5.00%	0.84	$0.11	$2.53
Bob Wickman	881.24	4.27%	-1.76	-$0.22	$1.83
Fernando Cabrera	553.66	2.11%	5.63	$0.73	$1.79
Matt Miller	585.82	2.04%	4.83	$0.63	$1.65
Jason Davis	830.27	2.77%	0.18	$0.02	$1.36
Scott Sauerbeck	786.81	2.46%	1.17	$0.15	$1.34
Kazuhito Tadano	439.56	0.28%	1.03	$0.13	$0.27
Jeremy Guthrie	1367.43	0.41%	-2.06	-$0.26	-$0.07
Brian Tallet	1783.15	0.32%	-2.88	-$0.36	-$0.22

COLORADO ROCKIES

Player	Season RA	%IP	RABA	$ValAA	MRP
Jeff Francis	721.83	12.95%	-9.56	-$1.15	$7.27
Jamey Wright	762.55	12.07%	-14.42	-$1.68	$6.16
Byung-Hyun Kim	699.81	10.43%	-5.13	-$0.63	$6.15
Jason Jennings	697.85	8.60%	-4.04	-$0.50	$5.09
Brian Fuentes	527.72	5.24%	7.52	$0.99	$4.30
Aaron Cook	623.35	5.87%	2.14	$0.27	$4.05
Joe Kennedy	774.26	6.48%	-8.60	-$1.04	$3.21
Shawn Chacon	720.03	5.12%	-3.68	-$0.46	$2.89
Mike DeJean	358.45	2.59%	8.62	$1.14	$2.70
Sun-Woo Kim	631.18	3.76%	1.04	$0.13	$2.55
Jay Witasick	440.60	2.52%	6.07	$0.79	$2.34
David Cortes	690.05	3.71%	-1.42	-$0.18	$2.24
Marcos Carvajal	708.65	3.74%	-2.21	-$0.28	$2.16
Jose Acevedo	825.50	4.51%	-8.57	-$1.03	$1.95
Ryan Speier	569.50	1.74%	1.68	$0.21	$1.32
Scott Dohmann	849.38	2.18%	-4.74	-$0.58	$0.88
Dan Miceli	637.29	1.29%	0.27	$0.03	$0.86
Randy Williams	781.62	1.55%	-2.18	-$0.27	$0.75
Blaine Neal	855.18	1.04%	-2.31	-$0.29	$0.41
Aquilino Lopez	85.71	0.28%	1.80	$0.23	$0.39
Zach Day	925.15	0.80%	-2.40	-$0.30	$0.24
Mike Esposito	1033.90	1.04%	-4.39	-$0.54	$0.18
Javier Lopez	293.25	0.14%	0.57	$0.07	$0.16
Bobby Seay	1049.12	0.82%	-3.63	-$0.45	$0.13
Chin-hui Tsao	1089.77	0.78%	-3.77	-$0.47	$0.08
Allan Simpson	2485.73	0.05%	-1.01	-$0.13	-$0.08
Matt Anderson	1451.47	0.70%	-6.28	-$0.77	-$0.24

DETROIT TIGERS

Player	Season RA	%IP	RABA	$ValAA	MRP
Jason Johnson	756.75	14.63%	6.64	$0.87	$8.55
Jeremy Bonderman	721.47	13.16%	10.53	$1.40	$8.32
Mike Maroth	815.16	14.56%	-1.72	-$0.22	$7.43
Nate Robertson	843.97	13.70%	-5.49	-$0.67	$6.52
Kyle Farnsworth	489.94	2.97%	9.13	$1.21	$2.79
Sean Douglass	883.17	6.08%	-4.77	-$0.59	$2.60
Chris Spurling	826.24	4.92%	-1.12	-$0.14	$2.44
Jamie Walker	718.69	3.39%	2.81	$0.36	$2.15
Fernando Rodney	730.04	3.06%	2.19	$0.28	$1.89
Franklyn German	920.93	4.11%	-4.75	-$0.58	$1.56
Craig Dingman	817.63	2.23%	-0.32	-$0.04	$1.13
Matt Ginter	915.22	2.44%	-2.68	-$0.33	$0.94
Ugueth Urbina	832.88	1.90%	-0.56	-$0.07	$0.93
Vic Darensbourg	765.49	1.55%	0.57	$0.07	$0.89
Wilfredo Ledezma	1067.66	3.46%	-8.98	-$1.08	$0.72
Jason Grilli	758.85	1.11%	0.48	$0.06	$0.65
Justin Verlander	783.18	0.79%	0.15	$0.02	$0.43
Mark Woodyard	744.14	0.42%	0.24	$0.03	$0.25
Roman Colon	1117.04	1.74%	-5.36	-$0.66	$0.25
Andrew Good	718.43	0.35%	0.29	$0.04	$0.22
Troy Percival	1177.70	1.74%	-6.39	-$0.78	$0.12
Jason Karnuth	480.92	0.12%	0.37	$0.05	$0.11
Doug Creek	1183.42	1.55%	-5.79	-$0.71	$0.09

FLORIDA MARLINS

Player	Season RA	%IP	RABA	$ValAA	MRP
Dontrelle Willis	535.78	16.38%	36.96	$5.58	$13.75
A. J. Burnett	589.14	14.49%	25.35	$3.63	$10.86
Josh Beckett	612.41	12.39%	18.93	$2.63	$8.82
Brian Moehler	712.53	10.98%	6.33	$0.83	$6.29
Todd Jones	435.19	5.06%	16.26	$2.23	$4.83
Jason Vargas	642.13	5.11%	6.37	$0.83	$3.40
Guillermo Mota	699.73	4.65%	3.24	$0.42	$2.74
Jim Mecir	610.68	3.00%	4.64	$0.60	$2.12
Ismael Valdez	866.76	3.52%	-3.12	-$0.39	$1.34
Al Leiter	1005.82	5.55%	-12.25	-$1.45	$1.27
Nate Bump	844.56	2.63%	-1.78	-$0.22	$1.08
Ron Villone	659.02	1.64%	1.78	$0.23	$1.05
Antonio Alfonseca	792.45	1.89%	-0.35	-$0.04	$0.89
John Riedling	852.34	1.92%	-1.44	-$0.18	$0.76
Chris Resop	695.37	1.18%	0.87	$0.11	$0.70
Josh Johnson	736.27	0.85%	0.30	$0.04	$0.46
Travis Smith	751.62	0.74%	0.15	$0.02	$0.39

(continued)

MRP Estimates for Pitchers (2005) (*continued*)

Player	Season RA	%IP	RABA	$ValAA	MRP
Randy Messenger	1061.52	2.57%	-7.03	-$0.85	$0.39
Matt Perisho	913.55	0.97%	-1.29	-$0.16	$0.31
Valerio de los Santos	1033.20	1.53%	-3.77	-$0.47	$0.27
Scott Olsen	1080.07	1.41%	-4.10	-$0.51	$0.17
Frank Castillo	908.57	0.30%	-0.38	-$0.05	$0.10
Yorman Bazardo	856.18	0.12%	-0.09	-$0.01	$0.05
Jim Crowell	1035.91	0.23%	-0.57	-$0.07	$0.04
Paul Quantrill	1409.85	0.37%	-2.22	-$0.28	-$0.11
Logan Kensing	1427.98	0.40%	-2.46	-$0.31	-$0.13
Chad Bentz	2831.31	0.14%	-2.71	-$0.34	-$0.29

HOUSTON ASTROS

Player	Season RA	%IP	RABA	$ValAA	MRP
Roy Oswalt	554.39	16.75%	32.04	$4.73	$13.55
Andy Pettitte	549.20	15.41%	30.25	$4.43	$12.55
Roger Clemens	528.76	14.64%	31.69	$4.67	$12.40
Brad Lidge	451.40	4.90%	14.32	$1.95	$4.55
Brandon Backe	841.13	10.35%	-9.28	-$1.12	$4.33
Chad Qualls	637.12	5.52%	6.09	$0.79	$3.71
Dan Wheeler	593.61	5.08%	7.77	$1.02	$3.71
Wandy Rodriguez	873.88	8.92%	-10.86	-$1.29	$3.40
Russ Springer	784.36	4.09%	-1.39	-$0.17	$1.97
Ezequiel Astacio	1082.88	5.61%	-18.34	-$2.09	$0.84
John Franco	534.93	1.04%	2.19	$0.28	$0.83
Mike Gallo	700.76	1.41%	0.67	$0.09	$0.83
Mike Burns	887.85	2.15%	-2.91	-$0.36	$0.76
Chad Harville	1017.10	2.65%	-6.96	-$0.85	$0.54
Travis Driskill	-20.64	0.07%	0.52	$0.07	$0.10
Brandon Duckworth	1109.60	1.13%	-3.99	-$0.49	$0.09
Scott Strickland	1480.59	0.28%	-1.99	-$0.25	-$0.11

KANSAS CITY ROYALS

Player	Season RA	%IP	RABA	$ValAA	MRP
Zack Greinke	774.50	12.95%	2.62	$0.34	$7.26
Runelvys Hernandez	843.96	11.30%	-5.48	-$0.67	$5.37
Jose Lima	980.80	11.93%	-21.96	-$2.45	$3.94
D. J. Carrasco	838.40	8.11%	-3.49	-$0.43	$3.91
Mike MacDougal	617.37	4.97%	8.74	$1.16	$3.82
Andrew Sisco	727.32	5.33%	3.57	$0.46	$3.31
Ambiorix Burgos	719.94	4.48%	3.33	$0.43	$2.83
Mike Wood	957.83	8.14%	-13.12	-$1.54	$2.81
Shawn Camp	673.30	3.47%	4.18	$0.54	$2.40

(*continued*)

MRP Estimates for Pitchers (2005) (*continued*)

Player	Season RA	%IP	RABA	$ValAA	MRP
J. P. Howell	878.18	5.14%	-4.24	-$0.52	$2.23
Jeremy Affeldt	750.42	3.52%	1.55	$0.20	$2.08
Kyle Snyder	694.28	2.55%	2.54	$0.33	$1.69
Denny Bautista	714.39	2.53%	2.01	$0.26	$1.61
Leo Nunez	901.03	3.80%	-3.99	-$0.49	$1.54
Jimmy Gobble	998.01	3.80%	-7.64	-$0.93	$1.10
Ryan Jensen	820.10	1.79%	-0.45	-$0.06	$0.90
Brian Anderson	934.96	2.17%	-3.01	-$0.37	$0.78
Steve Stemle	484.69	0.76%	2.33	$0.30	$0.71
Jaime Cerda	930.90	1.34%	-1.81	-$0.23	$0.49
Jonah Bayliss	851.53	0.83%	-0.46	-$0.06	$0.38
Nate Field	1085.82	0.47%	-1.36	-$0.17	$0.08
Chris Demaria	1251.33	0.64%	-2.88	-$0.36	-$0.02

LOS ANGELES ANGELS OF ANAHEIM

Player	Season RA	%IP	RABA	$ValAA	MRP
John Lackey	599.02	14.27%	30.25	$4.43	$11.65
Bartolo Colon	703.06	15.21%	17.04	$2.35	$10.01
Paul Byrd	699.81	13.95%	16.07	$2.20	$9.24
Jarrod Washburn	776.73	12.11%	5.01	$0.65	$6.76
Scot Shields	589.11	6.26%	13.87	$1.88	$5.08
Ervin Santana	808.89	9.13%	0.96	$0.12	$4.73
Kelvim Escobar	592.12	4.08%	8.91	$1.18	$3.27
Francisco Rodriguez	677.14	4.60%	6.29	$0.82	$3.16
Brendan Donnelly	782.18	4.46%	1.61	$0.21	$2.46
Kevin Gregg	842.53	4.39%	-0.96	-$0.12	$2.09
Esteban Yan	863.82	4.55%	-1.92	-$0.24	$2.05
Chris Bootcheck	634.04	1.28%	2.28	$0.29	$0.95
Joel Peralta	915.38	2.37%	-2.17	-$0.27	$0.91
Jake Woods	1071.32	1.89%	-4.57	-$0.56	$0.37
Jason Christiansen	536.52	0.25%	0.69	$0.09	$0.22
Bret Prinz	1379.30	0.20%	-1.10	-$0.14	-$0.04
Greg Jones	1313.89	0.36%	-1.72	-$0.21	-$0.04
Joe Saunders	1385.75	0.64%	-3.45	-$0.43	-$0.12

LOS ANGELES DODGERS

Player	Season RA	%IP	RABA	$ValAA	MRP
Derek Lowe	739.78	15.55%	3.80	$0.49	$8.38
Brad Penny	654.45	12.28%	13.06	$1.76	$8.00
Jeff Weaver	768.04	15.69%	-0.43	-$0.05	$7.91
Odalis Perez	724.50	7.61%	2.98	$0.38	$4.25
Duaner Sanchez	731.32	5.74%	1.87	$0.24	$3.16

(*continued*)

MRP Estimates for Pitchers (2005) (*continued*)

Player	Season RA	%IP	RABA	$ValAA	MRP
D. J. Houlton	904.17	9.04%	-12.06	-$1.43	$3.15
Giovanni Carrara	754.85	5.30%	0.53	$0.07	$2.76
Elmer Dessens	704.83	4.60%	2.67	$0.34	$2.68
Yhency Brazoban	864.15	5.09%	-4.84	-$0.60	$1.97
Steve Schmoll	781.00	3.27%	-0.50	-$0.06	$1.59
Franquelis Osoria	730.28	2.08%	0.70	$0.09	$1.15
Derek Thompson	604.20	1.26%	1.95	$0.25	$0.90
Kelly Wunsch	771.66	1.66%	-0.10	-$0.01	$0.83
Edwin Jackson	853.28	2.01%	-1.70	-$0.21	$0.80
Eric Gagne	542.60	0.93%	1.99	$0.25	$0.74
Jonathan Broxton	572.40	0.96%	1.78	$0.23	$0.72
Scott Erickson	1162.04	3.87%	-14.76	-$1.72	$0.20
Buddy Carlyle	1068.99	0.98%	-2.86	-$0.36	$0.13
Hong-Chih Kuo	984.00	0.37%	-0.78	-$0.10	$0.09
Wilson Alvarez	1149.71	1.68%	-6.21	-$0.76	$0.07

MILWAUKEE BREWERS

Player	Season RA	%IP	RABA	$ValAA	MRP
Doug Davis	717.62	15.49%	2.63	$0.34	$8.78
Ben Sheets	594.81	10.90%	15.23	$2.08	$8.02
Chris Capuano	802.47	15.23%	-10.34	-$1.23	$7.07
Tomokazu Ohka	701.01	8.78%	2.95	$0.38	$5.17
Victor Santos	846.67	9.85%	-11.04	-$1.31	$4.06
Derrick Turnbow	585.07	4.68%	7.00	$0.92	$3.47
Matt Wise	642.25	4.47%	4.13	$0.53	$2.97
Rick Helling	537.57	3.41%	6.71	$0.88	$2.74
Gary Glover	752.02	4.50%	-0.78	-$0.10	$2.35
Wes Obermueller	870.74	4.52%	-6.15	-$0.75	$1.71
Julio Santana	741.13	2.92%	-0.19	-$0.02	$1.57
Jorge de la Rosa	757.30	2.94%	-0.67	-$0.08	$1.52
Dana Eveland	727.60	2.20%	0.15	$0.02	$1.22
Justin Lehr	832.54	2.41%	-2.36	-$0.29	$1.02
Ricky Bottalico	908.59	2.90%	-5.05	-$0.62	$0.96
Jose Capellan	554.22	1.09%	1.97	$0.25	$0.85
Tommy Phelps	778.83	1.62%	-0.72	-$0.09	$0.79
Kane Davis	887.28	1.16%	-1.77	-$0.22	$0.41
Mike Adams	948.00	0.92%	-1.97	-$0.25	$0.26

MINNESOTA TWINS

Player	Season RA	%IP	RABA	$ValAA	MRP
Johan Santana	546.26	15.82%	37.22	$5.63	$14.40
Carlos Silva	700.81	12.86%	10.18	$1.36	$8.49

(*continued*)

MRP Estimates for Pitchers (2005) (*continued*)

Player	Season RA	%IP	RABA	$ValAA	MRP
Brad Radke	759.90	13.70%	2.68	$0.34	$7.95
Kyle Lohse	762.60	12.20%	2.05	$0.26	$7.03
Juan Rincon	483.87	5.26%	15.68	$2.15	$5.05
Joe Mays	849.36	10.65%	-7.55	-$0.92	$5.00
Joe Nathan	486.21	4.78%	14.14	$1.92	$4.56
Matt Guerrier	685.90	4.90%	4.61	$0.60	$3.31
Jesse Crain	758.43	5.44%	1.14	$0.15	$3.16
Scott Baker	677.36	3.67%	3.77	$0.49	$2.52
Terry Mulholland	778.19	4.03%	0.04	$0.01	$2.24
J. C. Romero	876.59	3.89%	-3.83	-$0.47	$1.69
Francisco Liriano	680.97	1.62%	1.61	$0.20	$1.10
Dave Gassner	765.73	0.53%	0.07	$0.01	$0.30
Travis Bowyer	1036.55	0.66%	-1.72	-$0.22	$0.15

NEW YORK METS

Player	Season RA	%IP	RABA	$ValAA	MRP
Pedro Martinez	542.08	15.12%	29.92	$4.38	$12.48
Tom Glavine	620.44	14.72%	17.72	$2.45	$10.33
Victor Zambrano	709.95	11.58%	3.68	$0.47	$6.68
Aaron Heilman	533.59	7.52%	15.52	$2.12	$6.16
Kris Benson	788.44	12.14%	-5.58	-$0.68	$5.82
Jae Weong Seo	619.46	6.29%	7.63	$1.00	$4.38
Roberto Hernandez	627.84	4.86%	5.49	$0.71	$3.32
Heath Bell	532.13	3.25%	6.76	$0.88	$2.63
Juan Padilla	536.65	2.53%	5.14	$0.67	$2.03
Kazuhisa Ishii	933.26	6.34%	-12.00	-$1.42	$1.97
Braden Looper	814.49	4.13%	-2.96	-$0.37	$1.84
Steve Trachsel	843.42	2.58%	-2.59	-$0.32	$1.06
Manuel Aybar	709.67	1.76%	0.56	$0.07	$1.02
Dae-Sung Koo	723.20	1.60%	0.30	$0.04	$0.90
Mike DeJean	944.73	1.79%	-3.59	-$0.45	$0.51
Royce Ring	788.90	0.75%	-0.35	-$0.04	$0.36
Jose Santiago	519.04	0.40%	0.88	$0.11	$0.33
Felix Heredia	479.44	0.19%	0.49	$0.06	$0.16
Mike Matthews	796.32	0.35%	-0.19	-$0.02	$0.16
Danny Graves	1086.21	1.41%	-4.82	-$0.59	$0.16
Shingo Takatsu	1070.04	0.54%	-1.74	-$0.22	$0.07
Tim Hamulack	3442.66	0.16%	-4.28	-$0.53	-$0.45

NEW YORK YANKEES

Player	Season RA	%IP	RABA	$ValAA	MRP
Randy Johnson	672.52	15.78%	15.94	$2.18	$11.10
Mike Mussina	703.66	12.56%	8.70	$1.15	$8.24
Mariano Rivera	408.47	5.47%	20.27	$2.83	$5.89
Chien-Ming Wang	687.54	8.13%	6.97	$0.91	$5.50
Kevin Brown	595.47	5.12%	9.20	$1.22	$4.10
Aaron Small	635.95	5.31%	7.35	$0.96	$3.95
Tom Gordon	677.72	5.64%	5.40	$0.70	$3.88
Carl Pavano	804.95	6.99%	-2.38	-$0.30	$3.65
Shawn Chacon	744.92	5.52%	1.50	$0.19	$3.31
Tanyon Sturtze	798.02	5.45%	-1.47	-$0.18	$2.90
Al Leiter	765.19	4.35%	0.28	$0.04	$2.49
Jaret Wright	885.69	4.45%	-5.18	-$0.64	$1.88
Felix Rodriguez	802.71	2.26%	-0.72	-$0.09	$1.19
Buddy Groom	749.48	1.80%	0.41	$0.05	$1.06
Paul Quantrill	844.70	2.24%	-1.67	-$0.21	$1.06
Scott Proctor	974.46	3.12%	-6.47	-$0.79	$0.99
Mike Stanton	653.29	0.98%	1.18	$0.15	$0.70
Alan Embree	754.68	1.00%	0.17	$0.02	$0.59
Wayne Franklin	793.03	0.89%	-0.19	-$0.02	$0.48
Steve Karsay	450.53	0.42%	1.37	$0.17	$0.41
Jason Anderson	1039.30	0.40%	-1.09	-$0.14	$0.09
Colter Bean	769.32	0.14%	0.00	$0.00	$0.08
Jorge DePaula	1256.67	0.47%	-2.32	-$0.29	-$0.02
Tim Redding	2146.87	0.07%	-0.98	-$0.12	-$0.08
Ramiro Mendoza	2435.24	0.07%	-1.19	-$0.15	-$0.11
Alex Graman	2978.49	0.09%	-2.05	-$0.26	-$0.20
Sean Henn	1506.85	0.79%	-5.92	-$0.73	-$0.27
Darrell May	1851.49	0.49%	-5.39	-$0.66	-$0.37

OAKLAND ATHLETICS

Player	Season RA	%IP	RABA	$ValAA	MRP
Danny Haren	678.65	14.96%	13.17	$1.78	$10.38
Barry Zito	743.37	15.74%	3.36	$0.43	$9.48
Joe Blanton	752.96	13.88%	1.59	$0.20	$8.18
Rich Harden	541.47	8.82%	20.23	$2.83	$7.86
Kirk Saarloos	712.01	11.01%	5.91	$0.77	$7.09
Justin Duchscherer	529.27	5.91%	14.29	$1.94	$5.30
Huston Street	509.54	5.40%	14.15	$1.92	$4.98
Kiko Calero	652.94	3.84%	4.40	$0.57	$2.76
Joe Kennedy	752.16	4.18%	0.51	$0.07	$2.47
Keiichi Yabu	749.42	4.00%	0.60	$0.08	$2.37
Jay Witasick	671.34	1.91%	1.82	$0.23	$1.32
Juan Cruz	912.76	2.25%	-3.45	-$0.43	$0.88

(continued)

MRP Estimates for Pitchers (2005) (*continued*)

Player	Season RA	%IP	RABA	$ValAA	MRP
Ricardo Rincon	987.43	2.57%	-5.92	-$0.72	$0.77
Ron Flores	552.47	0.60%	1.31	$0.17	$0.51
Octavio Dotel	887.51	1.05%	-1.34	-$0.17	$0.44
Seth Etherton	972.36	1.22%	-2.62	-$0.33	$0.38
Tim Harikkala	1014.99	0.88%	-2.26	-$0.28	$0.23
Santiago Casilla	559.00	0.21%	0.44	$0.06	$0.17
Ryan Glynn	1117.75	1.17%	-4.27	-$0.53	$0.16
Britt Reames	1249.96	0.39%	-1.97	-$0.25	-$0.01

PHILADELPHIA PHILLIES

Player	Season RA	%IP	RABA	$ValAA	MRP
Cory Lidle	588.21	12.87%	13.54	$1.83	$9.63
Brett Myers	668.93	15.00%	2.83	$0.36	$9.49
Jon Lieber	680.29	15.21%	1.02	$0.13	$9.38
Billy Wagner	465.66	5.41%	12.80	$1.73	$4.93
Vicente Padilla	834.18	10.24%	-16.18	-$1.87	$4.36
Ryan Madson	630.19	6.06%	3.66	$0.47	$4.13
Robinson Tejeda	659.06	5.97%	1.76	$0.22	$3.84
Aaron Fultz	589.73	5.04%	5.22	$0.68	$3.70
Geoff Geary	623.84	4.04%	2.71	$0.35	$2.78
Randy Wolf	782.91	5.57%	-5.75	-$0.70	$2.70
Ugueth Urbina	706.23	3.64%	-0.77	-$0.10	$2.12
Rheal Cormier	831.21	3.30%	-5.10	-$0.63	$1.40
Eude Brito	713.27	1.53%	-0.44	-$0.06	$0.88
Tim Worrell	782.05	1.18%	-1.21	-$0.15	$0.57
Aquilino Lopez	753.49	0.89%	-0.63	-$0.08	$0.46
Gavin Floyd	990.96	1.81%	-5.90	-$0.72	$0.42
Amaury Telemaco	836.04	0.75%	-1.19	-$0.15	$0.31
Terry Adams	1207.08	0.93%	-5.16	-$0.63	-$0.04
Pedro Liriano	1461.29	0.54%	-4.45	-$0.55	-$0.19

PITTSBURGH PIRATES

Player	Season RA	%IP	RABA	$ValAA	MRP
Mark Redman	704.04	12.42%	2.92	$0.37	$7.26
Kip Wells	848.23	12.67%	-15.48	-$1.80	$5.23
Zach Duke	508.15	5.90%	13.06	$1.76	$5.02
Josh Fogg	848.40	11.79%	-14.42	-$1.68	$4.85
Salomon Torres	676.35	6.59%	3.39	$0.44	$4.09
Dave Williams	840.76	9.66%	-11.07	-$1.32	$4.04
Rick White	615.40	5.22%	5.90	$0.77	$3.66
Ryan Vogelsong	695.66	5.66%	1.81	$0.23	$3.37
Brian Meadows	694.69	5.20%	1.71	$0.22	$3.10

(*continued*)

MRP Estimates for Pitchers (2005) (*continued*)

Player	Season RA	%IP	RABA	$ValAA	MRP
Mike Gonzalez	597.28	3.48%	4.57	$0.59	$2.52
Paul Maholm	625.48	2.88%	2.96	$0.38	$1.97
John Grabow	770.68	3.62%	-1.59	-$0.20	$1.81
Jose Mesa	812.32	3.95%	-3.39	-$0.42	$1.77
Ian Snell	827.40	2.92%	-2.96	-$0.37	$1.26
Oliver Perez	1087.18	7.17%	-26.07	-$2.84	$1.14
Matt Capps	267.65	0.28%	1.29	$0.16	$0.32
Tom Gorzelanny	965.88	0.42%	-1.01	-$0.13	$0.11
Bryan Bullington	678.95	0.09%	0.04	$0.01	$0.06
Mike Johnston	4425.68	0.07%	-2.60	-$0.32	-$0.28

SAN DIEGO PADRES

Player	Season RA	%IP	RABA	$ValAA	MRP
Jake Peavy	583.35	13.95%	28.41	$4.13	$10.56
Brian Lawrence	748.00	13.44%	7.25	$0.95	$7.10
Adam Eaton	763.61	8.84%	3.51	$0.45	$4.50
Woody Williams	881.41	10.97%	-7.40	-$0.90	$4.12
Scott Linebrink	567.12	5.06%	11.06	$1.48	$3.88
Rudy Seanez	515.31	4.14%	11.01	$1.47	$3.46
Trevor Hoffman	502.60	3.96%	10.99	$1.47	$3.38
Akinori Otsuka	687.52	4.31%	4.69	$0.61	$2.61
Clay Hensley	552.47	3.28%	7.60	$1.00	$2.56
Tim Stauffer	853.45	5.56%	-2.34	-$0.29	$2.23
Pedro Astacio	773.98	4.10%	1.24	$0.16	$2.03
Paul Quantrill	488.75	2.18%	6.31	$0.82	$1.88
Chris Hammond	862.01	4.03%	-2.01	-$0.25	$1.57
Chan Ho Park	807.41	3.14%	0.00	$0.00	$1.43
Darrell May	969.14	4.07%	-6.00	-$0.73	$1.07
Dennys Reyes	892.66	3.00%	-2.33	-$0.29	$1.05
Craig Breslow	899.00	1.12%	-0.93	-$0.12	$0.38
Chris Oxspring	965.59	0.82%	-1.19	-$0.15	$0.21
Scott Cassidy	987.47	0.85%	-1.39	-$0.17	$0.19
Brian Falkenborg	977.64	0.76%	-1.17	-$0.15	$0.18
Tim Redding	1186.46	2.04%	-7.04	-$0.86	$0.00
Randy Williams	1501.57	0.30%	-1.87	-$0.23	-$0.12
Sean Burroughs	2955.76	0.07%	-1.34	-$0.17	-$0.15

SAN FRANCISCO GIANTS

Player	Season RA	%IP	RABA	$ValAA	MRP
Noah Lowry	696.25	14.17%	7.41	$0.97	$8.43
Brett Tomko	718.69	13.20%	4.00	$0.52	$7.47
Jason Schmidt	714.56	11.91%	4.09	$0.53	$6.80

(*continued*)

MRP Estimates for Pitchers (2005) (*continued*)

Player	Season RA	%IP	RABA	$ValAA	MRP
Jeff Fassero	663.31	6.30%	5.33	$0.69	$4.02
Scott Eyre	540.66	4.73%	9.68	$1.29	$3.79
Brad Hennessey	860.72	8.19%	-8.92	-$1.07	$3.23
Kirk Rueter	898.65	7.43%	-10.85	-$1.29	$2.61
Scott Munter	618.22	2.68%	3.45	$0.44	$1.86
Tyler Walker	824.05	4.27%	-3.12	-$0.39	$1.86
Matt Cain	726.54	3.21%	0.72	$0.09	$1.78
LaTroy Hawkins	701.08	2.58%	1.23	$0.16	$1.52
Jason Christiansen	774.83	2.91%	-0.72	-$0.09	$1.44
Jeremy Accardo	649.01	2.06%	2.03	$0.26	$1.35
Jack Taschner	574.19	1.57%	2.70	$0.35	$1.18
Brian Cooper	611.68	1.23%	1.66	$0.21	$0.86
Kevin Correia	1042.43	4.04%	-11.58	-$1.37	$0.73
Matt Herges	789.81	1.45%	-0.57	-$0.07	$0.69
Jim Brower	911.81	2.10%	-3.34	-$0.41	$0.68
Jerome Williams	705.27	1.16%	0.50	$0.06	$0.67
Armando Benitez	950.77	2.08%	-4.10	-$0.51	$0.58
Alan Levine	1022.76	0.71%	-1.91	-$0.24	$0.13
Matt Kinney	1054.75	0.83%	-2.48	-$0.31	$0.12
Brandon Puffer	1233.53	0.48%	-2.30	-$0.29	-$0.04
Jesse Foppert	1463.40	0.71%	-4.99	-$0.61	-$0.25

SEATTLE MARINERS

Player	Season RA	%IP	RABA	$ValAA	MRP
Jamie Moyer	760.46	14.01%	4.79	$0.62	$8.12
Joel Pineiro	782.47	13.24%	1.64	$0.21	$7.29
Ryan Franklin	873.78	13.36%	-10.42	-$1.24	$5.91
Felix Hernandez	546.54	5.91%	14.52	$1.98	$5.15
Gil Meche	901.95	10.04%	-10.63	-$1.27	$4.10
Julio Mateo	752.13	6.19%	2.62	$0.34	$3.65
Shigetoshi Hasegawa	638.71	4.67%	7.23	$0.95	$3.45
Aaron Sele	915.56	8.13%	-9.70	-$1.16	$3.18
Eddie Guardado	704.74	3.94%	3.52	$0.45	$2.57
J. J. Putz	813.69	4.20%	-0.78	-$0.10	$2.15
Ron Villone	664.41	2.82%	3.65	$0.47	$1.98
Jeff Nelson	774.43	2.57%	0.52	$0.07	$1.44
Jeff Harris	952.17	3.76%	-5.85	-$0.72	$1.29
George Sherrill	740.68	1.33%	0.72	$0.09	$0.80
Rafael Soriano	262.12	0.51%	2.70	$0.35	$0.62
Matt Thornton	1164.74	3.99%	-14.62	-$1.70	$0.42
Scott Atchison	581.43	0.47%	0.99	$0.13	$0.38
Clint Nageotte	555.20	0.28%	0.67	$0.08	$0.24
Jorge Campillo	634.35	0.14%	0.22	$0.03	$0.10
Bobby Madritsch	1077.07	0.30%	-0.84	-$0.11	$0.05
Masao Kida	1609.94	0.14%	-1.13	-$0.14	-$0.07

ST. LOUIS CARDINALS

Player	Season RA	%IP	RABA	$ValAA	MRP
Chris Carpenter	517.02	16.72%	35.51	$5.33	$14.59
Matt Morris	658.07	13.33%	9.32	$1.24	$8.62
Mark Mulder	706.21	14.18%	3.02	$0.39	$8.25
Jeff Suppan	755.03	13.44%	-3.76	-$0.47	$6.98
Jason Marquis	820.64	14.32%	-13.50	-$1.58	$6.35
Al Reyes	543.98	4.34%	8.03	$1.06	$3.45
Julian Tavarez	634.91	4.54%	4.24	$0.55	$3.06
Jason Isringhausen	639.34	4.08%	3.63	$0.47	$2.73
Brad Thompson	668.38	3.80%	2.26	$0.29	$2.40
Randy Flores	637.95	2.88%	2.60	$0.33	$1.93
Cal Eldred	703.02	2.56%	0.63	$0.08	$1.50
Ray King	746.39	2.77%	-0.53	-$0.07	$1.47
Anthony Reyes	729.41	0.92%	-0.02	$0.00	$0.51
Gabe White	745.46	0.57%	-0.11	-$0.01	$0.31
Bill Pulsipher	652.94	0.28%	0.21	$0.03	$0.18
Tyler Johnson	699.80	0.19%	0.05	$0.01	$0.11
Jimmy Journell	1318.02	0.30%	-1.77	-$0.22	-$0.06
Kevin Jarvis	1465.68	0.23%	-1.70	-$0.21	-$0.08
Adam Wainwright	1821.91	0.14%	-1.53	-$0.19	-$0.11
Carmen Cali	1900.34	0.42%	-4.92	-$0.61	-$0.37

TAMPA BAY DEVIL RAYS

Player	Season RA	%IP	RABA	$ValAA	MRP
Scott Kazmir	699.15	13.08%	12.41	$1.67	$8.67
Mark Hendrickson	815.64	12.54%	-2.57	-$0.32	$6.39
Casey Fossum	787.38	11.45%	0.86	$0.11	$6.23
Doug Waechter	898.29	11.04%	-11.30	-$1.34	$4.57
Danys Baez	758.78	5.09%	1.82	$0.23	$2.96
Hideo Nomo	978.06	7.08%	-12.84	-$1.51	$2.27
Chad Orvella	709.19	3.52%	2.99	$0.38	$2.27
Seth McClung	1006.15	7.69%	-16.08	-$1.86	$2.25
Travis Harper	961.59	5.16%	-8.51	-$1.03	$1.73
Lance Carter	888.60	4.01%	-3.72	-$0.46	$1.68
Joe Borowski	734.18	2.48%	1.49	$0.19	$1.52
Trever Miller	856.26	3.12%	-1.89	-$0.24	$1.43
Jesus Colome	900.45	3.19%	-3.33	-$0.41	$1.29
Tim Corcoran	732.97	1.60%	0.98	$0.12	$0.98
Dewon Brazelton	1183.09	4.99%	-19.19	-$2.18	$0.48
Joe Beimel	818.68	0.77%	-0.18	-$0.02	$0.39
Franklin Nunez	823.23	0.35%	-0.10	-$0.01	$0.18
Lee Gardner	1119.77	0.51%	-1.65	-$0.21	$0.07
Jon Switzer	1147.46	0.28%	-0.98	-$0.12	$0.03
Rob Bell	1253.60	1.76%	-7.99	-$0.97	-$0.03
John Webb	1476.97	0.28%	-1.90	-$0.24	-$0.09

TEXAS RANGERS

Player	Season RA	%IP	RABA	$ValAA	MRP
Kenny Rogers	668.27	13.56%	13.38	$1.81	$9.60
Chris Young	666.10	11.44%	11.54	$1.55	$8.11
Chan Ho Park	712.82	7.62%	4.02	$0.52	$4.89
Kameron Loe	691.60	6.39%	4.77	$0.62	$4.28
Doug Brocail	575.06	5.09%	9.91	$1.32	$4.21
Francisco Cordero	587.55	4.79%	8.71	$1.15	$3.88
Joaquin Benoit	712.20	6.04%	3.23	$0.41	$3.88
John Wasdin	725.56	5.26%	2.09	$0.27	$3.28
Ryan Drese	731.66	4.84%	1.62	$0.21	$2.98
Pedro Astacio	815.93	4.65%	-2.48	-$0.31	$2.37
Juan Dominguez	842.64	4.88%	-3.95	-$0.49	$2.32
Brian Shouse	774.61	3.70%	-0.40	-$0.05	$2.08
C. J. Wilson	742.31	3.33%	0.75	$0.09	$2.01
Ricardo Rodriguez	941.25	3.96%	-7.22	-$0.88	$1.41
Erasmo Ramirez	752.13	1.60%	0.20	$0.02	$0.94
Nick Regilio	734.95	1.23%	0.37	$0.05	$0.75
R. A. Dickey	940.50	2.06%	-3.75	-$0.46	$0.73
Ron Mahay	993.89	2.48%	-5.87	-$0.72	$0.72
Steve Karsay	774.65	1.09%	-0.12	-$0.01	$0.61
Scott Feldman	474.48	0.65%	1.93	$0.25	$0.61
Josh Rupe	536.52	0.67%	1.58	$0.20	$0.58
James Baldwin	932.58	1.20%	-2.08	-$0.26	$0.44
Jason Standridge	491.75	0.16%	0.45	$0.06	$0.15
Kevin Gryboski	1072.83	0.67%	-2.14	-$0.27	$0.13
Matt Riley	1147.04	0.88%	-3.48	-$0.43	$0.09
Ryan Bukvich	1026.83	0.28%	-0.75	-$0.09	$0.07
Edinson Volquez	1194.28	0.88%	-3.91	-$0.48	$0.04
Michael Tejera	1586.72	0.14%	-1.18	-$0.15	-$0.06
Justin Thompson	2889.17	0.12%	-2.58	-$0.32	-$0.25
Carlos Almanzar	1935.98	0.35%	-4.19	-$0.52	-$0.30

TORONTO BLUE JAYS

Player	Season RA	%IP	RABA	$ValAA	MRP
Josh Towers	667.24	14.42%	15.35	$2.10	$10.24
Roy Halladay	527.21	9.79%	24.41	$3.48	$8.98
Gustavo Chacin	727.61	14.03%	6.29	$0.82	$8.75
David Bush	773.50	9.42%	-0.18	-$0.02	$5.30
Scott Downs	754.78	6.50%	1.11	$0.14	$3.81
Jason Frasor	709.23	5.16%	3.28	$0.42	$3.33
Ted Lilly	935.42	8.73%	-14.59	-$1.70	$3.23
Scott Schoeneweis	602.09	3.94%	6.81	$0.89	$3.10
Miguel Batista	755.94	5.16%	0.82	$0.10	$3.02
Pete Walker	817.67	5.80%	-2.73	-$0.34	$2.94

(continued)

MRP Estimates for Pitchers (2005) (*continued*)

Player	Season RA	%IP	RABA	$ValAA	MRP
Justin Speier	721.07	4.61%	2.37	$0.30	$2.90
Vinnie Chulk	807.00	4.98%	-1.80	-$0.22	$2.59
Dustin McGowan	831.97	3.13%	-1.93	-$0.24	$1.53
Shaun Marcum	615.69	0.55%	0.88	$0.11	$0.42
Brandon League	1146.58	2.47%	-9.44	-$1.13	$0.28
Chad Gaudin	1514.57	0.90%	-6.81	-$0.83	-$0.31
Justin Miller	3134.85	0.16%	-3.83	-$0.47	-$0.38
Matt Whiteside	2661.92	0.26%	-4.93	-$0.61	-$0.45

WASHINGTON NATIONALS

Player	Season RA	%IP	RABA	$ValAA	MRP
Esteban Loaiza	621.19	14.89%	22.43	$3.17	$10.44
John Patterson	661.53	13.60%	15.34	$2.09	$8.74
Livan Hernandez	765.93	16.90%	2.47	$0.32	$8.56
Gary Majewski	634.65	5.90%	8.14	$1.07	$3.98
Hector Carrasco	675.20	6.06%	6.05	$0.79	$3.76
Chad Cordero	692.19	5.10%	4.28	$0.55	$3.05
Luis Ayala	683.71	4.87%	4.48	$0.58	$2.97
Ryan Drese	699.36	4.10%	3.16	$0.41	$2.42
Joey Eischen	638.42	2.49%	3.35	$0.43	$1.66
Tony Armas	1015.80	6.95%	-15.31	-$1.78	$1.57
Jon Rauch	735.22	2.06%	0.89	$0.11	$1.12
Sun-Woo Kim	732.66	2.01%	0.92	$0.12	$1.10
Mike Stanton	709.18	1.90%	1.29	$0.16	$1.10
Tomokazu Ohka	950.92	3.70%	-5.90	-$0.72	$1.05
John Halama	675.57	1.46%	1.45	$0.19	$0.91
Jay Bergmann	654.92	1.35%	1.61	$0.20	$0.87
Zach Day	1031.77	2.47%	-5.81	-$0.71	$0.45
Darrell Rasner	496.64	0.50%	1.34	$0.17	$0.42
Joe Horgan	654.10	0.41%	0.49	$0.06	$0.27
Matt White	723.10	0.27%	0.15	$0.02	$0.15
C. J. Nitkowski	675.11	0.23%	0.23	$0.03	$0.14
T. J. Tucker	1219.38	0.87%	-3.59	-$0.44	-$0.05
Travis Hughes	1413.11	0.89%	-5.29	-$0.65	-$0.25
Claudio Vargas	1448.00	0.87%	-5.46	-$0.67	-$0.28
Antonio Osuna	4317.22	0.16%	-5.24	-$0.64	-$0.61

MRP Estimates for Top 35 Hitters (2006)

Rank	Player	Team	Season RS	%PA	RSAA	$ValAA	MRP
1	Albert Pujols	St. Louis Cardinals	1493.85	10.18%	77.33	$16.64	$21.23
2	Ryan Howard MVP_{NL}	Philadelphia Phillies	1384.75	10.82%	70.32	$14.73	$19.88
3	Miguel Cabrera	Florida Marlins	1357.02	10.92%	67.96	$14.11	$19.37
4	Travis Hafner	Cleveland Indians	1542.91	8.93%	67.53	$13.99	$18.08
5	David Ortiz	Boston Red Sox	1352.89	10.66%	60.32	$12.15	$17.44
6	Lance Berkman	Houston Astros	1320.14	10.21%	59.80	$12.02	$17.05
7	Carlos Beltran	New York Mets	1269.22	9.81%	52.43	$10.23	$15.18
8	Nick Johnson	Washington Nationals	1238.69	10.00%	50.39	$9.75	$14.85
9	Manny Ramirez	Boston Red Sox	1403.03	8.67%	53.42	$10.46	$14.71
10	Derek Jeter	New York Yankees	1193.69	11.08%	45.05	$8.52	$14.39
11	Jim Thome	Chicago White Sox	1288.35	9.65%	48.40	$9.29	$14.23
12	Vladimir Guerrero	Los Angeles Angels of Anaheim	1205.78	10.69%	44.76	$8.46	$14.10
13	Jason Bay	Pittsburgh Pirates	1125.01	11.08%	43.27	$8.12	$14.03
14	Grady Sizemore	Cleveland Indians	1125.10	11.92%	40.29	$7.47	$13.93
15	Garrett Atkins	Colorado Rockies	1125.62	10.95%	42.82	$8.02	$13.86
16	Jason Giambi	New York Yankees	1314.91	8.97%	47.35	$9.04	$13.60
17	David Wright	New York Mets	1135.54	10.51%	42.13	$7.87	$13.45
18	Alfonso Soriano	Washington Nationals	1068.69	11.59%	38.71	$7.12	$13.42
19	Joe Mauer	Minnesota Twins	1236.51	9.76%	43.88	$8.26	$13.36
20	Alex Rodriguez	New York Yankees	1184.83	10.44%	41.54	$7.74	$13.30
21	Jermaine Dye	Chicago White Sox	1234.03	9.67%	43.23	$8.11	$13.17
22	Justin Morneau MVP_{AL}	Minnesota Twins	1160.52	10.61%	39.64	$7.33	$13.02
23	Barry Bonds	San Francisco Giants	1322.73	8.03%	47.25	$9.02	$13.02
24	Matt Holliday	Colorado Rockies	1111.35	10.51%	39.59	$7.31	$12.95
25	Chase Utley	Philadelphia Phillies	1034.61	11.35%	34.06	$6.14	$12.39
26	Carlos Guillen	Detroit Tigers	1157.43	10.04%	37.17	$6.80	$12.20
27	Chipper Jones	Atlanta Braves	1311.17	7.59%	43.77	$8.23	$12.04
28	Andruw Jones	Atlanta Braves	1056.27	10.65%	34.25	$6.18	$12.00
29	Carlos Delgado	New York Mets	1100.67	9.82%	35.96	$6.54	$11.84
30	Miguel Tejada	Baltimore Orioles	1058.19	11.37%	30.82	$5.48	$11.79
31	Raul Ibanez	Seattle Mariners	1062.46	11.25%	30.99	$5.51	$11.76
32	Paul Konerko	Chicago White Sox	1108.34	10.18%	32.70	$5.86	$11.43
33	Frank Thomas	Oakland Athletics	1178.33	8.90%	34.83	$6.30	$11.06
34	Nick Swisher	Oakland Athletics	1056.95	10.70%	28.88	$5.09	$11.04
35	Mark Teixeira	Texas Rangers	1009.86	11.59%	25.83	$4.49	$11.03

MRP Estimates for Top 35 Pitchers (2006)

Rank	Player	Team	Season RA	%IP	RABA	$ValAA	MRP
1	Brandon Webb CY_{NL}	Arizona Diamondbacks	498.15	16.10%	38.07	$5.43	$16.00
2	Johan Santana CY_{AL}	Minnesota Twins	579.54	16.24%	33.69	$5.87	$15.25
3	Roy Halladay	Toronto Blue Jays	592.32	15.40%	29.99	$4.33	$14.06
4	Roy Oswalt	Houston Astros	541.50	15.03%	29.02	$4.50	$13.66
5	Aaron Harang	Cincinnati Reds	587.97	16.21%	23.76	$2.59	$13.43
6	John Smoltz	Atlanta Braves	597.18	16.10%	22.12	$3.76	$13.08
7	Chris Carpenter	St. Louis Cardinals	581.91	15.51%	23.68	$4.02	$13.00
8	Jeremy Bonderman	Detroit Tigers	610.07	14.78%	26.15	$4.30	$13.00
9	John Lackey	Los Angeles Angels of Anaheim	618.06	14.99%	25.32	$4.65	$12.98
10	Derek Lowe	Los Angeles Dodgers	583.73	14.93%	22.52	$3.20	$12.45
11	C. C. Sabathia	Cleveland Indians	598.49	13.54%	25.52	$4.31	$12.14
12	Kevin Millwood	Texas Rangers	656.59	15.02%	19.59	$2.51	$12.01
13	Bronson Arroyo	Cincinnati Reds	655.38	16.65%	13.19	$0.79	$11.94
14	Chien-Ming Wang	New York Yankees	670.88	15.10%	17.54	$3.34	$11.72
15	Curt Schilling	Boston Red Sox	639.46	14.15%	20.88	$3.07	$11.71
16	Jake Westbrook	Cleveland Indians	666.17	14.84%	17.94	$3.06	$11.63
17	Aaron Cook	Colorado Rockies	621.22	14.70%	16.66	$1.50	$11.33
18	Javier Vazquez	Chicago White Sox	652.79	13.99%	18.78	$2.57	$11.26
19	Mike Mussina	New York Yankees	641.49	13.67%	19.89	$3.65	$11.25
20	Erik Bedard	Baltimore Orioles	650.17	13.83%	18.93	$3.04	$11.19
21	David Bush	Milwaukee Brewers	637.65	14.73%	14.28	$2.13	$10.97
22	Jason Jennings	Colorado Rockies	642.85	14.65%	13.44	$0.99	$10.78
23	Chris Capuano	Milwaukee Brewers	672.03	15.52%	9.71	$1.42	$10.73
24	Zach Duke	Pittsburgh Pirates	668.01	15.00%	9.99	$1.46	$10.46
25	Danny Haren	Oakland Athletics	732.05	15.36%	8.44	$1.74	$10.44
26	Vicente Padilla	Texas Rangers	695.90	13.97%	12.73	$1.43	$10.27
27	Jon Garland	Chicago White Sox	715.94	14.58%	10.36	$1.20	$10.26
28	Jason Schmidt	San Francisco Giants	674.26	14.92%	9.00	$1.31	$10.26
29	Jose Contreras	Chicago White Sox	681.03	13.53%	14.34	$1.85	$10.25
30	Kelvim Escobar	Los Angeles Angels of Anaheim	663.11	13.03%	16.15	$3.01	$10.25
31	Jeff Francis	Colorado Rockies	654.52	13.75%	11.01	$0.67	$9.86
32	Jake Peavy	San Diego Padres	659.75	13.82%	10.35	$2.38	$9.80
33	Brad Penny	Los Angeles Dodgers	631.66	12.94%	13.32	$1.72	$9.74
34	Carlos Zambrano	Chicago Cubs	698.75	14.87%	5.33	$0.31	$9.68
35	Dontrelle Willis	Florida Marlins	720.97	15.58%	2.12	$0.95	$9.64

MRP Estimates for Top 35 Hitters (2007)

Rank	Player	Team	Season RS	%PA	RSAA	$ValAA	MRP
1	Alex Rodriguez	New York Yankees	1499.12	10.85%	77.24	$16.61	$23.77
2	David Ortiz	Boston Red Sox	1424.64	10.38%	66.18	$13.64	$20.49
3	Magglio Ordonez	Detroit Tigers	1387.74	10.66%	64.01	$13.08	$20.11
4	Albert Pujols	St. Louis Cardinals	1310.38	10.93%	62.95	$12.81	$20.02
5	David Wright	New York Mets	1274.18	11.21%	60.48	$12.19	$19.59
6	Prince Fielder	Milwaukee Brewers	1266.89	10.92%	58.11	$11.60	$18.80
7	Chipper Jones	Atlanta Braves	1375.71	9.41%	60.35	$12.16	$18.37
8	Miguel Cabrera	Florida Marlins	1256.78	10.72%	55.97	$11.08	$18.15
9	Hanley Ramirez	Florida Marlins	1205.65	11.13%	52.42	$10.23	$17.57
10	Matt Holliday	Colorado Rockies	1195.90	10.97%	50.62	$9.80	$17.04
11	Vladimir Guerrero	Los Angeles Angels of Anaheim	1263.98	10.65%	50.79	$9.84	$16.87
12	Carlos Pena	Tampa Bay Devil Rays	1331.76	9.75%	53.11	$10.39	$16.82
13	Barry Bonds	San Francisco Giants	1433.55	7.68%	53.67	$10.52	$15.59
14	Jorge Posada	New York Yankees	1330.96	9.02%	49.09	$9.44	$15.40
15	Ryan Howard	Philadelphia Phillies	1165.92	9.91%	42.76	$8.01	$14.55
16	Chase Utley	Philadelphia Phillies	1189.38	9.38%	42.65	$7.99	$14.17
17	Todd Helton	Colorado Rockies	1098.07	10.50%	38.15	$7.00	$13.93
18	Ichiro Suzuki	Seattle Mariners	1046.49	11.86%	30.76	$5.46	$13.28
19	Grady Sizemore	Cleveland Indians	1050.24	11.75%	30.93	$5.50	$13.25
20	Derrek Lee	Chicago Cubs	1062.88	10.37%	34.04	$6.14	$12.98
21	Curtis Granderson	Detroit Tigers	1092.92	10.62%	32.50	$5.82	$12.83
22	Adrian Gonzalez	San Diego Padres	996.43	11.38%	29.80	$5.27	$12.78
23	Lance Berkman	Houston Astros	1037.38	10.56%	31.98	$5.71	$12.68
24	Jim Thome	Chicago White Sox	1212.85	8.79%	37.41	$6.85	$12.64
25	Derek Jeter	New York Yankees	1048.50	10.94%	28.60	$5.03	$12.25
26	Ryan Braun	Milwaukee Brewers	1218.90	7.89%	38.20	$7.01	$12.22
27	Adam Dunn	Cincinnati Reds	1047.84	9.99%	31.29	$5.57	$12.16
28	Jimmy Rollins	Philadelphia Phillies	939.47	11.90%	24.39	$4.21	$12.06
29	Carlos Beltran	New York Mets	1035.16	10.03%	30.14	$5.34	$11.95
30	Carlos Lee	Houston Astros	973.27	11.02%	26.31	$4.58	$11.85
31	Victor Martinez	Cleveland Indians	1074.08	10.13%	29.09	$5.13	$11.81
32	Aaron Rowand	Philadelphia Phillies	999.28	10.47%	27.70	$4.85	$11.76
33	Nick Markakis	Baltimore Orioles	983.89	11.34%	22.32	$3.81	$11.29
34	Pat Burrell	Philadelphia Phillies	1054.01	9.15%	29.22	$5.16	$11.19
35	Brad Hawpe	Colorado Rockies	1036.13	9.33%	28.12	$4.94	$11.09

MRP Estimates for Top 35 Pitchers (2007)

Rank	Player	Team	Season RA	%IP	RABA	$ValAA	MRP
1	C. C. Sabathia	Cleveland Indians	550.85	16.48%	40.73	7.56	18.04
2	Brandon Webb	Arizona Diamondbacks	503.92	16.40%	32.87	5.89	17.75
3	Roy Halladay	Toronto Blue Jays	576.37	15.55%	30.07	5.33	16.13
4	Joe Blanton	Oakland Athletics	598.89	15.88%	32.73	5.87	15.76
5	Jake Peavy	San Diego Padres	523.15	15.04%	36.52	6.66	15.60
6	Josh Beckett	Boston Red Sox	540.17	13.95%	33.68	6.06	15.42
7	Tim Hudson	Atlanta Braves	547.90	15.40%	30.44	5.40	15.22
8	John Lackey	Los Angeles Angels of Anaheim	617.37	15.61%	30.34	5.38	14.91
9	Aaron Harang	Cincinnati Reds	579.23	15.98%	18.35	3.08	14.83
10	John Smoltz	Atlanta Braves	554.31	14.12%	27.03	4.72	13.73
11	Scott Kazmir	Tampa Bay Devil Rays	620.66	14.46%	22.26	3.80	13.68
12	James Shields	Tampa Bay Devil Rays	643.29	15.04%	19.68	3.32	13.60
13	Roy Oswalt	Houston Astros	572.83	14.47%	22.58	3.86	13.57
14	Brad Penny	Los Angeles Dodgers	571.09	14.34%	21.81	3.72	13.49
15	Gil Meche	Kansas City Royals	649.78	15.03%	14.76	2.43	13.41
16	Javier Vazquez	Chicago White Sox	656.10	15.04%	17.72	2.96	13.25
17	Danny Haren	Oakland Athletics	667.69	15.38%	21.43	3.65	13.22
18	Kelvim Escobar	Los Angeles Angels of Anaheim	616.19	13.64%	26.66	4.65	13.00
19	Fausto Carmona	Cleveland Indians	658.29	14.70%	20.86	3.54	12.88
20	Chien-Ming Wang	New York Yankees	638.52	13.74%	23.91	4.12	12.52
21	Erik Bedard	Baltimore Orioles	600.38	12.65%	24.37	4.20	12.40
22	Andy Pettitte	New York Yankees	688.39	14.84%	18.73	3.15	12.20
23	Greg Maddux	San Diego Padres	585.35	13.34%	24.59	4.25	12.16
24	Johan Santana	Minnesota Twins	703.86	15.24%	14.82	2.44	12.12
25	Justin Verlander	Detroit Tigers	671.05	13.93%	17.09	2.85	11.87
26	Jeff Francis	Colorado Rockies	642.00	14.63%	6.97	1.10	11.87
27	Adam Wainwright	St. Louis Cardinals	634.49	14.07%	15.87	2.63	11.59
28	Jon Garland	Chicago White Sox	702.05	14.46%	10.26	1.65	11.54
29	Matt Cain	San Francisco Giants	627.98	13.76%	14.67	2.42	11.49
30	Mark Buehrle	Chicago White Sox	692.40	13.95%	11.27	1.83	11.36
31	Carlos Silva	Minnesota Twins	702.50	14.06%	13.86	2.27	11.20
32	Ian Snell	Pittsburgh Pirates	662.77	14.37%	10.32	1.66	11.14
33	Derek Lowe	Los Angeles Dodgers	647.16	13.74%	10.24	1.65	11.02
34	Daisuke Matsuzaka	Boston Red Sox	723.34	14.23%	8.03	1.28	10.84
35	Felix Hernandez	Seattle Mariners	692.35	13.27%	17.15	2.86	10.80

MRP Estimates for Hitters (2007)

ARIZONA DIAMONDBACKS

Player	Season RS	%PA	RSAA	$ValAA	MRP
Eric Byrnes	816.71	11.44%	9.40	$1.51	$9.05
Orlando Hudson	851.11	9.85%	11.48	$1.86	$8.36
Conor Jackson	871.98	7.82%	10.74	$1.74	$6.89
Mark Reynolds	859.07	6.79%	8.45	$1.35	$5.83
Chris Young	666.26	10.23%	-6.99	-$1.03	$5.72
Stephen Drew	561.59	10.15%	-17.56	-$2.44	$4.26
Chris Snyder	742.93	6.23%	0.52	$0.08	$4.19
Chad Tracy	787.63	4.26%	2.26	$0.35	$3.16
Tony Clark	777.24	4.02%	1.71	$0.26	$2.91
Miguel Montero	546.45	4.00%	-7.53	-$1.10	$1.53
Carlos Quentin	486.52	4.31%	-10.70	-$1.54	$1.30
Augie Ojeda	651.89	2.16%	-1.79	-$0.27	$1.16
Scott Hairston	509.43	3.26%	-7.35	-$1.08	$1.07
Jeff Salazar	674.89	1.69%	-1.01	-$0.15	$0.96
Justin Upton	468.38	2.49%	-6.63	-$0.98	$0.66
Robby Hammock	414.82	0.80%	-2.57	-$0.39	$0.14
Emilio Bonifacio	447.23	0.44%	-1.27	-$0.19	$0.10
Jeff Cirillo	338.33	0.72%	-2.86	-$0.43	$0.05
Jeff Davanon	314.42	0.54%	-2.27	-$0.34	$0.01
Jason Smith	195.46	0.07%	-0.35	-$0.05	-$0.01
Alberto Callaspo	269.20	2.56%	-11.90	-$1.71	-$0.02
Donnie Sadler	-902.84	0.02%	-0.27	-$0.04	-$0.03
Brian Barden	-536.74	0.20%	-2.50	-$0.38	-$0.25

ATLANTA BRAVES

Player	Season RS	%PA	RSAA	$ValAA	MRP
Chipper Jones	1375.71	9.41%	60.35	$12.16	$18.37
Edgar Renteria	1032.72	8.52%	25.40	$4.40	$10.02
Kelly Johnson	962.48	9.54%	21.74	$3.70	$10.00
Jeff Francoeur	825.31	10.92%	9.91	$1.59	$8.80
Matt Diaz	1012.77	6.02%	16.76	$2.79	$6.76
Brian McCann	785.23	8.66%	4.39	$0.69	$6.40
Mark Teixeira	1330.31	3.77%	22.43	$3.83	$6.32
Andruw Jones	688.26	10.34%	-4.79	-$0.71	$6.11
Yunel Escobar	986.25	5.57%	14.02	$2.30	$5.97
Willie Harris	770.10	6.13%	2.18	$0.34	$4.38
Jarrod Saltalamacchia	755.22	2.40%	0.50	$0.08	$1.66
Scott Thorman	491.12	4.82%	-11.73	-$1.68	$1.49
Martin Prado	595.89	0.97%	-1.35	-$0.20	$0.44
Corky Miller	741.43	0.45%	0.03	$0.00	$0.30
Julio Franco	535.93	0.71%	-1.40	-$0.21	$0.25

(continued)

MRP Estimates for Hitters (2007) (*continued*)

Player	Season RS	%PA	RSAA	$ValAA	MRP
Clint Sammons	2814.94	0.05%	0.98	$0.15	$0.18
Craig Wilson	399.40	1.08%	-3.63	-$0.54	$0.17
Chris Woodward	272.08	2.37%	-10.96	-$1.58	-$0.02
Brayan Pena	190.26	0.52%	-2.82	-$0.42	-$0.08
Brandon Jones	-37.95	0.33%	-2.55	-$0.38	-$0.17
Pete Orr	109.69	1.08%	-6.76	-$1.00	-$0.28
Ryan Langerhans	-240.45	0.82%	-7.95	-$1.17	-$0.63

BALTIMORE ORIOLES

Player	Season RS	%PA	RSAA	$ValAA	MRP
Nick Markakis	983.89	11.34%	22.32	$3.81	$11.29
Brian Roberts	936.03	11.43%	17.04	$2.84	$10.38
Miguel Tejada	894.31	9.07%	9.73	$1.56	$7.55
Kevin Millar	880.14	8.97%	8.36	$1.33	$7.25
Aubrey Huff	831.50	9.63%	4.28	$0.67	$7.02
Melvin Mora	803.35	8.41%	1.37	$0.21	$5.76
Ramon Hernandez	716.70	6.53%	-4.59	-$0.69	$3.62
Corey Patterson	637.41	8.03%	-12.02	-$1.72	$3.58
Jay Payton	584.11	7.50%	-15.23	-$2.14	$2.81
Chris Gomez	750.86	2.95%	-1.07	-$0.16	$1.79
Tike Redman	878.08	2.22%	2.02	$0.31	$1.78
Jay Gibbons	476.30	4.63%	-14.39	-$2.03	$1.02
Freddie Bynum	699.94	1.61%	-1.40	-$0.21	$0.85
Luis Hernandez	584.41	1.13%	-2.30	-$0.35	$0.40
J. R. House	722.70	0.65%	-0.42	-$0.06	$0.37
Jon Knott	905.59	0.30%	0.36	$0.06	$0.26
Scott Moore	461.64	0.80%	-2.60	-$0.39	$0.13
Paul Bako	335.21	2.78%	-12.55	-$1.79	$0.04
Gustavo Molina	298.31	0.14%	-0.70	-$0.11	-$0.01
Alberto Castillo	299.29	0.57%	-2.80	-$0.42	-$0.04
Brandon Fahey	30.35	0.89%	-6.77	-$1.00	-$0.41

BOSTON RED SOX

Player	Season RS	%PA	RSAA	$ValAA	MRP
David Ortiz	1424.64	10.38%	66.18	$13.64	$20.49
Mike Lowell	1027.62	10.16%	24.45	$4.22	$10.92
Manny Ramirez	1044.19	8.85%	22.77	$3.90	$9.74
Kevin Youkilis	983.72	9.73%	19.13	$3.22	$9.63
Dustin Pedroia	936.50	9.04%	13.52	$2.21	$8.18
J. D. Drew	883.39	8.59%	8.28	$1.32	$6.99
Jason Varitek	861.11	8.06%	5.97	$0.94	$6.26

(*continued*)

MRP Estimates for Hitters (2007) (*continued*)

Player	Season RS	%PA	RSAA	$ValAA	MRP
Coco Crisp	688.31	9.20%	-9.08	-$1.32	$4.74
Julio Lugo	528.29	9.80%	-25.37	-$3.36	$3.11
Jacoby Ellsbury	1086.10	1.98%	5.91	$0.93	$2.24
Eric Hinske	674.80	3.39%	-3.81	-$0.57	$1.67
Alex Cora	600.63	3.61%	-6.73	-$0.99	$1.39
Wily Mo Pena	576.65	2.68%	-5.63	-$0.84	$0.93
Doug Mirabelli	497.17	1.98%	-5.73	-$0.85	$0.45
Brandon Moss	930.03	0.45%	0.65	$0.10	$0.40
Bobby Kielty	494.11	0.95%	-2.78	-$0.42	$0.21
David Murphy	3040.85	0.03%	0.70	$0.11	$0.13
Jeff Bailey	145.26	0.14%	-0.90	-$0.14	-$0.04
Royce Clayton	-918.48	0.09%	-1.59	-$0.24	-$0.18
Kevin Cash	42.70	0.51%	-3.82	-$0.57	-$0.23

CHICAGO CUBS

Player	Season RS	%PA	RSAA	$ValAA	MRP
Derrek Lee	1062.88	10.37%	34.04	$6.14	$12.98
Aramis Ramirez	1021.94	8.90%	25.58	$4.44	$10.31
Alfonso Soriano	955.97	9.84%	21.79	$3.71	$10.21
Mark DeRosa	828.87	9.16%	8.63	$1.38	$7.42
Jacque Jones	691.14	7.90%	-3.43	-$0.52	$4.69
Cliff Floyd	835.61	5.14%	5.19	$0.82	$4.20
Ryan Theriot	577.60	9.52%	-14.95	-$2.11	$4.18
Matt Murton	803.63	4.16%	2.87	$0.45	$3.19
Daryle Ward	1190.22	2.12%	9.67	$1.55	$2.95
Mike Fontenot	696.20	4.15%	-1.59	-$0.24	$2.49
Michael Barrett	653.81	3.69%	-2.98	-$0.45	$1.98
Jason Kendall	697.56	3.22%	-1.19	-$0.18	$1.94
Geovany Soto	1408.50	0.96%	6.45	$1.02	$1.65
Angel Pagan	671.13	2.57%	-1.63	-$0.25	$1.45
Cesar Izturis	425.98	3.30%	-10.19	-$1.47	$0.70
Felix Pie	396.71	3.10%	-10.46	-$1.51	$0.53
Craig Monroe	476.95	0.88%	-2.26	-$0.34	$0.24
Ronny Cedeno	375.72	1.28%	-4.58	-$0.68	$0.16
Eric Patterson	404.00	0.14%	-0.47	-$0.07	$0.02
Sam Fuld	36.68	0.14%	-1.00	-$0.15	-$0.06
Jake Fox	114.24	0.24%	-1.48	-$0.23	-$0.07
Scott Moore	-928.88	0.08%	-1.33	-$0.20	-$0.15
Koyie Hill	175.94	1.68%	-9.36	-$1.36	-$0.26
Henry Blanco	-9.16	0.93%	-6.88	-$1.01	-$0.40
Rob Bowen	-289.02	0.57%	-5.88	-$0.87	-$0.49

CHICAGO WHITE SOX

Player	Season RS	%PA	RSAA	$ValAA	MRP
Jim Thome	1212.85	8.79%	37.41	$6.85	$12.64
Paul Konerko	919.03	10.42%	13.76	$2.26	$9.13
Jermaine Dye	815.36	9.20%	2.61	$0.40	$6.47
Josh Fields	778.55	6.85%	-0.58	-$0.09	$4.43
A. J. Pierzynski	654.12	8.34%	-11.09	-$1.60	$3.91
Tadahito Iguchi	712.64	6.18%	-4.60	-$0.69	$3.39
Juan Uribe	566.96	9.23%	-20.31	-$2.77	$3.31
Rob Mackowiak	811.85	4.39%	1.09	$0.17	$3.07
Jerry Owens	548.62	6.38%	-15.20	-$2.14	$2.07
Darin Erstad	546.20	5.65%	-13.62	-$1.93	$1.80
Scott Podsednik	569.13	3.85%	-8.39	-$1.23	$1.31
Danny Richar	602.45	3.38%	-6.23	-$0.92	$1.31
Luis Terrero	724.13	2.28%	-1.43	-$0.22	$1.29
Alex Cintron	442.73	3.21%	-11.06	-$1.59	$0.53
Joe Crede	366.44	2.92%	-12.27	-$1.75	$0.17
Ryan Sweeney	412.73	0.80%	-3.01	-$0.45	$0.08
Pablo Ozuna	373.09	1.39%	-5.77	-$0.85	$0.06
Andy Gonzalez	318.05	3.52%	-16.53	-$2.31	$0.02
Donny Lucy	3.19	0.25%	-1.93	-$0.29	-$0.13
Brian N. Anderson	-4.58	0.31%	-2.47	-$0.37	-$0.17
Gustavo Molina	-526.03	0.34%	-4.52	-$0.67	-$0.45
Toby Hall	144.13	1.97%	-12.64	-$1.80	-$0.51

CINCINNATI REDS

Player	Season RS	%PA	RSAA	$ValAA	MRP
Adam Dunn	1047.84	9.99%	31.29	$5.57	$12.16
Ken Griffey	919.91	9.85%	18.24	$3.06	$9.55
Brandon Phillips	787.52	11.09%	5.87	$0.93	$8.24
Scott Hatteberg	945.61	6.59%	13.91	$2.28	$6.63
Edwin Encarnacion	783.90	8.79%	4.33	$0.68	$6.47
Josh Hamilton	997.37	5.33%	13.99	$2.30	$5.81
Alex Gonzalez	743.26	6.80%	0.59	$0.09	$4.57
Jeff Keppinger	967.16	4.36%	10.14	$1.63	$4.51
Norris Hopper	745.78	5.29%	0.59	$0.09	$3.58
Javier Valentin	625.95	4.19%	-4.55	-$0.68	$2.08
Jeff Conine	636.53	3.82%	-3.75	-$0.56	$1.96
Dave Ross	485.07	5.50%	-13.72	-$1.95	$1.68
Ryan Freel	506.24	4.80%	-10.97	-$1.58	$1.59
Joey Votto	964.44	1.41%	3.23	$0.50	$1.43
Jorge Cantu	939.90	1.07%	2.21	$0.34	$1.05
Ryan Hanigan	745.09	0.17%	0.02	$0.00	$0.12
Ryan Jorgensen	601.27	0.24%	-0.32	-$0.05	$0.11
Dewayne Wise	973.19	0.09%	0.23	$0.03	$0.10

(continued)

MRP Estimates for Hitters (2007) (*continued*)

Player	Season RS	%PA	RSAA	$ValAA	MRP
Buck Coats	345.29	0.60%	-2.34	-$0.35	$0.04
Jason Ellison	303.70	0.88%	-3.81	-$0.57	$0.01
Enrique Cruz	-894.48	0.02%	-0.26	-$0.04	-$0.03
Mark Bellhorn	-8.00	0.28%	-2.11	-$0.32	-$0.13
Pedro Lopez	46.37	0.74%	-5.11	-$0.76	-$0.27
Chad Moeller	-38.80	0.77%	-5.99	-$0.89	-$0.38
Juan Castro	61.59	1.55%	-10.42	-$1.51	-$0.48

CLEVELAND INDIANS

Player	Season RS	%PA	RSAA	$ValAA	MRP
Grady Sizemore	1050.24	11.75%	30.93	$5.50	$13.25
Victor Martinez	1074.08	10.13%	29.09	$5.13	$11.81
Travis Hafner	1016.78	10.35%	23.79	$4.09	$10.92
Ryan Garko	989.29	8.50%	17.19	$2.87	$8.47
Casey Blake	848.99	10.40%	6.45	$1.02	$7.88
Jhonny Peralta	840.75	10.16%	5.46	$0.86	$7.56
Franklin Gutierrez	842.47	4.73%	2.62	$0.41	$3.53
Trot Nixon	679.63	5.56%	-5.97	-$0.88	$2.78
Jason Michaels	732.08	4.63%	-2.55	-$0.38	$2.67
Asdrubal Cabrera	865.69	2.92%	2.30	$0.36	$2.28
Kelly Shoppach	819.56	2.78%	0.90	$0.14	$1.97
Kenny Lofton	745.60	3.08%	-1.28	-$0.19	$1.84
Josh Barfield	435.77	6.98%	-24.50	-$3.26	$1.34
David Dellucci	619.82	3.13%	-5.23	-$0.78	$1.28
Ben Francisco	845.49	1.04%	0.61	$0.09	$0.78
Luis Rivas	1146.92	0.17%	0.62	$0.10	$0.21
Chris Gomez	455.10	0.86%	-2.87	-$0.43	$0.14
Shin-Soo Choo	633.05	0.31%	-0.48	-$0.07	$0.13
Andy Marte	308.43	0.94%	-4.51	-$0.67	-$0.05
Mike Rouse	-110.90	1.19%	-10.72	-$1.55	-$0.76

COLORADO ROCKIES

Player	Season RS	%PA	RSAA	$ValAA	MRP
Matt Holliday	1195.90	10.97%	50.62	$9.80	$17.04
Todd Helton	1098.07	10.50%	38.15	$7.00	$13.93
Brad Hawpe	1036.13	9.33%	28.12	$4.94	$11.09
Garrett Atkins	897.02	10.53%	17.10	$2.85	$9.79
Troy Tulowitzki	864.21	10.50%	13.60	$2.23	$9.15
Kazuo Matsui	697.63	6.97%	-2.58	-$0.39	$4.21
Ryan Spilborghs	885.07	4.62%	6.95	$1.10	$4.15
Willy Taveras	731.51	6.28%	-0.19	-$0.03	$4.11

(*continued*)

MRP Estimates for Hitters (2007) (*continued*)

Player	Season RS	%PA	RSAA	$ValAA	MRP
Yorvit Torrealba	599.22	6.82%	-9.23	-$1.34	$3.15
Chris Iannetta	580.20	3.60%	-5.56	-$0.83	$1.55
Cory Sullivan	650.37	2.35%	-1.98	-$0.30	$1.25
Jamey Carroll	461.70	4.12%	-11.25	-$1.62	$1.10
Jeff Baker	477.23	2.45%	-6.30	-$0.93	$0.68
Seth Smith	2237.34	0.12%	1.85	$0.29	$0.37
Ian Stewart	418.69	0.71%	-2.24	-$0.34	$0.13
Omar Quintanilla	336.27	1.15%	-4.60	-$0.69	$0.08
Sean Barker	35.65	0.05%	-0.32	-$0.05	-$0.02
Edwin Bellorin	-902.84	0.03%	-0.50	-$0.08	-$0.06
Clint Barmes	233.03	0.60%	-3.01	-$0.45	-$0.06
Joe Koshansky	-76.79	0.23%	-1.87	-$0.28	-$0.13
John Mabry	118.11	0.60%	-3.70	-$0.55	-$0.16
Steve Finley	173.26	1.57%	-8.81	-$1.28	-$0.25
Geronimo Gil	-414.75	0.25%	-2.83	-$0.43	-$0.26

DETROIT TIGERS

Player	Season RS	%PA	RSAA	$ValAA	MRP
Magglio Ordonez	1387.74	10.66%	64.01	$13.08	$20.11
Curtis Granderson	1092.92	10.62%	32.50	$5.82	$12.83
Placido Polanco	1016.12	10.07%	23.08	$3.96	$10.60
Carlos Guillen	996.09	9.90%	20.70	$3.51	$10.04
Gary Sheffield	990.16	9.32%	18.93	$3.18	$9.33
Sean Casey	797.35	7.80%	0.81	$0.12	$5.27
Brandon Inge	645.08	9.07%	-12.87	-$1.83	$4.15
Ivan Rodriguez	664.37	8.09%	-9.93	-$1.44	$3.90
Marcus Thames	749.58	4.46%	-1.67	-$0.25	$2.69
Ryan Raburn	953.67	2.33%	3.88	$0.60	$2.14
Timo Perez	1262.74	1.51%	7.18	$1.14	$2.13
Craig Monroe	493.84	5.85%	-17.14	-$2.38	$1.47
Omar Infante	593.39	2.80%	-5.42	-$0.80	$1.04
Mike Rabelo	575.58	2.91%	-6.15	-$0.91	$1.01
Ramon Santiago	701.16	1.16%	-1.00	-$0.15	$0.62
Mike Hessman	763.69	0.90%	-0.21	-$0.03	$0.56
Brent Clevlen	-471.50	0.16%	-1.98	-$0.30	-$0.20
Cameron Maybin	137.65	0.83%	-5.41	-$0.80	-$0.25
Neifi Perez	177.88	1.12%	-6.80	-$1.00	-$0.27

FLORIDA MARLINS

Player	Season RS	%PA	RSAA	$ValAA	MRP
Miguel Cabrera	1256.78	10.72%	55.97	$11.08	$18.15
Hanley Ramirez	1205.65	11.13%	52.42	$10.23	$17.57
Dan Uggla	868.75	11.48%	15.39	$2.54	$10.11
Josh Willingham	960.15	9.52%	21.48	$3.65	$9.93
Jeremy Hermida	1042.34	7.63%	23.48	$4.03	$9.07
Cody Ross	1447.68	3.11%	22.14	$3.78	$5.83
Mike Jacobs	803.02	7.25%	4.96	$0.78	$5.56
Alfredo Amezaga	646.87	7.06%	-6.20	-$0.92	$3.74
Aaron Boone	964.62	3.59%	8.27	$1.32	$3.69
Miguel Olivo	534.23	7.39%	-14.81	-$2.09	$2.79
Matt Treanor	811.91	3.12%	2.41	$0.37	$2.43
Todd Linden	731.63	2.27%	-0.07	-$0.01	$1.49
Joe Borchard	449.57	3.18%	-9.08	-$1.32	$0.78
Jason Wood	542.24	2.00%	-3.85	-$0.58	$0.74
Alejandro De Aza	367.48	2.49%	-9.14	-$1.33	$0.31
Robert Andino	1022.93	0.20%	0.59	$0.09	$0.23
Paul Hoover	838.66	0.13%	0.13	$0.02	$0.10
Reggie Abercrombie	297.42	1.26%	-5.51	-$0.82	$0.01
John Gall	-382.66	0.08%	-0.88	-$0.13	-$0.08
Brett Carroll	77.57	0.84%	-5.49	-$0.81	-$0.26
Eric Reed	-386.17	0.33%	-3.71	-$0.56	-$0.34

HOUSTON ASTROS

Player	Season RS	%PA	RSAA	$ValAA	MRP
Lance Berkman	1037.38	10.56%	31.98	$5.71	$12.68
Carlos Lee	973.27	11.02%	26.31	$4.58	$11.85
Hunter Pence	1007.56	7.65%	20.89	$3.55	$8.59
Luke Scott	922.62	6.72%	12.64	$2.06	$6.49
Mike Lamb	885.65	5.58%	8.43	$1.35	$5.03
Mark Loretta	708.85	8.08%	-2.08	-$0.31	$5.02
Craig Biggio	524.33	8.78%	-18.45	-$2.55	$3.24
Ty Wigginton	827.60	2.96%	2.75	$0.43	$2.38
Brad Ausmus	528.19	6.28%	-12.96	-$1.85	$2.29
Chris Burke	542.89	5.74%	-11.00	-$1.58	$2.20
Morgan Ensberg	642.18	4.10%	-3.78	-$0.57	$2.13
Josh Anderson	940.64	1.19%	2.44	$0.38	$1.16
J. R. Towles	1279.93	0.70%	3.79	$0.59	$1.05
Eric Bruntlett	542.28	2.61%	-5.02	-$0.75	$0.97
Eric Munson	567.63	2.37%	-3.96	-$0.59	$0.97
Adam Everett	409.00	3.73%	-12.15	-$1.74	$0.72
Cody Ransom	887.56	0.73%	1.11	$0.17	$0.65
Orlando Palmeiro	495.86	1.93%	-4.61	-$0.69	$0.59
Jason Lane	388.41	3.04%	-10.51	-$1.52	$0.48
Humberto Quintero	319.14	0.90%	-3.74	-$0.56	$0.03

KANSAS CITY ROYALS

Player	Season RS	%PA	RSAA	$ValAA	MRP
Mark Teahen	764.06	9.90%	-2.27	-$0.34	$6.19
David DeJesus	698.22	11.45%	-10.17	-$1.47	$6.08
Mark Grudzielanek	769.87	7.92%	-1.36	-$0.21	$5.02
Alex Gordon	656.03	9.77%	-12.80	-$1.83	$4.62
Billy Butler	806.97	5.86%	1.17	$0.18	$4.05
Esteban German	706.23	6.60%	-5.33	-$0.79	$3.56
John Buck	669.83	6.50%	-7.62	-$1.12	$3.17
Ross Gload	714.71	5.64%	-4.08	-$0.61	$3.11
Joey Gathright	707.36	4.25%	-3.39	-$0.51	$2.30
Tony Pena	485.32	8.73%	-26.34	-$3.47	$2.29
Mike Sweeney	648.01	4.71%	-6.54	-$0.97	$2.14
Emil Brown	515.83	6.47%	-17.54	-$2.43	$1.83
Reggie Sanders	1061.80	1.38%	3.80	$0.59	$1.51
Ryan Shealy	415.01	3.08%	-11.45	-$1.65	$0.39
Jason Smith	430.83	1.45%	-5.16	-$0.77	$0.19
Fernando Cortez	626.40	0.26%	-0.42	-$0.06	$0.11
Craig Brazell	645.05	0.08%	-0.12	-$0.02	$0.04
Shane Costa	322.52	1.78%	-8.25	-$1.21	-$0.04
Paul Phillips	25.61	0.24%	-1.86	-$0.28	-$0.12
Justin Huber	-436.25	0.16%	-1.99	-$0.30	-$0.19
Angel Berroa	-262.89	0.21%	-2.22	-$0.34	-$0.20
Jason LaRue	228.41	3.18%	-17.74	-$2.46	-$0.36

LOS ANGELES ANGELS OF ANAHEIM

Player	Season RS	%PA	RSAA	$ValAA	MRP
Vladimir Guerrero	1263.98	10.65%	50.79	$9.84	$16.87
Casey Kotchman	1024.71	8.20%	19.48	$3.28	$8.69
Chone Figgins	1028.65	8.12%	19.61	$3.31	$8.66
Orlando Cabrera	813.41	11.31%	2.98	$0.46	$7.92
Garret Anderson	951.51	7.26%	11.94	$1.94	$6.73
Reggie Willits	863.88	8.36%	6.42	$1.02	$6.53
Gary Matthews	781.88	9.34%	-0.48	-$0.07	$6.09
Howie Kendrick	912.04	5.70%	7.12	$1.13	$4.89
Maicer Izturis	838.32	6.03%	3.10	$0.48	$4.46
Mike Napoli	914.43	4.24%	5.41	$0.85	$3.65
Kendry Morales	922.05	2.03%	2.75	$0.43	$1.77
Robb Quinlan	597.21	3.13%	-5.94	-$0.88	$1.18
Jeff Mathis	512.71	3.15%	-8.63	-$1.26	$0.82
Shea Hillenbrand	461.64	3.29%	-10.71	-$1.55	$0.63
Erick Aybar	411.04	3.40%	-12.80	-$1.83	$0.42
Juan Rivera	735.95	0.71%	-0.36	-$0.06	$0.41
Nathan Haynes	557.66	0.77%	-1.78	-$0.27	$0.24
Terry Evans	391.82	0.21%	-0.83	-$0.13	$0.01

(*continued*)

MRP Estimates for Hitters (2007) (*continued*)

Player	Season RS	%PA	RSAA	$ValAA	MRP
Matthew Brown	-80.13	0.11%	-0.98	-$0.15	-$0.07
Nick Gorneault	-351.94	0.08%	-0.92	-$0.14	-$0.09
Jose Molina	293.62	2.11%	-10.43	-$1.51	-$0.11
Ryan Budde	-62.75	0.29%	-2.47	-$0.37	-$0.18
Tommy Murphy	38.43	0.63%	-4.71	-$0.70	-$0.29
Brandon Wood	-21.05	0.53%	-4.30	-$0.64	-$0.29

LOS ANGELES DODGERS

Player	Season RS	%PA	RSAA	$ValAA	MRP
Russell Martin	933.50	9.88%	19.64	$3.31	$9.83
Jeff Kent	989.30	8.95%	22.80	$3.90	$9.81
James Loney	1069.24	5.97%	19.99	$3.38	$7.32
Luis Gonzalez	831.09	8.38%	8.09	$1.29	$6.82
Andre Ethier	836.01	8.04%	8.16	$1.30	$6.61
Juan Pierre	616.57	11.61%	-13.71	-$1.94	$5.71
Matt Kemp	1016.06	4.95%	13.94	$2.29	$5.56
Rafael Furcal	622.68	10.23%	-11.44	-$1.64	$5.10
Nomar Garciaparra	637.02	7.42%	-7.24	-$1.07	$3.83
Wilson Betemit	899.40	3.06%	5.04	$0.79	$2.81
Tony Abreu	633.50	2.84%	-2.87	-$0.43	$1.44
Andy LaRoche	647.66	1.83%	-1.59	-$0.24	$0.97
Delwyn Young	1354.44	0.57%	3.55	$0.55	$0.93
Olmedo Saenz	497.27	2.10%	-4.99	-$0.74	$0.64
Chin-Lung Hu	621.88	0.49%	-0.56	-$0.08	$0.24
Brady Clark	446.77	1.05%	-3.03	-$0.46	$0.24
Shea Hillenbrand	378.68	1.18%	-4.20	-$0.63	$0.15
Mark Sweeney	423.11	0.54%	-1.69	-$0.26	$0.10
Mike Lieberthal	311.20	1.31%	-5.53	-$0.82	$0.04
Marlon Anderson	351.44	0.46%	-1.77	-$0.27	$0.04
Wilson Valdez	275.51	1.27%	-5.85	-$0.87	-$0.03
Chad Moeller	-83.89	0.14%	-1.17	-$0.18	-$0.08
Ramon Martinez	158.25	2.34%	-13.50	-$1.92	-$0.37

MILWAUKEE BREWERS

Player	Season RS	%PA	RSAA	$ValAA	MRP
Prince Fielder	1266.89	10.92%	58.11	$11.60	$18.80
Ryan Braun	1218.90	7.89%	38.20	$7.01	$12.22
Corey Hart	1006.48	9.07%	24.67	$4.26	$10.25
J. J. Hardy	789.40	10.23%	5.61	$0.88	$7.63
Rickie Weeks	890.50	8.11%	12.65	$2.06	$7.41
Geoff Jenkins	790.71	7.44%	4.17	$0.65	$5.56

(*continued*)

MRP Estimates for Hitters (2007) (*continued*)

Player	Season RS	%PA	RSAA	$ValAA	MRP
Bill Hall	699.23	8.06%	-2.85	-$0.43	$4.89
Johnny Estrada	605.21	7.44%	-9.62	-$1.40	$3.51
Kevin Mench	697.81	4.94%	-1.82	-$0.28	$2.98
Gabe Gross	761.79	3.37%	0.92	$0.14	$2.36
Tony Graffanino	641.80	4.17%	-3.87	-$0.58	$2.17
Craig Counsell	528.35	5.35%	-11.04	-$1.59	$1.94
Joe Dillon	1053.67	1.31%	4.19	$0.66	$1.52
Damian Miller	515.98	3.30%	-7.22	-$1.06	$1.12
Tony Gwynn	551.10	2.16%	-3.97	-$0.59	$0.83
Mike Rivera	1063.42	0.24%	0.79	$0.12	$0.28
Vinny Rottino	266.14	0.14%	-0.68	-$0.10	-$0.01
Mel Stocker	-966.04	0.05%	-0.82	-$0.12	-$0.09
Laynce Nix	-966.04	0.19%	-3.27	-$0.49	-$0.36

MINNESOTA TWINS

Player	Season RS	%PA	RSAA	$ValAA	MRP
Justin Morneau	944.56	10.84%	17.08	$2.85	$10.00
Torii Hunter	940.20	10.55%	16.16	$2.68	$9.64
Michael Cuddyer	885.79	10.11%	9.99	$1.61	$8.28
Joe Mauer	951.29	7.64%	12.56	$2.05	$7.09
Jason Kubel	850.08	7.56%	4.77	$0.75	$5.74
Jason Bartlett	706.37	9.25%	-7.46	-$1.10	$5.01
Luis Castillo	746.11	6.23%	-2.55	-$0.38	$3.73
Mike Redmond	714.51	4.84%	-3.51	-$0.53	$2.66
Jason Tyner	674.40	5.32%	-6.00	-$0.89	$2.62
Jeff Cirillo	715.00	2.82%	-2.03	-$0.31	$1.56
Nick Punto	404.38	8.70%	-33.29	-$4.20	$1.54
Lew Ford	637.23	2.11%	-3.16	-$0.48	$0.92
Brian Buscher	602.85	1.53%	-2.81	-$0.42	$0.58
Tommy Watkins	1004.13	0.52%	1.13	$0.17	$0.52
Luis Rodriguez	429.25	2.81%	-10.05	-$1.45	$0.40
Jose Morales	4414.88	0.05%	1.77	$0.27	$0.30
Garrett Jones	430.79	1.36%	-4.86	-$0.72	$0.18
Chris Heintz	360.42	0.99%	-4.22	-$0.63	$0.02
Rondell White	320.46	1.93%	-9.01	-$1.31	-$0.04
Darnell McDonald	-224.80	0.18%	-1.81	-$0.27	-$0.16
Alexi Casilla	278.45	3.31%	-16.84	-$2.35	-$0.16
Matt LeCroy	-150.35	0.32%	-3.04	-$0.46	-$0.24
Josh Rabe	-27.59	0.50%	-4.10	-$0.61	-$0.28

NEW YORK METS

Player	Season RS	%PA	RSAA	$ValAA	MRP
David Wright	1274.18	11.21%	60.48	$12.19	$19.59
Carlos Beltran	1035.16	10.03%	30.14	$5.34	$11.95
Jose Reyes	854.43	12.06%	14.45	$2.38	$10.33
Moises Alou	1156.98	5.68%	23.97	$4.13	$7.87
Carlos Delgado	834.43	9.57%	9.55	$1.53	$7.85
Shawn Green	863.51	7.73%	9.96	$1.60	$6.70
Paul Lo Duca	641.28	7.69%	-7.18	-$1.06	$4.02
Damion Easley	946.39	3.44%	7.28	$1.16	$3.42
Luis Castillo	818.92	3.64%	3.07	$0.48	$2.88
Lastings Milledge	857.86	3.25%	4.00	$0.62	$2.77
Ruben Gotay	844.27	3.33%	3.65	$0.57	$2.76
Ramon Castro	1020.65	2.48%	7.08	$1.12	$2.76
Endy Chavez	688.99	2.60%	-1.19	-$0.18	$1.54
Marlon Anderson	1088.34	1.21%	4.29	$0.67	$1.47
Jose Valentin	605.12	2.89%	-3.74	-$0.56	$1.34
Carlos Gomez	435.88	2.19%	-6.55	-$0.97	$0.48
Ricky Ledee	655.71	0.68%	-0.53	-$0.08	$0.37
Mike Difelice	591.64	0.74%	-1.06	-$0.16	$0.33
Julio Franco	484.85	0.96%	-2.40	-$0.36	$0.27
David Newhan	404.35	1.31%	-4.32	-$0.65	$0.22
Jeff Conine	387.28	0.79%	-2.74	-$0.41	$0.11
Anderson Hernandez	632.49	0.05%	-0.05	-$0.01	$0.02
Chip Ambres	632.49	0.05%	-0.05	-$0.01	$0.02
Ben Johnson	117.93	0.47%	-2.92	-$0.44	-$0.13
Sandy Alomar	-261.37	0.35%	-3.45	-$0.52	-$0.29

NEW YORK YANKEES

Player	Season RS	%PA	RSAA	$ValAA	MRP
Alex Rodriguez	1499.12	10.85%	77.24	$16.61	$23.77
Jorge Posada	1330.96	9.02%	49.09	$9.44	$15.40
Derek Jeter	1048.50	10.94%	28.60	$5.03	$12.25
Hideki Matsui	1043.47	9.70%	24.87	$4.30	$10.70
Robinson Cano	1001.07	10.25%	21.94	$3.74	$10.50
Bobby Abreu	974.40	10.71%	20.07	$3.39	$10.46
Johnny Damon	830.35	9.27%	4.02	$0.63	$6.74
Melky Cabrera	746.06	9.38%	-3.84	-$0.58	$5.61
Jason Giambi	913.71	4.64%	5.88	$0.93	$3.99
Doug Mientkiewicz	903.48	2.94%	3.43	$0.53	$2.47
Andy Phillips	749.43	3.17%	-1.19	-$0.18	$1.91
Shelley Duncan	1042.54	1.27%	3.25	$0.51	$1.34
Jose Molina	851.68	1.09%	0.70	$0.11	$0.83
Josh Phelps	703.03	1.35%	-1.13	-$0.17	$0.72
Wilson Betemit	635.12	1.41%	-2.14	-$0.32	$0.61

(continued)

MRP Estimates for Hitters (2007) (*continued*)

Player	Season RS	%PA	RSAA	$ValAA	MRP
Miguel Cairo	554.22	1.85%	-4.32	-$0.64	$0.58
Bronson Sardinha	927.47	0.18%	0.26	$0.04	$0.16
Kevin Thompson	433.42	0.35%	-1.25	-$0.19	$0.04
Chris Basak	-986.16	0.02%	-0.27	-$0.04	-$0.03
Alberto Gonzalez	-436.42	0.23%	-2.81	-$0.42	-$0.27
Wil Nieves	25.70	1.01%	-7.70	-$1.13	-$0.46

OAKLAND ATHLETICS

Player	Season RS	%PA	RSAA	$ValAA	MRP
Jack Cust	1191.26	7.97%	32.21	$5.76	$11.01
Nick Swisher	1020.48	10.36%	24.17	$4.17	$11.00
Mark Ellis	853.50	10.09%	6.71	$1.06	$7.72
Shannon Stewart	799.74	9.90%	1.26	$0.19	$6.72
Dan Johnson	856.38	7.78%	5.39	$0.85	$5.98
Travis Buck	1038.59	5.25%	13.20	$2.16	$5.62
Eric Chavez	768.43	5.96%	-1.11	-$0.17	$3.76
Marco Scutaro	699.31	5.96%	-5.22	-$0.78	$3.15
Mike Piazza	734.99	5.17%	-2.69	-$0.41	$3.00
Kurt Suzuki	767.05	3.90%	-0.78	-$0.12	$2.45
Daric Barton	1492.49	1.32%	9.31	$1.49	$2.36
Jack Hannahan	927.13	2.66%	3.72	$0.58	$2.33
Bobby Crosby	496.33	5.88%	-17.08	-$2.38	$1.50
Milton Bradley	980.22	1.18%	2.28	$0.35	$1.13
Donnie Murphy	709.33	2.07%	-1.61	-$0.24	$1.12
Rob Bowen	1103.72	0.85%	2.69	$0.42	$0.98
Mark Kotsay	419.60	3.55%	-13.05	-$1.86	$0.48
Chris Snelling	1145.86	0.39%	1.41	$0.22	$0.48
Jason Kendall	337.88	4.90%	-22.02	-$2.98	$0.26
Jeff Davanon	498.90	1.12%	-3.21	-$0.48	$0.25
Adam Melhuse	543.58	0.47%	-1.15	-$0.17	$0.14
J. J. Furmaniak	578.99	0.35%	-0.72	-$0.11	$0.12
Todd Walker	442.22	0.82%	-2.82	-$0.42	$0.11
Danny Putnam	500.40	0.49%	-1.40	-$0.21	$0.11
Bobby Kielty	289.02	0.63%	-3.13	-$0.47	-$0.06
Ryan Langerhans	-348.28	0.08%	-0.89	-$0.14	-$0.08
Dee Brown	-975.89	0.05%	-0.83	-$0.13	-$0.10
Hiram Bocachica	-91.41	0.31%	-2.76	-$0.42	-$0.21
Kevin Thompson	-431.87	0.24%	-2.87	-$0.43	-$0.28

PHILADELPHIA PHILLIES

Player	Season RS	%PA	RSAA	$ValAA	MRP
Ryan Howard	1165.92	9.91%	42.76	$8.01	$14.55
Chase Utley	1189.38	9.38%	42.65	$7.99	$14.17
Jimmy Rollins	939.47	11.90%	24.39	$4.21	$12.06
Aaron Rowand	999.28	10.47%	27.70	$4.85	$11.76
Pat Burrell	1054.01	9.15%	29.22	$5.16	$11.19
Shane Victorino	769.34	7.80%	2.71	$0.42	$5.57
Jayson Werth	995.65	4.65%	12.14	$1.98	$5.04
Carlos Ruiz	704.01	6.56%	-2.01	-$0.30	$4.03
Greg Dobbs	764.70	5.48%	1.65	$0.25	$3.87
Tadahito Iguchi	843.29	2.39%	2.59	$0.40	$1.98
Wes Helms	534.81	4.71%	-9.41	-$1.37	$1.74
Rod Barajas	735.67	2.23%	0.02	$0.00	$1.48
Michael Bourn	701.14	2.03%	-0.68	-$0.10	$1.24
Chris Coste	658.13	2.10%	-1.60	-$0.24	$1.14
Abraham Nunez	454.03	4.39%	-12.32	-$1.76	$1.13
Russell Branyan	1168.94	0.14%	0.60	$0.09	$0.18
Chris Roberson	438.08	0.44%	-1.32	-$0.20	$0.09
Pete LaForest	-113.95	0.20%	-1.69	-$0.26	-$0.12

PITTSBURGH PIRATES

Player	Season RS	%PA	RSAA	$ValAA	MRP
Adam LaRoche	846.72	10.17%	11.40	$1.85	$8.56
Freddy Sanchez	811.84	10.51%	8.12	$1.29	$8.23
Jack Wilson	832.71	8.61%	8.45	$1.35	$7.03
Jose Bautista	754.37	9.88%	1.95	$0.30	$6.82
Jason Bay	726.17	9.88%	-0.83	-$0.13	$6.39
Xavier Nady	830.42	7.56%	7.25	$1.15	$6.14
Nate McLouth	865.95	6.15%	8.07	$1.29	$5.34
Ronny Paulino	636.73	7.95%	-7.78	-$1.14	$4.10
Ryan Doumit	856.93	4.49%	5.49	$0.86	$3.83
Josh Phelps	1525.46	1.53%	12.09	$1.97	$2.97
Chris Duffy	580.61	4.35%	-6.69	-$0.99	$1.88
Nyjer Morgan	841.14	1.90%	2.02	$0.31	$1.57
Steven Pearce	735.96	1.17%	0.02	$0.00	$0.78
Cesar Izturis	530.81	2.09%	-4.26	-$0.64	$0.74
Jose Castillo	411.31	3.70%	-11.97	-$1.71	$0.73
Rajai Davis	707.76	0.92%	-0.25	-$0.04	$0.57
Carlos Maldonado	882.23	0.48%	0.71	$0.11	$0.43
Matt Kata	464.73	1.45%	-3.91	-$0.59	$0.37
Humberto Cota	808.42	0.29%	0.21	$0.03	$0.22
Don Kelly	131.34	0.51%	-3.11	-$0.47	-$0.13
Brad Eldred	-141.07	0.76%	-6.62	-$0.98	-$0.48

SAN DIEGO PADRES

Player	Season RS	%PA	RSAA	$ValAA	MRP
Adrian Gonzalez	996.43	11.38%	29.80	$5.27	$12.78
Mike Cameron	806.42	10.29%	7.39	$1.17	$7.96
Brian Giles	884.45	8.73%	13.08	$2.14	$7.89
Kevin Kouzmanoff	855.66	8.44%	10.22	$1.65	$7.21
Khalil Greene	754.70	10.42%	2.09	$0.32	$7.19
Josh Bard	873.80	7.00%	9.75	$1.57	$6.19
Milton Bradley	1374.46	2.67%	17.09	$2.85	$4.61
Geoff Blum	659.53	5.85%	-4.39	-$0.66	$3.20
Marcus Giles	521.65	7.52%	-16.02	-$2.24	$2.72
Jose Cruz	665.49	4.63%	-3.20	-$0.48	$2.57
Scott Hairston	1220.81	1.50%	7.30	$1.16	$2.15
Terrmel Sledge	620.03	3.68%	-4.22	-$0.63	$1.80
Russell Branyan	777.74	2.31%	1.00	$0.15	$1.68
Rob Bowen	960.39	1.55%	3.50	$0.54	$1.57
Brady Clark	1009.25	0.90%	2.47	$0.38	$0.98
Morgan Ensberg	834.28	1.03%	1.02	$0.16	$0.84
Pete LaForest	1416.84	0.47%	3.24	$0.50	$0.82
Hiram Bocachica	547.87	1.07%	-2.01	-$0.30	$0.41
Chase Headley	545.25	0.33%	-0.63	-$0.10	$0.12
Craig Stansberry	694.62	0.16%	-0.06	-$0.01	$0.09
Paul McAnulty	334.48	0.68%	-2.72	-$0.41	$0.04
Oscar Robles	305.66	0.52%	-2.24	-$0.34	$0.01
Colt Morton	-1038.75	0.02%	-0.28	-$0.04	-$0.03
Rob Mackowiak	264.71	0.96%	-4.53	-$0.68	-$0.04
Brian Myrow	134.12	0.19%	-1.14	-$0.17	-$0.05
Jason Lane	-1038.75	0.03%	-0.56	-$0.09	-$0.06
Michael Barrett	242.07	2.15%	-10.59	-$1.53	-$0.11

SAN FRANCISCO GIANTS

Player	Season RS	%PA	RSAA	$ValAA	MRP
Barry Bonds	1433.55	7.68%	53.67	$10.52	$15.59
Randy Winn	848.50	10.51%	11.97	$1.95	$8.88
Bengie Molina	663.35	8.32%	-5.93	-$0.88	$4.61
Pedro Feliz	613.27	9.50%	-11.52	-$1.65	$4.61
Ryan Klesko	746.18	6.62%	0.77	$0.12	$4.48
Dave Roberts	645.14	7.12%	-6.36	-$0.94	$3.75
Omar Vizquel	485.33	9.26%	-23.07	-$3.10	$3.01
Ray Durham	502.52	8.50%	-19.73	-$2.70	$2.90
Kevin Frandsen	670.75	4.76%	-3.04	-$0.46	$2.69
Rich Aurilia	572.07	5.76%	-9.37	-$1.36	$2.44
Fred Lewis	849.73	2.90%	3.34	$0.52	$2.43
Dan Ortmeier	828.75	2.69%	2.53	$0.39	$2.17
Rajai Davis	767.99	2.61%	0.87	$0.13	$1.85

(continued)

MRP Estimates for Hitters (2007) (*continued*)

Player	Season RS	%PA	RSAA	$ValAA	MRP
Mark Sweeney	836.38	1.72%	1.75	$0.27	$1.41
Nate Schierholtz	664.93	1.88%	-1.31	-$0.20	$1.04
Guillermo Rodriguez	619.18	1.58%	-1.82	-$0.28	$0.76
Eliezer Alfonzo	494.95	1.08%	-2.58	-$0.39	$0.32
Eugenio Velez	1266.92	0.21%	1.11	$0.17	$0.31
Luis Figueroa	-25.90	0.08%	-0.61	-$0.09	-$0.04
Scott McClain	-111.36	0.18%	-1.50	-$0.23	-$0.11
Lance Niekro	1.33	0.29%	-2.12	-$0.32	-$0.13
Todd Linden	124.73	0.97%	-5.89	-$0.87	-$0.24

SEATTLE MARINERS

Player	Season RS	%PA	RSAA	$ValAA	MRP
Ichiro Suzuki	1046.49	11.86%	30.76	$5.46	$13.28
Raul Ibanez	988.97	10.24%	20.69	$3.51	$10.27
Jose Guillen	960.11	10.60%	18.35	$3.08	$10.07
Jose Vidro	931.13	10.07%	14.51	$2.39	$9.03
Adrian Beltre	892.76	10.29%	10.88	$1.76	$8.55
Kenji Johjima	811.76	8.26%	2.04	$0.32	$5.77
Yuniesky Betancourt	739.54	9.00%	-4.28	-$0.64	$5.30
Richie Sexson	665.67	7.91%	-9.60	-$1.39	$3.82
Jose Lopez	552.35	9.04%	-21.21	-$2.88	$3.08
Ben Broussard	785.34	4.25%	-0.07	-$0.01	$2.79
Jamie Burke	881.58	2.08%	1.97	$0.30	$1.67
Willie Bloomquist	622.70	3.03%	-4.98	-$0.74	$1.26
Jeff Clement	1980.61	0.31%	3.65	$0.57	$0.77
Mike Morse	1603.50	0.32%	2.63	$0.41	$0.62
Adam Jones	683.17	1.14%	-1.19	-$0.18	$0.57
Wladimir Balentien	4197.61	0.06%	2.20	$0.34	$0.38
Charlton Jimerson	6697.99	0.03%	1.90	$0.29	$0.32
Jason Ellison	465.52	0.77%	-2.49	-$0.38	$0.13
Rob Johnson	670.27	0.05%	-0.06	-$0.01	$0.02
Jeremy Reed	97.12	0.27%	-1.89	-$0.29	-$0.11
Nick Green	-996.65	0.11%	-2.01	-$0.30	-$0.23

ST. LOUIS CARDINALS

Player	Season RS	% PA	RSAA	$ValAA	MRP
Albert Pujols	1310.38	10.93%	62.95	$12.81	$20.02
Chris Duncan	929.82	6.96%	13.58	$2.22	$6.81
David Eckstein	768.69	7.79%	2.66	$0.41	$5.55
Ryan Ludwick	881.58	5.46%	8.02	$1.28	$4.88
Scott Rolen	717.48	7.10%	-1.21	-$0.18	$4.50

(continued)

MRP Estimates for Hitters (2007) (*continued*)

Player	Season RS	%PA	RSAA	$ValAA	MRP
Jim Edmonds	707.64	6.62%	-1.78	-$0.27	$4.09
Yadier Molina	694.12	6.38%	-2.58	-$0.39	$3.82
Aaron Miles	621.98	7.23%	-8.14	-$1.19	$3.58
Juan Encarnacion	775.75	4.94%	2.03	$0.31	$3.57
So Taguchi	724.67	5.47%	-0.54	-$0.08	$3.53
Rick Ankiel	944.06	3.06%	6.41	$1.01	$3.03
Scott Spiezio	767.04	4.14%	1.34	$0.21	$2.94
Skip Schumaker	903.95	3.03%	5.13	$0.80	$2.80
Brendan Ryan	779.36	3.20%	1.43	$0.22	$2.33
Adam Kennedy	381.14	4.93%	-17.41	-$2.42	$0.83
Gary Bennett	470.45	2.74%	-7.23	-$1.06	$0.74
Miguel Cairo	514.81	1.16%	-2.55	-$0.38	$0.38
Russell Branyan	523.41	0.63%	-1.33	-$0.20	$0.21
Preston Wilson	366.28	1.09%	-4.03	$0.60	$0.12
Brian Barden	324.35	0.40%	-1.65	-$0.25	$0.02
Kelly Stinnett	49.40	1.40%	-9.60	-$1.39	-$0.47

TAMPA BAY DEVIL RAYS

Player	Season RS	%PA	RSAA	$ValAA	MRP
Carlos Pena	1331.76	9.75%	53.11	$10.39	$16.82
B. J. Upton	1062.29	8.73%	24.03	$4.14	$9.90
Carl Crawford	900.07	9.94%	11.24	$1.82	$8.38
Brendan Harris	813.41	9.18%	2.42	$0.37	$6.43
Akinori Iwamura	821.41	8.91%	3.06	$0.48	$6.35
Delmon Young	688.82	10.85%	-10.65	-$1.54	$5.62
Ty Wigginton	809.32	6.64%	1.48	$0.23	$4.61
Jonny Gomes	794.47	6.28%	0.47	$0.07	$4.21
Greg Norton	713.38	3.82%	-2.82	-$0.42	$2.10
Dioner Navarro	514.02	6.91%	-18.88	-$2.60	$1.96
Elijah Dukes	668.89	3.50%	-4.14	-$0.62	$1.69
Josh Wilson	525.58	4.54%	-11.87	-$1.70	$1.29
Jorge Velandia	1193.62	0.96%	3.89	$0.61	$1.24
Raul Casanova	869.66	1.42%	1.17	$0.18	$1.12
Rocco Baldelli	466.35	2.39%	-7.66	-$1.12	$0.45
Joel Guzman	540.79	0.62%	-1.53	-$0.23	$0.18
Justin Ruggiano	223.77	0.24%	-1.35	-$0.20	-$0.05
Jorge Cantu	270.36	1.04%	-5.35	-$0.79	-$0.11
Dustan Mohr	-32.09	0.25%	-2.09	-$0.32	-$0.15
Shawn Riggans	-457.63	0.16%	-1.98	-$0.30	-$0.19
Josh Paul	183.15	1.83%	-11.06	-$1.59	-$0.38
Ben Zobrist	-32.42	1.67%	-13.71	-$1.94	-$0.84

TEXAS RANGERS

Player	Season RS	%PA	RSAA	$ValAA	MRP
Michael Young	836.48	11.14%	5.51	$0.87	$8.21
Ian Kinsler	842.87	9.11%	5.09	$0.80	$6.81
Mark Teixeira	1100.55	5.39%	16.91	$2.81	$6.37
Marlon Byrd	871.38	7.31%	6.16	$0.97	$5.79
Kenny Lofton	910.24	5.84%	7.20	$1.14	$5.00
Sammy Sosa	759.21	7.31%	-2.03	-$0.31	$4.51
Frank Catalanotto	796.04	6.07%	0.55	$0.08	$4.09
Brad Wilkerson	781.01	6.26%	-0.38	-$0.06	$4.07
Hank Blalock	1017.35	3.73%	8.60	$1.37	$3.84
Ramon Vazquez	575.06	5.55%	-11.77	-$1.69	$1.97
David Murphy	1071.96	1.77%	5.04	$0.79	$1.96
Nelson Cruz	554.47	5.34%	-12.43	-$1.78	$1.75
Gerald Laird	469.79	7.21%	-22.87	-$3.08	$1.68
Travis Metcalf	693.69	2.91%	-2.72	-$0.41	$1.51
Jarrod Saltalamacchia	638.40	2.83%	-4.21	-$0.63	$1.24
Jason Botts	588.73	3.06%	-6.06	-$0.90	$1.12
Victor Diaz	724.22	1.74%	-1.09	-$0.17	$0.98
Guillermo Quiroz	1227.47	0.18%	0.78	$0.12	$0.24
Chris Stewart	450.77	0.69%	-2.33	-$0.35	$0.11
Freddy Guzman	664.12	0.10%	-0.12	-$0.02	$0.05
Matt Kata	310.32	1.24%	-5.91	-$0.88	-$0.06
Adam Melhuse	300.77	1.17%	-5.71	-$0.85	-$0.07
Jerry Hairston	288.87	2.96%	-14.75	-$2.08	-$0.13
Kevin Mahar	-57.32	0.29%	-2.45	-$0.37	-$0.18
Desi Relaford	-196.26	0.45%	-4.43	-$0.66	-$0.36

TORONTO BLUE JAYS

Player	Season RS	%PA	RSAA	$ValAA	MRP
Alexis Rios	942.75	11.47%	17.87	$2.99	$10.56
Frank Thomas	979.01	10.07%	19.33	$3.26	$9.90
Aaron Hill	817.47	10.60%	3.23	$0.50	$7.49
Matt Stairs	1066.31	6.54%	18.25	$3.06	$7.37
Troy Glaus	936.38	7.36%	10.99	$1.78	$6.63
Vernon Wells	638.34	10.36%	-15.40	-$2.16	$4.67
Gregg Zaun	761.29	6.31%	-1.62	-$0.25	$3.92
Lyle Overbay	652.29	7.68%	-10.35	-$1.50	$3.57
Adam Lind	560.05	5.02%	-11.39	-$1.64	$1.67
Reed Johnson	505.91	4.95%	-13.93	-$1.97	$1.29
John McDonald	451.59	5.70%	-19.11	-$2.63	$1.13
Royce Clayton	544.27	3.39%	-8.23	-$1.20	$1.03
Russ Adams	635.44	1.11%	-1.69	-$0.26	$0.48
John-Ford Griffin	1491.22	0.23%	1.59	$0.25	$0.39
Joe Inglett	2484.31	0.08%	1.37	$0.21	$0.26

(continued)

MRP Estimates for Hitters (2007) (*continued*)

Player	Season RS	%PA	RSAA	$ValAA	MRP
Curtis Thigpen	419.69	1.78%	-6.52	-$0.96	$0.21
Howie Clark	364.13	0.92%	-3.89	-$0.58	$0.02
Jason Phillips	333.16	2.55%	-11.57	-$1.66	$0.02
Jason Smith	315.13	0.90%	-4.26	-$0.64	-$0.04
Ray Olmedo	289.89	0.87%	-4.33	-$0.65	-$0.07
Sal Fasano	270.61	0.79%	-4.08	-$0.61	-$0.09
Ryan Roberts	-52.29	0.26%	-2.17	-$0.33	-$0.16
Hector Luna	116.50	0.74%	-4.98	-$0.74	-$0.25

WASHINGTON NATIONALS

Player	Season RS	%PA	RSAA	$ValAA	MRP
Dmitri Young	1032.95	8.19%	24.44	$4.22	$9.62
Ryan Zimmerman	824.75	11.64%	10.50	$1.69	$9.37
Austin Kearns	819.90	10.87%	9.27	$1.49	$8.66
Ryan Church	895.39	8.55%	13.74	$2.25	$7.89
Ron Belliard	778.04	8.98%	3.90	$0.61	$6.53
Felipe Lopez	571.92	10.82%	-17.60	-$2.44	$4.70
Brian Schneider	599.64	7.69%	-10.38	-$1.50	$3.57
Cristian Guzman	995.08	3.10%	8.07	$1.29	$3.33
Wily Mo Pena	973.17	2.34%	5.58	$0.88	$2.42
Nook Logan	549.06	5.64%	-10.47	-$1.51	$2.21
D'Angelo Jimenez	829.63	2.06%	1.96	$0.30	$1.66
Jesus Flores	594.22	3.18%	-4.46	-$0.67	$1.43
Ryan Langerhans	567.03	3.02%	-5.05	-$0.75	$1.24
Tony Batista	686.29	1.90%	-0.92	-$0.14	$1.12
Robert Fick	494.10	3.56%	-8.57	-$1.25	$1.10
Chris Snelling	692.47	0.98%	-0.41	-$0.06	$0.59
Justin Maxwell	794.49	0.44%	0.26	$0.04	$0.33
Brandon Watson	564.96	0.31%	-0.52	-$0.08	$0.12
Josh Wilson	-34.72	0.40%	-3.10	-$0.47	-$0.20
Michael Restovich	-149.67	0.47%	-4.14	-$0.62	-$0.31
Kory Casto	-215.48	0.92%	-8.73	-$1.27	-$0.67

MRP Estimates for Pitchers (2007)

ARIZONA DIAMONDBACKS

Player	Season RA	%IP	RABA	$ValAA	MRP
Brandon Webb	503.92	16.40%	32.87	$5.89	$17.75
Doug Davis	740.31	13.37%	-6.70	-$0.99	$8.70
Micah Owings	713.29	10.60%	-2.28	-$0.34	$7.34

(*continued*)

MRP Estimates for Pitchers (2007) (*continued*)

Player	Season RA	%IP	RABA	$ValAA	MRP
Livan Hernandez	874.49	14.18%	-27.27	-$3.57	$6.64
Brandon Lyon	511.29	5.14%	9.89	$1.59	$5.25
Tony Pena	643.32	5.92%	3.12	$0.48	$4.75
Edgar Gonzalez	801.32	7.08%	-8.13	-$1.19	$3.96
Jose Valverde	592.28	4.46%	4.76	$0.75	$3.95
Randy Johnson	520.58	3.93%	7.19	$1.14	$3.94
Juan Cruz	619.92	4.23%	3.28	$0.51	$3.55
Dustin Nippert	651.20	3.14%	1.39	$0.21	$2.48
Doug Slaten	682.34	2.52%	0.29	$0.04	$1.86
Yusmeiro Petit	874.12	3.96%	-7.59	-$1.11	$1.79
Bob Wickman	430.89	0.46%	1.29	$0.20	$0.52
Jailen Peguero	1028.80	1.02%	-3.63	-$0.54	$0.22
Dana Eveland	802.87	0.35%	-0.40	-$0.06	$0.19
Bill Murphy	922.04	0.44%	-1.06	-$0.16	$0.16
Joe Kennedy	719.72	0.19%	-0.05	-$0.01	$0.13
Enrique Gonzalez	676.97	0.14%	0.02	$0.00	$0.10
Mike Schultz	200.20	0.07%	0.36	$0.06	$0.10
Augie Ojeda	419.49	0.07%	0.20	$0.03	$0.08
Brandon Medders	1179.14	2.03%	-10.48	-$1.51	$0.02
J. D. Durbin	841.87	0.05%	-0.08	-$0.01	$0.02
Jeff Cirillo	1230.11	0.07%	-0.40	-$0.06	-$0.01
Byung-Hyun Kim	1341.73	0.19%	-1.29	-$0.20	-$0.05

ATLANTA BRAVES

Player	Season RA	%IP	RABA	$ValAA	MRP
Tim Hudson	547.90	15.40%	30.44	$5.40	$15.22
John Smoltz	554.31	14.12%	27.03	$4.72	$13.73
Peter Moylan	632.28	6.18%	7.10	$1.13	$5.07
Chuck James	937.93	11.08%	-20.44	-$2.79	$4.27
Oscar Villarreal	687.18	5.24%	3.20	$0.50	$3.84
Buddy Carlyle	863.07	7.35%	-8.17	-$1.20	$3.47
Tyler Yates	675.64	4.53%	3.28	$0.51	$3.40
Rafael Soriano	720.99	4.94%	1.39	$0.21	$3.36
Kyle Davies	895.64	5.90%	-8.45	-$1.23	$2.51
Chad Paronto	690.78	2.77%	1.59	$0.25	$2.01
Bob Wickman	728.37	3.00%	0.62	$0.10	$2.01
Ron Mahay	659.00	1.92%	1.71	$0.26	$1.49
Mike Gonzalez	534.47	1.17%	2.46	$0.38	$1.13
Manny Acosta	755.91	1.63%	-0.10	-$0.02	$1.02
Jo-Jo Reyes	1063.67	3.48%	-10.72	-$1.55	$0.65
Octavio Dotel	453.95	0.53%	1.53	$0.24	$0.58
Jose Ascanio	899.43	1.10%	-1.61	-$0.24	$0.45
Macay McBride	894.64	1.03%	-1.46	-$0.22	$0.43

(*continued*)

MRP Estimates for Pitchers (2007) (*continued*)

Player	Season RA	%IP	RABA	$ValAA	MRP
Jeff Bennett	855.51	0.89%	-0.93	-$0.14	$0.42
Blaine Boyer	424.57	0.36%	1.16	$0.18	$0.41
Wilfredo Ledezma	761.10	0.64%	-0.07	-$0.01	$0.40
Mark Redman	1016.27	1.49%	-3.89	-$0.58	$0.36
Joey Devine	790.55	0.57%	-0.23	-$0.03	$0.33
Royce Ring	598.18	0.34%	0.51	$0.08	$0.30
Kevin Barry	536.35	0.14%	0.29	$0.04	$0.13
Steve Colyer	1418.63	0.25%	-1.67	-$0.25	-$0.10
Anthony Lerew	1387.74	0.80%	-5.02	-$0.75	-$0.25
Lance Cormier	1383.80	3.14%	-19.50	-$2.68	-$0.71

BALTIMORE ORIOLES

Player	Season RA	%IP	RABA	$ValAA	MRP
Erik Bedard	600.38	12.65%	24.37	$4.20	$12.40
Jeremy Guthrie	756.68	12.19%	4.62	$0.72	$8.61
Daniel Cabrera	854.26	14.20%	-8.34	-$1.22	$7.98
Chad Bradford	542.22	4.50%	11.25	$1.82	$4.75
Brian Burres	852.91	8.41%	-4.82	-$0.72	$4.73
Steve Trachsel	929.24	9.78%	-13.00	-$1.85	$4.48
Jamie Walker	693.89	4.26%	4.26	$0.67	$3.43
Chris Ray	732.09	2.97%	1.85	$0.29	$2.21
Kurt Birkins	694.10	2.38%	2.38	$0.37	$1.92
Rob Bell	901.21	3.68%	-3.88	-$0.58	$1.80
John Parrish	818.46	2.90%	-0.67	-$0.10	$1.77
Jon Leicester	795.26	2.22%	-0.01	$0.00	$1.44
Adam Loewen	853.54	2.11%	-1.22	-$0.19	$1.18
Danys Baez	1019.25	3.50%	-7.76	-$1.14	$1.12
James Hoey	890.38	1.72%	-1.62	-$0.25	$0.86
Scott Williamson	680.40	0.99%	1.13	$0.17	$0.82
Garrett Olson	1031.32	2.25%	-5.25	-$0.78	$0.67
Todd Williams	799.69	0.99%	-0.05	-$0.01	$0.64
Paul Shuey	990.32	1.79%	-3.46	-$0.52	$0.63
Radhames Liz	1036.77	1.72%	-4.11	-$0.61	$0.49
Victor Zambrano	943.54	0.86%	-1.26	-$0.19	$0.36
Jaret Wright	1018.44	0.72%	-1.58	-$0.24	$0.22
Rocky Cherry	1189.13	1.13%	-4.42	-$0.66	$0.07
Jim Johnson	910.03	0.14%	-0.16	-$0.02	$0.07
Fernando Cabrera	1214.53	0.70%	-2.89	-$0.43	$0.01
Cory Doyne	1409.11	0.26%	-1.56	-$0.24	-$0.07
Victor Santos	1588.88	0.99%	-7.81	-$1.15	-$0.51

BOSTON RED SOX

Player	Season RA	%IP	RABA	$ValAA	MRP
Josh Beckett	540.17	13.95%	33.68	$6.06	$15.42
Daisuke Matsuzaka	723.34	14.23%	8.03	$1.28	$10.84
Tim Wakefield	774.44	13.14%	0.63	$0.10	$8.92
Curt Schilling	704.15	10.49%	7.96	$1.27	$8.31
Julian Tavarez	770.73	9.36%	0.80	$0.12	$6.41
Jonathan Papelbon	464.73	4.05%	12.87	$2.10	$4.81
Hideki Okajima	582.95	4.80%	9.51	$1.53	$4.74
Mike Timlin	755.82	3.84%	0.91	$0.14	$2.72
Manny Delcarmen	663.07	3.06%	3.59	$0.56	$2.61
Javier Lopez	667.86	2.83%	3.18	$0.49	$2.39
Kason Gabbard	703.77	2.85%	2.17	$0.34	$2.25
Jon Lester	902.75	4.38%	-5.46	-$0.81	$2.13
Kyle Snyder	897.91	3.77%	-4.52	-$0.68	$1.86
Clay Buchholz	481.67	1.58%	4.74	$0.74	$1.80
Brendan Donnelly	430.40	1.44%	5.07	$0.80	$1.75
Joel Pineiro	749.93	2.36%	0.70	$0.11	$1.69
Eric Gagne	574.85	1.30%	2.68	$0.42	$1.28
Bryan Corey	550.60	0.65%	1.49	$0.23	$0.66
J. C. Romero	967.67	1.39%	-2.65	-$0.40	$0.54
Devern Hansack	1245.49	0.54%	-2.52	-$0.38	-$0.02

CHICAGO CUBS

Player	Season RA	%IP	RABA	$ValAA	MRP
Ted Lilly	677.66	14.31%	5.24	$0.82	$10.74
Carlos Zambrano	726.27	14.95%	-2.01	-$0.30	$10.05
Rich Hill	692.94	13.48%	2.81	$0.44	$9.78
Jason Marquis	763.64	13.25%	-6.89	-$1.01	$8.16
Bobby Howry	570.18	5.62%	8.28	$1.32	$5.19
Carlos Marmol	481.10	4.79%	11.45	$1.86	$5.14
Sean Marshall	739.20	7.14%	-1.91	-$0.29	$4.66
Michael Wuertz	682.85	5.00%	1.56	$0.24	$3.70
Ryan Dempster	745.41	4.61%	-1.53	-$0.23	$2.97
Scott Eyre	717.22	3.62%	-0.15	-$0.02	$2.48
Will Ohman	640.28	2.51%	1.88	$0.29	$2.02
Angel Guzman	539.35	2.09%	3.75	$0.58	$2.02
Kerry Wood	492.33	1.68%	3.82	$0.60	$1.74
Kevin Hart	357.71	0.76%	2.78	$0.43	$0.95
Rocky Cherry	593.42	1.04%	1.28	$0.20	$0.91
Neal Cotts	658.64	1.15%	0.65	$0.10	$0.90
Steve Trachsel	880.63	1.20%	-2.06	-$0.31	$0.52
Clay Rapada	431.71	0.02%	0.06	$0.01	$0.02
Carmen Pignatiello	1183.04	0.14%	-0.67	-$0.10	$0.00
Sean Gallagher	1232.40	1.02%	-5.43	-$0.81	-$0.08

(continued)

MRP Estimates for Pitchers (2007) (*continued*)

Player	Season RA	%IP	RABA	$ValAA	MRP
Billy Petrick	1348.69	0.67%	-4.39	-$0.66	-$0.17
Wade Miller	1360.48	0.95%	-6.31	-$0.93	-$0.25

CHICAGO WHITE SOX

Player	Season RA	%IP	RABA	$ValAA	MRP
Javier Vazquez	656.10	15.04%	17.72	$2.96	$13.25
Jon Garland	702.05	14.46%	10.26	$1.65	$11.54
Mark Buehrle	692.40	13.95%	11.27	$1.83	$11.36
Jose Contreras	745.92	13.12%	3.43	$0.53	$9.50
Bobby Jenks	440.48	4.51%	15.24	$2.52	$5.56
John Danks	934.63	9.65%	-16.05	-$2.25	$4.35
Matt Thornton	642.95	3.91%	5.13	$0.81	$3.46
Boone Logan	819.74	3.52%	-1.73	-$0.26	$2.15
Gavin Floyd	982.34	4.86%	-10.45	-$1.51	$1.83
Ehren Wassermann	486.22	1.60%	4.65	$0.73	$1.81
Mike MacDougal	825.54	2.94%	-1.62	-$0.24	$1.76
Nick Masset	806.34	2.73%	-0.97	-$0.15	$1.72
David Aardsma	762.30	2.24%	0.21	$0.03	$1.56
Lance Broadway	412.09	0.72%	2.62	$0.41	$0.89
Ryan Bukvich	1015.19	2.48%	-6.16	-$0.91	$0.80
Dewon Day	913.91	0.83%	-1.21	-$0.18	$0.39
Andrew Sisco	985.36	0.97%	-2.12	-$0.32	$0.35
Heath Phillips	994.37	0.51%	-1.15	-$0.17	$0.17
Mike Myers	1117.67	0.95%	-3.36	-$0.50	$0.15
Bret Prinz	1384.32	0.23%	-1.43	-$0.22	-$0.06
Charlie Haeger	1405.11	0.78%	-5.07	-$0.75	-$0.20

CINCINNATI REDS

Player	Season RA	%IP	RABA	$ValAA	MRP
Aaron Harang	579.23	15.98%	18.35	$3.08	$14.83
Bronson Arroyo	686.09	14.53%	0.07	$0.01	$10.70
Matt Belisle	693.20	12.26%	-0.87	-$0.13	$8.88
Kyle Lohse	666.34	9.08%	1.96	$0.30	$6.97
Dave Weathers	566.65	5.36%	6.87	$1.09	$4.98
Mike Stanton	642.30	3.98%	1.88	$0.29	$3.20
Bobby Livingston	682.02	3.88%	0.19	$0.03	$2.88
Jared Burton	592.29	2.97%	2.99	$0.46	$2.62
Homer Bailey	735.57	3.12%	-1.64	-$0.25	$2.06
Jon Coutlangus	703.70	2.83%	-0.52	-$0.08	$2.00
Eric Milton	705.47	2.16%	-0.44	-$0.07	$1.52
Victor Santos	888.16	3.38%	-7.29	-$1.07	$1.46

(*continued*)

MRP Estimates for Pitchers (2007) (*continued*)

Player	Season RA	%IP	RABA	$ValAA	MRP
Todd Coffey	916.16	3.52%	-8.64	-$1.26	$1.38
Gary Majewski	661.34	1.59%	0.43	$0.07	$1.23
Kirk Saarloos	898.31	2.95%	-6.67	-$0.98	$1.22
Brad Salmon	691.27	1.66%	-0.08	-$0.01	$1.20
Marcus McBeth	622.39	1.36%	0.93	$0.14	$1.13
Bill Bray	527.99	0.99%	1.67	$0.26	$0.97
Mike Gosling	955.67	2.28%	-6.55	-$0.97	$0.75
Eddie Guardado	743.97	0.94%	-0.58	-$0.09	$0.61
Tom Shearn	1025.41	2.26%	-8.18	-$1.20	$0.52
Rheal Cormier	1212.61	0.21%	-1.16	-$0.18	-$0.01
Elizardo Ramirez	1202.95	1.12%	-6.21	-$0.92	-$0.04
Phil Dumatrait	1346.45	1.24%	-8.77	-$1.28	-$0.30
Ricky Stone	1876.16	0.37%	-4.65	-$0.69	-$0.38

CLEVELAND INDIANS

Player	Season RA	%IP	RABA	$ValAA	MRP
C. C. Sabathia	550.85	16.48%	40.73	$7.56	$18.04
Fausto Carmona	658.29	14.70%	20.86	$3.54	$12.88
Paul Byrd	775.13	13.15%	3.60	$0.56	$8.91
Jake Westbrook	733.27	10.39%	7.11	$1.13	$7.73
Rafael Betancourt	420.41	5.42%	20.33	$3.44	$6.93
Rafael Perez	565.00	4.15%	9.68	$1.56	$4.21
Joe Borowski	729.47	4.49%	3.24	$0.50	$3.36
Aaron Laffey	589.15	3.37%	7.07	$1.12	$3.28
Cliff Lee	926.37	6.65%	-8.04	-$1.18	$3.04
Tom Mastny	814.29	3.95%	-0.43	-$0.07	$2.44
Jensen Lewis	473.97	2.00%	6.46	$1.02	$2.31
Jeremy Sowers	910.54	4.60%	-4.85	-$0.72	$2.19
Aaron Fultz	696.22	2.53%	2.65	$0.41	$2.02
Jason Stanford	571.98	1.80%	4.07	$0.64	$1.79
Roberto Hernandez	835.70	1.78%	-0.57	-$0.09	$1.04
Fernando Cabrera	1045.90	2.30%	-5.48	-$0.81	$0.64
Jason Davis	819.59	0.77%	-0.12	-$0.02	$0.47
Mike Koplove	508.46	0.41%	1.18	$0.18	$0.45
Edward Mujica	967.56	0.89%	-1.43	-$0.22	$0.34
Matt Miller	480.92	0.07%	0.22	$0.03	$0.08
Juan Lara	2306.70	0.09%	-1.31	-$0.20	-$0.15

COLORADO ROCKIES

Player	Season RA	%IP	RABA	$ValAA	MRP
Jeff Francis	642.00	14.63%	6.97	$1.10	$11.87
Aaron Cook	660.56	11.28%	3.14	$0.49	$8.77
Josh Fogg	765.22	11.26%	-9.48	-$1.38	$6.91
Taylor Buchholz	562.17	6.37%	8.47	$1.35	$5.97
Manuel Corpas	546.24	5.30%	7.96	$1.27	$5.10
Jason Hirsh	824.84	7.63%	-11.29	-$1.62	$4.02
Ubaldo Jimenez	721.49	5.57%	-2.08	-$0.32	$3.79
Rodrigo Lopez	723.92	5.39%	-2.15	-$0.33	$3.64
Brian Fuentes	613.89	4.16%	3.24	$0.50	$3.54
Jeremy Affeldt	638.22	4.01%	2.07	$0.32	$3.25
Jorge Julio	641.95	3.58%	1.71	$0.26	$2.88
Matt Herges	611.21	3.31%	2.67	$0.41	$2.82
LaTroy Hawkins	676.90	3.76%	0.39	$0.06	$2.81
Franklin Morales	560.36	2.67%	3.60	$0.56	$2.49
Zach McClellan	396.04	0.95%	2.96	$0.46	$1.13
Mark Redman	629.58	1.34%	0.82	$0.13	$1.10
Ryan Speier	601.97	1.22%	1.11	$0.17	$1.06
Ramon Ramirez	646.71	1.18%	0.50	$0.08	$0.93
Tom Martin	836.26	1.75%	-2.80	-$0.42	$0.88
Denny Bautista	450.36	0.59%	1.49	$0.23	$0.65
Elmer Dessens	874.17	1.29%	-2.59	-$0.39	$0.58
Tim Harikkala	438.50	0.22%	0.60	$0.09	$0.25
Josh Newman	89.71	0.14%	0.87	$0.13	$0.22
Alberto Arias	963.13	0.50%	-1.47	-$0.22	$0.15
Juan Morillo	944.39	0.25%	-0.69	-$0.11	$0.09
Darren Clarke	640.88	0.09%	0.04	$0.01	$0.07
Bobby Keppel	1268.42	0.27%	-1.69	-$0.26	-$0.04
Ramon Ortiz	1218.89	0.88%	-5.03	-$0.75	-$0.06
Dan Serafini	3816.50	0.02%	-0.68	-$0.10	-$0.08
Byung-Hyun Kim	1382.65	0.41%	-3.04	-$0.46	-$0.13

DETROIT TIGERS

Player	Season RA	%IP	RABA	$ValAA	MRP
Justin Verlander	671.05	13.93%	17.09	$2.85	$11.87
Jeremy Bonderman	731.82	12.04%	7.53	$1.20	$8.99
Nate Robertson	795.06	12.28%	-0.01	$0.00	$7.95
Jason Grilli	657.06	5.51%	7.52	$1.19	$4.77
Chad Durbin	939.20	8.82%	-12.60	-$1.80	$3.91
Todd Jones	667.52	4.23%	5.34	$0.84	$3.59
Bobby Seay	510.96	3.20%	8.99	$1.44	$3.52
Zach Miner	679.98	3.71%	4.22	$0.66	$3.07
Fernando Rodney	678.01	3.50%	4.06	$0.63	$2.91
Tim Byrdak	690.15	3.11%	3.23	$0.50	$2.52

(continued)

MRP Estimates for Pitchers (2007) (*continued*)

Player	Season RA	%IP	RABA	$ValAA	MRP
Kenny Rogers	848.66	4.35%	-2.31	-$0.35	$2.47
Andrew Miller	890.07	4.42%	-4.16	-$0.62	$2.24
Joel Zumaya	767.96	2.33%	0.62	$0.10	$1.60
Mike Maroth	1058.91	5.41%	-14.13	-$2.00	$1.49
Yorman Bazardo	635.15	1.64%	2.59	$0.40	$1.46
Jair Jurrjens	869.67	2.12%	-1.57	-$0.24	$1.13
Wilfredo Ledezma	973.86	2.47%	-4.37	-$0.65	$0.94
Aquilino Lopez	834.45	1.20%	-0.47	-$0.07	$0.70
Jordan Tata	818.94	0.97%	-0.23	-$0.04	$0.59
Macay McBride	999.48	1.22%	-2.48	-$0.37	$0.41
Eulogio De La Cruz	968.49	0.46%	-0.80	-$0.12	$0.18
Jose Mesa	1159.68	0.81%	-2.92	-$0.44	$0.08
Jose Capellan	1202.87	0.97%	-3.91	-$0.58	$0.04
Clay Rapada	2519.14	0.16%	-2.71	-$0.41	-$0.31
Virgil Vasquez	1493.28	1.15%	-7.98	-$1.17	-$0.43

FLORIDA MARLINS

Player	Season RA	%IP	RABA	$ValAA	MRP
Sergio Mitre	630.90	10.32%	13.31	$2.18	$8.54
Dontrelle Willis	862.29	14.22%	-13.26	-$1.89	$6.87
Lee Gardner	494.43	5.15%	13.38	$2.19	$5.41
Matt Lindstrom	487.15	4.64%	12.39	$2.02	$4.92
Scott Olsen	938.27	12.24%	-20.34	-$2.78	$4.76
Kevin Gregg	678.05	5.82%	4.87	$0.76	$4.35
Justin Miller	583.47	4.27%	7.46	$1.18	$3.84
Byung-Hyun Kim	921.82	7.60%	-11.43	-$1.64	$3.00
Renyel Pinto	821.04	4.07%	-2.18	-$0.33	$2.15
Taylor Tankersley	758.73	3.28%	0.20	$0.03	$2.04
Rick VandenHurk	983.59	5.66%	-11.87	-$1.70	$1.74
Randy Messenger	556.51	1.64%	3.29	$0.51	$1.54
Wes Obermueller	943.95	4.09%	-7.01	-$1.03	$1.45
Armando Benitez	875.97	2.29%	-2.43	-$0.37	$1.02
Logan Kensing	525.78	0.92%	2.12	$0.33	$0.90
Henry Owens	847.00	1.59%	-1.25	-$0.19	$0.78
Chris Seddon	757.92	1.20%	0.08	$0.01	$0.75
Anibal Sanchez	944.16	2.08%	-3.57	-$0.54	$0.72
Ricky Nolasco	907.78	1.48%	-2.02	-$0.31	$0.59
Josh Johnson	830.83	1.09%	-0.69	-$0.10	$0.56
Marcos Carvajal	626.42	0.28%	0.37	$0.06	$0.23
Erasmo Ramirez	734.42	0.23%	0.07	$0.01	$0.15
Harvey Garcia	1061.89	0.85%	-2.43	-$0.37	$0.14
Jason Wood	463.19	0.07%	0.20	$0.03	$0.07

(*continued*)

MRP Estimates for Pitchers (2007) (*continued*)

Player	Season RA	%IP	RABA	$ValAA	MRP
Nate Field	547.52	0.07%	0.14	$0.02	$0.07
Ross Wolf	1244.29	0.85%	-3.92	-$0.59	-$0.09
Daniel Barone	1247.82	2.84%	-13.16	-$1.87	-$0.18
Jorge Julio	1482.43	0.64%	-4.44	-$0.66	-$0.29
Mauro Zarate	1834.81	0.35%	-3.56	-$0.53	-$0.34
Carlos Martinez	3092.90	0.19%	-4.18	-$0.62	-$0.54

HOUSTON ASTROS

Player	Season RA	%IP	RABA	$ValAA	MRP
Roy Oswalt	572.83	14.47%	22.58	$3.86	$13.57
Wandy Rodriguez	692.30	12.47%	4.41	$0.69	$9.06
Woody Williams	882.80	12.83%	-20.16	-$2.75	$5.85
Chad Qualls	655.35	5.65%	4.10	$0.64	$4.42
Chris Sampson	842.34	8.31%	-9.65	-$1.40	$4.18
Brad Lidge	678.56	4.57%	2.25	$0.35	$3.41
Matt Albers	898.19	7.56%	-13.04	-$1.86	$3.22
Dave Borkowski	742.33	4.89%	-0.74	-$0.11	$3.17
Jason Jennings	887.42	6.76%	-10.93	-$1.57	$2.96
Brian Moehler	753.24	4.08%	-1.07	-$0.16	$2.57
Dan Wheeler	680.11	3.39%	1.62	$0.25	$2.52
Trever Miller	768.14	3.16%	-1.30	-$0.20	$1.92
Mark McLemore	805.61	2.39%	-1.89	-$0.29	$1.32
Juan Gutierrez	732.70	1.45%	-0.08	-$0.01	$0.96
Dennis Sarfate	117.18	0.57%	3.49	$0.54	$0.92
Brandon Backe	868.99	1.96%	-2.80	-$0.42	$0.90
Rick White	884.13	2.00%	-3.17	-$0.48	$0.87
Travis Driskill	747.38	0.41%	-0.08	-$0.01	$0.26
Troy Patton	990.59	0.87%	-2.31	-$0.35	$0.24
Felipe Paulino	1091.09	1.30%	-4.77	-$0.71	$0.17
Stephen Randolph	1418.89	0.91%	-6.34	-$0.94	-$0.32

KANSAS CITY ROYALS

Player	Season RA	%IP	RABA	$ValAA	MRP
Gil Meche	649.78	15.03%	14.76	$2.43	$13.41
Brian Bannister	672.15	11.48%	8.55	$1.37	$9.73
Zack Greinke	614.38	8.49%	11.52	$1.87	$8.01
Odalis Perez	745.90	9.55%	-0.35	-$0.05	$6.91
Joakim Soria	440.15	4.80%	15.38	$2.54	$5.93
Joel Peralta	608.51	6.10%	8.66	$1.38	$5.78
Jorge de la Rosa	842.09	9.04%	-9.55	-$1.39	$5.22
David Riske	723.60	4.85%	0.97	$0.15	$3.68

(*continued*)

MRP Estimates for Pitchers (2007) (*continued*)

Player	Season RA	%IP	RABA	$ValAA	MRP
John Bale	486.18	2.78%	7.56	$1.20	$3.17
Jimmy Gobble	697.65	3.74%	1.77	$0.27	$2.98
Brandon Duckworth	735.69	3.25%	0.23	$0.04	$2.40
Leo Nunez	764.53	3.04%	-0.71	-$0.11	$2.11
Ryan Braun	814.55	2.73%	-2.09	-$0.32	$1.69
Kyle Davies	960.57	3.48%	-8.04	-$1.18	$1.40
Octavio Dotel	690.67	1.60%	0.88	$0.13	$1.29
Billy Buckner	888.78	2.37%	-3.67	-$0.55	$1.20
John Thomson	527.52	0.74%	1.70	$0.26	$0.79
Luke Hochevar	687.25	0.88%	0.52	$0.08	$0.72
Neal Musser	996.56	1.72%	-4.63	-$0.69	$0.59
Jason Standridge	1158.26	0.54%	-2.36	-$0.36	$0.05
Todd Wellemeyer	1219.33	1.09%	-5.52	-$0.82	$0.02
Luke Hudson	2533.53	0.14%	-2.64	-$0.40	-$0.27
Scott Elarton	1346.77	2.57%	-16.49	-$2.30	-$0.34

LOS ANGELES ANGELS OF ANAHEIM

Player	Season RA	%IP	RABA	$ValAA	MRP
John Lackey	617.37	15.61%	30.34	$5.38	$14.91
Kelvim Escobar	616.19	13.64%	26.66	$4.65	$13.00
Jered Weaver	723.85	11.22%	10.34	$1.67	$8.53
Joe Saunders	755.15	7.48%	4.64	$0.73	$5.30
Dustin Moseley	704.15	6.41%	7.12	$1.13	$5.06
Ervin Santana	912.77	10.45%	-9.33	-$1.36	$5.02
Francisco Rodriguez	558.64	4.69%	11.76	$1.91	$4.82
Chris Bootcheck	703.84	5.39%	6.00	$0.95	$4.25
Scot Shields	705.09	5.37%	5.91	$0.93	$4.23
Bartolo Colon	824.94	6.92%	-0.34	-$0.05	$4.17
Darren Oliver	684.13	4.48%	5.84	$0.92	$3.68
Justin Speier	680.43	3.48%	4.66	$0.73	$2.88
Jason Bulger	454.23	0.44%	1.54	$0.24	$0.51
Hector Carrasco	1112.25	2.67%	-7.49	-$1.10	$0.49
Chris Resop	1054.42	0.30%	-0.67	-$0.10	$0.08
Greg Jones	1216.18	0.61%	-2.31	-$0.35	$0.01
Rich Thompson	1816.48	0.47%	-4.47	-$0.67	-$0.41
Marcus Gwyn	2214.04	0.37%	-4.94	-$0.74	-$0.54

LOS ANGELES DODGERS

Player	Season RA	%IP	RABA	$ValAA	MRP
Brad Penny	571.09	14.34%	21.81	$3.72	$13.49
Derek Lowe	647.16	13.74%	10.24	$1.65	$11.02

(*continued*)

MRP Estimates for Pitchers (2007) (*continued*)

Player	Season RA	%IP	RABA	$ValAA	MRP
Chad Billingsley	674.94	10.14%	4.68	$0.73	$7.64
Mark Hendrickson	660.63	8.46%	5.14	$0.81	$6.57
Jonathan Broxton	485.02	5.65%	13.56	$2.22	$6.05
Randy Wolf	644.90	7.08%	5.44	$0.86	$5.68
Takashi Saito	438.85	4.43%	12.72	$2.08	$5.07
Joe Beimel	527.43	4.64%	9.13	$1.46	$4.61
Brett Tomko	754.08	7.17%	-2.48	-$0.37	$4.52
Rudy Seanez	696.78	5.24%	1.25	$0.19	$3.76
David Wells	732.89	2.67%	-0.35	-$0.05	$1.77
Eric Stults	778.74	2.67%	-1.59	-$0.24	$1.58
Hong-Chih Kuo	698.06	2.09%	0.47	$0.07	$1.50
Scott Proctor	769.64	2.21%	-1.11	-$0.17	$1.34
Chin-hui Tsao	728.98	1.70%	-0.15	-$0.02	$1.14
D. J. Houlton	791.86	1.93%	-1.41	-$0.21	$1.11
Jason Schmidt	874.96	1.77%	-2.80	-$0.42	$0.79
Roberto Hernandez	852.54	1.40%	-1.89	-$0.29	$0.67
Eric Hull	505.49	0.46%	1.01	$0.16	$0.47
Yhency Brazoban	710.06	0.12%	0.01	$0.00	$0.08
Jonathan Meloan	1105.40	0.50%	-1.98	-$0.30	$0.05
Esteban Loaiza	1535.22	1.57%	-13.01	-$1.85	-$0.76

MILWAUKEE BREWERS

Player	Season RA	%IP	RABA	$ValAA	MRP
Jeff Suppan	691.54	14.31%	6.16	$0.97	$10.41
David Bush	731.76	12.90%	0.37	$0.06	$8.56
Ben Sheets	683.33	9.78%	5.02	$0.79	$7.24
Yovani Gallardo	577.75	7.64%	11.98	$1.95	$6.98
Chris Capuano	735.96	10.39%	-0.14	-$0.02	$6.83
Francisco Cordero	425.95	4.38%	13.53	$2.22	$5.11
Claudio Vargas	863.43	9.30%	-11.98	-$1.72	$4.42
Carlos Villanueva	810.71	7.91%	-6.02	-$0.89	$4.33
Brian Shouse	448.93	3.30%	9.44	$1.51	$3.69
Derrick Turnbow	658.84	4.71%	3.57	$0.56	$3.66
Matt Wise	640.37	3.72%	3.50	$0.55	$3.00
Chris Spurling	736.74	3.46%	-0.07	-$0.01	$2.27
Manny Parra	549.29	1.82%	3.37	$0.53	$1.73
Scott Linebrink	718.51	1.75%	0.28	$0.04	$1.20
Seth McClung	459.02	0.83%	2.29	$0.35	$0.90
Greg Aquino	761.09	0.97%	-0.26	-$0.04	$0.60
Elmer Dessens	816.89	1.04%	-0.85	-$0.13	$0.55
Mitch Stetter	477.04	0.35%	0.89	$0.14	$0.37
Jose Capellan	936.80	0.83%	-1.68	-$0.25	$0.29
Ray King	820.58	0.42%	-0.36	-$0.05	$0.22
Grant Balfour	1826.57	0.19%	-2.04	-$0.31	-$0.19

MINNESOTA TWINS

Player	Season RA	%IP	RABA	$ValAA	MRP
Johan Santana	703.86	15.24%	14.82	$2.44	$12.12
Carlos Silva	702.50	14.06%	13.86	$2.27	$11.20
Scott Baker	664.10	10.00%	13.62	$2.23	$8.60
Boof Bonser	861.27	12.04%	-6.87	-$1.01	$6.64
Joe Nathan	501.60	4.99%	14.74	$2.43	$5.63
Matt Guerrier	664.85	6.12%	8.30	$1.32	$5.23
Ramon Ortiz	760.14	6.33%	2.67	$0.41	$4.44
Matt Garza	725.01	5.78%	4.42	$0.69	$4.37
Pat Neshek	673.28	4.89%	6.22	$0.98	$4.10
Juan Rincon	892.84	4.16%	-3.65	-$0.55	$2.08
Kevin Slowey	955.18	4.64%	-6.92	-$1.02	$1.92
Glen Perkins	708.16	2.00%	1.86	$0.29	$1.56
Dennys Reyes	788.31	2.04%	0.30	$0.05	$1.34
Sidney Ponson	1012.74	2.62%	-5.39	-$0.80	$0.85
Carmen Cali	965.35	1.46%	-2.32	-$0.35	$0.57
Nick Blackburn	805.56	0.81%	-0.02	$0.00	$0.51
Jesse Crain	1034.27	1.13%	-2.57	-$0.39	$0.33
Julio DePaula	1237.26	1.39%	-5.92	-$0.88	-$0.01
Jason Miller	1925.52	0.28%	-3.06	-$0.46	-$0.29

NEW YORK METS

Player	Season RA	%IP	RABA	$ValAA	MRP
John Maine	739.89	13.15%	3.20	$0.50	$8.57
Tom Glavine	805.82	13.79%	-5.38	-$0.80	$7.67
Oliver Perez	769.62	12.19%	-0.52	-$0.08	$7.40
Jorge Sosa	729.31	7.76%	2.67	$0.41	$5.18
Orlando Hernandez	863.90	10.17%	-9.64	-$1.40	$4.84
Aaron Heilman	635.59	5.92%	7.37	$1.17	$4.83
Billy Wagner	568.17	4.70%	8.90	$1.42	$4.35
Pedro Feliciano	617.44	4.41%	6.25	$0.99	$3.72
Mike Pelfrey	811.34	5.01%	-2.22	-$0.34	$2.73
Guillermo Mota	759.37	4.08%	0.23	$0.03	$2.54
Pedro Martinez	328.62	1.93%	8.08	$1.29	$2.52
Joe Smith	645.14	3.05%	3.52	$0.55	$2.44
Aaron Sele	772.53	3.70%	-0.26	-$0.04	$2.23
Scott Schoeneweis	881.87	4.06%	-4.55	-$0.68	$1.79
Ambiorix Burgos	781.02	1.63%	-0.25	-$0.04	$0.96
Brian Lawrence	890.36	2.00%	-2.40	-$0.36	$0.85
Philip Humber	890.55	0.48%	-0.58	-$0.09	$0.20
Willie Collazo	961.95	0.39%	-0.74	-$0.11	$0.12
Carlos Muniz	747.07	0.16%	0.03	$0.00	$0.10
Jon Adkins	463.19	0.07%	0.20	$0.03	$0.07
Lino Urdaneta	2801.82	0.07%	-1.35	-$0.20	-$0.17

(continued)

MRP Estimates for Pitchers (2007) (*continued*)

Player	Season RA	%IP	RABA	$ValAA	MRP
Chan Ho Park	1674.67	0.28%	-2.40	-$0.36	-$0.21
Jason Vargas	1387.77	0.71%	-4.24	-$0.63	-$0.22
Dave Williams	2099.46	0.30%	-3.79	-$0.57	-$0.41

NEW YORK YANKEES

Player	Season RA	%IP	RABA	$ValAA	MRP
Chien-Ming Wang	638.52	13.74%	23.91	$4.12	$12.52
Andy Pettitte	688.39	14.84%	18.73	$3.15	$12.20
Mike Mussina	692.30	10.48%	12.83	$2.09	$8.51
Mariano Rivera	466.53	4.92%	16.67	$2.77	$5.85
Roger Clemens	715.27	6.82%	6.85	$1.08	$5.27
Philip Hughes	781.92	5.01%	1.82	$0.28	$3.34
Luis Vizcaino	802.61	5.19%	0.86	$0.13	$3.30
Joba Chamberlain	387.51	1.65%	6.87	$1.09	$2.14
Kyle Farnsworth	903.89	4.14%	-3.34	-$0.50	$2.01
Mike Myers	761.91	2.81%	1.56	$0.24	$1.96
Ron Villone	866.22	2.92%	-1.30	-$0.20	$1.57
Scott Proctor	974.17	3.74%	-5.55	-$0.82	$1.44
Brian Bruney	956.70	3.45%	-4.53	-$0.68	$1.41
Ian Kennedy	692.20	1.31%	1.60	$0.25	$1.06
Kei Igawa	1130.29	4.67%	-13.91	-$1.97	$0.84
Matt DeSalvo	941.86	1.91%	-2.24	-$0.34	$0.81
Darrell Rasner	945.99	1.70%	-2.06	-$0.31	$0.72
Carl Pavano	712.82	0.78%	0.80	$0.12	$0.60
Sean Henn	1106.85	2.53%	-6.97	-$1.03	$0.48
Jose Veras	736.66	0.64%	0.51	$0.08	$0.47
Chris Britton	942.98	0.88%	-1.04	-$0.16	$0.37
Ross Ohlendorf	696.75	0.43%	0.51	$0.08	$0.35
Jim Brower	762.17	0.23%	0.13	$0.02	$0.16
Edwar Ramirez	1180.75	1.45%	-5.02	-$0.75	$0.11
Tyler Clippard	1207.22	1.86%	-6.92	-$1.02	$0.08
Colter Bean	1277.17	0.21%	-0.91	-$0.14	-$0.02
Jeff Karstens	1393.06	1.01%	-5.58	-$0.83	-$0.24
Chase Wright	1807.70	0.69%	-6.54	-$0.97	-$0.58

OAKLAND ATHLETICS

Player	Season RA	%IP	RABA	$ValAA	MRP
Joe Blanton	598.89	15.88%	32.73	$5.87	$15.76
Danny Haren	667.69	15.38%	21.43	$3.65	$13.22
Chad Gaudin	826.94	13.76%	-2.08	-$0.31	$8.26
Lenny DiNardo	821.65	9.07%	-0.90	-$0.14	$5.51

(*continued*)

MRP Estimates for Pitchers (2007) (*continued*)

Player	Season RA	%IP	RABA	$ValAA	MRP
Alan Embree	633.57	4.70%	8.10	$1.29	$4.24
Joe Kennedy	859.91	6.97%	-3.28	-$0.49	$3.84
Huston Street	550.45	3.45%	8.74	$1.40	$3.58
Dallas Braden	794.06	4.99%	0.84	$0.13	$3.24
Andrew Brown	523.69	2.88%	8.03	$1.28	$3.10
Santiago Casilla	769.29	3.50%	1.43	$0.22	$2.40
Kiko Calero	764.31	2.81%	1.28	$0.20	$1.95
Ruddy Lugo	740.24	2.60%	1.80	$0.28	$1.90
Jay Marshall	843.26	2.90%	-0.90	-$0.14	$1.67
Rich Harden	745.16	1.77%	1.14	$0.18	$1.28
Colby Lewis	978.40	2.60%	-4.22	-$0.63	$0.98
Esteban Loaiza	714.94	1.02%	0.95	$0.15	$0.78
Jay Witasick	818.06	1.04%	-0.07	-$0.01	$0.63
Ron Flores	925.84	1.22%	-1.36	-$0.21	$0.55
Dan Meyer	918.86	1.13%	-1.17	-$0.18	$0.52
Justin Duchscherer	996.93	1.13%	-2.03	-$0.31	$0.39
Erasmo Ramirez	673.45	0.21%	0.28	$0.04	$0.17
Connor Robertson	808.97	0.14%	0.00	$0.00	$0.09
Jerry Blevins	1064.83	0.32%	-0.80	-$0.12	$0.08
Shane Komine	1129.01	0.53%	-1.64	-$0.25	$0.08

PHILADELPHIA PHILLIES

Player	Season RA	%IP	RABA	$ValAA	MRP
Cole Hamels	635.40	12.57%	10.07	$1.62	$10.32
Jamie Moyer	784.71	13.67%	-10.07	-$1.46	$8.00
Kyle Kendrick	738.04	8.30%	-2.12	-$0.32	$5.43
Jon Lieber	620.56	5.35%	5.10	$0.80	$4.49
Adam Eaton	933.42	11.09%	-25.15	-$3.34	$4.33
Brett Myers	652.89	4.71%	2.93	$0.45	$3.71
Kyle Lohse	699.23	4.18%	0.60	$0.09	$2.99
Ryan Madson	670.70	3.84%	1.68	$0.26	$2.91
Geoff Geary	760.25	4.61%	-2.24	-$0.34	$2.86
Clay Condrey	653.80	3.43%	2.10	$0.32	$2.69
J. D. Durbin	792.68	4.44%	-3.63	-$0.54	$2.54
Antonio Alfonseca	742.20	3.41%	-1.02	-$0.15	$2.21
J. C. Romero	664.01	2.49%	1.26	$0.19	$1.91
Freddy Garcia	861.74	3.98%	-6.08	-$0.90	$1.87
Tom Gordon	804.85	2.74%	-2.59	-$0.39	$1.52
Francisco Rosario	727.78	1.80%	-0.27	-$0.04	$1.21
Jose Mesa	909.50	2.67%	-5.41	-$0.80	$1.07
Yoel Hernandez	559.52	1.05%	1.66	$0.26	$0.98
Mike Zagurski	789.90	1.46%	-1.15	-$0.18	$0.84

(*continued*)

MRP Estimates for Pitchers (2007) (*continued*)

Player	Season RA	%IP	RABA	$ValAA	MRP
John Ennis	686.79	0.53%	0.14	$0.02	$0.39
Kane Davis	992.97	0.77%	-2.23	-$0.34	$0.21
Zack Segovia	883.37	0.34%	-0.60	-$0.09	$0.15
Joseph Bisenius	623.15	0.14%	0.13	$0.02	$0.11
Fabio Castro	1105.82	0.82%	-3.33	-$0.50	$0.08
Anderson Garcia	431.71	0.05%	0.14	$0.02	$0.05
Matt Smith	1832.66	0.27%	-3.16	-$0.48	-$0.27
J. A. Happ	2049.36	0.27%	-3.77	-$0.57	-$0.36
Brian Sanches	1615.82	1.01%	-9.37	-$1.36	-$0.63

PITTSBURGH PIRATES

Player	Season RA	%IP	RABA	$ValAA	MRP
Ian Snell	662.77	14.37%	10.32	$1.66	$11.14
Tom Gorzelanny	673.46	13.93%	8.52	$1.36	$10.55
Paul Maholm	735.78	12.27%	-0.15	-$0.02	$8.07
Matt Capps	509.00	5.46%	12.31	$2.00	$5.60
Zach Duke	775.95	7.41%	-3.06	-$0.46	$4.43
Shawn Chacon	736.78	6.63%	-0.14	-$0.02	$4.35
Damaso Marte	498.98	3.13%	7.37	$1.17	$3.23
Tony Armas	900.18	6.70%	-11.09	-$1.60	$2.82
Matt Morris	746.89	4.28%	-0.53	-$0.08	$2.74
Shane Youman	742.02	3.96%	-0.29	-$0.04	$2.57
Salomon Torres	720.47	3.64%	0.51	$0.08	$2.48
John Grabow	716.98	3.57%	0.63	$0.10	$2.45
Franquelis Osoria	730.18	1.95%	0.09	$0.01	$1.30
John Wasdin	662.30	1.36%	0.98	$0.15	$1.05
John Van Benschoten	925.85	2.69%	-5.15	-$0.77	$1.01
Romulo Sanchez	794.66	1.24%	-0.75	-$0.11	$0.71
Jonah Bayliss	1002.88	2.60%	-6.99	-$1.03	$0.69
Bryan Bullington	905.68	1.17%	-2.01	-$0.30	$0.47
Juan Perez	975.76	0.85%	-2.05	-$0.31	$0.25
Danny Kolb	1401.96	0.21%	-1.38	-$0.21	-$0.07
Dave Davidson	2113.05	0.14%	-1.90	-$0.29	-$0.20
Masumi Kuwata	1343.18	1.45%	-8.83	-$1.29	-$0.33
Marty McLeary	1601.78	0.53%	-4.61	-$0.69	-$0.34
Brian Rogers	2846.45	0.14%	-2.92	-$0.44	-$0.35
Josh Sharpless	2083.88	0.30%	-4.01	-$0.60	-$0.40

SAN DIEGO PADRES

Player	Season RA	%IP	RABA	$ValAA	MRP
Jake Peavy	523.15	15.04%	36.52	$6.66	$15.60
Greg Maddux	585.35	13.34%	24.59	$4.25	$12.16
Chris Young	614.07	11.65%	18.34	$3.07	$9.99
Heath Bell	466.25	6.31%	18.70	$3.14	$6.98
Justin Germano	753.44	8.98%	2.37	$0.37	$5.67
Cla Meredith	593.65	5.37%	9.48	$1.52	$4.74
David Wells	845.30	7.99%	-4.80	-$0.71	$3.98
Trevor Hoffman	518.53	3.86%	9.54	$1.53	$3.88
Justin Hampson	534.43	3.59%	8.34	$1.33	$3.51
Kevin Cameron	620.30	3.91%	5.92	$0.93	$3.28
Doug Brocail	765.23	5.17%	0.79	$0.12	$3.17
Jack Cassel	586.33	1.53%	2.80	$0.44	$1.36
Joe Thatcher	564.28	1.41%	2.89	$0.45	$1.31
Clay Hensley	935.15	3.37%	-4.86	-$0.72	$1.23
Brett Tomko	802.59	1.84%	-0.36	-$0.06	$1.02
Scott Linebrink	994.00	3.03%	-6.05	-$0.90	$0.85
Wilfredo Ledezma	855.27	0.96%	-0.67	-$0.10	$0.46
Royce Ring	893.99	1.01%	-1.07	-$0.16	$0.42
Mike Thompson	957.45	1.06%	-1.75	-$0.26	$0.34
Aaron Rakers	473.04	0.07%	0.20	$0.03	$0.07
Tim Stauffer	2283.74	0.52%	-7.32	-$1.08	-$0.83

SAN FRANCISCO GIANTS

Player	Season RA	%IP	RABA	$ValAA	MRP
Matt Cain	627.98	13.76%	14.67	$2.42	$11.49
Tim Lincecum	633.00	10.06%	10.22	$1.65	$8.29
Barry Zito	794.11	13.53%	-8.05	-$1.18	$7.75
Matt Morris	673.34	9.40%	5.76	$0.91	$7.11
Noah Lowry	792.14	10.73%	-6.18	-$0.91	$6.16
Kevin Correia	675.18	7.00%	4.16	$0.65	$5.26
Vinnie Chulk	536.11	3.65%	7.24	$1.15	$3.55
Brad Hennessey	722.44	4.70%	0.57	$0.09	$3.19
Jack Taschner	703.77	3.44%	1.06	$0.16	$2.43
Steve Kline	669.96	3.16%	2.05	$0.32	$2.40
Patrick Misch	624.36	2.77%	3.06	$0.47	$2.30
Russ Ortiz	722.65	3.37%	0.40	$0.06	$2.28
Randy Messenger	700.60	2.80%	0.95	$0.15	$1.99
Jonathan Sanchez	806.83	3.58%	-2.58	-$0.39	$1.97
Brian Wilson	524.07	1.63%	3.43	$0.53	$1.61
Scott Atchison	798.82	2.11%	-1.36	-$0.21	$1.19
Tyler Walker	451.05	0.98%	2.79	$0.43	$1.08
Scott Munter	561.82	0.74%	1.27	$0.20	$0.68
Armando Benitez	876.10	1.19%	-1.68	-$0.26	$0.53

(continued)

MRP Estimates for Pitchers (2007) (*continued*)

Player	Season RA	%IP	RABA	$ValAA	MRP
Travis Blackley	1140.89	0.60%	-2.43	-$0.37	$0.03
Erick Threets	1055.57	0.16%	-0.51	-$0.08	$0.03
Dan Giese	1352.72	0.64%	-3.95	-$0.59	-$0.17

SEATTLE MARINERS

Player	Season RA	%IP	RABA	$ValAA	MRP
Felix Hernandez	692.35	13.27%	17.15	$2.86	$10.80
Miguel Batista	800.95	13.46%	3.51	$0.55	$8.59
Jarrod Washburn	831.46	13.50%	-0.39	-$0.06	$8.02
Jeff Weaver	870.27	10.23%	-4.06	-$0.61	$5.50
J. J. Putz	518.22	5.00%	14.73	$2.43	$5.50
Cha Seung Baek	635.73	5.11%	9.36	$1.50	$4.60
Sean Green	662.20	4.74%	7.49	$1.19	$4.06
Eric O'Flaherty	592.59	3.65%	8.17	$1.30	$3.53
George Sherrill	616.87	3.19%	6.40	$1.01	$2.95
Horacio Ramirez	955.98	6.83%	-8.28	-$1.21	$2.85
Brandon Morrow	806.85	4.41%	0.91	$0.14	$2.78
Ryan Rowland-Smith	697.53	2.70%	3.36	$0.52	$2.15
Sean White	844.64	2.46%	-0.38	-$0.06	$1.41
Chris Reitsma	899.88	1.65%	-1.12	-$0.17	$0.81
Julio Mateo	653.95	0.84%	1.39	$0.21	$0.72
John Parrish	600.47	0.72%	1.56	$0.24	$0.68
Ryan Feierabend	1109.52	3.44%	-9.18	-$1.34	$0.67
Jon Huber	735.41	0.79%	0.70	$0.11	$0.58
Jorge Campillo	945.12	0.93%	-1.03	-$0.16	$0.39
Jason Davis	1088.35	1.79%	-4.42	-$0.66	$0.38
Jake Woods	1001.39	0.75%	-1.23	-$0.19	$0.25
Rick White	791.25	0.37%	0.13	$0.02	$0.24
Mark Lowe	1737.94	0.19%	-1.63	-$0.25	-$0.15

ST. LOUIS CARDINALS

Player	Season RA	%IP	RABA	$ValAA	MRP
Adam Wainwright	634.49	14.07%	15.87	$2.63	$11.59
Braden Looper	786.14	12.19%	-4.37	-$0.65	$7.11
Kip Wells	810.44	11.33%	-6.76	-$1.00	$6.22
Russ Springer	481.02	4.60%	12.10	$1.97	$4.92
Ryan Franklin	628.96	5.57%	6.59	$1.04	$4.60
Randy Flores	486.26	3.83%	9.89	$1.59	$4.05
Jason Isringhausen	636.75	4.55%	5.03	$0.79	$3.70
Anthony Reyes	854.97	7.47%	-7.72	-$1.13	$3.62
Brad Thompson	936.33	9.01%	-16.48	-$2.30	$3.43

(*continued*)

MRP Estimates for Pitchers (2007) (*continued*)

Player	Season RA	%IP	RABA	$ValAA	MRP
Todd Wellemeyer	769.16	4.44%	-0.85	-$0.13	$2.69
Troy Percival	551.33	2.79%	5.41	$0.85	$2.64
Joel Pineiro	805.32	4.44%	-2.42	-$0.37	$2.45
Kelvin Jimenez	652.74	2.93%	2.78	$0.43	$2.30
Tyler Johnson	779.60	2.65%	-0.78	-$0.12	$1.56
Brian Falkenborg	734.09	1.30%	0.20	$0.03	$0.86
Troy Cate	732.33	1.11%	0.19	$0.03	$0.74
Chris Carpenter	427.97	0.42%	1.32	$0.20	$0.47
Randy Keisler	943.43	1.20%	-2.29	-$0.35	$0.42
Josh Hancock	865.71	0.88%	-1.01	-$0.15	$0.41
Scott Spiezio	1010.72	0.07%	-0.18	-$0.03	$0.02
Aaron Miles	1599.18	0.14%	-1.16	-$0.18	-$0.09
Mike Maroth	1222.51	2.65%	-12.27	-$1.75	-$0.09
Andy Cavazos	1294.16	1.39%	-7.43	-$1.09	-$0.22
Dennis Dove	2087.60	0.21%	-2.74	-$0.41	-$0.29
Mark Mulder	1576.55	0.77%	-6.21	-$0.92	-$0.45

TAMPA BAY DEVIL RAYS

Player	Season RA	%IP	RABA	$ValAA	MRP
Scott Kazmir	620.66	14.46%	22.26	$3.80	$13.68
James Shields	643.29	15.04%	19.68	$3.32	$13.60
Andy Sonnanstine	702.52	9.14%	6.44	$1.02	$7.26
Edwin Jackson	833.14	11.26%	-7.07	-$1.04	$6.66
Jason Hammel	853.05	5.95%	-4.94	-$0.74	$3.33
Gary Glover	840.32	5.41%	-3.79	-$0.57	$3.13
Casey Fossum	927.68	5.32%	-8.46	-$1.24	$2.41
Al Reyes	855.80	4.25%	-3.65	-$0.55	$2.36
J. P. Howell	808.73	3.57%	-1.35	-$0.21	$2.24
Brian Stokes	937.41	4.36%	-7.37	-$1.08	$1.91
Scott Dohmann	777.37	2.29%	-0.14	-$0.02	$1.54
Shawn Camp	882.96	2.80%	-3.18	-$0.48	$1.44
Jae Weong Seo	969.62	3.64%	-7.35	-$1.08	$1.42
Dan Wheeler	703.24	1.75%	1.22	$0.19	$1.38
Grant Balfour	671.63	1.54%	1.57	$0.24	$1.29
Jae Kuk Ryu	766.71	1.63%	0.08	$0.01	$1.13
Jon Switzer	734.99	1.33%	0.50	$0.08	$0.98
Juan Salas	973.90	2.54%	-5.24	-$0.78	$0.97
Tim Corcoran	1008.68	1.21%	-2.93	-$0.44	$0.39
Jay Witasick	1076.21	1.14%	-3.54	-$0.53	$0.26
Josh Wilson	997.20	0.07%	-0.16	-$0.02	$0.02
Ruddy Lugo	1353.27	0.75%	-4.44	-$0.66	-$0.14
Jeff Ridgway	9582.76	0.02%	-1.89	-$0.29	-$0.27
Chad Orvella	1785.48	0.56%	-5.79	-$0.86	-$0.46

TEXAS RANGERS

Player	Season RA	%IP	RABA	$ValAA	MRP
Kevin Millwood	742.24	12.08%	2.72	$0.42	$8.82
Kameron Loe	754.71	9.51%	0.92	$0.14	$6.75
Joaquin Benoit	558.59	5.74%	12.14	$1.97	$5.92
Vicente Padilla	834.54	8.41%	-6.11	-$0.90	$4.95
Brandon McCarthy	769.67	7.11%	-0.41	-$0.06	$4.88
C. J. Wilson	633.12	4.78%	6.44	$1.02	$4.32
Jamey Wright	795.30	5.39%	-1.73	-$0.26	$3.48
Frank Francisco	720.96	4.15%	1.84	$0.28	$3.16
Willie Eyre	824.01	4.76%	-2.93	-$0.44	$2.87
Akinori Otsuka	444.54	2.26%	7.44	$1.18	$2.72
Eric Gagne	582.92	2.33%	4.35	$0.68	$2.28
Robinson Tejeda	1016.65	6.67%	-17.34	-$2.41	$2.24
Wes Littleton	793.85	3.36%	-1.03	-$0.16	$2.18
Ron Mahay	725.43	2.73%	1.09	$0.17	$2.06
Mike Wood	890.01	3.55%	-4.60	-$0.69	$1.79
Edinson Volquez	755.32	2.38%	0.21	$0.03	$1.68
Kason Gabbard	884.86	2.82%	-3.51	-$0.53	$1.44
John Rheinecker	963.12	3.52%	-7.21	-$1.06	$1.40
Scott Feldman	950.13	2.73%	-5.23	-$0.78	$1.13
Luis Mendoza	627.56	1.12%	1.57	$0.24	$1.01
John Koronka	671.01	0.72%	0.69	$0.11	$0.60
A. J. Murray	1063.48	1.96%	-6.04	-$0.89	$0.49
Bill White	872.44	0.65%	-0.73	-$0.11	$0.34
Armando Galarraga	1229.41	0.61%	-2.92	-$0.44	$0.00
Bruce Chen	1271.48	0.70%	-3.66	-$0.55	-$0.05

TORONTO BLUE JAYS

Player	Season RA	%IP	RABA	$ValAA	MRP
Roy Halladay	576.37	15.55%	30.07	$5.33	$16.13
Dustin McGowan	636.39	11.71%	15.41	$2.55	$10.68
A. J. Burnett	731.51	11.44%	3.84	$0.60	$8.55
Shaun Marcum	817.87	10.98%	-6.08	-$0.90	$6.73
Josh Towers	772.92	7.39%	-0.67	-$0.10	$5.03
Jesse Litsch	802.71	7.66%	-3.05	-$0.46	$4.87
Casey Janssen	602.23	5.02%	8.37	$1.34	$4.80
Brian Tallet	535.13	4.30%	10.14	$1.63	$4.59
Jeremy Accardo	584.97	4.65%	8.57	$1.37	$4.57
Jason Frasor	552.54	3.93%	8.57	$1.37	$4.07
Scott Downs	567.82	4.00%	8.09	$1.29	$4.04
Brian Wolfe	693.85	3.13%	2.26	$0.35	$2.51
Tomokazu Ohka	970.37	3.87%	-8.21	-$1.20	$1.51
Gustavo Chacin	981.58	1.88%	-4.22	-$0.63	$0.69
Jordan De Jong	576.47	0.62%	1.20	$0.18	$0.61

(continued)

MRP Estimates for Pitchers (2007) (*continued*)

Player	Season RA	%IP	RABA	$ValAA	MRP
Jamie Vermilyea	382.35	0.41%	1.63	$0.25	$0.53
Brandon League	825.92	0.81%	-0.51	-$0.08	$0.48
Joe Kennedy	578.20	0.48%	0.93	$0.14	$0.47
Josh Banks	839.52	0.50%	-0.39	-$0.06	$0.29
Ty Taubenheim	1136.93	0.35%	-1.33	-$0.20	$0.04
Lee Gronkiewicz	1154.63	0.28%	-1.11	-$0.17	$0.03
B. J. Ryan	1300.01	0.30%	-1.64	-$0.25	-$0.04
Victor Zambrano	1915.48	0.74%	-8.76	-$1.28	-$0.73

WASHINGTON NATIONALS

Player	Season RA	%IP	RABA	$ValAA	MRP
Saul Rivera	566.68	6.43%	11.52	$1.87	$5.98
Jon Rauch	578.51	6.04%	10.12	$1.63	$5.49
Shawn Hill	650.30	6.73%	6.55	$1.04	$5.33
Matt Chico	923.70	11.55%	-19.70	-$2.70	$4.66
Jay Bergmann	837.36	7.97%	-6.86	-$1.01	$4.06
Chad Cordero	717.39	5.18%	1.64	$0.25	$3.56
Chris Schroder	514.17	3.13%	7.23	$1.15	$3.16
Jesus Colome	735.33	4.56%	0.64	$0.10	$3.00
Tim Redding	845.72	5.81%	-5.47	-$0.81	$2.88
Mike Bacsik	1004.94	8.16%	-20.41	-$2.79	$2.40
Micah Bowie	822.20	3.96%	-2.82	-$0.42	$2.09
Luis Ayala	725.53	2.92%	0.69	$0.11	$1.97
Jason Simontacchi	915.27	4.89%	-7.94	-$1.16	$1.94
Billy Traber	705.63	2.74%	1.18	$0.18	$1.93
Levale Speigner	890.43	2.77%	-3.82	-$0.57	$1.18
John Lannan	856.32	2.40%	-2.51	-$0.38	$1.14
Jonathan Albaladejo	492.80	0.99%	2.49	$0.39	$1.02
Ray King	964.44	2.33%	-4.91	-$0.73	$0.74
Winston Abreu	944.90	2.09%	-4.01	-$0.60	$0.72
Joel Hanrahan	1073.04	3.53%	-11.18	-$1.61	$0.62
Ryan Wagner	893.42	1.09%	-1.53	-$0.23	$0.45
John Patterson	1097.52	2.16%	-7.38	-$1.08	$0.28
Jerome Williams	1127.51	2.07%	-7.68	-$1.13	$0.18
Ross Detwiler	216.55	0.07%	0.36	$0.06	$0.10
Chris Booker	3064.44	0.07%	-1.57	-$0.24	-$0.20
Arnie Munoz	1919.61	0.37%	-4.20	-$0.63	-$0.41

Endnotes

1. Thomas Carlyle, "Occasional Discourse on the Negro Question," *Fraser's Magazine for Town and Country*, December 1849, Vol. 40: 670–679. For a history on the role of economists in the nineteenth-century debates on race and slavery, see *How the Dismal Science Got Its Name: Classical Economics and the Ur-Text of Racial Politics* by David M. Levy.

2. See Stephen Jay Gould's section "The Model Batter: The Extinction of .400 Hitting and the Improvement of Baseball" in *Full House*, p. 78.

3. Quote from Ken Rosenthal, "Mets Get Shot with Mighty Clemens at the Bat," in *The Sporting News*, June 13, 2002.

4. Quote from Ken Rosenthal, "Mets Get Shot with Mighty Clemens at the Bat," in *The Sporting News*, June 13, 2002.

5. Baker's comments came after an interleague matchup between the Giants and Yankees, in which Roger Clemens plunked Barry Bonds after hinting he would do so before the game. Baker referred to Clemens as "Roger the Dodger." Though this idea has long been a part of traditional baseball wisdom, three economists—Brian Goff, Bill Shughart, and Bob Tollison—first proposed and tested the theory in a 1997 article in the economics journal *Economic Inquiry*.

6. Economists Akihiko Kawaura and Sumner La Croix (2002) identified this similarity in the Japanese game.

7. This hypothesis was offered in two separate papers: one by Greg Trandel, Larry White, and Peter Klein (1998); the other by Steven Levitt (1998). Both papers were published as responses to the Goff, Shughart, and Tollison (1997) paper discussed in footnote 4.

8. "Teams Touchy After Incident Sunday," ESPN.com, August 27, 2004, and Retroseet game-logs (http://www.retrosheet.org/boxesetc/VHOU02004.htm).

9. This data, as well as the game-by-game data discussed in the chapters, are available at Retrosheet (www.retrosheet.org).

10. *The Armchair Economist,* p. 3.
11. Quote from Steve Henson, "Win Is Big in Grand Scheme," in *The Los Angeles Times,* April 25, 2006.
12. Jason Stark, "The Book on Hooks," www.espn.com, May 10, 2004.
13. This calculation is made from the averages of all of the statistics. One hundred points of OPS is about a one standard deviation difference in OPS.
14. *The Economist as Preacher and Other Essays,* p. 10
15. All data on handedness comes from *The Lahman Baseball Database 5.2* (www.baseball1.com).
16. This list actually overcounts the lefties, because the old rules of the game only required players to be listed at a position in the lineup, not to play in the game. So some of these lefties never saw any playing time, though official baseball rules credit them with a game played at that position.
17. While other tables exist with some minor differences, the Lindsey tables will be fine for this example. See *The Numbers Game* by Alan Schwarz (2004) for a description of this data-gathering project. For an excellent description of how these tables can be used, see *Curve Ball* by James Albert and Jay Bennett (2001).
18. Why are steals of third base rare? Table 37 shows the "breakeven" points, where the expected gains equal the expected costs, for stealing third base at each base/out configuration. They are expressed as the percentage of stealing success needed to offset the lost runner and out if the runner is caught. As you can see, a runner needs to have a pretty high success rate to justify swiping the bag. For example, with no outs and a runner on second base, a runner needs to be successful more than 83 percent of the time to justify the risk of stealing. Why is such a high success rate necessary? According to Table 4, the runner risks an expected 1.194 runs (if he just stays on second base) to increase the team's expected runs by 0.196 (1.39 − 1.194 = 0.196). If he fails, he loses 0.96 expected runs (0.234 − 1.194 = −0.96). Wagering nearly one run to gain 0.2 runs is a perilous strategy. Because the potential gains are so low and the losses are quite high, it's only worth taking the risk to steal third if a player can make it safely more than 83 percent of the time in this circumstance. The average breakeven point for all of the base/out states is 67 percent, so it's no surprise that teams are reluctant to steal third in almost every situation.
19. Right-handers may throw out some runners lefties will miss, but there will be plenty that lefties will get too. Plus, runners will not attempt to steal with every

Table 37: Breakeven Points for Stealing Third

Base/Out State	Breakeven
2nd, 0 out	83%
2nd, 1 out	65%
2nd, 2 out	84%
1st and 2nd, 0 out	62%
1st and 2nd, 1 out	51%
1st and 2nd, 2 out	59%
Mean	67%

opportunity. Furthermore, some lefties have stronger arms than right-handers, and it is possible for the strong arm of a lefty to compensate for the throwing-angle disadvantage. Therefore, if the benefits from being right-handed at catcher are real, they have to be small.

20. *The New Bill James Historical Abstract,* 2003, p. 41.
21. Quote from Travis Haney, "La Russa Badmouths Braves," *Augusta Chronicle,* May 2, 2005.
22. *Atlanta Journal-Constitution,* May 2, 2005.
23 Mazzone and Freeman, p. 196.
24. "Spahn & Sain," Gerald V. Hern, *Boston Post,* September 14, 1948.
25. Mazzone and Freeman, *Tales from the Braves Mound,* pp.13–14.
26. Merron, "Rock of Atlanta." *ESPN.com E-Ticket,* September, 17–18, 2005.
27. Merron, "Rock of Atlanta." *ESPN.com E-Ticket,* September, 17–18, 2005.
28. I use the three-year pitcher park factor from The Lahman Baseball Database, which is based on home and away batting performances by teams (www.baseball1.com).
29. Mazzone and Freeman, *Tales from the Braves Mound,* pp. 14–15.
30. Mazzone and Freeman, *Tales from the Braves Mound,* p. 186.
31. Mazzone and Freeman, *Tales from the Braves Mound,* p. 190.
32. Mazzone and Freeman, *Tales from the Braves Mound,* p. 175.
33. Merron, "Rock of Atlanta." *ESPN.com E-Ticket,* September, 17–18, 2005.
34. Thomas Stinson, "Renowned Mileage of Retreads," *Atlanta Journal-Constitution,* October 22, 2005. p. E1.
35. Merron, "Rock of Atlanta," *ESPN.com E-Ticket,* September, 17–18, 2005.
36. Thomas Stinson, "Renowned Mileage of Retreads," *Atlanta Journal-Constitution,* October 22, 2005.
37. Gary Curtright, "Coach's Style's a Change-up for Pitchers" *Atlanta Journal-Constitution,* February 10, 2006.
38. Merron, "Rock of Atlanta," *ESPN.com E-Ticket,* September, 17–18, 2005.
39. Merron, "Rock of Atlanta," *ESPN.com E-Ticket,* September, 17–18, 2005.
40. Merron, "Rock of Atlanta," *ESPN.com E-Ticket,* September, 17–18, 2005.
41. Eric Mack, *CBS.sportsline.com,* January 24, 2006.
42. Mark Feinsand, "Yankees Sign Jaret Wright," *MLB.com,* December 29, 2004.
43. *The Report of the Independent Members of the Commissioner's Blue Ribbon Panel on Baseball Economics,* July 2000, p. 5.
44. *The Report of the Independent Members of the Commissioner's Blue Ribbon Panel on Baseball Economics,* July 2000, p. 43.
45. I used this same method in an earlier study, "Quantifying the Market Size Advantage in MLB," in *The Hardball Times,* March 27, 2004.
46. Posnanski, "Bill James Finally Gets Enough of Royals," *Kansas City Star,* November 10, 2002.
47. Ritter, *The Glory of Their Times.*
48. Schmidt and Berri (2003) find some support for Gould's hypothesis in major-league baseball.
49. Note that in the past, the new talent was not equally distributed across all clubs; however, in the last two rounds of expansion, MLB made an effort to

encourage success among expansion teams. Of the four new teams, only one (Tampa Bay) has not made the playoffs. The other teams have been quite competitive, with Florida winning the World Series twice and Arizona winning it once.

50. Coeffcient of Variation of X = (Standard Deviation of X)/(Mean of X).

51. Additionally, the coefficient of variation is preferred to the standard variation because it eliminates any influence of a rising and falling of the mean values that can raise and lower the standard deviation even when the dispersion of performance does not change.

52. Interestingly, Gould's study of the variation of batting averages ended just as the batting talent dispersion bottomed out.

53. Economist Art De Vany (forthcoming) argues that these great feats are expected given the non-normal distribution of home run hitting.

54. My use of decades to denote eras is arbitrary. I do this only because most baseball historians discuss baseball history in decades. For an example, see *The New Bill James Historical Abstract*. However, it can be useful to break eras into other time periods

55. Barro, *Getting It Right: Market Choices in a Free Society*, p. 154.

56. *Boston Globe*, January 14, 2005. It was not until 2006 that the owners and the MLBPA agreed to test and punish the use of amphetamines.

57. "Goodby to Some Old Baseball Ideas," *LIFE*, 1954.

58. Michael Lewis, *Moneyball*, p. 128.

59. Hakes and Sauer, 2006, p. 184.

60. p. 36.

61. James and Neyer, *The Neyer/James Guide to Pitching*, p. 436.

62. In this model each player receives a 1 or 0 for each conference variable. This means that a pitcher pitching in the ACC with have a 1 for the ACC variable, while pitchers in other conferences will have the value of 0 for ACC. They will receive a 1 for their conference variable. Each player in a conference will receive the weight of his conference only, because 1 × weight = weight and 0 × weight = 0.

63. For an earlier discussion of this, see my article "Moneyball and Efficient Efficiency" in *The Hardball Times*, July 26, 2005.

64. Michael Lewis, *Moneyball*, pp. 37–38.

65. Run production based on OPS. Run prevention based on Fielding Independent Pitching (FIP), a predicted ERA based solely on strikeouts, walks, and home runs.

66. Frederic Bastiat, *That Which Is Seen, and That Which Is Not Seen*.

67. Statisticians Jim Albert and Jay Bennett find minimal evidence for clutch ability in these situations, and any observed effect is very weak (*Curve Ball*, 2001).

68. I am not claiming to have discovered the importance of these statistics. The values I present mirror past findings of many sabermetricians. I am merely trying to demonstrate the relative importance of each statistic with recent data.

69. *The Hidden Game of Baseball*, 1984.

70. *The Bill James Baseball Abstract*, 1987.

71. The nature of the data used to estimate the regression results creates some complicated problems. For those readers who are familiar with some advanced regression techniques: I estimated the model using random effects and cor-

rected for first-order serial correlation. I used the pitcher's team's seasonal BABIP for all pitchers to proxy defense, assumed the impact of age on ERA to be U-shaped (quadratic), and used indicator variables equal to 1 or 0 to identify the league and year in which the pitcher's stats were posted. I made a correction for the propensity of a pitcher's home park to yield runs. So pitchers with an unfriendly home park (such as Coors Field in Denver) are not punished, and pitchers with friendly home parks are not rewarded. See my study article in *Journal of Sports Economics*, "Does the Baseball Labor Market Properly Value Pitchers?" (forthcoming). Also, you can find some similar findings in my article "Another Look At DIPS" in *The Hardball Times*, May 24, 2005.

72. For the remainder of the analysis I exclude hit batters, because they are such rare events that don't strongly correlate from year to year.

73. Michael Lewis, *Moneyball*, p. 236.

74. *Principles of Economics*, p. 43.

75. "Pay and Performance in Major League Baseball," *American Economic Review*, 1974.

76. The relationship between winning and revenue is a quadratic function, with increasing dollar value added for each win beyond seventy-one.

77. Total Revenue = $(0.126 \times$ Run Difference$) + (0.000665 \times$ Run Difference$^2) + (3.88 \times$ MSA Population$) + 109.022$; Adj. $R^2 = .52$. All estimates are statistically significant at the 5 percent level. I use the 2004 season to estimate the impact of the run differential on revenue as reported in the 2005 *Forbes Business of Baseball* report. Estimates using several seasons of data did not yield much different results. The model is simple, but more complicated specifications—including the interaction between wins and population and per capita income—performed no better. While other factors may have some slight importance, they should not bias the relationship between wins and revenue.

78. Runs Scored = $(3012.54 \times$ OBP$) + (1688.17 \times$ SLG$) + (29.18 \times$ AL$) -966.04$; Adj. $R^2 = .93$. All estimates are statistically significant at the 5 percent level.

79. Runs Allowed = $(-25.83 \times$ K9$) + (60.65 \times$ BB9$) + (249.5 \times$ HR9$) - (4196.21 \times$ Team Outs on Balls in Play percent$) + (26.64 \times$ AL$) + 3419.59$; Adj. $R^2 = .91$. All estimates are statistically significant at the 5 percent level. Reported estimates in this edition include a correction, and therefore differ slightly from estimates reported in the first edition.

80. *The Fielding Bible* by John Dewan presents an experimental new system for objectively evaluating defense. Dewan estimates that Perez made twenty more plays than the average shortstop in 2005, which translates to about 9.2 runs. Using our runs-to-dollars conversion, this translates to approximately $1.22 million, which is close to the amount Cedeno would have added with his bat, $1.85 million.

81. Berri, Schmidt, and Brook, *The Wages of Wins*, p. 189.

82. Helyar, *Lords of the Realm: The Real History of Baseball.*

83. All price data from www.teammarketing.com. Rodney Fort compiles the many years of this data on his Web site (http://www.rodneyfort.com/SportsData/BizFrame.htm).

84. *An Inquiry into the Nature and Causes of the Wealth of Nations*, Oxford University Press, 1976, pp. 26–27.

85. Figure 22 graphically demonstrates exactly how price discrimination eliminates

deadweight loss. A single-price monopolist maximizes its profits by producing the output where the additional revenue of selling an additional unit—known as marginal revenue (MR)—equals the cost of producing an additional unit—known at the marginal cost (MC). Thus, the monopolist in this example produces Qm amount of output, while it sells each unit for the price of Pm. The rectangle A measures the profits captured by the monopolist. Triangles B and C represent two untapped profit opportunities to the monopolist.

From zero to Qm, every consumers pays price Pm, although according to the demand curve (D), which captures the consumer willingness-to-pay for the product at different prices, some consumers are willing to pay more and less. Triangle B represents that revenue lost to a seller charging Pm, because some consumers would be willing to pay a higher price. Qm to Q* is the quantity of the product that consumers would be willing to purchase if the price were less than Pm and greater than P*. To the left of Q* the price that would be received by the seller exceeds the marginal cost of producing those units. If the monopolist could sell the goods to these customers at a price lower than Pm, it would do so because the additional revenue would exceed the additional cost. Triangle C represents the uncaptured revenue from units the monopolist doesn't sell. This area is equal to the deadweight loss.

Together, the areas of Triangle B and C equal the total uncaptured revenue available to the monopolist if it could charge different prices to different consumers using price discrimination. Triangle B differs from C because B represents revenue lost from individuals who consume the product. We are not concerned with these individuals, because they valued these units at least as much as the amount they paid for them. The loss of revenue in Triangle C is much worse than the loss reflected in Triangle B, because the lost revenue of Triangle C also means that some sellable products will not be sold.

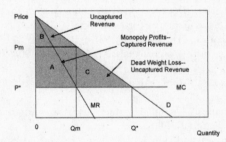

86. Ticket price data from www.teammarketing.com.
87. *Capitalism, Socialism, and Democracy,* p. 99.
88. Anyone interested in doing serious research with multiple regression analysis would be wise to acquire software that is designed to handle some common problems the empirical researcher faces. I typically use the regression package Stata, but R, SPSS, Limdep, and SAS all work well.
89. This assumes the data are distributed in a certain manner. Different regression estimators are needed for different types of data to interpret the statistical significance of coefficient estimates.

Bibliography

Albert, James, and Jay Bennett. *Curve Ball: Baseball, Statistics, and the Role of Chance in the Game.* New York: Copernicus, 2001.

Barro, Robert. *Getting It Right: Market Choices in a Free Society.* Cambridge: MIT Press, 1996.

Bastiat, Frédéric. "That Which Is Seen, and That Which Is Not Seen," 1850.

Berri, David J., Martin B. Schmidt, and Stacey L. Brook. *The Wages of Wins.* Stanford: Stanford University Press. 2006.

Bradbury, John Charles. "Another Look at DIPS." *The Hardball Times,* May 24, 2005.

Bradbury, John Charles. "Does the Baseball Labor Market Properly Value Pitchers?" *Journal of Sports Economics,* forthcoming.

Bradbury, John Charles. "The Mazzone Effect Revisited." *The Baseball Analysts,* March 17, 2005. (http://baseballanalysts.com/archives/2005/03/the_mazzone_eff 1.php).

Bradbury, John Charles. "Moneyball and Efficient Efficiency." *The Hardball Times,* July 26, 2005.

Bradbury, John Charles. "Quantifying the Market Size Advantage in MLB." *The Hardball Times,* March 27, 2004.

Bradbury, John Charles, and Douglas J. Drinen. "Crime and Punishment in Major League Baseball: The Case of the Designated Hitter and Hit Batters," *Economic Inquiry,* forthcoming.

Bradbury, John Charles, and Douglas J. Drinen. "The Designated Hitter, Moral Hazard, and Hit Batters: New Evidence from Game-Level Data," *Journal of Sports Economics,* August 2006.

Bradbury, John Charles, and Douglas J. Drinen. "Pigou at the Plate: Externalities in Major League Baseball," *Journal of Sports Economics,* (forthcoming).

Carlyle, Thomas. "Occasional Discourse on the Negro Question." *Fraser's Magazine for Town and Country*, December 1849, Vol. 40: 670–679.

Canseco, Jose. *Juiced: Wild Times, Rampant 'Roids, Smash Hits, and How Baseball Got Big*. New York: Regan Books, 2005.

De Vany, Arthur. "Steroids, Home Runs and the Law of Genius." *Economic Inquiry*, forthcoming.

Dewan, John. *The Fielding Bible*. Skokie, IL: ACTA Sports, 2006.

Fainaru-Wada, Mark, and Lance Williams. *Game of Shadows: Barry Bonds, BALCO, and the Steroids Scandal that Rocked Professional Sports*. New York: Gotham, 2006.

Goff, Brian L., William F. Shughart, and Robert D. Tolison. "Batter Up! Moral Hazard and the Effects of the Designated Hitter Rule on Hit Batsmen." *Economic Inquiry*, 1997, Vol. 35: 16–26.

Goff, Brian L., William F. Shughart, and Robert D. Tolison. "Moral Hazard and the Effects of the Designated Hitter Rule Revisited." *Economic Inquiry*, 1998, Vol. 36: 688–692.

Gould, Stephen Jay. *Full House: The Spread of Excellence from Plato to Darwin*. New York: Three Rivers Press, 1996.

Hakes, Jahn K., and Raymond D. Sauer. "An Economic Evaluation of the Moneyball Hypothesis," *Journal of Economic Perspectives*, 2006, Vol. 20: 178–185.

Helyar, John. *Lords of the Realm: The Real History of Baseball*. New York: Balantine Books, 1995.

James, Bill. *The New Bill James Historical Abstract*. New York: Free Press, 2003.

James, Bill, and Rob Neyer. *The Neyer/James Guide to Pitching*, New York: Fireside, 2004.

Kawaura, Akihiko, and Sumner La Croix. "Baseball in Japan and North America: Same Game, Same Rules, Same Results?" Manuscript, University of Hawaii. 2002.

Landsburg, Steven. *The Armchair Economist: Economics and Everyday Life*. New York: The Free Press, 1993.

Levitt, Steven D. "The Hazards of Moral Hazard." *Economic Inquiry*, 1998, Vol. 36: 685–687.

Levitt, Steven D., and Stephen Dubner. *Freakonomics: A Rogue Economist Explores the Hidden Side of Everything*, New York: William Morrow, 2005.

Levy, David M. *How the Dismal Science Got Its Name: Classical Economics and the Ur-Text of Racial Politics*. The University of Michigan Press, 2001.

Lindsey, George. "An Investigation of Strategies in Baseball." *Operations Research*, 1963, Vol. 11: 447–501.

Marshal, Alfred. *Principles of Economics*. Amherst, NY: Prometheus Books, 1997.

Mazzone, Leo, and Scott Freeman. *Leo Mazzone's Tales from the Braves Mound*. Champaign, IL: Sports Publishing, L.L.C., 2003.

Merron, Jeff. "Rock of Atlanta." *ESPN.com E-Ticket*, September 17–18, 2005.

Posnanski, Joe. "Bill James Finally Gets Enough of Royals." *Kansas City Star*, November 10, 2002.

Quirk, James, and Rodney Fort. *Pay Dirt: The Business of Professional Team Sports*. Princeton University Press, 1992.

Ritter, Lawrence S. *The Glory of Their Times: The Story of the Early Days of Baseball Told By the Men Who Played It*. New York: Vintage, 1985.

Rosenthal, Ken. "Mets Get Shot with Mighty Clemens at the Bat." *The Sporting News,* June 13, 2002.

Schell, Michael J. *Baseball's All-Time Best Sluggers: Adjusted Batting Performance from Strikeouts to Home Runs.* Princeton University Press, 2005.

Schmidt, Martin B., and David J. Berri. "On the Evolution of Competitive Balance: The Impact of Increasing Global Search." *Economic Inquiry,* October 2003.

Schumpeter, Joseph A. *Capitalism, Socialism, and Democracy.* New York: Harper, 1950.

Schwarz, Alan. *The Numbers Game: Baseball's Lifelong Fascination with Statistics.* New York: Thomas Dunne Books, 2004.

Scully, Gerald. "Pay and Performance in Major League Baseball." *American Economic Review,* Vol. 65: 915–930.

Stigler, George J. *The Economist as Preacher and Other Essays.* Chicago: The University of Chicago Press, 1982.

Thorn, John, and Pete Palmer. *The Hidden Game of Baseball: A Revolutionary Approach to Baseball and Statistics.* New York: Dolphin, 1984.

Trandel, Gregory A., Lawrence H. White, and Peter G. Klein. "The Effect of the Designated Hitter Rule on Hit Batsmen: Pitcher's Moral Hazard or the Team's Cost-Benefit Calculation." *Economic Inquiry,* 1998, Vol. 36: 679–684.

Tullock, Gordon. "The Welfare Costs of Tariffs, Monopolies, and Theft." *Western Economic Journal,* 1967, Vol. 5: 224–232.

Index

Note: Page numbers in *italics* indicate charts and graphs.